Y0-BRM-341

FRANZ JOSEPH HAYDN

GARLAND COMPOSER
RESOURCE MANUALS
(VOL. 31)

GARLAND REFERENCE LIBRARY
OF THE HUMANITIES
(VOL. 740)

GARLAND COMPOSER RESOURCE MANUALS

General Editor: Guy A. Marco

1. *Heinrich Schütz: A Guide to Research* by Allen B. Skei
2. *Josquin Des Prez: A Guide to Research* by Sydney Robinson Charles
3. *Sergei Vasil'evich Rachmaninoff: A Guide to Research* by Robert Palmieri
4. *Manuel de Falla: A Bibliography and Research Guide* by Gilbert Chase and Andrew Budwig
5. *Adolphe Adam and Léo Delibes: A Guide to Research* by William E. Studwell
6. *Carl Nielsen: A Guide to Research* by Mina F. Miller
7. *William Byrd: A Guide to Research* by Richard Turbet
8. *Christoph Willibald Gluck: A Guide to Research* by Patricia Howard
9. *Girolamo Frescobaldi: A Guide to Research* by Frederick Hammond
10. *Stephen Collins Foster: A Guide to Research* by Galvin Elliker
11. *Béla Bartók: A Guide to Research* by Elliott Antokoletz
12. *Antonio Vivaldi: A Guide to Research* by Michael Talbot
13. *Johannes Ockeghem and Jacob Obrecht: A Guide to Research* by Martin Picker
14. *Ernest Bloch: A Guide to Research* by David Z. Kushner
15. *Hugo Wolf: A Guide to Research* by David Ossenkop
16. *Wolfgang Amadeus Mozart: A Guide to Research* by Baird Hastings
17. *Nikolai Andreevich Rimsky-Korsakov: A Guide to Research* by Gerald R. Seaman
18. *Henry Purcell: A Guide to Research* by Franklin B. Zimmerman
19. *G. F. Handel: A Guide to Research* by Mary Ann Parker-Hale
20. *Jean-Philippe Rameau: A Guide to Research* by Donald Foster
21. *Ralph Vaughan Williams: A Guide to Research* by Neil Butterworth
22. *Hector Berlioz: A Guide to Research* by Jeffrey A. Langford and Jane Denker Graves
23. *Claudio Monteverdi: A Guide to Research* by K. Gary Adams and Dyke Kiel
24. *Carl Maria von Weber: A Guide to Research* by Donald G. Henderson and Alice H. Henderson
25. *Orlando di Lasso: A Guide to Research* by James Erb
26. *Giovanni Battista Pergolesi: A Guide to Research* by Marvin E. Paymer and Hermine W. Williams
27. *Claude Debussy: A Guide to Research* by James Briscoe
28. *Gustav and Alma Mahler: A Guide to Research* by Susan M. Filler
29. *Franz Liszt: A Guide to Research* by Michael Saffle
30. *Ludwig van Beethoven: A Guide to Research* by Theodore Albrecht
31. *Franz Joseph Haydn: A Guide to Research* by Floyd K. Grave and Margaret G. Grave

FRANZ JOSEPH HAYDN
A Guide to Research

Floyd K. Grave
Margaret G. Grave

GARLAND PUBLISHING, INC. • NEW YORK & LONDON
1990

Library of Congress Cataloging-in-Publication Data

Grave, Floyd K. (Floyd Kersey), 1945-
Franz Joseph Haydn : a guide to research / Floyd K. Grave and Margaret G. Grave
p. cm. — (Garland composer resource annuals ; vol. 31)
(Garland reference library of the humanities ; vol. 740)
Includes indexes.
ISBN 0-8240-8487-X (alk. paper)
1. Haydn, Joseph, 1732–1809—Biography. I. Grave, Margaret G., 1943- . II. Title. III. Series. IV. Series: Garland composer resource manuals ; v. 31.
ML134.H272G74 1990
016.78'092—dc20 90-3533
CIP

Printed on acid-free, 250-year-life paper
Manufactured in the United States of America

CONTENTS

ACKNOWLEDGMENTS

Preparation of this volume has been aided by a grant from the Rutgers University Research Council. The assistance provided by the following individuals and organizations is also gratefully acknowledged: Georg Feder, director of the Joseph Haydn Institute, Cologne; Jan LaRue, Professor Emeritus, New York University; Roger Tarman and the staff of the Blanche and Irving Laurie Music Library, Rutgers University, who patiently responded to many inquiries and requests for information; and Channan Willner, Fran Barulich, and their fellow-librarians of the New York Public Library, Music Research Collection, whose generous contribution of bibliographical expertise helped guide and inform the progress of our work.

INTRODUCTION

By the end of his long and productive career, Franz Joseph Haydn had won virtually universal applause as the greatest of living composers. Favorite works were cherished by audiences throughout Europe and the New World, and critics extolled his accomplishments as models of excellence in composition. But the number of works on which his reputation rested was small. Major portions of his life's work were all but unknown, and because succeeding generations neglected to examine his oeuvre in detail, his musical legacy remained clouded in obscurity until well into the twentieth century. Autographs and other authentic sources were lost and scattered; there was no comprehensive catalogue of his works; and the surviving early prints and manuscript copies encompassed a hopelessly confusing array of spurious attributions, unauthentic arrangements, and sources whose provenance, filiation, and chronology were uncertain at best.

As late as 1935, the British scholar Donald Francis Tovey felt compelled to dub Haydn "the inaccessible" (item 993). Indeed, it was only after the Second World War that decisive steps were taken toward bibliographical control of the sources and publication of reliable, scholarly editions of the works. Haydn research as an organized discipline is thus a recent phenomenon, and the body of Haydn literature, though growing rapidly, nevertheless remains small by comparison with that devoted to the other Viennese masters, Mozart and Beethoven.

As may be expected, given the long-dormant state of research on Haydn, few studies have appeared that convey a unified or comprehensive understanding of the composer's life, music, or historical significance.

Until now, much scholarly energy has been concentrated on the discovery and examination of sources and on the struggle with problems of chronology and authenticity. A relatively small number of critical and analytical studies have addressed topics of special pertinence to Haydn's music, including folk influence, wit and humor, motivic unity, and processes of thematic development. In a manner that seems to reflect the composer's own predilections, much of this material takes the form of intricate variations on familiar themes; and much of it involves animated debate among scholars whose independence of mind mirrors that which we have come to associate with Haydn's own personality and musical idiom.

Sadly, work on this research guide has coincided with the death of two scholars whose leadership in Haydn studies, beginning in the 1930s, has been largely responsible for launching that era of post-war achievements on which our present state of knowledge rests: the Austrian-born Karl Geiringer and the Danish scholar Jens Peter Larsen. Our project has also come at a time when the *Joseph Haydn Werke*, an authoritative complete edition undertaken by the Joseph Haydn Institute in Cologne, is finally nearing completion.

It may be said that a plateau has been reached and that a phase in the history of Haydn research is drawing to a close. The landscape of the composer's oeuvre has come into full view at last, and while questions of dating, authenticity, and chronology remain, efficacious methods for addressing them have been developed. Major directions and points of view have been delineated and, with a reasonable degree of coherence and consistency, can be isolated and categorized in a way that can serve as a guide to the researcher.

Our procedure in confronting this task has been to provide annotated entries for a broad selection of writings spanning the gamut of Haydn research from the late eighteenth century to the present, to divide them into discrete subject areas, and to supply a limited number of cross references for items whose content suggests inclusion in more than one category. Primarily addressing the trained student-researcher for whom the basic tools of musical scholarship are familiar, we have limited the scope of this guide to material that deals directly and extensively with Haydn and his music.

Unavoidably, much has been left out. Notably absent is the wealth of background and peripheral literature which, however relevant to the study of Haydn and his age, does not actually discuss the composer directly. In the main, we have omitted standard reference sources, textbooks, most general books on music history, prefaces and critical notes to editions of Haydn's music, and a substantial number of pedagogically oriented books and articles that are intended primarily for performers and that offer relatively little by way of critical insight or usefulness to the researcher.

In selecting items for inclusion, our aim has been to represent the work of major Haydn scholars, past and present; to cover all genres and principal areas of inquiry; and to emphasize relatively recent research. In general, preference has been given to accessible books and to scholarly articles in journals most likely to be found in the collection of a large university library. The vast majority of these writings are either in German or English, and while some important contributions in French and Italian are represented, those in other languages (notably Hungarian, Czech, Russian, Swedish, and Danish) have been excluded, regardless of their scholarly merit.

Although we have omitted numerous books and articles whose content has been superseded or absorbed in more recent literature, some of the older material has been retained in light of its historical interest. We have chosen to include some of the best-known and most frequently cited non-specialist books; but articles in education journals, regional periodicals rarely found in American libraries, and eighteenth- and nineteenth-century periodicals not available in reprint have generally been excluded. Where available, information on reprints, different versions, and multiple editions has been included, although no attempt has been made to provide comprehensive coverage in this regard. For convenient reference, we have appended a list of Haydn's compositions based on that furnished by Georg Feder in *The New Grove Haydn* (item 269).

Franz Joseph Haydn

I

FRANZ JOSEPH HAYDN (1732-1809)

BIOGRAPHICAL SKETCH

Though hampered by a scarcity of surviving documents, especially having to do with the composer's early years, Haydn's biographers have succeeded in tracing a profile of his life and the principal stations of his career: early musical training, struggles as a young professional musician in Vienna, the long term of service as Esterházy kapellmeister, the triumphant sojourns in London, and the crowning accomplishments and accolades of the late years. Sources on which scholars must rely, including Haydn's 1776 autobiographical sketch (item 189) and the early accounts by Albert Christoph Dies and Georg August Griesinger (item 183), are not free of contradictions; but the outlines are clearly discernible, and they afford a basis for gaining some understanding of Haydn's personality, artistic development, and musical contribution.

Haydn's father, Mathias (1699-1763), was born in the town of Hainburg, in a section of eastern Austria close to the Hungarian border. The son of a wheelwright, he settled in the border village of Rohrau by 1727. There he pursued his father's trade, was evidently prosperous, and eventually became mayor of the town. In 1728 he married Anna Maria Koller (1707-54), daughter of a Rohrau farmer. Joseph was the second of twelve children. His musically talented brother Michael was the sixth.

According to the composer's own account, his father was an enthusiastic amateur musician. Though Mathias did not read music, he was fond of singing and accompanying himself on the harp. By the age of five, the young Joseph himself was able to participate in the family's music-making, and the parents, encouraged by such early signs of artistic promise, chose to send the child to school in Hainburg, where he could receive training under the care of a schoolmaster cousin, Johann Mathias Franck.

Attending his cousin's school at Hainburg, Haydn learned to play harpsichord and violin, and he sang in the church choir. But his term of study there turned out to be of brief duration. Before long, his proficiency as a singer came to the attention of Johann Georg Reutter the younger, who had recently assumed directorship of the St. Stephen's Cathedral choir in Vienna. Reutter had stopped at Hainburg in search of able young singers, and upon hearing the boy sing, promptly accepted him into the choir.

At St. Stephen's, where Haydn was recognized as a good though not outstanding singer, activity centered on vocal training and performance. The extent of instruction in theory and composition he might have received is uncertain, and probably no more than minimal. But the eight years or so spent with the cathedral choir did acquaint him with an important repertory of sacred music, including works of Caldara, Fux, Bonno, and Reutter himself. In the mid-1740s, a time when Joseph was approaching maturity and suffering the deterioration of his singing voice, Michael Haydn, vocally more gifted than his older sibling, was admitted to the choir and probably had little difficulty upstaging his brother. By the end of the decade, Joseph was dismissed from St. Stephen's and obliged to fend for himself.

As recounted in Haydn's autobiographical sketch and amplified by Dies and Griesinger, the young musician suffered hardship and deprivation following his release from the cathedral choir. Unable to find suitable steady employment, he made ends meet by playing dance music, making arrangements of compositions for various instruments, teaching, and taking part in the traditional Viennese street serenades. In this way he became intimately familiar with that popular, *galant*, Austrian chamber music idiom which contributed so importantly to his own early development as a composer.

Added to the practical experience gained during this time was the rigorous program of self-instruction Haydn imposed on himself despite the effort of eking out a living. Texts he studied included Johann Joseph Fux's famous counterpoint treatise *Gradus ad Parnassum* and Johann Mattheson's widely read *Der vollkommene Kapellmeister.* (The early biographers also describe a decisive encounter with the work of C.P.E. Bach, but his acquaintance with Bach's treatise as well as his music may actually have occurred no earlier than the decade of the 1760s.)

Before long, fresh opportunities presented themselves. A building in which Haydn had taken an apartment, the Michaelerhaus, happened to be the residence of the court poet Metastasio. (By coincidence, the Michaelerhaus was also the home of the dowager Princess Esterházy, mother of Haydn's future patron.) Through Metastasio, Haydn met the famous composer and teacher Nicola Porpora and was engaged for a brief time as the illustrious musician's valet and accompanist.

More promising in terms of the progress of Haydn's career was his acquaintance in the late 1750s with Karl Joseph Edler von Fürnberg. This nobleman invited Haydn to take part in chamber music performances at Weinzierl, his country home; and by 1759, Fürnberg had recommended him to another patron, Count Karl Joseph Franz Morzin. Morzin, who lived in Vienna but spent the summer months at Lukaveč, his estate in Bohemia, promptly appointed Haydn as music director of his orchestra. It was reportedly for Morzin's Lukaveč ensemble that Haydn wrote his first symphony.

In 1760, Haydn made the unfortunate step of marrying someone with whom he proved utterly incompatible. The daughter of a wigmaker, Maria Anna Keller (1729-1800) was something of a second choice, her older, more desirable sister Josepha having entered a convent. Though scholars hold differing views on the nature of the couple's relationship, it is clear that their marriage was unsatisfactory. She exhibited little understanding of his profession (Griesinger reported Haydn's complaint that "it's all the same to her if her husband is a cobbler or an artist"). They had no children, and for extended periods, especially in later years, they lived apart. In letters, he referred to her as an "infernal beast," and as the composer readily acknowledged, his affections were often directed toward other women.

It was through Count Morzin that Prince Paul Anton Esterházy came to know of Haydn. The Esterházys, among the richest and most influential of the Hungarian nobility, were famous as patrons of music and the fine arts. Gregor Joseph Werner (1695-1766) had served as kapellmeister at the family residence in Eisenstadt (located south of Vienna in the Burgenland) since 1728, and now Haydn was to be engaged as assistant conductor, with the understanding that he would eventually replace his older colleague as head of the musical establishment.

The date of Haydn's engagement at Eisenstadt is uncertain. His contract bore the date 1761, but he may have been employed by the Esterházy family as early as 1760. According to the terms of that famous contract (quoted in its entirety in major modern biographies), it was understood that Haydn would be subordinate to Werner, who was a composer primarily of sacred music, in matters pertaining to the choir. Otherwise, he was given sole direction of musical activities. Duties assigned to him included the instruction of the vocalists, "in order that they may not forget in the country what they have been taught with much trouble and expense in Vienna." In accordance with prevailing custom, he was obliged to supply compositions for his employer on request. This music was not to be copied, but must be retained for the sole use of the prince, and no pieces were to be written for any other person without his employer's knowledge and consent.

The instrumental ensemble Haydn was charged with supervising consisted of a mere 10-15 musicians (the number eventually reached 20-25 under Haydn's stewardship). Among its members were several outstanding performers, including the violinist Luigi Tomasini and the cellist Anton Kraft. While Haydn's activities centered on instrumental performance and composition at the start of his tenure in Eisenstadt, circumstances were destined to change before long. Paul Anton died in March 1762 (less than a year after the signing of Haydn's initial contract), and his son Nikolaus ("the Magnificent") became Haydn's new patron. Nikolaus, more actively involved in musical matters than his predecessor, appears to have been a demanding though appreciative patron; and among the tasks he assigned the composer was that of supplying a vast quantity of chamber music for the prince's own favorite instrument, the baryton. Early in his reign, following a sojourn in

France, Nikolaus undertook the building of a new palace whose magnificence was to mirror that of Versailles. Situated in the swamplands on the Neusiedler Lake, Eszterháza, as it was called, was initially intended as a summer resort but soon became the prince's residence for the greater part of the year. Consequently, it became the center of Haydn's activities as well.

In 1766, the death of Werner (whose relations with Haydn had been strained, to say the least) and the move to Eszterháza entailed major changes in the nature of Haydn's career. Now there were more opportunities to write sacred music; but more important was the new emphasis on operatic activity, which came to demand an increasingly large share of the kapellmeister's time and energy. Doubtless related to this change in circumstance was an important development in Haydn's compositional style, as witnessed in a number of symphonies and other instrumental works that featured unprecedented rhythmic intensity, vivid textural and dynamic contrasts, and a marked preference for minor keys. Extending from the late 1760s through the early 1770s, this imperfectly understood phase has been customarily labeled *Sturm und Drang,* after the contemporaneous German literary movement. While reflecting his increasing absorption in theater music, it may also have been the product of a special effort of Haydn's to expand and deepen his technical and expressive resources.

In 1779, the engagement of a violinist named Antonio Polzelli and his young wife Luigia, a singer, turned out to be an unexpectedly significant event in Haydn's personal life. Haydn evidently became amorously involved with Polzelli's wife. Though neither of the Polzellis proved to be a fully satisfactory musician, both were kept on until the disbanding of the Esterházy music establishment in 1790; and for Luigia, Haydn took special pains to revise difficult arias and to supply numerous so-called "insertion arias," specially suited to her vocal limitations, for operatic productions at the Eszterháza opera theater.

Meanwhile, restrictions of his contract notwithstanding, Haydn's music circulated widely in manuscript copies, and this dissemination of his work enabled him to earn an extraordinary degree of international recognition despite his social and geographical isolation. Then in 1779, under circumstances that remain unclear, his contract was redrawn and a conspicuous change was made: whereas the original arrangement specified that the prince should hold exclusive rights over Haydn's compositions, this stipulation was now dropped. The alteration in his contract occurred at around the time he entered relations with Artaria, the newly established Viennese publisher. It also coincided with a fundamental change in his outlook and approach to his occupation as a composer. Prior to this time, his music was written primarily with local use in mind. From now on, it would be designed to address the needs of his publishers and the international market they served.

While Haydn's regular duties permitted minimal contact with the world beyond the confines of Eszterháza, he did make occasional visits to Vienna. These excursions enabled him to keep abreast of current developments and, more importantly, to make the acquaintance of the city's most gifted musician, W.A. Mozart. Though they evidently spent little time together, the two artists did become friends and readily expressed deepest admiration for each other's work. The younger composer's famous series of six string quartets, inspired by Haydn's quartets of Op. 33, bore a fond dedication to the older master; and Haydn, for his part, declared to Mozart's father that "before God and as an honest man I tell you that your son is the greatest composer known to me either in person or by name. He has taste and, what is more, the greatest knowledge of composition."

It was perhaps lucky for Haydn that toward the mid-1780s, his patron tired of the operatic activity that had been such a prominent feature of life at Eszterháza up to this time (Haydn's last opera for Eszterháza was his *Armida*, composed in 1783). In any event, the change left him with more time to pursue other interests, most notably the job of supplying instrumental music for eager European publishers.

In 1785, very likely at Mozart's instigation, Haydn joined the Masonic lodge *Zur wahren Eintracht*. While some scholars have detected Masonic influence in *The Creation* and other works, it is doubtful that Haydn was captivated by the ritual and mystique of the fraternal order as was his friend. He certainly did not become comparably involved.

The social contact which he craved was of a different sort; and to some extent it found fulfillment in the ardent but subdued intensity of his friendship with Marianne von Genzinger, the musically knowledgeable wife of the Esterházy physician Peter von Genzinger. A singer and pianist, she established initial contact with Haydn in 1789. The two corresponded frequently thereafter and enjoyed each other's company at musical gatherings in the von Genzinger home in Vienna.

Haydn's letters to Marianne reflect feelings of growing dissatisfaction with his personal and professional circumstances. It was clear that he was ready for a change, and the chance to strike out in a new direction came with the death of his patron in 1790. Anton, Nikolaus' son and successor, shared little of his father's passion for music. For Haydn, this meant virtual release from obligations as court kapellmeister, and though he retained his title and salary, he was now free to leave Eszterháza and take up residence in Vienna.

Not long after moving, Haydn received a visit from Johann Peter Salomon, who had come to Vienna to seek out the famous artist after learning of his patron's death. Salomon, born in Bonn in 1745, enjoyed international recognition as a virtuoso violinist. Having left the Continent for England in 1781, he had been occupied since 1786 with directing a series of subscription concerts in London. His aim now was to adorn his concerts with the most famous of living composers. "My name is Salomon," he is reported to have declared. "I have come from London to fetch you; we shall conclude our accord tomorrow." As specified in the agreement reached with Salomon, Haydn was to supply a new opera, six new symphonies to be performed in concerts under his direction, and various smaller compositions.

Haydn arrived in England on New Year's Day, 1791, and found himself caught up in a busy social life totally different from his reclusive Eszterháza existence. "Everyone wants to know me," he wrote to Marianne, and he soon found himself receiving far more invitations than he could accept. Musically there was much stimulation. Impressed by the large orchestras, by such events as the Handel Commemoration at Westminster Abbey in May 1791, and by the general vitality of London musical life, Haydn participated in numerous events and attended many others.

The Salomon concerts were central to Haydn's London activities. The first of these under the composer's direction took place on March 11 in the Hanover Square rooms. Burney, impressed by the "electrical effect on all present," reported that there was "such a degree of enthusiasm as almost amounted to frenzy." Subsequent weekly concerts took place on Fridays, the series extending into June. Haydn's symphonies were featured (though actually only two of the new London symphonies were heard in the first season) along with other instrumental music of his and works by other composers. One aspect of this first London engagement that did not turn out successfully involved the opera he had agreed to write: though Haydn had completed the commissioned work, *L'anima del filosofo*, by May 1791, plans for its performance were abandoned.

The recipient of honors and much praise following the conclusion of the first season, Haydn was invited by Burney in July to receive the honorary degree of Doctor of Music from Oxford. The second season, no less successful than the first, extended from February to May 1792. It was enlivened by a friendly musical rivalry between the composer and the renowned Ignaz Pleyel, a former pupil of his who had been engaged by a competing group, the Professional Concerts. During the time that intervened between the two seasons, Rebecca Schroeter, widow of the composer Johann Samuel Schroeter, became Haydn's pupil. As poignantly documented in the copies of her letters that Haydn kept, teacher and pupil enjoyed an affectionate and lasting relationship.

Haydn returned to Vienna in June 1792 and settled down temporarily to a relatively quiet existence. In November 1792, the young Ludwig van Beethoven arrived and for a brief time was his pupil. Although Haydn's music was to exert decisive influence on the development of Beethoven's style in the following years, relations between master and scholar were reportedly strained at the time of this initial encounter. The younger composer, possibly dissatisfied with instruction he was receiving, turned to other teachers for the guidance in basic compositional technique which he sought.

Having reached an agreement with Salomon in autumn 1793 for a return engagement in London, Haydn departed for his second visit to the British Isles in January 1794, accompanied by his loyal assistant Johann Elssler. Like the previous concert series, the 1794 season involved weekly concerts in which Haydn's appearance and the performance of his symphonies were featured attractions. This time, however, there was no rival group, the Professional Concerts having been discontinued in 1793. After the 1794 series, Salomon discontinued his own venture. But Haydn, still immensely popular with London audiences, was engaged for a 1795 season by a new enterprise, the Opera Concerts. Drawing on an orchestra of no fewer than 60 performers, this series was held in the concert hall of the King's Theatre under the direction of the virtuoso violinist J.B. Viotti.

Fending off entreaties to remain in England, Haydn departed in August 1795. He returned to Vienna to face altered circumstances. Paul Anton, having outlived his father by only a few years, had died in January 1794. His successor, Nikolaus, chose to reestablish the Esterházy orchestra, and for Haydn this meant resumption of kapellmeister duties, though on a much smaller scale than under the previous Prince Nikolaus. Now, his chief responsibility consisted of supplying a mass each year to celebrate the name-day of his patron's wife, Princess Maria Hermenegild. Haydn dutifully fulfilled this request by supplying six masses from 1796 to 1802. Conceived on a grand scale, these works stand alongside the twelve London symphonies as major achievements of the composer's later years.

The post-London period also encompassed two of the most ambitious of all Haydn's works, *The Creation* and *The Seasons*, both inspired by the Handelian oratorio tradition with which Haydn had become familiar during his sojourns in England. Other notable compositions from this time included eight string quartets (Op. 76 and 77) plus a two-movement quartet fragment (published as Op. 103), a substantial number of part-songs and vocal canons, and the famous "Emperor Hymn," ("Gott, erhalte Franz den Kaiser!").

Evidently exhausted by these taxing creative efforts, Haydn ceased composing by 1803. No longer active as Esterházy kapellmeister, he spent the remaining years of his life in Vienna. His last public appearance as conductor took place in December 1803, and the last concert he attended before his death in the spring of 1809 was an 1808 performance of *The Creation*, led by Antonio Salieri.

While complaining of ever-increasing frailty in his last years, Haydn nevertheless managed to continue playing the role of international celebrity to which he had become accustomed. He received illustrious visitors, honors were bestowed upon him, and various collected-edition projects were undertaken. In connection with one of these ventures, Breitkopf & Härtel's "complete works," he made the acquaintance of Georg August Griesinger, counsellor to the Saxon Legation in Vienna.

Griesinger's original mission was to secure Haydn's authorization for the Breitkopf & Härtel series, but he then made regular visits to the composer from 1799 on, with the intention of collecting material for a biography. Having a similar idea in mind, Albert Christoph Dies began visiting the aging artist in 1805. Meanwhile, the task of preparing a "catalogue of all those compositions which I recall having made from my 18th to my 73rd year" was undertaken by Elssler under Haydn's supervision. By virtue of these endeavors, the composer was granted the opportunity to review his life's work, and through the information he supplied to his visitors and collaborators, to help lay a foundation for posterity's judgment of his accomplishment.

II

NOTES ON THE HISTORY OF HAYDN RESEARCH: CHANGING PERCEPTIONS OF THE COMPOSER AND HIS CONTRIBUTION

Despite the professional hardships he suffered, first as an impecunious free-lance musician in Vienna, then later as a responsibility-laden, spiritually isolated kapellmeister in the Austro-Hungarian hinterland, Joseph Haydn lived to enjoy an unprecedented degree of artistic good fortune. The customary fate of the artist, whose creative innovations meet with confusion and hostility on the part of contemporaries, was, by and large, not shared by him. Reservations about whimsical and prankish qualities in his instrumental music notwithstanding, Haydn's musical language posed few obstacles to listeners' comprehension. Moreover, his maturation as an artist coincided with the early growth of a vital music-publishing industry whose practitioners soon acquired an unquenchable appetite for his music. Evidently endowed with good business sense in addition to a phenomenally fertile musical imagination, Haydn used the new medium of dissemination to advantage, and it enabled him to share the products of his art on an international scale.

Critics who came to know the music of Haydn in the 1770s and 80s were impressed by its polished craftsmanship, its directness and simplicity of utterance, and the novelty of its invention.

As early as 1772, Charles Burney ranked Haydn among the best Viennese composers of quartets and symphonies, and in Gerber's lexicon of 1790, his music is described as unmistakably original, universal in its appeal, and witty and accessible, despite the richness and complexity of its subordinate parts (item 179). Curiously, though attention was directed mainly toward instrumental works, one of the most detailed of the early critiques, published in Carl Friedrich Cramer's *Magazin der Musik* 1 (1783), concerns a vocal composition, the secular cantata "Ah, come il core" (item 907). Describing the piece in terms that became watchwords of early Haydn criticism, the writer perceives the work as a perfect whole and admires the noble simplicity, restraint, and directness of expression that typify the setting of the text.

The subject of Haydn's special affinity for musical wit stands out with special prominence in early critiques. This trait, whereby listeners' expectations and the manipulation of commonplace materials furnished a basis for accomplishing the unexpected, was an aspect of his music that did not win immediate or universal admiration. To Joseph II, his music was characterized by "tricks and nonsense." Carl Junker's essay on Haydn in *Zwanzig Componisten: Eine Skizze* (1776) dwells at length on the aesthetically problematical elements of whim and caprice that informed his music (item 192). As Haydn himself noted in a reference to the Berlin critics in his autobiographical sketch, it was primarily in the north that his idiosyncrasies were misunderstood. Charles Burney's friend from Hamburg, quoted in book 4 of *A General History of Music* (1789), wrote in 1772 of Haydn (along with Dittersdorf and Fils) that "their mixture of serious and comic was disliked, particularly as there is more of the latter than the former in their works; and as for rules, they knew but little of them" (item 169).

By the end of the eighteenth century, most of the earlier doubts on the part of critics had dissipated. Benefiting from greater familiarity with Haydn's style, audiences were perhaps able to hear moments of novelty and surprise less as aberrations than as logically justifiable parts of an artfully designed, coherent plan. In his *Mémoires* (1789), Grétry marveled at Haydn's ability to extract a wealth of material from a single motive (item 184). Praising the symphonies for their inherent eloquence and drama, he urged that they be studied by composers of opera. In the *Dictionnaire historique des musiciens* of Choron and Fayolle (1810), the element of surprise in the quartets is applauded, and the symphonies are extolled as models for all aspects of musical expression (item 173). Haydn's stature as a preeminent master of variation was emphasized by Abbé Vogler, and Heinrich Christoph Koch drew on his music to illustrate modern compositional procedure. In the *Cours complet d'harmonie et de composition* (1806), Jérôme-Joseph de Momigny chose the *Drumroll* Symphony as the subject for an elaborate experiment in critical analysis that included the detailed examination of structural hierarchy, thematic contrast and development, orchestration, and expressive content.

By the start of the nineteenth century, Haydn's reputation had reached its zenith, and the reverence with which his art was regarded found reflection in the early biographical accounts by Dies, Griesinger, and Carpani. Dwelling on the universal appeal and accessibility of his music, these writers conveyed the image of a benign, paternal figure whose homespun wisdom, humility, and integrity seemed to accord perfectly with the folk-inspired optimism, innocence, and humor with which his music was identified.

But with the changing attitudes of a younger, Romantically inclined generation, this kind of admiration, based as it was on an idealized picture of the man and a somewhat simplistic view of his accomplishment, proved to be Haydn's undoing. In the context of a greatly increased emotional range that characterized much nineteenth-century music, the clarity and buoyancy of Haydn's language, features that had enhanced his popularity among late eighteenth-century listeners, now seemed out of step. The number of works on which his reputation was based, never very large, dwindled to a few favorite symphonies and excerpts from the oratorios; and these came to be heard by a younger generation of critics as outmoded fixtures in an increasingly stagnant repertoire. The songs were largely overlooked. The keyboard music was thought to be unpianistic, and to an age caught up in the mystique of Cecilianism, his sacred music sounded unchurchly.

Under such conditions, Haydn's music all too easily became the symbol of reactionary attitudes. As such, it was scorned by advocates of liberation from the stifling constraints of tradition. Critics understood the symphonies to be harmless and playful, but not truly capable of monumental expression, and they denounced the oratorios on the grounds of their all-too-literal approach to tone-painting. His idiom was felt to be pleasing to the ear and obedient to the rules of art but lacking in depth and artistic merit. Viewing the composer as essentially a predecessor to the weightier, more modern accomplishments of Mozart and Beethoven, critics came to identify "Papa" Haydn with an age whose illustrious, epoch-making achievements deserved to be honored, yet whose values had been superseded.

The nineteenth-century tendency toward a patronizing, monolithic view of the composer finds reflection in François Joseph Fétis' *Biographie universelle des musiciens* (1833-44), where his music is described as simple and symmetrical, the man himself as pious and sincere, though incapable of writing effectively for church or theater (item 60). Thomas Busby, in his *General History of Music, from the Earliest Times to the Present* (1819), observes that Haydn's "heart and mind were superstitious, impassioned, affectionate, friendly, simple, and honourable," and concludes that his genius, "original and powerful, but limited in its range, was incapable of superior excellence in the sublimer sphere of composition, but shone with an unequalled lustre, in the tract to which his judgment generally restricted his exertions" (item 170). More pointedly, Robert Schumann declared in 1841 that "one can learn nothing new from him," that his music, however familiar and respected, no longer possessed deep interest for the present day.

Such attitudes were destined to change under pressure from major developments in the latter part of the nineteenth century. A growing wave of enthusiasm for musical scholarship, led principally by the Germans, brought to light vast quantities of newly discovered source material, and with the development of increasingly sophisticated research methods, an impressive series of critical editions for the works of major composers was undertaken. In addition to the *Gesamtausgaben* for Beethoven, Mozart, Lassus, Palestrina, Schubert, Schumann, Schütz, and Victoria, there appeared monumental catalogues, bibliographies, thematic indexes, and important books on composers' lives and works, including Otto Jahn's ambitious study of Mozart and Philipp Spitta's exemplary biography of J.S. Bach.

Among those engaged in this rising tide of research was

the German organist and music historian Carl Ferdinand Pohl. During a sojourn in Great Britain, Pohl had written an important documentary study, *Mozart und Haydn in London* (1867; item 278). Subsequently appointed archivist of the Gesellschaft der Musikfreunde in Vienna, he was called upon to do a biography of Haydn (item 277). He assumed the task reluctantly, and confessed that he would have preferred to see the job done by his friend Otto Jahn.

The result of Pohl's subsequent exertions was a two-volume work (1875, 1882) that traced the composer's life and offered an account of his music up to the time of his departure for London in late 1790 (a third volume was eventually supplied by Hugo Botstiber in 1927). Following what Spitta described as an "antiquarian" approach, Pohl's study turned out to be more a chronicle of Haydn's times than the thoroughly revised interpretation of the artist and his works that was so urgently needed. As the author himself was doubtless aware, his accomplishment was limited both in degree of penetration into factual, historical material and in the depth of its critical insights into the music.

In Pohl's defense, it may be noted that he faced virtually insurmountable obstacles, the extent of which would only become clear to a later generation: an utter lack of bibliographical control over the Haydn sources, immense problems of authenticity and chronology, and the absence of reliable biographical documents for extended periods in the composer's career. In fact, Pohl did succeed in furnishing a welcome compilation of available knowledge about Haydn and his age; and until very recently, his book stood out as the most authoritative biographical study available.

Whatever the merits and drawbacks of Pohl's achievement, his study was scarcely destined to inspire a large-scale Haydn revival; and in the absence of any other major effort, neglect of the composer's musical legacy persisted. The contrast with other German masters is striking. Whereas complete editions for Bach, Mozart, Handel, and Beethoven were available before the end of the nineteenth century, the task of undertaking a definitive Haydn edition did not even get started until 1907. Under the guidance of Eusebius Mandyczewski, several volumes were produced before the project came to a halt with the onset of the First World War. Scarcely able to regain momentum in the following decades, the endeavor was abandoned again in the 1930s with fewer than a dozen volumes published.

Yet signs of renewed interest were apparent in the early years of the twentieth century, a trend partly attributable to changes in the cultural environment in which the music of Haydn's day was studied and heard. Evidence of a new outlook can be seen in such efforts as the multi-volume critical study of Mozart by Théodore de Wyzewa and Georges de St. Foix, with its penetrating insights into the music, including Haydn's, with which their protagonist came in contact. In 1909, Wyzewa published a landmark essay on the "Romantic crisis" in Haydn's music (item 783); and Sir Henry Hadow's essay on the composer for the *Oxford History of Music*, which took pains to defend him against the Romantics' charge that his music was old-fashioned, went so far as to identify Haydn's accomplishment with "the turning of a new page in the history of music" (item 62).

The development of fresh approaches within the discipline of historical musicology proved helpful in promoting a rebirth of enthusiasm for Haydn. In the writings of Guido Adler, Wilhelm Fischer, and others, the concept of a Viennese Classical period was explored and elaborated, and theories of its evolution became closely associated with his music. Adler, in a 1932 essay, "Haydn and the Viennese Classical School" (item 653), emphasized the importance of the composer's early works as a factor in eighteenth-century stylistic evolution, and he observed that Haydn's idiom displayed traits that were to become identified with Classical style: popular and folk inspiration, variation principle, and unified motivic development.

Given Haydn's newly acquired status as a key player in the development of a Classical style, his traditional depiction as a paternal figure took on a deeper, more sophisticated meaning. In Adler's essay, the theme of paternity persists (Haydn is characterized as Beethoven's true father in music), but he is no longer cloaked patronizingly in the guise of a precursor. Instead, he appears as a seeker, an innovator whose pathbreaking experiments proved decisively important to the history of the art.

In the decade of the 1930s, increased interest in Haydn was reflected in the publication of new editions of previously unavailable works and in the undertaking of scholarly studies, notably in the special issues of scholarly journals dedicated to the bicentennial celebration of the composer's birth. The time was ripe for a reappraisal of Haydn's contribution and for the construction of a new foundation for research and appreciation. Yet efforts in this direction were hindered by the scarcity of reliable editions, and by the fact that sources on which such editions might be based lay unexamined and uncatalogued. Much of the composer's oeuvre remained virtually unknown, so that when alleged Haydn compositions surfaced, there was no secure foundation on which rudimentary questions of chronology and authenticity could be decided.

The stage was set for what the Danish scholar Jens Peter Larsen later depicted as a crisis in Haydn research. Matters came to a head in 1933 with Adolf Sandberger's assertion that he had identified a large number of hitherto unrecognized symphonies by Haydn (item 491). Unfortunately, as Larsen emphasized in the course of the ensuing debate, the claim was based essentially on guesswork. Whatever the merits of scholarship by intuition, such an approach was scarcely appropriate for attributing works to a composer for whom an authentic canon had never been successfully delineated.

The young Larsen, soon destined to become the principal leader of Haydn research, used his dispute with Sandberger as an opportunity to establish principles by which the future of Haydn studies might be guided. At issue was the methodology of modern scholarship and the importance, repeatedly underscored by Larsen, of insisting on a comprehensive knowledge of pertinent sources as a prerequisite for appraising a composer's contribution or for judging the authenticity of newly discovered music.

Calling attention to the inherent problems of Haydn research--including large quantities of unauthentic material, stylistic diversity within the composer's oeuvre (especially among the early works), and general scarcity of reliable documentary evidence--Larsen put together the results of his own investigations in a major, crucially important study. *Die Haydn-Überlieferung* (item 478), and the accompanying *Drei Haydn Kataloge* (item 41; a publication in facsimile of the three authentic thematic catalogues of Haydn's music), constituted a masterpiece of scholarly method. Incorporating a compact, systematic examination of the surviving sources, including autographs, prints, manuscript copies, and catalogue references, Larsen's monograph has retained its value to this day as an indispensable reference for Haydn scholars.

Larsen was by no means alone in his dedication to Haydn research. During the years between the wars, Anthony van Hoboken had assembled a large private collection of first and early editions, including more than 1,000 prints of Haydn works. Hoboken was thus in a position to appreciate the frustration that had been expressed early in the previous century by Ernst Ludwig Gerber, who had struggled with the problem of representing Haydn's oeuvre in his *Neues historisch-biographisches Lexikon der Tonkünstler* (1812) and had deplored the unavailability of a thematic catalogue by which the composer's largely unknown works could be identified and placed in chronological order (item 180). Assuming responsibility for this immense task, Hoboken initiated what turned out to be a thirty-year project of preparing his definitive *Thematisch-bibliographisches Werkverzeichnis* of Haydn's works.

Meanwhile, an older contemporary of Larsen's, the Viennese scholar Karl Geiringer, was appointed to succeed Mandyczewski as museum curator and librarian of the Gesellschaft der Musikfreunde in 1930. In this role, he was invited to contribute a volume on Haydn in connection with the 1932 bicentennial celebration. The resulting monograph (item 241) provided the basis for a later, more extended book, first published in 1946 and repeatedly revised thereafter (item 242). Geiringer's biography proved to be a well-balanced, eminently readable account of the composer's life and works; as such, it has furnished an invaluable resource for English- as well as German-speaking readers.

The numerous revisions to which Geiringer subjected his study testify to the astonishing acceleration of Haydn research following the Second World War. Blessed by the dedication of several energetic scholars, work on Haydn expanded to a new order of magnitude. Much of the fresh impetus came from the industry and enthusiasm of H.C. Robbins Landon, a student of Geiringer's at Boston University (1945-47) who went on to become an ardent and tireless champion of the Haydn legacy. Delving into an intensive study of the Haydn symphony sources in the late 1940s, Landon founded the Haydn Society in 1949, encouraged the performance and recording of lesser-known Haydn works, and proceeded with the noble intention of publishing a complete edition. While the Haydn Society's efforts were short-lived (five volumes were published before the venture came to a halt in 1951), Landon's study of Haydn's music continued unabated. Concentrating on the symphonies, he acquired a broad familiarity with their sources, including a wealth of previously unexamined manuscripts in the Austrian and Eastern European monastery and court collections. Results of this research were then applied to his *Symphonies of Joseph Haydn* (1955; item 964) and to a resumption of the defunct Haydn Society's project of publishing a modern edition of the symphonies. (The final volume of Landon's edition, based in part on Haydn Society symphony volumes that had been taken over by Universal Edition, appeared in 1967.)

Following the demise of the Haydn Society, responsibility for preparing a complete edition passed to the Joseph Haydn Institute, established at Cologne in 1955. Larsen, who had been director of the Haydn Society, became head of the newly formed organization. He was succeeded in that position in 1961 by its current chief, Georg Feder.

Under Feder's leadership, the lack of bibliographical control of the sources, identified by Larsen as the principal hindrance to progress in Haydn research, has been attacked head-on. Guiding a team of talented archivists, Feder has supervised the methodical, deliberate progress of the *Joseph Haydn Werke*, now scheduled for completion by approximately the year 2000. The projected total number of volumes stands at no fewer than 100. With each volume undertaken, the aim has been to represent authentic sources as precisely as possible and to supply each with a detailed critical commentary that includes description of the sources, filiation, variant readings, and critical evaluation based on provenance, notational style, and musical plausibility. In addition to preparing the volumes of the complete edition, the institute has undertaken publication of a periodical, *Haydn-Studien* (item 72), as a vehicle for disseminating information on its researches and discoveries.

Other post-war developments, not directly related to the Cologne institute's activities, have helped accelerate the advancement of Haydn research. The year 1957 saw the appearance of the first volume of Hoboken's thematic catalogue (item 28; two subsequent volumes, which appeared in 1971 and 1978 respectively, profited from the results of source research undertaken by Feder and his colleagues). In 1961, the Hungarian scholars Dénes Bartha and László Somfai published their pathbreaking study, *Haydn als Opernkapellmeister* (item 535). Based upon documents associated with the Esterházy music establishment, the book furnished a new perspective on the composer by revealing the previously unrecognized extent of his involvement in the direction of operatic productions for his patron.

In the field of instrumental music, traditionally beset by problems of authenticity and chronology, increased familiarity with sources of the period has led to further clarification of Haydn's oeuvre and its historical position. A leading role has been played by Jan LaRue, whose vast "Union Thematic Catalogue of 18th-Century Symphonies" now encompasses more than 16,000 sources (see item 44). Addressing the central problem of mistaken attribution, a critically important issue in Haydn research, this venture has involved extensive first-hand examination of sources in addition to the assembling of information from eighteenth-century printed and manuscript catalogues, modern printed catalogues for individual composers and collections, and catalogues of library holdings.

In the waning years of the twentieth century, major tasks have reached completion. Landon has managed to assemble an overwhelming amount of information in his five-volume *Haydn: Chronicle and Works* (item 259); the final volume of Hoboken's catalogue has become available; and Irmgard Becker-Glauch's detailed study of the Haydn prints has appeared in *RISM* A/I/4 (1974; item 8). Thanks to the continued progress of the *Joseph Haydn Werke*, major source problems have been resolved, and the authentic canon of the composer's works has been firmly established.

Thus the condition of Haydn scholarship has changed drastically in a relatively brief span of time, and from the vastly increased quantity of information that has become available, a historical figure of unexpected complexity has emerged. New questions have arisen in the fields of biography and stylistic criticism. The issue of Haydn's artistic development--the changes in outlook and technique that his music underwent in the course of his career--has been tackled afresh. Endowed with a new appreciation for his musical legacy and its transmission, scholars have undertaken the reexamination of his role as a teacher and his influence on younger contemporaries. Landon has identified the existence of several Haydn "schools," and Douglas Johnson has shown how the study of the composer's late symphonic style can shed new light on Beethoven's early development (item 332). Other topics being newly addressed include Haydn's relations with his Esterházy patrons, the nature of his business practices, his sense of his own worth and historical importance, and his place within the political, cultural, and social history of his day.

As with other great masters, our interpretation of Haydn changes from one generation to the next as it reflects changing values, attitudes, and fashions. That Haydn represents something of an extreme case is attributable to traits of his artistic personality, conditions under which particular works of his were created, and the circumstances under which different facets of his output have been variously cherished or relegated to obscurity. More than two and a half centuries after Haydn's birth, we have come full circle. But if our appreciation of his worth as the master of an inimitably popular, universal style is less fervent than that of critics and audiences of his own day, it is nevertheless based on a clearer understanding of his entire output.

Doubtless our image of Haydn will continue to change and evolve. But whereas changes of attitude in the past were conditioned by, and largely dependent on, the rediscovery of forgotten sources, this is a phase that has essentially drawn to a close. Now it can at least be said that subsequent developments in our understanding of Haydn's oeuvre will be based on virtually full awareness of its scope. Belatedly, but decisively, a foundation has been laid on which critical judgments of the composer's music and its significance can be formed.

III

BASIC RESOURCES

Bibliographies

Restricted to independently published bibliographical studies, this listing excludes bibliographies that accompany encyclopedia articles on Haydn, most notably those in *Die Musik in Geschichte und Gegenwart* (item 64) and *The New Grove Dictionary* (item 63). The bibliography in the latter is updated in *The New Grove Haydn* (item 269). Also worthy of mention are the relatively recent, extended bibliographies in Vignal's *Joseph Haydn* (item 302) and in the fifth volume of Landon's *Haydn: Chronicle and Works* (item 259).

1. Brown, A. Peter, in collaboration with Brown, Carol Vanderbilt. "Joseph Haydn in Literature: A Survey." *Notes* 31 (1974-75):530-47.

   Offers bibliographical guidance to "those unfamiliar with the research terrain for Haydn." Calls attention to important studies or research tools, classified under the headings Special Publications, Biographies, Stylistic Studies, Bibliographies of Works, Instrumental Works, Vocal Works, and Performance Practice.

2. ———, and Berkenstock, James T., in collaboration with Brown, Carol Vanderbilt. "Joseph Haydn in Literature: A Bibliography." *Haydn-Studien* 3 (1973-74):173-352.

Designed as "a beginning contribution to bibliographic control of the Haydn literature," constitutes by far the most ambitious bibliographical study to date. Encompasses 2,285 items, principally books, articles, theses, and dissertations pertaining specifically to Haydn. Excludes general anthologies of letters, general music histories, histories of the Classical period, most genre histories, concert notes, and libretti. Furnishes a single alphabetical listing, with detailed indexes of topics, proper names and places, and works.

3. Hatting, Carsten E., and Krabbe, Niels. "Bibliografi over Professor Jens Peter Larsens skrifter." In *Festskrift Jens Peter Larsen, 14. VI. 1902–1972,* edited by Nils Schiørring, Henrik Glahn, and Carsten E. Hatting, pp. 1-10. Copenhagen: Wilhelm Hansen, 1972.

A single chronological listing of Larsen's publications spanning the years 1929–70.

4. Heller, Friedrich C. "Haydn-Nachlese." *Österreichische Musikzeitschrift* 38 (1983):54–58.

A discussion and list of several recent Haydn studies and editions of his works, chiefly from the anniversary year 1982.

5. Surian, Elvidio. *A Checklist of Writings on 18th-Century French and Italian Opera (Excluding Mozart).* Hackensack, NJ: Joseph Boonin, 1970. xiv, 121 pp.

Covers dictionaries, general chronologies, general bibliographies, eighteenth-century writings on opera, travel reports and memoirs, librettos and librettists, singing and singers, theatrical productions, studies on individual composers, and studies on individual cities. The section devoted to Haydn encompasses 22 items.

6. Walter, Horst. "Haydn-Bibliographie 1973–1983." *Haydn-Studien* 5 (1982–85):205–306.

Providing a sequel to the Brown/Berkenstock bibliography (item 2), encompasses more than 700 items. Features an extended critical introduction that discusses major contributions to the literature within the years covered. Furnishes a chronological list of Haydn letters and other documents rediscovered in the years 1965–83.

Catalogues and Indexes

Major landmarks within this category include the magisterial three-volume catalogue of Haydn's works prepared by Anthony van Hoboken (item 28), whose numerical system of categorization has been universally recognized; Jens Peter Larsen's facsimile edition of the early Haydn thematic inventories, *Drei Haydn Kataloge* (item 41), reprinted with preface and commentary in English as *Three Haydn Catalogues* (item 43); and Irmgard Becker-Glauch's catalogue for *RISM* A/I/4 (item 8). In addition to smaller, specialized catalogues and related studies pertinent to Haydn, this section includes a sampling of publishers' catalogues and inventories of archival collections in which Haydn is well represented. Attention should also be called to the "Thematic Catalogue of the Authentic Symphonies" in Landon, *The Symphonies of Joseph Haydn* (item 964).

7. Albrecht, Otto E. *A Census of Autograph Music Manuscripts of European Composers in American Libraries.* Philadelphia: University of Pennsylvania Press, 1953. xvii, 331 pp.

   Organized alphabetically by composer, includes listings for 19 Haydn manuscripts. Provides a description of each item and information on current and former owners, where available.

8. Becker-Glauch, Irmgard. "Haydn, Franz Joseph." In *International Inventory of Musical Sources (RISM).* A/I/4: *Einzeldrucke vor 1800,* pp. 140-279. Kassel: Bärenreiter, 1974.

   This rigorously researched inventory of Haydn sources divides into four categories: *Gesamtausgaben,* Vocal Music, Instrumental Works, and Arrangements.

9. Brook, Barry S., ed. *The Breitkopf Thematic Catalogue: The Six Parts and Sixteen Supplements, 1762-1787.* New York: Dover, 1966. xxvii pp., 888 cols., lxxxi pp.

   Reprint of the dated thematic catalogues of manuscript and printed music available from Breitkopf. The editor's introduction offers commentary on the catalogue and its utility, including its use in establishing terminal datings for undated works. An index, likewise supplied by the editor, directs the reader to numerous works attributed to Haydn.

10. ———. *Thematic Catalogues in Music: An Annotated Bibliography.* Hillsdale, NY: Pendragon, 1972. xxxvi, 347 pp.

A listing of all thematic catalogues, both printed and in manuscript, known to the author. Includes a substantial representation of catalogues in which Haydn is represented, in addition to those devoted exclusively to Haydn.

11. Bryant, Stephen C., and Chapman, Gary W. *A Melodic Index to Haydn's Instrumental Music: A Thematic Locator for Anthony van Hoboken's 'Thematisch-bibliographisches Werkverzeichnis,' Vols. I & III.* New York: Pendragon, 1982. xvii, 100 pp.

Using a system of alphabetic notation, presents incipits in two separate lists: one represents original keys, while the other involves transposition to C major or minor. For each entry, gives key, Hoboken number, page number in the Hoboken catalogue, and location on the page.

12. Dearling, Robert. "Annotations to the Breitkopf Thematic Catalogue and Supplements." *The Haydn Yearbook* 9 (1975):256-302.

Provides supplementary information on symphonies, trios, overtures, and related instrumental works listed by Breitkopf. Arranged by genre, then by the order in the Dover reprint (item 9), then composer, collection number, and number within the collection. For any work listed, the information given includes known references to the work in standard texts on the composer, differences in instrumentation, and, where applicable, conflicting attributions. Contains numerous entries for Haydn.

13. Deutsch, Otto Erich. "Haydn als Sammler." *Österreichische Musikzeitschrift* 14 (1959):188-93.

Surveys the catalogues of music and books owned by Haydn. The earliest is Johann Elssler's "Verzeichnis musikalischer Werke theils eigner, theils fremder Composition" (not before 1807); but Ignaz Sauer's auction catalogue of 1809, the "Inventur und Schätzung der Joseph Haydnschen Kunstsachen," is more inclusive. Among items from the catalogues selected for discussion is Haydn's parrot, for which the author includes Sauer's full catalogue description and a passage from Dies.

14. ———. "Haydns Musikbücherei." In *Musik und Verlag: Karl Vötterle zum 65. Geburtstag am 12. April 1968,* edited by Richard Baum and Wolfgang Rehm, pp. 220-21. Kassel: Bärenreiter, 1968.

A list of music books in Haydn's library, based on a catalogue of 1807 and the *Nachlass* inventory.

15. ———. "Theme and Variations, with Bibliographical Notes on Pleyel's Haydn Editions." *The Music Review* 12 (1951):68-71.

Discusses origins and early uses of the term "thematic catalogue," and questions the appropriateness of the word "thematic" to designate the opening bars of a work. Briefly describes Pleyel's editions of Haydn's string quartets, which included a thematic catalogue. Notes that in the second edition, the word *thématique* was dropped.

16. Feder, Georg. "Joseph Haydns Skizzen und Entwürfe: Übersicht der Manuskripte, Werkregister, Literatur- und Ausgabenverzeichnis." *Fontes Artis Musicae* 26 (1979):172-88.

An inventory of manuscripts, arranged by library, with information on the sources and references to facsimiles, transcriptions, and literature. Source information includes identification by Hoboken number (where possible), description of the nature of the sketch or draft, writing material used, number of pages, and placement in the source. Provides an index (by Hoboken number, in numerical order) and a bibliography of literature and editions.

17. Flotzinger, Rudolf. "Ein handschriftliches Exzerpt aus dem Haydn-Verzeichnis von Elssler." *Haydn-Studien* 5 (1982-85):191-97.

Reports on the discovery (in Friedrich Ambrosi's *Nachlass*) of a non-thematic inventory based on Elssler's thematic catalogue. Reproduces its contents, and compares totals by genre with those represented by the Elssler catalogue itself and excerpts in Dies, Griesinger, and Bertuch. Proposes a relative chronology of the excerpts (all supposedly from 1805), placing the Ambrosi source between Dies and Griesinger; Bertuch is placed last. Determines that the manuscript is accurate with respect to its model, and that it sometimes provides additional information.

18. Fuchs, Alois. *Thematisches Verzeichnis der sämtlichen Kompositionen von Joseph Haydn.* Edited by Richard Schaal. Wilhelmshaven: Heinrichshofen, 1968. xi, 204 pp.

A photographic reproduction of the 1839 manuscript catalogue. Schaal's preface furnishes information on Fuchs, places the catalogue in the context of other early Haydn catalogues, and offers an appraisal of its significance.

19. Geiringer, Karl. *A Thematic Catalogue of Haydn's Settings of Folksongs from the British Isles.* Superior, WI: Research Microfilm Publishers, 1953. 438 cards.

Available in microfilm as RMP Studies in Musicology, Series A, II, constitutes the photographic reproduction of a 438-item card catalogue, preceded by a reprint of Geiringer's 1949 study published in *The Musical Quarterly* (item 559). Information supplied for items represented includes incipit, title, Elssler catalogue number, manuscript and printed sources, first line of text, poet, and miscellaneous information on multiple versions and alternative texts.

20. Gerlach, Sonja. "Haydns 'chronologische' Sinfonienliste für Breitkopf & Härtel." *Haydn-Studien* 6/2 (1988):116-29.

A fresh look at the list, which survives only in a copy by Pohl and which has no incipits, but rather a system of numbers referring presumably to a lost Breitkopf catalogue. Gives a table of concordances with entries in an extant Breitkopf catalogue, and attempts to decode the numerical list. Concludes from available evidence that the date 1757 can be assigned to the symphony Hob. I:1. Includes facsimile pages from the list and the extant Breitkopf catalogue.

21. Harich, János. "Inventare der Esterházy-Hofmusikkapelle in Eisenstadt." *The Haydn Yearbook* 9 (1975):5-125.

Offers a concise history of the Esterházys, beginning with the sixteenth century, as a backdrop for discussion and transcription of the 1721 inventory of church music, Werner's inventory of 1737-38, the thematic catalogue of 1740, the catalogue of 1759, Haydn's opera list of 1784, and J.N. Hummel's catalogue of 1806. Discusses the significance of the inventories as a reflection of contemporary events and musical practices at the court. Includes a summary in English.

22. *Haydn-Museum Eisenstadt: Katalog.* Eisenstadt: Amt der Burgenländischen Landesregierung, 1980. 85 pp. plus illustrations.

A catalogue of all items on display at the Haydn-Museum, prefaced by a history of the Haydn house and a floor plan. Includes discussions of such relevant topics as Haydn portraits exhibited, the Haydn autographs, Eszterháza castle, and Haydn's relations with the Polzelli family. Contains 22 illustrations and a family tree for the Esterházy family from 1687 to 1833. Translated by Günther Stefanits, in somewhat altered form, as *Haydn-Museum Eisenstadt: Catalogue* (Eisenstadt: Amt der Burgenländischen Landesregierung, 1982).

23. Hirsch, Ferdinand. *Zeitgenössische Drucke und Handschriften der Werke Joseph Haydns in der Musikbibliothek der Stadt Leipzig.* Leipzig: Musikbibliothek der Stadt Leipzig, 1962. 57 pp.

The collection represented includes printed editions of symphonies, string quartets, sonatas, masses, oratorios, arias, and songs; volumes from early collected editions; libretti; portraits; and manuscripts. Most sources date from the last quarter of the eighteenth century. A brief physical description accompanies each listed source. Several facsimiles; no index.

24. Hoboken, Anthony van. "Die Entstehung des *Thematischen Verzeichnisses der Werke von Joseph Haydn.*" *Acta Musicologica* 29 (1957):106-7.

An account of the origins and development of the author's catalogue (item 28).

25. ———. "Die Entwicklung des Haydn-Werkverzeichnisses." In *Festschrift für einen Verleger: Ludwig Strecker zum 90. Geburtstag,* edited by Carl Dahlhaus, pp. 72-75. Mainz: B. Schott's Söhne, 1973.

Aspects of the development and publication of the Hoboken catalogue.

26. ———. "The First Thematic Catalog of Haydn's Works." *Notes* 9 (1951-52):226-27.

Describes the structure and scope of the then forthcoming catalogue.

27. ———. "The First Thematic Catalog of Haydn's Works--Volume II." *Notes* 28 (1971-72):209-11.

A description of the structure and contents, with miscellaneous pieces of information about several of the vocal works.

28. ———. *Joseph Haydn: Thematisch-bibliographisches Werkverzeichnis.* 3 vols. Mainz: B. Schott's Söhne, 1957-78. xxi, 848 pp.; 602 pp.; 424 pp.

Divides into five parts, distributed among the volumes as follows: volume 1, 1957: 1) instrumental music, subdivided into 20 categories; volume 2, 1971: 2) vocal music, subdivided into 11 categories; 3) arrangements and pasticcios; volume 3, 1978: 4) early Haydn collections, early anthologies in which Haydn is represented, and various other indexes: opus numbers, publishers, nicknames, dedicatees and sponsors, locations of autograph manuscripts, titles and text incipits, abbreviations; 5) addenda, corrigenda, general index. Designates each category by Roman numeral, and each work within a category by Arabic number in accordance with existing modern catalogues, where available (elsewhere, follows numberings in the 1805 Haydn catalogue). Designates and arranges unauthentic works by group, key, and Arabic number (e.g. I:D4). Individual entries supply relevant information on date, scoring, catalogue references, manuscript copies, editions, arrangements, and references in Haydn correspondence and in the Haydn literature.

29. ———. "Zum Haydn-Katalog." *Österreichische Musikzeitschrift* 14 (1959):202-5.

A response to letters and reviews that pointed out errors in the first volume of item 28. To show how easily errors can arise in source research, describes problems encountered during preparation of the second volume with respect to insertion arias attributed to Haydn.

30. Holm, Anna-Lena. *Index of Titles and Text Incipits to Anthony van Hoboken: 'Joseph Haydn. Thematisch-bibliographisches Werkverzeichnis. 2. Vokalwerke.' (Mainz 1971).* Strandvägen: Swedish Music History Archive, 1978. 53 pp.

A single alphabetical list encompassing all titles and text incipits in the Hoboken volume. Gives page references in the catalogue.

31. Hopkinson, Cecil, and Oldman, C.B. "Haydn and Beethoven in Thomson's Collections." *Edinburgh Bibliographical Society Transactions* 2/1 (1938-39):1-64.

Contains a thematic catalogue of 187 settings by Haydn of Scottish, Welsh, and Irish songs for the publisher Thomson. For each entry, supplies the edition or editions in which the song was published, the volume and page number, and the publication date. The catalogue is preceded by a history of the Scottish collections, a list of the different editions, a short bibliography, collations, and facsimiles of selected title pages.

32. ———. "Haydn and Beethoven in Thomson's Collections: Addenda et Corrigenda." *Edinburgh Bibliographical Society Transactions* 3/2 (1949-50, 1950-51):121-24.

Two pages of corrections for Haydn material in item 31.

33. ———. "Haydn's Settings of Scottish Songs in the Collections of Napier and Whyte." *Edinburgh Bibliographical Society Transactions* 3/2 (1949-50, 1950-51):85-120.

A supplement to item 31. The thematic catalogue adds 221 Scottish settings published by Napier and Whyte. Introductory material discusses the history of both firms, the musical layout of Napier's volumes, and Haydn's contributions. Among further material included are collations and cross references to settings that appear also in Thomson.

34. Hörwarthner, Maria. "Joseph Haydns Bibliothek--Versuch einer literarhistorischen Rekonstruktion." In *Joseph Haydn und die Literatur seiner Zeit* (item 79), pp. 157-207.

Provides an annotated reconstruction of an 1809 manuscript list of Haydn's books. Contains complete bibliographical references, and furnishes commentary on how each item (92 in all) may have related to the composer and his work. An index categorizes the items as either nonfiction (by topic or genre) or fiction (by language). Concludes with remarks on the nature of the library in light of contemporary tastes.

* Jerger, Wilhelm. *Die Haydndrucke aus dem Archiv der 'Theater- und Musik-Liebhabergesellschaft zu Luzern' nebst Materialien zum Musikleben in Luzern um 1800.* Freiburg in der Schweiz: Universitätsverlag, 1959. 45 pp.

Cited as item 465.

35. Johansson, Cari. *French Music Publishers' Catalogues of the Second Half of the Eighteenth Century.* 2 vols. Stockholm, 1955. xiii, 228 pp.; 146 facsimiles.

Offers facsimiles and commentary for non-thematic catalogues of nine French music publishers. For each publisher, the text volume provides historical background and chronological discussion of the catalogues. Datings for catalogues are provided on the basis of published announcements of works listed; these datings may be used in turn to place other, unadvertised works that appear in the catalogues. Numerous references to Haydn.

36. ———. *J.J. & B. Hummel Music-Publishing and Thematic Catalogues.* 3 vols. Stockholm, 1972. xvii, 136 pp.; 56 facsimiles; 76 facsimiles.

Provides background information on the brothers Hummel, and discusses methods of dating their prints. The text volume offers commentary on the non-thematic catalogues of 1762-1814, with references to dated, published announcements of works contained in the catalogues; it also offers brief discussion of the thematic catalogue (1768-74) and a list of plate numbers with terminal datings. Two volumes of facsimiles contain the non-thematic catalogues and the thematic catalogue, respectively. In both catalogues and text, Haydn is given substantial representation.

37. *Katalog der Sammlung Anthony van Hoboken in der Musiksammlung der österreichischen Nationalbibliothek.* Vol. 6: *Joseph Haydn, Symphonien (Hob. I, Ia);* Vol. 7: *Joseph Haydn, Instrumentalmusik (Hob. II-XI).* Edited by Karin

Breitner. Tutzing: Hans Schneider, 1987-89. xiii, 248 pp.; xiii, 219 pp.

Encompassing a total of 975 entries, these two volumes represent the holdings in Hoboken's private collection for individual prints and printed collections of Haydn's instrumental music within the designated Hoboken categories (I-XI). Individual entries are furnished with detailed documentary information including catalogue numbers, contents of title pages, instrumental parts, format, watermarks, plate numbers, and dating. A substantial number of title pages reproduced in facsimile.

38. Lachmann, Robert. "Die Haydn-Autographen der Staatsbibliothek zu Berlin." *Zeitschrift für Musikwissenschaft* 14 (1931-32):289-98.

A chiefly non-thematic inventory, incorporating operas and other theatrical pieces, non-dramatic vocal works, instrumental compositions, and letters. Identifies the musical sources with numbers from the Breitkopf & Härtel *Gesamtausgabe* and other pre-Hoboken resources.

39. Landon, H.C. Robbins. "Doubtful and Spurious Quartets and Quintets Attributed to Haydn." *The Music Review* 18 (1957):213-21.

A catalogue containing then-new information on three groups of works: quartets and quintets published in sets of 6 (6 sets), single string quartets (32 works), and single string quintets (10 works). Thematic incipits are provided for the sets and for single works not cited in Larsen's *Drei Haydn Kataloge* (item 41). For each work, information is given on attributions and sources, with indication (where applicable) of correct or probable author.

40. ———. "Haydn and Authenticity: Some New Facts." *The Music Review* 16 (1955):138-40.

A supplement to Larsen's *Drei Haydn Kataloge* (item 41). In catalogue form, reports on "new sources through which it was possible to ascribe to the correct, or probably correct author a number of non-symphonic works hitherto attributed to Joseph Haydn." Identifies some as authentic Haydn works.

41. Larsen, Jens Peter, ed. *Drei Haydn Kataloge in Faksimile*

mit Einleitung und ergänzenden Themenverzeichnissen. Copenhagen: Einar Munksgaard, 1941. 138 pp.

Reproduces in facsimile the three thematic catalogues dating from Haydn's day that were written or supervised by Haydn himself: the "Entwurf-Katalog" (begun ca. 1765), the "Kees-Katalog" (completed in the years 1790-92), and the "Haydn-Verzeichnis" (prepared by Johann Elssler in 1805). Gives background and descriptive information on the catalogues, which represent a principal foundation of modern Haydn research. See item 43 for an expanded English version.

* ———. "The Haydn Tradition." In Jens Peter Larsen. *Handel, Haydn, and the Viennese Classical Style,* translations by Ulrich Krämer, pp. 185-224. Ann Arbor: UMI Research Press, 1988.

Cited as item 477.

* ———. *Die Haydn-Überlieferung.* Copenhagen: Einar Munksgaard, 1939. Reprint, with foreword by the author. Munich: Kraus International Publications, 1980. xviii, 335 pp.

Cited as item 478.

* ———. "Haydn und das 'kleine Quartbuch'." *Acta Musicologica* 7 (1935):111-23.

Cited as item 479.

42. ———. "Probleme der chronologischen Ordnung von Haydns Sinfonien." In *Festschrift Otto Erich Deutsch zum 80. Geburtstag am 5. September 1963,* edited by Walter Gerstenberg, Jan LaRue, and Wolfgang Rehm, pp. 90-104. Kassel: Bärenreiter, 1963.

Considers the question of how to organize a thematic catalogue, and in this context, examines Hoboken's catalogue of Haydn's works (item 28). Calls attention to unevenness in source representation and to inconsistent treatment of chronology for the different genres. Pays particular attention to chronology of the symphonies, pointing out Hoboken's heavy reliance on Mandyczewski's catalogue and his occasional use of unsubstantiated datings. Discusses five chronological indexes for the symphonies that appeared between 1950 and 1956; and for comparative purposes, provides a table in which the datings from these indexes appear alongside those of Mandyczewski and Hoboken.

43. ———, ed. *Three Haydn Catalogues (Drei Haydn Kataloge).* 2d facs. ed., with a survey of Haydn's oeuvre. New York: Pendragon, 1979. xlvi, 119 pp.

Translation of item 41, with a newly added survey of works that gives a summary appraisal of authenticity within each genre.

44. LaRue, Jan. *A Catalogue of 18th-Century Symphonies.* Vol. 1: *Thematic Identifier.* Bloomington: Indiana University Press, 1988. xvi, 352 pp.

Spanning the time-period ca. 1720-ca. 1810, uses an alphabetical-numeric system to list melodic incipits for the 16,558 works represented. Furnishes a composer's identification number and name for each entry. To be followed by *Composers' Worklists* volumes with incipits in full musical notation. Databases also to be made available on microfilm or compact disk.

45. ———. "Haydn Listings in the Rediscovered Leuckart Supplements: Breslau, 1788-92." In *Studies in Eighteenth-Century Music: A Tribute to Karl Geiringer on His Seventieth Birthday,* edited by H.C. Robbins Landon and Roger E. Chapman, pp. 310-14. New York: Oxford University Press, 1970.

Describes the contents of the supplements, which begin at the time Breitkopf ceased issuing supplements to that firm's thematic catalogue. Composers most heavily represented include Pleyel, Hoffmeister, Haydn, Koželuch, and Mozart. Includes a comparison of Leuckart's lists of music by 27 composers for each of the 10 supplements, and a summary of Haydn works represented: 20 symphonies, 33 quartets, and 10 solo keyboard sonatas.

46. ———. "Ten Rediscovered Sale-Catalogues: Leuckart's Supplements, Breslau 1787-1792." In *Musik und Verlag: Karl Vötterle zum 65. Geburtstag am 12. April 1968,* edited by Richard Baum and Wolfgang Rehm, pp. 424-32. Kassel: Bärenreiter, 1968.

Offers description and analysis of the supplements and discusses their significance as bibliographical tools. Provides a representative sample (1791) of categories included. Compares the supplements to Breitkopf's and notes, among other things, fundamental differences in emphases and sources of supply. Shows how the supplements give evidence of efficient collection of publications from widely dispersed sources.

47. *Österreichische Nationalbibliothek. Katalog des Archivs für Photogramme musikalischer Meisterhandschriften Widmung Anthony van Hoboken,* part 1. Edited by Agnes Ziffer. Vienna: Georg Prachner, 1967. xxiv, 482 pp.

The collection in question, comprising photographic reproductions of manuscripts by the great composers, was initiated by Anthony van Hoboken under the stimulus of Heinrich Schenker. Housed in the Österreichische Nationalbibliothek since 1927, it was donated to the library in 1957 and has enjoyed subsequent expansion. Among the Haydn entries (pp. 193-238; catalogue nos. 1178-1452), letters, London notebooks, thematic catalogues, and a wide diversity of vocal and instrumental compositions are represented.

48. Pazdírek, Franz. "Haydn Josef (1732-1809)." In *Universal-Handbuch der Musikliteratur,* 12:238-70. Vienna, 1904-10. Reprint. Hilversum: Frits Knuf, 1967. 5:583-615.

An alphabetical listing of printed Haydn compositions. Identifies publishers, and gives information on instrumentation, format, and price.

49. Radant, Else. "A Facsimile of Hummel's Catalogue of the Princely Music Library in Eisenstadt, with Transliteration and Commentary." *The Haydn Yearbook* 11 (1980):5-182.

An inventory of all music owned by the Esterházy family, prepared by Johann Nepomuk Hummel for Nikolaus II. The 114-page catalogue, organized primarily by genre, begins with Hummel's own compositions, and was declared by Hummel to be correct and to have been brought up to date as of 24 March 1806. The transliteration is followed by an annotated list of operas in the inventory, arranged alphabetically by composer, with specification of premieres, early publications, and related information.

50. Rokseth, Yvonne. "Manuscrits de Joseph Haydn à la Bibliothèque du Conservatoire de Paris." *Revue de musicologie* 14 (1933):40-41.

Addenda and corrections to the list of autographs in the Saint-Foix article, item 51.

51. Saint-Foix, Georges de. "Les Manuscrits et les copies d'oeuvres de Joseph Haydn à la Bibliothèque du Conservatoire (Fonds Malherbe)." *Revue de musicologie* 13 (1932):206-13.

Annotated list of Haydn autographs and of copies contained in the collection.

52. Schmid, Manfred Hermann. *Die Musikaliensammlung der Erzabtei St. Peter in Salzburg, Katalog.* Part 1: *Leopold und Wolfgang Amadeus Mozart, Joseph und Michael Haydn.* Salzburg, 1970. 300 pp.

For Joseph Haydn's works (pp. 76-102), provides detailed decriptions of early manuscript and printed sources (mainly eighteenth and early nineteenth century), grouped under the headings of instrumental works, vocal works, and collections.

53. Vécsey, Jenő, ed. *Haydn Compositions in the Music Collection of the National Széchényi Library, Budapest, published on the Occasion of the 150th Anniversary of Haydn's Death (1809-1959).* Translated by Sándor Országh. Budapest: Hungarian Academy of Sciences, 1960. xxiii, 167 pp.

Introductory matter discusses Haydn's relationship to Hungary, the neglect of certain genres in his musical output, and vast holdings of Haydn materials at the library (only a portion of these are represented in the Music Collection). The text contains photographs of selected documents and sources, followed by a listing of all Haydn compositions, in each instance by genre: autographs, contemporary manuscript copies, and contemporary printed editions. Four indexes provide access to the works and names. Originally published in Hungarian in 1959. Also published in German as *Haydns Werke in der Musiksammlung der Nationalbibliothek Széchényi in Budapest, hrsg. anlässlich der 150-sten Jahreswende seines Todes, 1809-1959* (Budapest: Ungarische Akademie der Wissenschaften, 1959).

54. *Verzeichnis von musikalischen Autographen, revidirten Abschriften und einigen seltenen gedruckten Original-Ausgaben vornemlich der reichen Bestände aus dem Nachlasse Joseph Haydn's und Ludwig van Beethoven's ... im Besitze von August Artaria in Wien.* Vienna: [Artaria], 1893. 26 pp.

Haydn listings comprise a diversity of full scores and fragments of vocal and instrumental works, including material from several of the operas. No incipits, and little in the way of detailed description of contents for the items listed.

Articles in Dictionaries and Encyclopedias

This listing describes a selection of Haydn articles in major reference books on music, the most recent, accessible, and comprehensive of which is that prepared by Jens Peter Larsen and Georg Feder for *The New Grove Dictionary* (item 63), available in modified form as *The New Grove Haydn* (item 269). Haydn entries in late eighteenth- and early nineteenth-century reference books are included below under the category "Early Accounts."

55. Brenet, Michel [Marie Bobillier]. "Les Grandes Classiques." In *Encyclopédie de la musique et dictionnaire du conservatoire.* Part 1: *Histoire de la musique,* edited by Albert Lavignac, 2:1014-60. Paris: Delagrave, 1913.

The biographical discussion of Haydn, pp. 1025-34, places special emphasis on his youth and the early years of his Esterházy employment.

56. Bücken, Ernst. *Handbuch der Musikwissenschaft.* Vol. 4: *Die Musik des Rokokos und der Klassik.* Wildpark-Potsdam: Akademische Verlagsgesellschaft Athenaion, 1927. 247 pp.

A lavishly illustrated volume that strives for an overview of contributions by major and secondary figures to the evolution of styles in eighteenth-century music. Discussion of Haydn, pp. 191-205, portrays him as the embodiment of humanistic ideals of the age and emphasizes the influence of C.P.E. Bach in his artistic development. Divides his creative output into three periods: early (to

1770), middle (1770-90), and late, and links the start of the middle period to the onset of the so-called "Romantic crisis." While discerning no marked discontinuity between middle and late works, sees the London symphonies, late masses, oratorios, and later sets of string quartets as an artistic summit attained after long ascent. Relegates the theatrical works to the periphery of Haydn's accomplishment.

57. Della Croce, Luigi. "Haydn, Franz Joseph." In *Dizionario enciclopedico universale della musica e dei musicisti.* Vol. 3: *Le biografie,* edited by Alberto Basso, pp. 481-525. Turin: Unione Tipografico-Editrice Torinese, 1986.

Includes an overview of the history of Haydn's reputation and of the publication of his works. Organizes discussion of the music by genre, and provides a detailed, tabular listing of works. Offers a concise, topically organized bibliography.

58. Eitner, Robert. "Haydn, Joseph." In *Biographisch-bibliographisches Quellen-Lexikon der Musiker und Musikgelehrten der christlichen Zeitrechnung bis zur Mitte des XIX. Jahrhunderts,* 5:59-72. Leipzig, Breitkopf & Härtel, 1901. Reprint. Graz: Akademische Druck- und Verlagsanstalt, 1959.

Includes an extended list of nineteenth-century biographical accounts, a chronological list of works after Pohl, and a catalogue of prints and manuscripts of works by Haydn, organized by category, with information on location of sources.

59. Feder, Georg. "Haydn, Franz Joseph." In *Riemann Musik Lexikon, Ergänzungsband, Personenteil A-K,* 12th ed., edited by Carl Dahlhaus, pp. 499-504. Mainz: B. Schott's Söhne, 1972.

Reports updated research on Haydn's output: newly discovered authentic works and pieces no longer attributed to Haydn. List of editions; bibliography (see item 61).

60. Fétis, François Joseph. "Haydn (François-Joseph)." In *Biographie universelle des musiciens et bibliographie générale de la musique,* 2d ed., 4:254-70. Paris: Didot, 1874. Reprint. Brussels: Culture et Civilization, 1963.

First published in 1839 (Brussels: Leroux). Recounts the major anecdotes from early biographies, and describes important events in Haydn's life, without attempting a portrayal of his character. Extolling the purity, clarity, and naturalness of the instrumental works, asserts that they lack the passion of Mozart's and the energy of Beethoven's. Offers a deprecating assessment of the operas and sacred music, and values the late oratorios less highly than the great instrumental compositions. Provides a list of works by category and a short bibliography of published biographical studies.

61. Geiringer, Karl. "Haydn, Franz Joseph." In *Riemann Musik Lexikon, Personenteil A-K,* 12th ed., edited by Wilibald Gurlitt, pp. 750-54. Mainz: B. Schott's Söhne, 1959.

A concise summary of Haydn's life and an overview of his output. Provides a listing of published editions of compositions and a short bibliography (see item 59).

62. Hadow, William H. *The Oxford History of Music.* Vol. 5: *The Viennese Period.* 2d ed. London: Oxford University Press, 1931. vii, 350 pp.

Covers major developments from C.P.E. Bach to Schubert. Organized according to the principal musical forms. Includes background on eighteenth-century musical tastes, musical instruments and vocal technique. Examines questions of stylistic change, and places great emphasis on the importance of folksong as an inspiration to Haydn, who in this sense represents a major turning point in the history of Western music. Originally published in 1904 (Oxford: Clarendon).

63. Larsen, Jens Peter, and Feder, Georg. "Haydn, (Franz) Joseph." In *The New Grove Dictionary of Music and Musicians,* edited by Stanley Sadie, 8:328-407. London: Macmillan, 1980.

A concise, authoritative account, with a list of works prepared by Georg Feder. Emphasis is biographical rather than critical. Discussion of Haydn's life divides into five segments (early life, 1761-75, 1776-90, London, late years). Summarizes revised views of Haydn's personality, and examines his artistic development by concentrating on his contribution in the major genres: symphony, quartet, opera, mass, and oratorio. Includes an extended bibliography.

64. ———, and Landon, H.C. Robbins. "Haydn, Franz Joseph." In *Die Musik in Geschichte und Gegenwart,* edited by Friedrich Blume, 5: cols. 1857-1933. Kassel: Bärenreiter, 1956.

Major features include a detailed, factual account of Haydn's life, with numerous references to early sources of biographical information; a comprehensive list of works; a catalogue of contemporary prints (organized, in the main, by opus number); a summary list of modern editions, prepared by Richard Schaal, and a large bibliography compiled by Wilhelm Pfannkuch. Divides Haydn's creative accomplishment into three periods: to 1760; 1760-90; Vienna and London works after 1790. Offers a summary overview of Haydn's stylistic development and characteristic traits in the different genres.

65. Loewenberg, Alfred. *Annals of Opera: 1597-1940.* Revised by Harold Rosenthal. 3d ed. Totowa, NJ: Rowman and Littlefield, 1978. xxv, 1756 cols.

Organized chronologically (by year and within each year). Each entry supplied with information on text, location and date of subsequent performances, and pertinent bibliography. Furnishes indexes of operas, composers, and librettists, as well as a general index. First published in 1943 (Cambridge: W. Heffer & Sons).

66. *Neues Handbuch der Musikwissenschaft.* Vol. 5: *Die Musik des 18. Jahrhunderts.* Edited by Carl Dahlhaus. Laaber: Laaber-Verlag, 1985. vi, 434 pp.

Discussion of Haydn, pp. 278-91, offers a fresh look at his role in the development of eighteenth-century instrumental genres. Examines the symphonies, baryton trios, and keyboard trios, in addition to string quartets. Exploring questions of stylistic models and innovation, places particular emphasis on the historical importance of the early quartet publications Op. 1 and 2.

67. *New Oxford History of Music.* Vol. 7: *The Age of Enlightenment: 1745-1790,* edited by Egon Wellesz and Frederick Sternfeld. New York: Oxford University Press, 1973. xx, 724 pp.

Although the treatment of different genres is neither consistent nor unified in approach, and the range of topics and repertory is too broad to permit either a comprehensive overview or penetrating stylistic criticism, the book is nonetheless useful in placing Haydn's output in the context of contemporaries' achievements. Includes a chapter by H.C. Robbins Landon devoted to the operas of Haydn (item 873). Other chapters in which Haydn's music is covered, though in less detail, include "Church Music and Oratorio" by Edward Olleson; "Solo Song" by Rosemary Hughes; "The Concerto" by Wellesz and Sternfeld, based on material submitted by Jan LaRue; "The Rise of Chamber Music" by Karl Geiringer; "Keyboard Music" by Philip Radcliffe; and "Instrumental Masterworks and Aspects of Formal Design" by Frederick Sternfeld.

68. Stieger, Franz. *Opernlexikon,* part 2. 3 vols. Tutzing: Hans Schneider, 1977. 1194 pp.

Provides a list (pp. 480-81) of Haydn's operas, oratorios, and miscellaneous vocal pieces. Names the librettists as well as the date (or year) and place of first performance.

Special Publications

Items listed below consist of major, recent compilations that feature Haydn-related studies. Most prominent in terms of size, diversity, and participation by major scholars are the published papers of major congresses held in celebration of the anniversary years 1959 and 1982. Also included here are the two periodicals devoted to Haydn (*Haydn-Studien* and *The Haydn Yearbook*), but not the special anniversary volumes or fascicles of general music journals, for which the bibliography in *The New Grove Haydn* (item 269) furnishes a separate listing. In all instances, selected individual articles are annotated under the appropriate topic headings.

69. *Beiträge zur Musikgeschichte des 18. Jahrhunderts.* Edited by Friedrich Heller. Jahrbuch für österreichische Kulturgeschichte, 1/2. Eisenstadt: Institut für österreichische Kulturgeschichte, 1971. 190 pp.

A collection devoted largely to articles pertaining directly or indirectly to Haydn. Topics featured include the history of the Esterházy music establishment, Haydn in nineteenth-century Viennese music criticism, the baryton, and Haydn in London. Contributors include Otto Biba, Harald Dreo, Clemens Höslinger, Alfred Lessing, H.C. Robbins Landon, and Friedrich Heller.

70. *Bericht über die Internationale Konferenz zum Andenken Joseph Haydns, Budapest, 17.-22. September 1959.* Edited by Bence Szabolcsi and Dénes Bartha. Budapest: Akadémiai Kiadó, 1961. 186 pp.

A diversity of papers by such scholars as Dénes Bartha, Heinrich Besseler, Gustav Fellerer, Karl Geiringer, H.C. Robbins Landon, François Lesure, Ernst Fritz Schmid, Horst Seeger, and Bence Szabolcsi. Features discussions of regional traditions (including Russian, Hungarian, and Romanian), in addition to such topics as sacred music, opera, and vocal ornamentation.

71. *Haydnfest: Music Festival, September 22-October 11, 1975; International Musicological Conference, October 4-11, 1975.* Edited by Jens Peter Larsen and Howard Serwer. Washington, D.C.: John F. Kennedy Center for the Performing Arts, 1975. 49 pp.

A program of events for the festival and conference. In addition to several illustrations and facsimiles, offers background essays on Haydn's contributions to the major vocal and instrumental genres by leading scholars: Paul Henry Lang, Jens Peter Larsen, James Webster, Georg Feder, Eva Badura-Skoda, and Irmgard Becker-Glauch.

72. *Haydn-Studien* 1- (1965-).

Edited by Georg Feder, and published by the Joseph Haydn Institute in Cologne. Consecutively numbered volumes encompass four fascicles each, but a volume spans several years. Features the results of source research undertaken in connection with preparation of the complete edition (*Joseph Haydn Werke*), yet also includes a wide range of biographical, critical, and analytical studies.

73. *Haydn Studies: Proceedings of the International Haydn Conference, Washington, D.C., 1975.* Edited by Jens Peter Larsen, Howard Serwer, and James Webster. New York: W.W. Norton, 1981. xvii, 590 pp.

Written versions of papers presented and transcriptions of the panel discussions. Topics featured in the conference sessions include biography, iconography, chronology, authenticity, performance, stylistic criticism, and studies of the different genres. Indexes of Haydn compositions and doubtful and spurious works named; list of participants; bibliography of specialist studies cited.

74. *The Haydn Yearbook/Das Haydn Jahrbuch* 1- (1962-).

Published on a (nearly) annual basis, under the editorial direction of H.C. Robbins Landon. Encompasses studies that have to do indirectly as well as directly with Haydn. Features contributions by leading Haydn scholars, with emphasis falling principally on biographical and documentary material. Includes pertinent book reviews, as well as information on auctions, exhibitions, recordings, and editions.

75. *Joseph Haydn.* Edited by Heinz-Klaus Metzger and Rainer Riehn. Munich: Text + Kritik, 1985. 97 pp.

An unorthodox mélange of new and old literary, critical, and theoretical pieces by Hennes Holz, Heinrich Schenker, Klaus-K. Hübler, Hans Rudolf Zeller, Peter Gülke, and Gesine Schröder.

76. *Joseph Haydn: Bericht über den Internationalen Joseph Haydn Kongress, Proceedings of the International Joseph Haydn Congress, Wien, Hofburg, 5.-12. September 1982.* Edited by Eva Badura-Skoda. Munich: G. Henle, 1986. xviii, 641 pp.

Encompasses an opening lecture by Jens Peter Larsen, a closing paper by Georg Feder, and sessions on performance practice, lied and oratorio, style and compositional technique, "musica usualis" of the time of Haydn, opera, instrumental works, church music, documentation and bibliography, and problems of authenticity and chronology.

77. *Joseph Haydn in seiner Zeit, Eisenstadt, 20. Mai-26. Oktober 1982.* Edited by Gerda Mraz, Gottfried Mraz, and Gerald Schlag. Eisenstadt: Amt der Burgenländischen Landesregierung, [1982]. 591 pp., 56 plates.

Lavish catalogue of 1,044 items featured in the 1982 Eisenstadt Haydn exhibition, accompanied by 56 plates (30 in color), a chronology, and 33 papers by major scholars whose topics mirror the interdisciplinary focus of the exhibition: regional eighteenth-century history, economy and society, the Church, science and education, visual arts, literature, theater, and musical environment. Papers concerned directly with Haydn include studies by Otto Biba, A. Peter Brown, Maria Hörwarthner, Clemens Höslinger, H.C. Robbins Landon, Horst Walter, and Herbert Zeman.

78. *Joseph Haydn: Tradition und Rezeption. Bericht über die Jahrestagung der Gesellschaft für Musikforschung, Köln 1982.* Edited by Georg Feder, Heinrich Hüschen, and Ulrich Tank. Regensburg: Gustav Bosse, 1985. xvii, 266 pp.

Contains papers delivered at the annual meeting of the Gesellschaft für Musikforschung in 1982, grouped by colloquia on the following topics: Haydn and the string quartet, Haydn and opera, and Haydn and sacred music. Contributors include Horst Walter, Wulf Konold, Gerhard Allroggen, Howard Smither, and Ulrich Tank.

79. *Joseph Haydn und die Literatur seiner Zeit.* Edited by Herbert Zeman. Jahrbuch für österreichische Kulturgeschichte, 6. Eisenstadt: Institut für österreichische Kulturgeschichte, 1976. 270 pp.

A diverse collection of essays encompassing literary traditions, fashions, and influences to which Haydn was exposed. Topics include central-European popular-song traditions, the Viennese popular comedy, German lieder and the Greiner circle, late eighteenth-century German enthusiasm for British literature, and the contents of Haydn's library. Contributors include Herbert Zeman, Leopold Schmidt, Erika Kanduth, Roswitha Strommer, and Maria Hörwarther. An appendix reproduces correspondence among Karolina von Greiner, Lorenz Leopold Kaschka, and Johann Caspar Lavater. Emphasizing the overall coherence of the volume, the editor's preface cites its significance as a contribution toward a new, more sophisticated image of the composer than that of the traditional "Papa Haydn."

80. *Joseph Haydn und seine Zeit.* Edited by Gerda Mraz. Jahrbuch für österreichische Kulturgeschichte, 2. Eisenstadt: Institut für österreichische Kulturgeschichte, 1972. 160 pp.

Consists of papers delivered at an international symposium on the theme of Joseph Haydn and his times (Eisenstadt, 1971), sponsored by the Institut für österreichische Kulturgeschichte. Includes papers dealing with peripheral areas not directly related to Haydn or to music (e.g. political history, painting, literature). Contributors include Georg Feder, Jens Peter Larsen, László Somfai, and Herbert Zeman.

81. *Der junge Haydn: Wandel von Musikauffassung und Musikaufführung in der österreichischen Musik zwischen Barock und Klassik. Bericht der internationalen Arbeitstagung des Instituts für Aufführungspraxis der Hochschule für Musik und darstellende Kunst in Graz, 29.6.-2.7.1970.* Edited by Vera Schwarz. Graz: Akademische Druck- und Verlagsanstalt, 1972. 264 pp.

A collection of papers read at the first international research conference of the Institut für Aufführungspraxis. Particular emphasis on matters of performance practice and performance medium. Other topics addressed include style change in eighteenth-century Austrian music, folk music, Haydn's early sacred works, and Viennese theater traditions. Featured contributors include Jens Peter Larsen, Rudolf Pečman, Walther Wünsch, Akio Mayeda, Eva Badura-Skoda, Irmgard Becker-Glauch, László Somfai, Eduard Melkus, Gernot Gruber, Georg Feder, Horst Walter, and Vera Schwarz.

IV

HAYDNIANA

Published Correspondence and Documents

By far the most extensive collections of Haydn letters are the volume of translated correspondence edited by Landon (item 107) and Dénes Bartha's German-language compilation (item 87). Other entries listed here include articles that offer substantial background information on Haydn documents, and studies that reproduce letters and other materials not incorporated in the major collections of correspondence. Additional mention should be made of the many contemporary documents, some supplied with English translation, that are incorporated in the volumes of Landon's *Haydn: Chronicle and Works* (item 259).

82. "Acta Musicalia." *The Haydn Yearbook* 14 (1983):9–128.

Consists of documents 36 to 100 of the *Acta Musicalia* from the Esterházy archives, presented in transcription and English translation, with commentary in both German and English (see item 85). Contains a variety of items dating from 1745 to 1811, among them numerous letters to Prince Nikolaus Esterházy and others (including ten from Haydn), some contracts (including Haydn's contract with Prince Anton), and several promises of pension.

83. "Acta Musicalia." *The Haydn Yearbook* 15 (1984):93–180.

Presents documents 101 to 152 of the *Acta Musicalia* in

the Esterházy archives. These are given in transcription with commentary, both in German and in English translation. They consist of assurances of pension, employment contracts, miscellaneous documents, and letters (including a 1791 letter from Antonio Salieri to Prince Anton). While none of the items is addressed to or written by Haydn, they shed pertinent light on daily life at the Esterházy court.

84. "Acta Musicalia." *The Haydn Yearbook* 16 (1985):99-203.

Publishes transcriptions, with commentary, of documents 153 to 174 from the *Acta Musicalia* of the Esterházy archives. Dating from 1721 to 1825, the documents consist of pay lists, contracts, assurances, reports, letters, and the like. Documents and commentary given in German and English translation.

85. "The 'Acta Musicalia' of the Esterházy Archives." *The Haydn Yearbook* 13 (1982):5-96.

The first in a series of articles that plans to publish all documents in the *Acta Musicalia* from the Esterházy archives (material now at the National Széchényi Library in Budapest). This first installment contains numbers 1 through 35 in transcription and English translation. Only two documents pertain directly to Haydn: a contract of 1771 witnessed by Haydn, and a contract of service (1762) issued by Prince Nikolaus for Haydn and others.

* Angermüller, Rudolph. "Sigismund Ritter von Neukomm (1778-1858) und seine Lehrer Michael und Joseph Haydn: Eine Dokumentation." *Haydn-Studien* 3 (1973-74):29-42.

Cited as item 157.

86. Artaria, Franz, and Botstiber, Hugo. *Joseph Haydn und das Verlagshaus Artaria, nach den Briefen des Meisters an das Haus Artaria & Compagnie dargestellt.* Vienna: Artaria & Co., 1909. 101 pp.

A history of Haydn's relationship to the firm from 1779 until his death in 1809. Presents the history in three distinct phases: 1779-90, 1790-99, and 1799-1809, drawing on the contents of letters by Haydn known to the authors. Provides the reader with relevant information on the firm's early history, and concludes with a catalogue of Haydn works published by Artaria.

87. Bartha, Dénes, ed. *Joseph Haydn: Gesammelte Briefe und Aufzeichnungen.* Kassel: Bärenreiter, 1965. 599 pp.

Resting largely on the body of correspondence assembled by Landon (item 107), includes an expanded representation of material from the Esterházy archives, and encompasses a total of 384 items. Like the Landon volume, stands mid-way between a collection of letters and a documentary biography, with notes and commentary in the main body of the text. Provides a detailed history of the rediscovery and publication of Haydn material, and includes a chronological list of letters and documents.

* ———, and Somfai, László. *Haydn als Opernkapellmeister: Die Haydn-Dokumente der Esterházy Opernsammlung.* Budapest: Ungarische Akademie der Wissenschaften, 1960. 470 pp.

Cited as item 535.

88. Biba, Otto, ed. *"Eben komme ich von Haydn ...": Georg August Griesingers Korrespondenz mit Joseph Haydns Verleger Breitkopf & Härtel, 1799–1819.* Zurich: Atlantis, 1987. 281 pp.

An annotated edition of the letters (1799–1819), based on copies and excerpts prepared by Carl Ferdinand Pohl; letters unavailable to Pohl are supplied from other sources. As distilled by Pohl, provides a picture not only of Haydn, but also of Viennese musical life, cultural life in general, and Griesinger himself. Includes illustrations from the collection of the Gesellschaft der Musikfreunde, which also houses the Pohl manuscript.

89. ———. "Haydniana in den Sammlungen der Gesellschaft der Musikfreunde in Wien." *Österreichische Musikzeitschrift* 37 (1982):174–78.

A survey of Haydniana acquired by the Gesellschaft since shortly after its inception in 1812. Discusses musical sources (including autographs), letters, documents, musical instruments, and miscellaneous items, many from the collections of such notable figures as Griesinger, Archduke Rudolf, Brahms, Pohl, and Hoboken. Ranks the collection as second only to that of the Esterházy archives.

90. Blume, Friedrich. "Haydn als Briefschreiber." In Friedrich Blume. *Syntagma Musicologicum: Gesammelte Reden und Schriften,* edited by Martin Ruhnke, pp. 564-70. Kassel: Bärenreiter, 1963. Previously published in *Neue Zürcher Zeitung,* 13 March 1960.

Surveys the publication of Haydn letters prior to the *Collected Correspondence* (item 107). Assesses the Landon compilation, and with reference to letters it includes, lists persons with whom Haydn corresponded most frequently and describes the breadth of his circle of correspondents. Compares Haydn's epistolary style with that of Mozart, an uninhibited and born letter-writer.

91. Croll, Gerhard. "Mitteilungen über die 'Schöpfung' und die 'Jahreszeiten' aus dem Schwarzenberg-Archiv." *Haydn-Studien* 3 (1973-74):85-92.

Comments on entries in the Schwarzenberg account books for 1798-1801 concerned with performances of *The Creation* and *The Seasons* in Vienna. Entries include such items as honoraria for Haydn, expenditures for cavalry and police guards, an order for printed scores of *The Creation,* and payment to the wax-chandler for candles.

92. Cudworth, Charles. "The Vauxhall 'Lists'." *The Galpin Society Journal* 20 (1967):24-42.

Description of a program book in the Minet Library, London, that lists songs and instrumental music performed at Vauxhall Gardens in the summer seasons of 1790 and 1791. Offers background on the concerts and presents excerpts from the lists. Four appendices include typical Vauxhall programs as well as lists of the symphonic composers, named overtures, and concerted music represented. Among symphonic composers, Haydn's name occurs most frequently, appearing 85 times in 1790 and 65 times in 1791.

93. Elvers, Rudolf. "Ein nicht abgesandter Brief Zelters an Haydn." In *Musik und Verlag: Karl Vötterle zum 65. Geburtstag am 12. April 1968,* edited by Richard Baum and Wolfgang Rehm, pp. 243-45. Kassel: Bärenreiter, 1968.

Transcribes the draft of a letter to Haydn, apparently written in 1802. In it, Zelter offers Haydn the first printed copy of a 16-voice mass by the deceased Fasch.

The letter, however, was never sent: Zelter had the work engraved, but it was not actually printed until seven years after Zelter's death.

* Feder, Georg. "Aus Roman Hoffstetters Briefen." *Haydn-Studien* 1 (1965-67):198-201.

Cited as item 599.

94. ———. "Unbekannte Spezifikationen und Quittungen von J. Haydn." *Haydn-Studien* 5 (1982-85):184-90.

Contains transcriptions (some with commentary) for nine previously unknown documents from the Esterházy archives in Forchtenstein. They consist of full or partial autographs dating from 1773 to 1789.

95. ———. "Ein vergessener Haydn-Brief." *Haydn-Studien* 1 (1965-67):114-16.

Cites a neglected letter in which Haydn offers his Op. 33 quartets for sale. Describes two related letters and recalls Dénes Bartha's conjecture that Haydn dispatched a whole set of such letters. According to his letter of 5 April 1784 to Artaria, he appears to have sold more than 16 copies by subscription.

96. ———. "Zwei unbekannte Haydn-Briefe." *Haydn-Studien* 4 (1976-80):49-51.

Elucidates the contents of two letters from the Esterházy archives in Forchtenstein: the first, addressed to a court official in 1768, concerns formation of a trumpet and drum ensemble; the second, written to Prince Nikolaus in 1784, has to do with Haydn's garden.

97. ———, and Franken, Franz Hermann. "Ein wiedergefundener Brief Haydns an Artaria & Co." *Haydn-Studien* 5 (1982-85):55-59.

Reports on a newly rediscovered letter of 1788, in which Haydn requests that Artaria send a "Freyle von Kärger" (i.e. Antonia Karger) two arias from his oratorio, presumably *Il ritorno di Tobia.* Describes the condition of the letter, provides both transcription and facsimile, and makes allusion to circumstances that may have prompted the request. Also suggests that extant manuscript copies of two arias from the oratorio, bearing Artaria's name, may be those sent to Antonia Karger.

98. ———, and Gerlach, Sonja. "Haydn-Dokumente aus dem Esterházy-Archiv in Forchtenstein." *Haydn-Studien* 3 (1973-74):92-105.

Gives the contents of nine miscellaneous documents (1761-84) relating to Haydn personally or to the Esterházy musical establishment. Offers commentary on each.

* ———, and Thomas, Günter. "Documente zur Ausstattung von *Lo speziale, L'infedeltà delusa, La fedeltà premiata, Armida,* und andern Opern Haydns." *Haydn-Studien* 6/2 (1988):88-115.

Cited as item 855.

99. Gotwals, Vernon. "Joseph Haydn's Last Will and Testament." *The Musical Quarterly* 47 (1961):331-53.

Drawing on Griesinger and Dies, discusses Haydn's attitude toward money, his generosity, and his financial circumstances, which improved substantially from the time he first went to London. Addresses the complex question of currencies in Haydn's time, and describes economic problems caused by inflation and the French invasions of Vienna in 1805 and 1809. Includes tables on currencies, comparative prices, and Haydn's finances. Against this background, concludes with an annotated translation of Haydn's revised will of 7 February 1809.

100. Harich, János. "Haydn Documenta (I)." *The Haydn Yearbook* 2 (1963-64):2-44.

Describes a planned series of articles (items 101-4 listed below) involving transcription of selected documents from the Esterházy archives in Eisenstadt and Budapest. Also provides historical background on the rebuilding of the opera house at Eszterháza (it had been destroyed by fire in 1779) and on theatrical events of 1780: the court at Eszterháza and its personnel, the musicians employed in 1780, the strolling players, and other miscellaneous information. Written in German, with a summary in English.

101. ———. "Haydn Documenta (II)." *The Haydn Yearbook* 3 (1965):122-52.

Transcribes 50 documents from the Esterházy archives,

the majority dating from 1780. Among them are lists of chamber musicians, receipts, and various bills (e.g. for music paper, strings, bassoon reeds); some pertain to Haydn.

102. ———. "Haydn Documenta (III)." *The Haydn Yearbook* 4 (1968):39-101.

Transcribes 121 documents from the Esterházy archives, 1761-1808. Typical among them are payrolls, a variety of receipts, a bookbinder's invoices (for binding works by Haydn and Burgsteiner), and tailor's bills for musicians. Haydn is well represented.

103. ———. "Haydn Documenta (IV)." *The Haydn Yearbook* 7 (1970):47-168.

Transcribes 75 Esterházy archive documents. Includes several payrolls for the musicians (for payment in cash and in kind, e.g. salt, wood, beef), as well as commissions, reports, and petitions. Among the musicians heavily represented are Antonio Polzelli and the new kapellmeister, Johann Fuchs.

104. ———. "Haydn Documenta (V)." *The Haydn Yearbook* 8 (1971):70-163.

Transcribes 142 documents from the years 1759 to 1824. Includes many documents on the Tomasini family, most especially, Luigi and Anton. Also includes some Haydn documents, written to or by Haydn.

* Hase, Hermann von. *Joseph Haydn und Breitkopf & Härtel: Ein Rückblick bei der Veranstaltung der ersten vollständigen Gesamtausgabe seiner Werke.* Leipzig: Breitkopf & Härtel, 1909. 64 pp.

Cited as item 433.

* *Haydn-Autographe aus dem Haydn-Haus Eisenstadt (Faksimile-Drucke).* Edited by A.J. Ohrenberger and A. Hahn. Eisenstadt: Amt der Burgenländischen Landesregierung, 1976. 13 sheets.

Cited as item 462.

105. Klein, Rudolf. "Der Applausus-Brief." *Österreichische Musikzeitschrift* 14 (1959):198-200.

Concerns the 1768 letter (partially reproduced in facsimile) that accompanied delivery of the *Applausus* cantata for performance (probably) in Zwettl. Identifying this as the only Haydn letter known to discuss problems of performance practice in detail, comments on its references to matters of tempo, cadences in recitative, and dynamics.

106. Landon, Christa. "Ein Dokument zur 'Schöpfung'." *Haydn-Studien* 4 (1976-80):113.

Reproduces the contents of documents concerning Baron Brown's request (1798) of Emperor Franz to break with tradition and allow a performance of *The Creation* at the court theater on Whit-Sunday, and Franz's wish to maintain the tradition of refraining from festive productions on that holiday.

107. Landon, H.C. Robbins, ed. *The Collected Correspondence and London Notebooks of Joseph Haydn.* London: Barrie and Rockliff, 1959. xxix, 367 pp.

Includes translations by Landon of approximately 350 items, supplementing Haydn's letters with miscellaneous documents and letters to Haydn from acquaintances with whom he corresponded. Richly supplied with annotations throughout, especially in the section on the London notebooks. A biographical introduction provides background on relevant personalities. Contains 28 plates, including facsimiles of letters from different periods of Haydn's life. An appendix furnishes a catalogue of sources.

108. ———. "Four New Haydn Letters." *The Haydn Yearbook* 13 (1982):213-19.

Concerns letters to Artaria (29 August 1788), John Bland (12 April 1790), J.G. Graeff (incomplete, 1797), and Neukomm (25 April 1807). For each, gives the original text, a translation, and an analysis of contents.

* ———. "Haydniana (I)." *The Haydn Yearbook* 4(1968):199-206.

Cited as item 469.

109. ———. "Haydniana (II)." *The Haydn Yearbook* 7 (1970):307-19.

Presents facsimiles, transcriptions, and commentary for three Haydn letters and an affidavit. Two of the documents have never before been published: a letter to Madame Pointner, wife of the Esterházy porter in Vienna, and an affidavit for the publisher Sieber which certified that neither Haydn nor Artaria had sold 50 copies of the quartets sold to Sieber. Speculates that the unnamed quartets were those of the Op. 76 set.

110. ———. "A Haydn Letter to Dr. Burney." *The Haydn Yearbook* 16 (1985):247.

Reports on a previously unknown letter of 9 June 1795, sold at auction at Sotheby's in London. The letter, given in the original Italian and English translation, expresses Haydn's regrets to Burney at having to decline an invitation.

111. ———. "More Haydn Letters in Autograph." *The Haydn Yearbook* 14 (1983):200-205.

Concerns a letter to Bland (12 April 1790); a letter to Artaria (17 May 1781), previously published in incomplete and corrupt form; another letter to Artaria (16 November 1788); and a receipt written by Haydn for Georg Halbig, a Viennese instrument maker, given here in facsimile, transcription, and translation for the first time.

112. ———. "New Haydn Letters." *The Haydn Yearbook* 15 (1984):214-18.

Gives a transcription and English translation for an unpublished letter of 6 November 1805. Also provides an English translation for a letter to August Hartung transcribed in item 123 and the address of another letter to Hartung.

113. Larsen, Jens Peter. "A Haydn Contract." *The Musical Times* 117 (1976):737-38.

Explains the import of a 1796 contract between Haydn and the music dealer Frederick Augustus Hyde, which states, among other things, that Haydn should write 55 compositions in 16 groups for specified fees. The document clarifies information in Griesinger's letters to Breitkopf & Härtel; it permits confirmation of certain later editions as authentic; and since Rebecca Schroeter signed the contract as a witness, it helps support the assumption that Haydn resumed contact with her during his second visit to London.

114. Nohl, Ludwig. *Musiker-Briefe.* Leipzig: Duncker und Humblot, 1867. x, 354 pp.

The section devoted to Haydn (pp. 73-174) reproduces a diverse selection of correspondence consisting of 82 letters from the years 1776-1808. Includes the 1776 autobiographical sketch and the sketch for the *Journal des Luxus und der Moden* (item 162).

115. Olleson, Edward. "Georg August Griesinger's Correspondence with Breitkopf & Härtel." *The Haydn Yearbook* 3 (1965):5-53.

An edition of excerpts from Griesinger's letters that pertain to Haydn. Draws heavily on transcriptions of the letters made by C.M. Brand before their destruction in World War II. Draws also on material from Pohl, volume 3 (item 277) and Hermann von Hase's *Joseph Haydn und Breitkopf & Härtel* (item 433). Supplies dates for undated excerpts in Pohl and von Hase, and chronicles the role played by Griesinger in Haydn's association with the publisher.

116. Pfohl, Ferdinand. "Joseph Haydn, der Leopoldsorden und die sancta simplicitas." *Zeitschrift für Musik* 104 (1937):66-68, 212.

Comments on a previously unpublished document in which Count Chotek, after attending the famous performance of *The Creation* on 27 March 1808, petitions the Emperor Franz to confer the Order of Leopold on Haydn. The reply, which first came in 1814, indicated that Haydn did not fulfill the requirements for membership (artists were excluded).

117. Platz, Nora, and Walter, Horst. "Neukomms Bemerkungen über Haydns Grab." *Haydn-Studien* 3 (1973-74):154-58.

Reproduces the contents of an autograph document by Neukomm, a Haydn pupil, which discusses a stone tablet ordered by Neukomm in 1814 and placed at Haydn's original grave site. As depicted here, the tablet bore a simple inscription and a riddle canon for five voices. Discusses Neukomm's curious remark about the removal of Haydn's remains to Rohrau and comments on a faulty reproduction of the canon circulated in the *Allgemeine Wiener Musik-Zeitung.*

118. Radant, Else. "Ignaz Pleyel's Correspondence with Hoffmeister & Co." *The Haydn Yearbook* 12 (1981):122-74.

Transcribes 19 documents, including letters, drafts of letters, and bills, from 1800 to 1805. Among the main topics are Hoffmeister's negotiations with Haydn over the French rights (for Pleyel) to *The Creation* and Pleyel's attempt to collect money owed him by Hoffmeister & Kühnel. Provides a translation for most documents, and includes occasional commentary. Contains a note on currencies and a glossary with information about paper.

* Reich, Willi, ed. *Joseph Haydn: Chronik seines Lebens in Selbstzeugnissen.* Zurich: Manesse, 1962. 352 pp.

Cited as item 203.

* ———. *Joseph Haydn: Leben, Briefe, Schaffen.* Lucerne: Josef Stocker, 1946. 264 pp.

Cited as item 204.

119. Reinöhl, Fritz von. "Neues zu Beethovens Lehrjahr bei Haydn." *Neues Beethoven-Jahrbuch* 6 (1935):36-47.

Tells of the discovery of letters pertaining to the continuation of Beethoven's studies with Haydn: one letter each by Haydn and Beethoven to the Elector in Bonn and the Elector's response to Haydn. Provides background and commentary on the letters and reproduces their texts in full. Proposes that the negative tone of the Elector's response was prompted by reports from van Swieten and Waldstein of Beethoven's dissatisfaction with Haydn.

120. Rifkin, Joshua. "Ein Haydn-Zitat bei Bossler." *Haydn-Studien* 4 (1976-80):55-56.

Cites Haydn's letter to Boyer (1783), in which the publisher was commissioned to print three symphonies. Shows that an announcement by Bossler of a similar commission (1783) describes the symphonies in nearly identical words (see item 501). Concludes that Bossler's description is quoted from a letter by Haydn, and confirms Larsen's conjecture that the symphonies are numbers 76-78, apparently the very works offered to Boyer.

121. Sandberger, Adolf. "Ein unbekannter Brief von Josef Haydn." *Zeitschrift für Musik* 105 (1938):1326-28.

Offers a facsimile and transcription of a letter of 28 July 1787, then housed at the Preussischer Staatsarchiv. Proposes that it was addressed to either Johann Michael Schmidt or Georg Anton Kreusser (both at the Mainz court) and not to Schmidt's successor, Vincenzo Righini, as suggested by Karl Schweickert.

122. Scott, Marion M. "Haydn: Relics and Reminiscences in England." *Music and Letters* 13 (1932):126-36.

Descriptions of selected Haydn materials chosen for their special interest: autograph and manuscript scores, early editions, portraits, musical instruments, and reminiscences. Includes excerpts from a letter by the Rev. C.J. Latrobe to Vincent Novello (22 November 1828), hitherto unpublished, containing an account of Haydn's first meeting with the writer's wife.

* Searle, Arthur. "Haydn Autographs and 'Authentic' Manuscript Copies in the British Library." *Early Music* 10 (1982):495-504.

Cited as item 497.

123. Staehelin, Martin. "Ein unbekannter Brief Joseph Haydns." *Haydn-Studien* 5 (1982-85):110-17.

Transcribes an autograph letter previously overlooked by researchers. Written on 1 September 1799 to August Hartung of Brunswick, it expresses thanks for a group of subscriptions from Brunswick to *The Creation*. In the author's commentary, subscribers are further identified and discussed. Facsimiles of the letter and address are included.

124. Tank, Ulrich. "Die Dokumente der Esterházy-Archive zur fürstlichen Hofkapelle in der Zeit von 1761 bis 1770." *Haydn-Studien* 4 (1976-80):129-333.

An edition of all material in the Esterházy archives pertaining to Haydn and the musical establishment. Draws on holdings in Budapest and Eisenstadt, chronologically arranged in faithful transcription (documents accessible in modern publication are listed but not transcribed). Includes a list of the 576 documents in question, an index of names and subjects, and facsimiles of five documents.

125. Thomas, Günter. "Griesingers Briefe über Haydn: Aus seiner Korrespondenz mit Breitkopf & Härtel." *Haydn-Studien* 1 (1965-67):49-114.

For the period 1799-1819, gives the text of the correspondence relevant to Haydn in chronological order, with annotations and explanatory commentary interspersed. Includes a well-documented biographical sketch of Griesinger.

126. ———. "Kostüme und Requisiten für die Uraufführung von Haydns 'Le pescatrici'." *Haydn-Studien* 5 (1982-85):64-70.

Transcribes a four-page bill of 12 September 1770 for various opera costumes and props for an unspecified opera. According to circumstantial evidence, the opera can only be *Le pescatrici.* Discusses the costumes for each character, as deduced from the fabrics and trimmings listed. Compares the findings with information in a 1775 inventory of opera costumes housed at Eszterháza, and notes discrepancies between bill and inventory.

127. Unverricht, Hubert. "Die gesammelten Briefe und Tagebücher Joseph Haydns." *Die Musikforschung* 16 (1963):53-62.

Offers a critique of Landon's volume of *Collected Correspondence* (item 107), summarizing its scope and citing its importance as the first comprehensive edition. Makes note of shortcomings and errors, as well as omissions. Furnishes transcriptions or summaries for 14 items missing from Landon: 10 by Haydn, the remainder by Prince Nikolaus, Nicholas Simrock, and Johann Fuchs. For each item, lists ownership of the source, place of publication or previous mention, and source used for the transcription. Further addenda provided in item 128.

128. ———. "Unveröffentlichte und wenig bekannte Briefe Joseph Haydns." *Die Musikforschung* 18 (1965):40-45.

Transcribes six letters by Haydn not published in Landon's volume of *Collected Correspondence* (item 107) and an autograph draft by Kuffner of a reply to Haydn.

Includes a table with information, where applicable, on ownership of the source, place of publication, and source used for the transcription.

129. Walter, Horst. "Ein Billet Haydns vom 6. November 1805." *Haydn-Studien* 3 (1973-74):43-44.

Speculates on the identity of the note's recipient, suggesting Magdalena Edle von Kurzböck as a possibility.

130. ———. "Drei kleine Haydn-Dokumente in Abschrift C.F. Pohls." *Haydn-Studien* 6/2 (1988):159-61.

Transcribes the texts of three documents and supplies annotations, including explanatory notes on the contents. One of these documents, a receipt from Haydn for Breitkopf & Härtel, has apparently not been published before.

* Wirth, Helmut. "Ein unbekanntes Schriftstück von Johann Elssler aus dem Jahre 1811." *Haydn-Studien* 5 (1982-85):137-39.

Cited as item 565.

Iconography

This section encompasses both picture books and scholarly studies concerned with contemporary portraits of Haydn and other iconographical issues. It also includes biographical volumes whose primary usefulness for the researcher resides in their illustrations.

131. Brown, A. Peter. "An Addendum to Weinmann's 'Eine Variante zu einem Porträt Joseph Haydns'." *The Haydn Yearbook* 9 (1975):303-5.

Examines the portrait that accompanied "An Account of Joseph Haydn, a Celebrated Composer of Music. (With an Excellent Engraved Likeness of Him.)," which appeared in *The European Magazine* (October 1784). Identifies this likeness as a variant of the Mansfeld engraving published by Artaria in 1781. Proposes that the variant described in an article by Alexander Weinmann (item 155) was actually based on the London engraving.

132. Garas, Klára. "Kunstwerke in Haydns Nachlass." In *Joseph Haydn in seiner Zeit* (item 77), pp. 196-97.

A brief description of the collection of more than 200 engravings, drawings, silhouettes, and other pieces of artwork in Haydn's legacy, most of which were acquired in the course of the London sojourns.

133. Huss, Manfred. *Joseph Haydn: Klassiker zwischen Barock und Biedermaier.* Eisenstadt: Roetzer, 1984. 408 pp.

A pictorial biography, based on the latest research, that aims to depict Haydn according to recent views on the Haydn image. Intersperses the text with 320 illustrations, mainly black and white, that pertain to Haydn, his music, contemporaries, and environment. Appends a chronological survey, which coordinates events in history with Haydn's life and works. Further material includes an index of illustrations (with sources), a selective list of critical editions, a list of doubtful and unauthentic works, and genealogies of Haydn and the Esterházy family.

134. Klein, Rudolf, and Lessing, Erich. *Joseph Haydn.* Freiburg im Breisgau: Herder, 1981. 120 pp.

Biographical narrative, with 40 color plates distributed within the text. Includes photographs of Haydn landmarks and portraits of the composer and contemporaries.

135. Ladenburger, Michael. "Joseph Haydn in zeitgenössischen Abbildungen." In *Joseph Haydn in seiner Zeit* (item 77), pp. 301-10.

Offers a descriptive survey of the major, known portraits of Haydn. Includes reference to the descriptions of Haydn's appearance in the accounts of Dies and Griesinger. Considers the question of portraits for which Haydn actually modelled as opposed to those based on existing depictions, and suggests that those in the latter group tell us less about Haydn than about the times and circumstances by which the portraitist was influenced.

136. Landon, H.C. Robbins. *Haydn: A Documentary Study.* London: Thames and Hudson, 1981. 224 pp.

Lavish iconography, with biographical narrative interspersed among the 220 illustrations (44 in color). Divides into four chapters on the early years (1732-65), the Eszterháza years (1766-90), the visits to England (1791-95), the late years in Vienna (1796-1809). Features numerous quotations from letters and contemporary documents. Includes a chronology and genealogical tables. Also published in German as *Joseph Haydn: Sein Leben in Bildern und Dokumenten* (Vienna: Fritz Molden, 1981), and in French as *Haydn* (Paris: Chêne/Hachette, 1981).

137. ———. "Das Haydn-Porträt von Loutherbourg." *Österreichische Musikzeitschrift* 23 (1968):185-89.

Recounts steps that led to the discovery of the long-elusive portrait in a tableau entitled *Appollini.* Drawn by Philipp Jakob Loutherbourg the younger and engraved by John Landseer, *Appollini* contains medallion portraits of Haydn, Mozart, and other musicians of the time. The article includes reproductions of both the full engraving and the Haydn portrait (see item 148).

138. ———. "The 'Loutherbourg' Haydn Portrait." In H.C. Robbins Landon. *Essays on the Viennese Classical*

Style: Gluck, Haydn, Mozart, Beethoven, pp. 39-43. London: Barrie & Rockliff, 1970.

Translation of item 137.

139. ———. "A New Haydn Portrait." *Soundings,* no. 8 (1979-80), pp. 2-5.

Describes steps taken to locate James Tassie's 1792 likeness of Haydn, preserved in the Tassie collection at the Scottish National Portrait Gallery in the form of a plaster cast of a lost medallion. Includes a photograph of the reproduction.

140. Larsen, Jens Peter. "Zur Frage der Porträtähnlichkeit der Haydn-Bildnisse." *Studia Musicologica Academiae Scientiarum Hungaricae* 12 (1970):153-66.

Examines the known representations of Haydn in approximate chronological order and assesses their faithfulness. Reports on the reactions of Haydn and others to several of these likenesses. Draws upon verbal descriptions of Haydn in early biographies (those of Griesinger, Dies, Carpani), all of which depict Haydn in his later years. Includes a few photographic representations; otherwise refers to Somfai (item 147).

141. Lenneberg, Hans. "A Negative Contribution to Haydn Iconography: The Longhi Portrait." *The Haydn Yearbook* 2 (1963-64):64-73.

Shows that the Brooklyn Museum portrait, alleged by Joseph Muller (item 142) to be a Haydn likeness by Alessandro Longhi, bears no resemblance to other representations of the composer and might not even be Longhi's. Includes a reproduction of the portrait.

142. Muller, Joseph. "Haydn Portraits." *The Musical Quarterly* 18 (1932):282-98.

Colorful discussion of selected likenesses of Haydn. Identifies a painting in the Brooklyn Museum as an Alessandro Longhi portrait of Haydn, ca. 1762. Contains several reproductions and a catalogue of Haydn portraits, which excludes items such as statues, busts, and models not used for graphic reproductions.

143. Müller-Blattau, Joseph, and Harden-Rauch, Philipp. *Haydn:*

Bilder aus seinem Leben. 3d ed. Stuttgart: E. Schreiber, 1970. 64 pp.

A biographical sketch, followed by 54 black-and-white illustrations and commentary. Among the illustrations are portraits of Haydn and contemporaries, facsimiles of autographs, title pages of prints, and architectural landmarks. Originally published in 1963 (Stuttgart: E. Schreiber).

144. Petzoldt, Richard, and Crass, Eduard. *Joseph Haydn: Sein Leben in Bildern.* Leipzig: Verlag Enzyklopädie, 1959. 52 pp. plus 111 plates.

A concise biographical overview, preceded by an account of nineteenth-century attitudes toward Haydn and the twentieth-century revival of interest in his works. Illustrations include portraits of contemporaries; pertinent depictions of scenes from London, Vienna, and Eisenstadt; title pages, letters, and miscellaneous Haydn documents.

145. Somfai, László. "Ein authentisches Haydn-Bild aufgefunden." *Österreichische Musikzeitschrift* 20 (1965):304–5.

Identifies a newly discovered Haydn portrait as the third attempt by Vincenz Georg Kininger at a suitable model drawing for an engraving in Breitkopf & Härtel's *Oeuvres complettes.* It served as the basis also for the engraving in Pleyel's *Collection complette des quatuors* and the Haydn profile in a medallion (1801) by Nicolas Marie Gatteaux. Includes a reproduction of the drawing.

146. ———. *Joseph Haydn: His Life in Contemporary Pictures.* Translated by Mari Kuttna and Károly Ravasz. New York: Taplinger, 1969. xxii, 244 pp.

Translation of item 147.

147. ———. *Joseph Haydn: Sein Leben in zeitgenössischen Bildern.* Kassel: Bärenreiter, 1966. xviii, 245 pp.

Iconographical study, divided into four chronological periods: 1732-60, 1761-90, 1791-95, and 1795-1809. Contains 394 illustrations (black and white) of Haydn, his surroundings, patrons, friends, associates, musical sources, and documents. Identifies the illustrations, sometimes with additional commentary, and supplies relevant quotations from contemporary sources such as Griesinger, Dies, Haydn's correspondence, and newspapers. Opens with an essay on Haydn, and furnishes a list of authentic Haydn representations as well as an inventory of sources for the illustrations.

148. ———. "Zur Authentizität des Haydn-Porträts von Loutherbourg." *Österreichische Musikzeitschrift* 23 (1968):276-77.

Demonstrates that the Haydn portrait in Loutherbourg's *Appollini* (see item 137) is copied from Thomas Hardy's engraving (1792) of his Haydn portrait. Reproduces the Hardy engraving and Loutherbourg portrait side by side.

149. Struck, Gustav. "Ein neues Haydn-Bild als Beitrag zur Haydn-Ikonographie." *Musica* 7 (1953):97-100.

Reports on a copy of Christian Ludwig Seehas' 1785 portrait in the Bärenreiter library at Kassel. Proposes that the copy, in which Haydn's facial features are more realistic, was also painted by Seehas. Includes a biographical sketch of Seehas, discussion of other notable Haydn portraits, and photographic reproductions of portraits by Seehas (Kassel copy), Hoppner, and Guttenbrunn (engraved by Schiavonett).

150. Tenschert, Roland. *Joseph Haydn, 1732-1809: Sein Leben in Bildern.* Leipzig: Bibliographisches Institut, 1935. 38 pp. plus 44 plates.

Biographical sketch, followed by 44 photographic plates (black and white) that serve to illustrate the text.

151. "Ein unbekanntes Haydn-Portrait." *Acta Mozartiana* 29 (1982):75, 95.

Calls attention to a previously unknown portrait from the Galéria hlavneho mesta in Bratislava, shown at the exhibition "Joseph Haydn in seiner Welt" in Eisenstadt. Includes a description from the exhibition catalogue (No. 261) and a photographic reproduction (p. 75).

152. Unverricht, Hubert. "Ein unbeachteter authentischer Schattenriss Joseph Haydns von 1785." *Österreichische Musikzeitschrift* 27 (1972):68-70.

Reproduces a silhouette from the title page of Bossler's edition of three sonatas, Op. 40 (Hob. XV:3-5), which first came to light in 1968. Suggests that the silhouette was published separately also, and may have been represented in Lavater's collection. Judges it to be the best likeness of Haydn up to 1791, and notes its resemblance to a silhouette by Löschenkohl and to an anonymous one published in Somfai's iconography (see item 147).

153. Vogel, Emil. "Joseph Haydn-Portraits." *Jahrbuch der Musikbibliothek Peters* 5 (1898):11-26.

The first survey to organize iconographical material chronologically, according to original versions. For each portrait, includes a description and discussion of subsequent likenesses for which it served as a model. An appendix lists painters, sculptors, copper engravers, and lithographers named in the article, and makes reference to the relevant originals.

154. Volkmann, Hans. "Das Haydn-Bildnis der Musikbibliothek Peters." *Jahrbuch der Musikbibliothek Peters* 38 (1931):78-80. Previously published as "Joseph Haydn und Dresden" in *Wissenschaftliche Beilage des Dresdner Anzeigers* 8 (1931):193-95.

With reference to an anonymous pastel portrait (presumably by Daniel Caffé) cited in Vogel's article (item 153), calls attention to a closely related engraving by Sichling, traditionally believed to have been based on the lost painting by Roesler. Proposes that the pastel itself was based on the Roesler--either the original, or Roesler's drawing, or an early engraving--and that Sichling copied the pastel. This would help account for certain differences between his engraving and those by Trière and Blaschke, both after Roesler. Adduces evidence to identify the painter in question as Johann Carl Roessler of Dresden and not the Viennese Franz Roesler proposed by Botstiber.

155. Weinmann, Alexander. "Eine Variante zu einem Porträt Joseph Haydns." *The Haydn Yearbook* 6 (1969):192-95.

Compares the well-known engraving by Johann Ernst Mansfeld (1781) with another portrayal published in *Journal von und für Deutschland* 3 (1786) and clearly derived from the former. Reproduces both engravings (see item 131).

V

BIOGRAPHICAL RESEARCH

Early Accounts

Concerned with eighteenth- and early nineteenth-century writings devoted to Haydn and his acquaintances, this section encompasses early biographies, monographs, history texts, published essays, travel reports, and diaries, as well as articles in almanacs, encyclopedias, and dictionaries. It excludes early analyses of specific compositions, which are incorporated under the category "Music Analysis and Criticism."

156. Angermüller, Rudolph. *Sigismund Neukomm: Werkverzeichnis, Autobiographie, Beziehungen zu seinen Zeitgenossen.* Munich: Emil Katzbichler, 1977. 276 pp.

Offers a chronology of Neukomm's life and a discussion of his relationship with Michael and Joseph Haydn. Includes a richly annotated edition of the 1858 autobiographical sketch.

157. ———. "Sigismund Ritter von Neukomm (1778-1858) und seine Lehrer Michael und Joseph Haydn: Eine Dokumentation." *Haydn-Studien* 3 (1973-74):29-42.

An account of Neukomm's close relationship to his teachers, heavily documented by material from his biographical sketch, his thematic catalogue (1804-58), and selections (including new information) from a collection of more than 100 letters in copy, donated by August Nibio to the Internationale Stiftung Mozarteum in 1965. For many of the letters, current location is unknown.

158. [Arnold, Ignaz T.F.C.]. *Joseph Haydn: Seine kurze Biographie und ästhetische Darstellung seiner Werke.* New ed. Erfurt: Müllersche Buchhandlung, 1825. 272 pp.

The text divides into three parts: a rambling, informal biographical narrative; an essay on the style and expressive qualities of Haydn's music; and a discussion of particular works and genres. Observes that often his works scarcely have any theme, and that they seem to begin in the middle, rather than with a true beginning, but that nevertheless they exhibit masterful coherence and organization. Proposes that his spirit is not of the sentimental or moving type, but is marked rather by whim and exuberance. Describes Haydn as a master of the realm of triumphant joviality. Discussion of the works concentrates on *The Creation* and *The Seasons,* with briefer descriptive commentary on *The Seven Last Words, Il ritorno di Tobia, Orfeo ed Euridice,* and other vocal works. For the instrumental genres, gives only summary descriptions. Originally published in 1810 by Müller in Erfurt.

159. ———. "Wolfgang Amadeus Mozart und Joseph Haydn: Versuch einer Parallele." In *Gallerie der berühmtesten Tonkünstler des achtzehnten und neunzehnten Jahrhunderts: Ihre kurzen Biographien, charakterisirende Anekdoten und ästhetische Darstellung ihrer Werke,* 2d ed., 1:1-118. Erfurt: Johann Karl Müller, 1816.

Mentions Haydn's admiration for Mozart, refers to Mozart's quartets dedicated to Haydn, and contrasts the two composers' upbringing and early training. Discussion of Haydn proper ("Joseph Haydn: Karakterzüge aus seinem Leben") mentions his international fame, recounts biographical anecdotes, and offers fragments of biographical information, notably from the time of the English sojourns. Depicts Haydn as humble, generous, and gifted with a sense of humor and self-knowledge. Discussion of the music emphasizes string quartets and symphonies, and points out the mixture of accessibility and complexity that typifies his music. First published in 1810 by Müller in Erfurt.

160. Balsano, Maria Antonella. "'Le Haydine' di Carpani, ovvero lettere per la salvezza della musica." *Nuova rivista musicale italiana* 12 (1978):317-41.

Deplores scholars' habit of comparing the Italian

biographer's work unfavorably to the contemporaneous accounts by Dies and Griesinger. Depicts Carpani as an articulate spokesman for his times, applauds his philosophical approach, and defends his attempt to place Haydn's accomplishment in a historical context. Examines the author's concept of musical rhetoric as a tool for criticizing Haydn's music.

161. ———. "Un 'nemico d'Haydn' a Palermo." *Chigiana* 36 (1979):235-55.

Chiefly concerned with Antonino Pisani's *Pensieri sul dritto uso della musica strumentale,* published in 1817, which contrasts the Italians' gift for melody with the Germans' proclivity for harmony. Shows that Pisani's negative assessment of Haydn reflects his reading of Carpani's *Le Haydine* (item 172) and not any direct knowledge of his music. Includes discussion of the study and performance of Haydn's works in the Palermo conservatory in the course of the nineteenth century.

162. [Bertuch, Carl]. "[Haydns Jugendgeschichte]." *Journal des Luxus und der Moden* (July 1805), pp. 448-52.

A sketch of Haydn's youth based on an account given by Haydn to the author.

163. Beyle, Marie Henri [Louis-César-Alexandre Bombet, Stendhal]. *Lives of Haydn, Mozart and Metastasio.* Translated, introduced and edited by Richard N. Coe. London: Calder & Boyars, 1972. xxxii, 370 pp.

Originally published under the pseudonym of Louis-César-Alexandre Bombet as *Lettres écrits de Vienne en Autriche, sur le célèbre compositeur Joseph Haydn, suivies d'une vie de Mozart, et de considerations sur Métastase et l'état présent de la musique en France et en Italie* (Paris: Didot, 1814), then revised and published under the new title *Vies de Haydn, de Mozart et de Métastase* in 1817 and translated into English the same year. For the portion on Haydn, Beyle plagiarized Carpani's biography (item 172), translating from the Italian into French, but with changes and additions. The modern edition, in a new and corrected translation from *Vies de Haydn,* includes annotations and a biographical index identifying names mentioned in the text.

164. ——— [Louis-César-Alexandre Bombet, Stendhal]. *Vies*

de Haydn, de Mozart, et de Métastase. Reprinted in Stendhal. *Oeuvres complètes,* vol. 41. Edited by Daniel Muller. Geneva: Edito-Service, 1970. lxxv, 535 pp.

Originally published in 1817. The reprint incorporates a preface by Romain Rolland (1913) and an editorial introduction (pp. lv–lxxv) by Daniel Muller that discusses origins of the work, early editions, contemporary reactions, and relationship to Carpani's *Le Haydine.*

165. Brenet, Michel [Marie Bobillier]. "Stendhal, Carpani et la vie de Haydn." *S.I.M. Revue musicale* 5 (1909):430–38.

Recounts the story of Stendhal's plagiarism (see items 163-64) of Carpani's work (item 172), and reports on nineteenth-century critical reactions. Describes differences between the Stendhal and the Carpani, and assesses the nature of the changes made.

166. Brown, A. Peter. "The Earliest English Biography of Haydn." *The Musical Quarterly* 59 (1973):339–54.

Concerns the anonymous critical-biographical essay, accompanied by an engraved portrait, that appeared in *The European Magazine* in 1784. Gives likely sources for certain information it contains, and suggests Thomas Busby as the possible author. Observes that the existence of German and Swedish translations, as well as copies of the engraving, reflect wide distribution of the essay's contents. Notes the widespread influence of this unreliable piece, notably in the perpetuation of an inappropriate emphasis on stylistic similarities between C.P.E. Bach and Haydn. Furnishes an annotated, corrected reading of the essay, with its engraving.

167. ———. "Marianna Martines' Autobiography as a New Source for Haydn's Biography during the 1750's." *Haydn-Studien* 6/1 (1986):68–70.

Transcribes the entire document, which suggests that the writer became Haydn's pupil in 1751 or 1752, and emphasizes its value in shedding light on early years of Haydn's career. Proposes on the basis of the document that Haydn may have established himself in an inner circle of musical and literary activity at court as early as 1751.

168. Burney, Charles. *Dr. Burney's Musical Tours in Europe.*

Vol 2: *An Eighteenth-Century Musical Tour in Central Europe and The Netherlands.* Modern edition by Percy A. Scholes. London: Oxford University Press, 1959. ix, 268 pp.

An edition of *The Present State of Music in Germany, The Netherlands, and United Provinces,* second edition (London: T. Becket, 1775). First published in 1773 (London: Becket, Robson & Robinson). A colorful, insightful account, with numerous references to composers and compositions. Cities covered include Mannheim, Augsburg, Munich, Berlin, and Hamburg. Devotes three chapters to Vienna, with discussion of St. Stephen's Cathedral, street-singing, Hasse, Salieri, Gluck, and Metastasio. The main references to Haydn concern L'Augier's promise of an introduction and Burney's highly favorable reaction to a performance of Haydn quartets.

169. ———. *A General History of Music from the Earliest Ages to the Present Period (1789).* Modern edition, with critical and historical notes by Frank Mercer. London: G.T. Foulis, 1935. Reprint. 2 vols. New York: Dover, 1957. 817 pp.; 1098 pp.

Includes a report on Haydn supplied by Sir Robert Keith (2:958-60). Underscores the composer's numerous pieces for baryton, activities as an opera composer, and reputation as a composer of church music. Makes note of characteristic features of surprise and novelty in his music, and remarks on the North Germans' hesitancy to appreciate these qualities. Originally published in 1776-89 (London).

170. Busby, Thomas. *A General History of Music, from the Earliest Times to the Present,* vol. 2. London: G. and W.B. Whittaker, 1819. Reprint. New York: Da Capo, 1968. iv, 523 pp.

Provides an anecdotal account of Haydn's life, with little specific discussion of his music. Proposes that he was not a great vocal composer, and that his genius, though original and powerful, was limited and "incapable of superior excellence in the sublimer spheres of composition."

171. Carpani, Giuseppe. "Geschichte der heutigen Instrumental-Musik mit vorzüglicher Rücksicht auf Haydn's Verdienste um dieselbe, nebst einer Charakteristik

seiner Werke in diesem Fache, und ihrem speziellen Verzeichnisse." *Wiener allgemeine musikalische Zeitung,* no. 15 (10 April 1813), cols. 217-23; no. 22 (29 May 1813), cols. 327-33. Reprint. Edited by Ignaz Franz von Schönholz. Vienna: Hermann Böhlaus Nachf., 1986.

Excerpts in translation from item 172.

172. ———. *'Le Haydine,' ovvero Lettere sulla vita e le opere del celebre maestro Giuseppe Haydn.* 2d ed. Padua: Minerva, 1823. Reprint. Bologna: Forni, 1969. xii, 307 pp.

First published in 1812 (Milan: C. Buccinelli). Conceived in a florid, rhetorical style, takes the form of seventeen letters from the years 1808-11. Rather than following a chronologically organized narrative, offers reflections on the composer's life and the nature of his creative achievement. Features comparisons with predecessors and contemporaries, including artists, poets, and philosophers as well as musicians.

173. Choron, Alexandre Étienne, and Fayolle, François Joseph. "Haydn (Joseph)." In *Dictionnaire historique des musiciens, artistes et amateurs, morts ou vivans,* 1:319-23. Paris: Valade, 1810. Reprint. Hildesheim: Georg Olms, 1971.

Describes Haydn's early tribulations and struggles. Then discusses such masterworks as the *Farewell* Symphony, *Surprise* Symphony, *The Seven Last Words, The Creation,* and *The Seasons.* Mentions the honorary doctorate from Oxford. Bestows special praise on the symphonies: the ingenuity of their creation from simple materials, their masterful orchestration, and their majestic eloquence.

174. Deutsch, Otto Erich. "Joseph Haydn und Kaiser Joseph II." In Otto Erich Deutsch. *Musikalische Kuckuckseier und andere Wiener Musikgeschichten,* edited by Rudolf Klein, pp. 42-48. Vienna: Jugend und Volk, 1973. Previously published in *Musikbuch aus Österreich* 7 (1910):25-29.

Furnishes three assessments of Haydn by Joseph II, two of them reported by Johann Friedrich Reichardt in his *Vertraute Briefe* of 1810 (item 205) and in the *Allgemeine musikalische Zeitung* of October 1813, and one by Carl Ditters von Dittersdorf in his autobiography (item 176).

175. Dies, Albert Christoph. *Biographische Nachrichten von Joseph Haydn.* Modern edition by Horst Seeger. Berlin: Henschelverlag, [1959]. 233 pp.

Designed in the form of an account of 30 visits to the aging composer undertaken between April 1805 and August 1808, this vividly penned narrative features the recollection of memorable incidents from Haydn's life and travels. Portrays the composer as a simple, noble-spirited, fatherly figure. While devoting little attention to the music, places emphasis on qualities of wit and humor in his artistic personality. An afterword (derived from item 212) links Dies with the humanistic, progress-embracing middle-class spirit of the age of Herder and Goethe. This edition gives the complete text of the Vienna 1810 publication; also includes several illustrations and a small number of endnotes, but no index. Foreword by Arnold Zweig. See item 183 for an English translation.

176. Dittersdorf, Carl Ditters von. *Lebensbeschreibung, seinem Sohne in die Feder diktiert.* Modern edition by Norbert Miller. Munich: Kösel, 1967. 359 pp.

Annotated edition of a work originally published in 1801 (Leipzig: Breitkopf & Härtel). Contains several references to Haydn, including Dittersdorf's description of how he and Haydn, in their youth, frequently met to evaluate new music "in a spirit of inquiry." Also records Dittersdorf's assessment of Haydn's instrumental music in a meeting with Joseph II. Translated by A.D. Coleridge as *The Autobiography of Karl von Dittersdorf, Dictated to His Son* (London: Richard Bentley and Son, 1896; reprint, New York: Da Capo, 1970).

177. Forkel, Johann Nikolaus. "Haydn (Joseph)." *Musikalischer Almanach für Deutschland,* 1782, p. 64; 1783, pp. 38-40; 1784, pp. 80-82; 1789, pp. 77-78. Reprint. 4 vols. Hildesheim: Georg Olms, 1974.

The 1782 reference consists of a single short paragraph identifying Haydn as Esterházy kapellmeister and mentioning the publication of keyboard sonatas, symphonies, and quartets in Vienna and Amsterdam. The next year (1783) offers a biographical sketch and mentions the *Stabat mater* and *Il ritorno di Tobia* in addition to publications of instrumental music. The 1784 volume reprints the biographical sketch, adding mention of *L'infedeltà delusa* and the four-hand sonata *Il maestro e scolare.* The last volume supplies merely a supplementary paragraph with references to sets of symphonies and quartets, collections of arias, and *The Seven Last Words.*

178. Fröhlich, Joseph. "Haydn, Joseph." In *Allgemeine Encyklopädie der Wissenschaften und Künste,* section 2/3, edited by G. Hassel and A.G. Hoffmann, pp. 239–56. Leipzig: Johann Friedrich Gleditsch, 1828. Reprinted as *Joseph Haydn.* Edited by Adolf Sandberger. Regensburg: Gustav Bosse, 1936. 72 pp.

Based on the accounts by Dies, Griesinger, and other early biographers, with corrections entered in brackets. Provides a concise portrayal of the composer's life and an assessment of his artistic personality and contribution. Emphasizes his natural simplicity, unassuming and peasant-like spirit, piety, and humor. Contrasts his artistic spirit to Mozart's, and bestows particular praise on the manifestations of Haydn's genius in his instrumental music.

179. Gerber, Ernst Ludwig. "Haydn (Joseph)." In *Historisch-biographisches Lexicon der Tonkünstler,* 1: cols. 609–12. Leipzig: J.G.I. Breitkopf, 1790. Reprint. Edited by Othmar Wessely. Graz: Akademische Druck- u. Verlagsanstalt, 1977.

Draws on Forkel's *Musikalischer Almanach* (item 177) for information on Haydn's early life. Identifies him as one of the greatest composers of the day, and emphasizes aspects of ingenuity and unmistakable originality in his style. Applauds the perfection of his quartets and symphonies, and the universality of his appeal. Cites the inexhaustible wealth of his inspiration, and observes that his art is fresh, astonishing, and also accessible despite contrapuntal complexity. Defends his music against critics' complaints of frivolity, and asserts that his expression is always exalted and grand, even when seemingly light-hearted. Mentions the wide dissemination of his works, and singles out his sacred and theater music for special praise as representative of the highest levels of excellence.

180. ------. "Haydn (Joseph)." In *Neues historisch-biographisches Lexikon der Tonkünstler,* 2: cols. 535–605. Leipzig: A. Kühnel, 1812. Reprint. Edited by Othmar Wessely. Graz: Akademische Druck- u. Verlagsanstalt,

1966.

Supplements the earlier account (item 179) by providing an extended list of Haydn's compositions, organized by genre, with information on publications and arrangements. Supplies anecdotes about his youth and early adulthood in Vienna, information on Esterházy performing personnel, the London sojourns, and background on the composition and early performances of the late oratorios. Emphasizes the great quantity, diversity, and originality of his output and the universal acclaim earned by his music.

181. Gotwals, Vernon. "The Earliest Biographies of Haydn." *The Musical Quarterly* 45 (1959):439–59.

A comparison of the Haydn biographies by Griesinger, Dies, and Carpani that aims to "recall the circumstances surrounding the writing of each book and to make a tentative evaluation of the relative worth of the three as source materials for Haydn's biography." Includes excerpts from the biographies, some chosen to contrast the three biographers' treatments of the same event. Concludes that Griesinger is the most reliable, that Dies' depiction is more detailed and life-like, and that Carpani, while least reliable, is the most entertaining to read.

182. ———. "Haydn in London Again." *The Music Review* 22 (1961):189–94.

Presents an English translation by Philip Keppler of passages from Carpani's *Le Haydine* (item 172) that concern Haydn's experiences in London. Excerpts in question, from Letter XIII, 29 July 1809, supposedly represent stories told by Haydn to Carpani.

183. ———, ed. *Haydn: Two Contemporary Portraits.* 2d ed. Madison: University of Wisconsin Press, 1968. xv, 275 pp.

Originally published as *Joseph Haydn: Eighteenth-Century Gentleman and Genius* (Madison: University of Wisconsin Press, 1963), consists of Gotwals' translations of the early biographies by Griesinger (item 185) and Dies (item 175). Features a biographical introduction on the authors and extensive notes on the text.

184. Grétry, André Ernest Modeste. *Mémoires ou essais sur la*

musique. 3 vols. Paris: Verdiere, 1812. 441 pp.; 419 pp.; 516 pp.

References to Haydn in volume 1 include pp. 185, 244, 348. Noting his popular appeal and the richness of his instrumental compositions, admires the eloquence of his symphonic language. Volume 1 was published in Paris, 1789. An expanded version in three volumes appeared in 1797.

185. Griesinger, Georg August. *Biographische Notizen über Joseph Haydn*. Modern edition by Franz Grasberger. Vienna: Paul Kaltschmid, 1954. 79 pp.

Originally appeared in the *Allgemeine musikalische Zeitung* 11 (1808-9): cols. 641-49, 657-68, 673-81, 689-99, 705-13, 721-33, 737-47, 776-81. Expanded and published separately as *Biographische Notizen über Joseph Haydn* (Leipzig: Breitkopf & Härtel, 1810), reprinted in 1981 (Hildesheim: Gerstenberg). Based on the author's personal acquaintance with the aging composer. Describing him as the founder of an epoch in music, gives a succinct account of his career, including early adventures, Esterházy employment, and London sojourns. Major emphasis falls on the London period and later years in Vienna. Furnishes a character portrayal that emphasizes his piety, modesty, generosity of spirit, and humor. Briefly treats his work habits, aesthetic outlook, and his assessments of other composers. See item 183 for an English translation.

186. Haas, Robert. "Abt Stadlers vergessene Selbstbiographie." *Mozart-Jahrbuch* (1957), pp. 78-84.

Transcribes the text of this forgotten document, which includes a brief section of anecdotes about Mozart and Haydn (those on Haydn concern *The Seven Last Words* and the calling card).

187. ———. "Von dem Wienerischen Geschmack in der Musik." In *Festschrift Johannes Biele zum sechzigsten Geburtstage überreicht*, edited by Erich H. Müller, pp. 59-65. Leipzig: Fr. Kistner & C.F.W. Siegel, 1930.

Reproduces the text of an anonymous article from the *Wienerisches Diarium* of 1766. The article, which offers insights into the emerging Viennese Classical period, addresses theoretical and aesthetic issues, and offers critiques of selected composers. Among them is Haydn, characterized as the "favorite of the nation" and deemed the musical counterpart of Gellert. His style is described in general terms, and brief assessments are given of various genres.

188. "Hayden (in Salzburg)." *Musikalisches Handbuch auf das Jahr 1782 (Alethinopel),* pp. 19-21.

Defines two styles or epochs in Haydn's compositional output, the first characterized by unbridled humor, the second, by more restrained humor. Credits Haydn with developing a virtually new form for the minuet and with a deft blending of harmony with melody in his accompaniments.

189. Haydn, Joseph. "Selbstbiographie [1776]." In Willi Kahl, ed. *Selbstbiographien deutscher Musiker des 18. Jahrhunderts,* pp. 75-86. Cologne: Staufen, 1948. Reprint. Amsterdam: Frits Knuf, 1972.

Facsimile reprint from a 1912 program booklet purported to be the first completely accurate edition of the 1776 document, first published in 1836. Richly annotated, with an introductory essay (pp. 75-82) on the autobiographical sketch and its significance as a reflection of the writer's artistic personality. Originating with a scheme of Ignaz de Lucca's, whose article on Haydn appeared in *Das gelehrte Österreich* 1 (1776):309, takes the form of a letter to one "Mademoiselle Leonore," who eventually married the Esterházy court official Lechner. Evidently de Lucca conveyed his request for information to the court official Zoller, who in turn asked Leonore to approach Haydn. The letter alludes to early family music-making, studies with Reutter and Porpora, and employment with Morzin and Esterházy. In mentioning his own accomplishments, places remarkable emphasis on vocal music: the operas *Le pescatrici, L'incontro improvviso,* and *L'infedeltà delusa;* the oratorio *Il ritorno di Tobia,* and the *Stabat Mater.* While devoting little attention to instrumental works, complains at some length about negative assessments of his chamber compositions on the part of Berlin critics. Other editions include those by Willi Reich (item 203), pp. 9-13, and Landon (item 261), pp. 397-99 (in English). Item 196 provides an annotated Italian translation.

190. Hoboken, Anthony van. *Discrepancies in Haydn Biographies.* Translated by Donald Mintz. Washington, D.C.: Library of Congress, 1962. 23 pp.

A lecture delivered in the Whittall Pavilion, Library of Congress, 18 May 1962. Laments the relative dearth of surviving, accurate information on Haydn's life. Compares the accounts of Griesinger and Dies, and deplores the relative neglect of the latter. Discussion of errors and contradictions in other accounts includes the writings of Carpani, Beyle, Mayr (in a program booklet for a performance of *The Creation,* Bergamo, 1809), Fröhlich, Pohl, von Seeburg, Jacob, and Sondheimer.

191. "Joseph Haydn." *Magazin der Musik* 2/1 (1784-85):585-94. Reprint. Hildesheim: Georg Olms, 1971.

Annotated translation by Carl Friedrich Cramer of an article originally published in *The European Magazine.* In it, the anonymous author falsely claims that Haydn retaliated against his enemies by mimicking their style and that his Op. 13 and 14 were written with the specific purpose of ridiculing C.P.E. Bach. Attributes some of the eccentricities of Haydn's music to the whims of Prince Esterházy, and while finding his output uneven, extols his instrumental music and bestows special praise on his vocal works, particularly the *Stabat Mater.*

192. Junker, Carl Ludwig. *Zwanzig Componisten: Eine Skizze.* Berne: Typographische Gesellschaft, 1776. 109 pp.

More an essay on aesthetics than a biographical sketch, the discussion of Haydn, pp. 55-67, focuses on issues of whim and humor. Censures Haydn for the predominance of caprice in his music, and disparages his symphonies for the limited scope of their expressive language. Haydn also figures prominently in the essay on Dittersdorf (pp. 28-36), whose style is purported to have been influenced by Haydn.

193. Kalkbrenner, Friedrich. "Memoir of Mr. Frederick Kalkbrenner Reprinted from *The Quarterly Musical Magazine and Review,* Volume VI (1824)." Submitted by Peter Riethus. *The Haydn Yearbook* 12 (1981):180-91.

Describes the author's encounter with Beethoven in the course of a 1796 journey from Prague to Vienna, where he was introduced to Haydn. Then describes a longer Viennese sojourn, starting in 1803, during which he studied with Haydn. Recounts Haydn's critique of a string quartet by the author and reports on the composer's reminiscences from the time of the latter's stay in England.

194. Kelly, Michael. *Reminiscences.* Modern edition by Roger Fiske. London: Oxford University Press, 1975. xx, 396 pp.

Recounts pertinent anecdotes from the Irish singer's experiences, including that of Storace's quartet party at which the players supposedly included Haydn (first violin), Dittersdorf (second violin), Mozart (viola), and Vanhal (cello). First published in 1826 (London: H. Colburn), reprinted in 1968 (New York: DaCapo).

195. LeBreton, Joachim. "Notice historique sur la vie et les ouvrages de Joseph Haydn, lue dans la séance publique de l'Institut, du 6 Octobre 1810." In *Bibliographie musicale de la France et de l'étranger,* edited by César Gardeton, pp. 350-71. Paris: Niogret, 1822.

More a portrayal of the artist and his accomplishment than a chronicle, gives relatively few specific dates or biographical details. Cites Haydn's courage and persistence in overcoming obstacles, and celebrates his achievement in elevating himself from obscurity to a position of artistic preeminence. Offers concise stylistic commentary on his output in the different genres. Mentions his studies of Mattheson, Fux, and the sonatas of C.P.E. Bach. Suggests that he would have benefitted from study in Italy and from familiarity with the French tradition of musical drama. Calling attention to such works as *Il ritorno di Tobia, The Creation,* and *The Seasons,* proclaims the master's immortality. First published as a separate monograph in 1810 ([Paris]: Baudouin, Imprimeur de l'Institue de France).

196. Le Castel, Sophie. "Schizzo autobiografico di Franz Joseph Haydn (1732-1809)." *Nuova rivista musicale italiana* 17 (1983):567-75.

Reproduces the text of the 1776 sketch. Supplies copious annotations and a brief commentary emphasizing the value of the document as an authentic reflection of Haydn's character. Remarks on the small number of compositions mentioned, and suggests that the information supplied in the sketch complements that transmitted in the early biographies of Dies and Griesinger.

197. Loft, Abram, trans. "Excerpts from the Memoirs of J.W. Tomaschek." *The Musical Quarterly* 32 (1946):244-64.

Includes a description of a visit paid by Tomaschek and Preindl to Haydn in Vienna during 1808. Also contains a brief assessment of Haydn's vocal works, in which *The Creation* is deemed inferior in poetic worth to *The Seven Last Words.*

198. Mörner, C.-G. Stellan. "Haydniana aus Schweden um 1800." *Haydn-Studien* 2 (1969-70):1-33.

Cites evidence of the late eighteenth-century sale and performance of Haydn's works in Sweden, and provides information on Haydn anecdotes and biographical articles in Swedish journals. Gives a substantial excerpt from Johan Fredrik Berwald's account of his 1799 sojourn in Vienna, including references to his encounter with Haydn. Discusses the Haydn pupil Paul Struck, and cites Struck's correspondence with Peter Frigel, Secretary of the Royal Music Academy in Stockholm, from the time of the former's stay in Vienna (1796-99). Offers information on Fredrik Samuel Silverstolpe, and gives a translation of his "Die mehrjährige Bekanntschaft eines Schweden mit Joseph Haydn."

199. Neubacher, Jürgen. "Haydns Aufenthalt in Wiesbaden: Ein dokumentarischer Beleg." *Haydn-Studien* 5 (1982-85): 190-91.

Cites reports in a Wiesbaden periodical that give factual support to an anecdote told by Dies concerning Haydn's encounter with several Prussian officers during a one-night stopover in Wiesbaden in 1794.

200. Nichols, David C. "A Mexican Tribute to Haydn." *The Haydn Yearbook* 13 (1982):231-32.

Provides the text of an anonymous tribute paid to the deceased Haydn in the Mexican cultural chronicle *Diario de México* in April of 1810. Also includes two short, laudatory references to Haydn that appeared in the *Diario* in 1806.

201. Olleson, Edward. "Haydn in the Diaries of Count Karl von Zinzendorf." *The Haydn Yearbook* 2 (1963-64):45-63.

Attempts to represent all information in Zinzendorf's diaries that has some bearing on Haydn or his music. Passages quoted span the years 1772-1809. Despite

Zinzendorf's musical limitations, he provides valuable social commentary on musical life in Vienna.

202. Radant, Else, ed. "The Diaries of Joseph Carl Rosenbaum, 1770-1829." *The Haydn Yearbook* 5 (1968):7-158.

An annotated, abridged version of the diaries from 1797 to 1810, in a translation by Eugene Hartzell. Includes all passages that comment on Haydn, his works, and acquaintances. Also retains passages that illuminate Rosenbaum's personality and create "a picture of the times as seen from the perspective of the man-in-the-street." A foreword provides biographical material on Rosenbaum (a successful businessman and one-time Esterházy employee, implicated in the theft of Haydn's skull), as well as background on the Esterházy and Imperial families and commentary on Vienna in Haydn's time: historical events, culture, and socio-economic conditions.

203. Reich, Willi, ed. *Joseph Haydn: Chronik seines Lebens in Selbstzeugnissen.* Zurich: Manesse, 1962. 352 pp.

Includes the "Selbstbiographie" (pp. 9-13) prepared by Haydn in 1776 for *Das gelehrte Oesterreich,* along with numerous letters and topically organized fragments excerpted from Dies, Griesinger, Pohl, and other biographical sources.

204. ———. *Joseph Haydn: Leben, Briefe, Schaffen.* Lucerne: Josef Stocker, 1946. 264 pp.

Divides into the three sections announced in the title. Part 1 draws primarily on the early biographies of Dies and Griesinger. Part 2 offers a selection of biographically significant letters, notably the correspondence with Marianne von Genzinger and Luigia Polzelli. Part 3 concerns the early recognition of artistic merit and historical significance in Haydn's works, with passages from the writings of Schubart, Gerber, Pastor Triest, Zelter, Rochlitz, Nägeli, and Fröhlich.

205. Reichardt, Johann Friedrich. *Vertraute Briefe geschrieben auf einer Reise nach Wien und den österreichischen Staaten zu Ende des Jahres 1808 und zu Anfang 1809.* Amsterdam: Im Kunst- und Industrie-Comtoir, 1810. Modern edition by Gustav Gugitz. 2 vols. Munich: Georg Müller, 1915. 357 pp.; 324 pp.

In describing Viennese musical life, makes numerous references in passing to Haydn's music, especially to quartets. Among passages of special interest are Reichardt's recollection of a visit with Haydn (11th letter), his touching grief over Haydn's failing health and his tribute to Haydn's music (27th letter), and his thoughts on Joseph II's assessment of Haydn (34th letter).

206. Sainsbury, John S. "(Haydn, Joseph)." In *A Dictionary of Musicians from the Earliest Ages to the Present Time*, 1:340–53. London, 1825. Reprint. New York: Da Capo, 1966.

The biographical account emphasizes Haydn's early years: childhood, employment at St. Stephen's, encounter with Kurz-Bernardon, early professional struggles, and eventual Esterházy employment. Offers little information on the London sojourns. Identifies Haydn as an innovator, and observes that "in music, as in every thing else, we have little idea of what the world was even a hundred years back." Describes him as "greatest of the great" as a symphonist, among the greatest in church music, and an imitator in the field of theater music. Identifies *The Seven Last Words* as his finest work, and reports that while most of the baryton compositions had burned, those that remained were "useless." Portrays Haydn as pious, diligent, amiable, content with his station, and indifferent to material status, comfort, and reward.

207. Sandberger, Adolf. "Zur Einbürgerung der Kunst Joseph Haydns in Deutschland." *Neues Beethoven-Jahrbuch* 6 (1935):5–25.

Discusses and quotes extensively from outstanding late eighteenth- and nineteenth-century writings and commentaries on Haydn, including those of Gerber, Griesinger, Dies, Carpani, Grétry, Pastor Triest (in the *Allgemeine musikalische Zeitung,* 1801), Bertuch (in *Journal des Luxus und der Moden,* 1805), Zelter, Reichardt, Arnold, and Fröhlich.

208. Schenk, Johann Baptist. "Autobiographische Skizze." *Studien zur Musikwissenschaft* 11 (1924):75–85.

An annotated printing of Schenk's autobiography, originally written as a letter to Aloys Fuchs and considered unreliable, in which he writes of how he assisted Haydn in instructing Beethoven.

209. Schönfeld, Johann Ferdinand von. *Jahrbuch der Tonkunst von Wien und Prag.* Vienna: [Schönfeld], 1796. Reprint, with afterword and index by Otto Biba. Munich: Emil Katzbichler, 1976. xiv, 194 pp.

Principal discussion of Haydn is incorporated in chapter 2, "Virtuosen und Dilettanten von Wien," pp. 20-23. Remarks on the international fame and universal recognition accorded his works, and asserts that the symphonies have contributed most to his immortality. Observes that he has imitators, despite the fact that his art is inimitable. Finds the keyboard works enjoyable and easy to play, the quartets ingenious. Proposes that while vocal music is not his forte, the sacred music, notably his *Seven Last Words,* is better than the theater works.

210. Schubart, Christian Friedrich Daniel. *Ideen zu einer Ästhetik der Tonkunst.* Degen: Vienna, 1806. Reprint. Hildesheim: Georg Olms, 1969. 402 pp.

Discussion of Haydn, pp. 226-27, ranks him with Mozart as an epoch-making genius, and remarks on the fire and originality of his symphonic style. Observes that his keyboard works, loved by connoisseurs, are incomparably instructive for performers and entertaining for listeners. Praises the craft and spirit embodied in the masses.

211. Seeger, Horst. "Zur musikhistorischen Bedeutung Albert Christoph Dies' und seiner Haydn-Biographie von 1810." In *Bericht über die Internationale Konferenz zum Andenken Joseph Haydns* (item 70), pp. 131-35.

Asserts that Dies' biography is no less trustworthy than Griesinger's, as evidenced in the catalogue of works, and explains why it is a Classical-realist, rather than a Romantic work. Attributes the traditional reservations about Dies to Pohl's treatment of a critique by Neukomm, but shows that Neukomm's purpose was merely to supplement Dies' information. Includes a biographical sketch of Dies and brief description of a neglected 1811 essay that suggested to the government ways in which to advance the arts. Another version published in *Beiträge zur Musikwissenschaft* 1/3 (1959):24-31 as "Zur musikhistorischen Bedeutung der Haydn-Biographie von Albert Christoph Dies (1810)," with Neukomm's commentary.

212. Sondheimer, Robert. *Die Theorie der Sinfonie und die Beurteilung einzelner Sinfoniekomponisten bei den Musikschriftstellern des 18. Jahrhunderts.* Leipzig: Breitkopf & Härtel, 1925. 99 pp.

Traces several stages in the development of eighteenth-century thought on the symphony, and presents an overview of references to the genre in writings by Vogler, Burney, de Brosses, Hiller, Arteaga, Schubart, Junker, Reichardt, Gerber, Stockhausen, and Sulzer. Includes references to Haydn. An index has been supplied by Eugene K. Wolf and Jan LaRue in "A Bibliographical Index to Robert Sondheimer's 'Die Theorie der Sinfonie'," *Acta Musicologica* 37 (1965):79-86.

213. Tschulik, Norbert. "Musikartikel aus dem Wienerischen Diarium von 1766: Ein Beitrag zur Geschichte des musikalischen Journalismus im 18. Jahrhundert." *Studien zur Musikwissenschaft* 30 (1979):91-106.

Discusses excerpts from music articles in the *Wiener Diarium* of 1766, with particular emphasis on the anonymous article "Von dem Wienerischen Geschmack in der Musik." Includes the text of a critique of Haydn from this article, and speculates on the identity of its author. Discusses at length the arguments for and against Dittersdorf's authorship.

214. Unger, Max. "Joseph Haydn und August Wilhelm Iffland." *Die Musik* 8/16 (1908-9):232-42.

Reproduces extracts from Iffland's account of his visit with Haydn on 7 September 1808, originally published in his *Almanach fürs Theater* (1811). Provides background on the visit, discusses critiques of the report, and gives information on a related account (Iffland's letter to Heinrich Schmidt, published in 1856).

215. Vignal, Marc. "A Side-Aspect of Sigismund Neukomm's Journey to France in 1809." *The Haydn Yearbook* 2 (1963-64):81-87.

Reproduces the "Notice biographique sur Joseph Haydn traduite de l'allemand de Sigismond Neukomm en 1809," a letter from the Haydn pupil to his friend George Frederic Joseph Rossel, a Montbéliard lawyer. Mainly concerned with biographical generalizations, the document attests to Haydn's great popularity in the early nineteenth century.

Modern Biography

From the flawed, incomplete, but nonetheless historically significant biography by Carl Ferdinand Pohl (item 277) to the immensely ambitious *Haydn: Chronicle and Works* of Landon (item 259), this section covers both the major scholarly biographies (such as Geiringer's, item 242) and a sampling of the most widely disseminated non-specialist books on Haydn. Also incorporated here are biographically oriented journal articles and studies such as James Webster's (items 303, 304) that address Haydn scholarship and the methodology of biographical research.

216. Barbaud, Pierre. *Haydn.* Paris: Éditions du Seuil, 1957. 191 pp.

A not very coherently organized collection of information and discussion of Haydn's life and his music, designed for the musically knowledgeable amateur. Numerous illustrations pertinent to Haydn and his milieu, including contemporary engravings, portraits, and photographs of landmarks. Critical analysis of various works, thumbnail sketches of contemporaries with whom Haydn was associated. Chronological tables of the Haydn symphonies and string quartets. Also published in an English translation by Kathrine Sorley Walker (New York: Grove Press, [1959]).

217. ———. *Joseph Haydn in Selbstzeugnissen und Bilddokumenten.* Translated by Clarita Waege and Hortensia Weiher-Waege. Reinbek bei Hamburg: Rowohlt, 1960. 175 pp.

A German version of item 216, with some differences in text and illustrations. Features not in the French edition include a catalogue of works and a section devoted to quotations on Haydn, present and past (e.g. Gerber, Mozart, Stendhal, Mörike, Wagner, Křenek, and Richard Benz).

218. Bartha, Dénes. "Zur Abstammung Joseph Haydns." *Acta Musicologica* 7 (1935):152-58.

Argues against E.F. Schmid's contention (item 284) that

Tétény-Tadten, birthplace of Haydn's great grandfather Caspar, had been among those villages of the *Heidebogen* populated by Swabians in the early 17th century. Adduces evidence to show that the town was still strictly Hungarian at the time Caspar left for Hainburg, ca. 1650; but concludes that Caspar's nationality cannot be established with certainty, since no records from Tétény have been found for him. With regard to the name Haydn, points out that Caspar was a *Burgknecht* in Tétény, and that *Burgknechte* of his district did not yet make use of surnames. In all likelihood, he acquired the surname in Hainburg--the name a reflection of his origins *auf der Haydt.*

219. Biba, Otto. "Nachrichten zur Musikpflege in der gräflichen Familie Harrach." *The Haydn Yearbook* 10 (1978):36-44.

Offers miscellaneous addenda, concerning the cultivation of music by members of the Harrach family, to information in a 1932 study by E.F. Schmid. Pays particular attention to Count Karl Leonhard Harrach (1765-1831), a recognized musical patron and accomplished amateur, who cultivated a close relationship with Haydn and paid tribute to him with a monument on his castle grounds in Rohrau.

220. Botstiber, Hugo. "Haydn and Luigia Polzelli." *The Musical Quarterly* 18 (1932):208-15.

Traces the relationship between Haydn and Luigia Polzelli, employed as a singer at the Esterházy court from 1779 to 1790. With occasional reference to letters and documents, describes the financial aid and career support given to her and her family, both before and after her husband's death. Also discusses the amorous relationship between Polzelli and Haydn, who allegedly was the father of her son Antonio. Reportedly a translation of "War Antonio Polzelli Haydns Sohn?" in *Österreichische Kunst* 3/3-4 (1932):17-19.

221. Brenet, Michel [Marie Bobillier]. *Haydn.* 2d ed. Paris: Félix Alcan, 1910. 207 pp.

Divided into separate sections on life and works. The portrayal of the man and his accomplishment exemplifies the traditional romantic image, whereby the moral content of his music could be understood in terms of the "simplicity, kindness, and tranquil endurance" that formed the basis of his character. Providing an overview of his contributions to the different genres, views the operatic and sacred works with condescension. Characterizes Haydn as a writer of musical "prose" rather than "poetry," and identifies him as one of the greatest masters of pure music and of instrumental scene-painting. First published in 1909 (Paris: Félix Alcan).

222. ———. *Haydn.* Translated by C. Leonard Leese, with commentary by Sir W.H. Hadow. London: Westminster, 1926. Reprint. New York: Benjamin Blom, 1972. xii, 143 pp.

Translation of item 221.

223. Bronnenmeyer, Walter. "Haydn, Mozart und ein dunkler Punkt." *Acta Mozartiana* 35 (1988):1-6.

Questions why Haydn neglected to use the influence he had at the Esterházy court and in Vienna to extend help to Mozart, and offers evidence to suggest that he must have been aware of Mozart's difficult circumstances.

224. Chailley, Jacques. "Joseph Haydn and the Freemasons." In *Studies in Eighteenth-Century Music: A Tribute to Karl Geiringer on His Seventieth Birthday,* edited by H.C. Robbins Landon and Roger E. Chapman, pp. 117-24. New York: Oxford University Press, 1970.

Speculates on the nature and degree of Haydn's involvement with Freemasonry. Disputes biographers' claims that no Masonic meaning is to be found in *The Creation,* and declares the need for a major study of the Masonic impact on Haydn's music. Pays special attention to the interaction between Haydn and Mozart as reflected in the latter's composition of his quartets dedicated to Haydn. Attributes Masonic significance to the Op. 54 quartets (for example the tonal scheme of No. 1, which modulates from E flat to G) and the late Piano Sonata in E flat.

225. Colombati, Claudia. "Concetto di libertà in Haydn e nel suo tempo: Aspetti nella vita e nell'arte." *Chigiana* 36 (1979):153-72.

Through quotations from Haydn's correspondence, detects an expression of yearning for liberation from the condition of servitude. Comparing his situation with Mozart's and Beethoven's, probes aspects of his character and artistic personality. Invokes Kant as well as Rousseau, and ponders conflicting forces by which his creativity was shaped: *Sturm und Drang* on one hand, rationalism on the other. Sees an expression of artistic freedom in the qualities of adventure, experimentation, and liberation from conventional procedure witnessed in his approach to composition.

226. Croll, Gerhard. "I fratelli Haydn." *Chigiana* 36 (1979):53-64.

Furnishes information on Michael Haydn, including aspects of his career, his relationship with Joseph, his musical output, and his visits to Vienna; but also discusses musical endeavors of Johann Haydn, none of whose compositions are known to survive. Recounts anecdotes involving Joseph and the two brothers.

227. Dack, James. "The Church Music of Karl Schiringer, Double-Bass Player in the Esterhazy 'Kapelle' 1767-1790." *The Haydn Yearbook* 9 (1975):329-40.

Describes circumstances under which this performer-composer (one of the longest-serving members of the Esterházy orchestra) wrote his small repertory of works: mass, *Te Deum, Regina Coeli, Salve Regina,* two Advent arias, five *Ave Reginas,* and a church sonata. Proposing that Schiringer was required to supply sacred music for the castle chapel at Eisenstadt as Haydn became increasingly involved with operatic activity at Eszterháza, suggests that the hiatus in Haydn's church-music output (1782-96) was more a consequence of his employer's passion for opera than of any alleged prohibition against instrumental music in church.

228. Dawson, R.V. "Haydn and Mozart." *The Musical Quarterly* 16 (1930):498-509.

Examines the relationship between an artist's life and works, and attempts to show how differences between Haydn and Mozart--with respect to their childhood, attitude towards religion, and relationship to national consciousness--accounted for differences in their music.

229. Deutsch, Otto Erich. *Admiral Nelson und Joseph Haydn: Ein britisch-österreichisches Gipfeltreffen.* Edited by Gitta Deutsch and Rudolf Klein. Vienna: Österreichischer Bundesverlag, 1982. 136 pp.

An account of Nelson, his relationship to Lady Hamilton, and his delayed return to England following his victory at Abukir. Contains a description of his meeting with Haydn during a visit to Eisenstadt (summer of 1800) in the company of Lord and Lady Hamilton and Emily Knight. Includes numerous illustrations, among them a facsimile page of the *Nelson* Mass.

230. ———. "Haydn bleibt Lehrling: Nach den Freimaurer-Akten des Österreichischen Staatsarchivs." *Musica* 13 (1959):289–90. Previously published in *Neue Freie Presse*, 14 March 1933, as "Der 'Lehrling' Haydn."

Draws on documentary evidence to examine Haydn's relationship to the Freemasons. Transcribes his petition for membership (29 December 1784), and recounts events leading to his induction on 11 February 1785. According to surviving records, Haydn subsequently failed to attend meetings, and thus never progressed beyond the level of apprentice. In 1787 he seems to have been quietly removed from the register of members.

231. ———. "Haydn und Nelson." *Österreichische Musikzeitschrift* 23 (1968):13–17. Previously published in *Die Musik* 24 (1931-32):436–40.

Addresses the issue of the naming of Haydn's *Nelson* Mass and the question of whether the music was inspired by Nelson's victory at Abukir in 1798 (Haydn was working on the mass when news of the victory reached Eisenstadt). Recounts details of a four-day visit paid by Nelson and a company of friends (the Hamiltons and Emily Knight) to Eisenstadt in 1800. During the visit, Haydn's newly-written "Nelson Aria," set to Emily Knight's "The Battle of the Nile," was sung by Lady Hamilton, with Haydn accompanying at the keyboard (cf. account in item 229).

232. Dreo, Harald. "Die fürstlich Esterházysche Musikkapelle von ihren Anfängen bis zum Jahre 1766." In *Beiträge zur Musikgeschichte des 18. Jahrhunderts* (item 69), pp. 80–115.

An annotated history of the Esterházy musical establishment at Eisenstadt, from its beginnings under Paul Esterházy up to Haydn's appointment as first kapellmeister. Includes music examples, documents, and illustrations.

233. Feder, Georg. "Haydn und Bach: Versuch eines musikhistorischen Vergleichs." In *Bachiana et Alia Musicologica: Festschrift Alfred Dürr zum 65. Geburtstag am 3. März 1983,* edited by Wolfgang Rehm, pp. 75-87. Kassel: Bärenreiter, 1983.

Begins with the premise that historical relationships need not be direct or immediate and that parallels between composers may exist in merely a shared musical tradition, or the influence of an intellectual movement, or common elements in their lives. In this light, examines biographical similarities, the question of J.S. Bach's influence on Haydn, the earlier traditions to which both composers were heir, Bach's and Haydn's thoughts on the nature of true sacred style, and their respective positions in the history of music.

234. ———. "Haydn und Eisenstadt." *Österreichische Musikzeitschrift* 25 (1970):213-21.

A concise but broadly ranging overview of Haydn's artistic and personal connections with the town. Includes reference to Haydn's residences, Eisenstadt compositions, and acquaintances. Supplies information on performers for whom particular works were written.

235. ———. "Die Philharmonische Akademie von Modena und ihr Mitglied Joseph Haydn." In *Festschrift Martin Ruhnke zum 65. Geburtstag,* pp. 94-105. Neuhausen-Stuttgart: Hänssler, 1986.

From the limited sources available, outlines the history and purpose of the organization, and includes selected lists (1775, 1796) of professional musicians in its service. Describes known references to Haydn's affiliation, and adds a previously overlooked, official source that confirms his membership: the calendar of events for the court of Modena, which first lists Haydn as a member in 1780. Names all the Academy's *maestri,* including Haydn, cited in the calendars of 1780, 1781, and 1796.

236. Franken, Franz Hermann. *Die Krankheiten grosser Komponisten,* vol. 1. Wilhelmshaven: Florian Noetzel, 1986. 303 pp.

Medical histories of Haydn, Beethoven, Bellini, Mendelssohn, Chopin, and Schumann. Discussion of Haydn, pp. 13-59, draws on item 237.

237. ———. *Krankheit und Tod grosser Komponisten.* Baden-Baden: Gerhard Witzstrock, 1979. viii, 280 pp.

A collection of medical histories of Haydn, Mozart, Beethoven, Schubert, Mendelssohn, Chopin, and Rossini. The section on Haydn, pp. 5-34, includes a biographical sketch, discussion of the false "Papa Haydn" image, a description of Haydn's physical appearance, his medical history, and the story of the theft and recovery of his skull. Investigation of his medical history divides into two parts. The first, from his birth to 1799, describes minor illnesses as reported in Haydn's letters and other sources; it pays particular attention to his polyp and the famous story of the surgeon John Hunter's comical attempt to remove it. The second part, from 1799 to 1809, concerns more serious problems, and proposes diagnoses based once again on contemporary sources. Contains several illustrations.

238. Fuchs, Ingrid, and Vobraba, Leopold. "Studien zur Biographie von Karl Friberth." *Studien zur Musikwissenschaft* 34 (1983):21-59.

A documented biographical study of a singer at the Esterházy court. Friberth had close associations with Haydn, notably in his role as *primo uomo* for six of Haydn's operas, his authorship of the libretto for *L'incontro improvviso,* and his performance at the premiere of *Il ritorno di Tobia* (1775) as well as its 1784 revival.

239. Geck, Martin. "Haydn in London." *Neue Zeitschrift für Musik* 126 (1965):157-58.

A brief account of Haydn's achievements during the London sojourns.

240. Geiringer, Karl. "Haydn and His Viennese Background." In *Haydn Studies* (item 73), pp. 3-13.

Depicts the economic and social climate in Vienna during Haydn's early years, and describes musical influences that helped mold his style. Briefly surveys the music he composed in Vienna prior to serving Count Morzin at Lukaveč, and examines his personal and professional ties to Vienna both during and after his years at Eisenstadt and Eszterháza.

241. ———. *Joseph Haydn.* Potsdam: Akademische Verlagsgesellschaft Athenaion, 1932. 160 pp.

Incorporated in Ernst Bücken's *Grossen Meister der Musik* series, this concise, boldly executed attempt at a comprehensive treatment of the composer and his accomplishment comprises a biographical essay, a discussion of eighteenth-century stylistic developments pertinent to the study of Haydn, and an overview of each of the major instrumental and vocal genres (string quartets, other chamber music without keyboard, symphonies, overtures, concertos, keyboard sonatas, other keyboard works, violin sonatas, keyboard trios, operas, solo cantatas and songs, masses, other sacred works, and cantatas and oratorios). While covering vocal works in less detail than the instrumental, emphasizes aspects of originality and ingenuity in all genres. Concludes that Haydn's life and works are inseparable, that he composed out of inner necessity, and that his works furnish a key to the understanding of his personality. Suggests that in light of the qualities of simplicity and contentment that characterized his personality, he was unsuited to the realm of theater music.

242. ———, in collaboration with Geiringer, Irene. *Haydn: A Creative Life in Music.* 3d ed., revised and enlarged. Berkeley: University of California Press, 1982. xii, 403 pp.

Until the appearance of Landon's five-volume study (item 259), the most authoritative English-language biography. The first edition (New York: W.W. Norton, 1946) was based on Geiringer's *Joseph Haydn* (item 241). Both the second edition (1968) and the third have drawn upon the advances of post-war Haydn research. Part 1 divides into ten chapters, representing stations of Haydn's career and his development as an artist. Part 2 offers an introductory essay on the Haydn sources, followed by five chapters corresponding to Geiringer's categorization of style periods: youth (1750-60); a phase of transition (1761-70); a Romantic crisis (1771-80); maturity (1781-90); consummate mastery (1791-1803). Strives for balanced treatment of each genre within a style period, favoring generalizations rather than critical analysis of individual works. Relatively few music examples. The depiction of Haydn as an artist emphasizes such qualities as his "truly mundane spirit," "healthy sensuality," "noble humanity," and "radiant joyfulness."

243. Giese, Alexander. "Einige Bemerkungen über Joseph Haydn als Freimaurer und die Freimaurerei seiner Zeit." In *Joseph Haydn in seiner Zeit* (item 77), pp. 168–71.

Argues that Haydn's failure to participate in activities of the Freemasons had more to do with external circumstances than with any intrinsic lack of interest. Cites numerous acquaintances who were Freemasons, notes Haydn's interest in Mozart's Masonic music, and makes reference to purported Masonic elements in *The Creation.*

244. Graschitz, Horst. *Joseph Haydn und Eisenstadt.* Eisenstadt: Verlag Nentwich Inh. Eva Lattner, 1982. 128 pp.

An engagingly written, non-scholarly account of Haydn's life, with little discussion of the music. Includes a brief chapter on the town of Eisenstadt, with photographs and historical background on important landmarks. Does not provide an index.

245. Gutkas, Karl. "Österreich und Europa zur Zeit Joseph Haydns." In *Joseph Haydn und seine Zeit* (item 80), pp. 9–24.

Provides a sketch of eighteenth-century history and culture, and of political events as they impinged on Haydn's life.

246. Hadden, J. Cuthbert. *Haydn.* Rev. ed. London: J.M. Dent, 1934. xv, 237 pp.

Originally published in 1902 (London: E.P. Dutton). Concentrates on Haydn's life (with special emphasis on the London visits) rather than on description of the music. Transmits the traditional view of the methodical, industrious, modest, and pious artist, unspoiled by success.

247. Hadow, William H. *A Croatian Composer: Notes Toward the Study of Joseph Haydn.* London: Seeley & Co., 1897. Reprint. Freeport, NY: Books for Libraries, 1972. 98 pp. Another reprint in William H. Hadow. *Collected Essays,* pp. 65–106. London: Oxford University Press, 1928.

Derives from two studies by František Š. Kuhač: a collection of South Slavonic folksongs and a pamphlet on Haydn. Speculating on Haydn's ethnic background, cites melodic correspondences and affinities in addition to biographical information in support of the composer's alleged Croatian origins.

248. Harich, János. "Das fürstlich Esterházy'sche Fideikommiss." *The Haydn Yearbook* 4 (1968):5-38.

A richly documented description of economic life at the Esterházy court in Haydn's time. Supplies specific information on court administration, employees' salaries, and the cost of food, clothing, and housing. Making note of Haydn's position as castle organist and his activities as a teacher, discusses Haydn's salary and supplementary earnings. Includes three facsimiles of court documents pertaining to Haydn.

249. Hoboken, Anthony van. "Joseph Haydns Schwager." In *Festschrift Josef Stummvoll,* edited by Josef Mayerhöfer and Walter Ritzer, in collaboration with Maria Razumovsky, pp. 788-93. Vienna: Brüder Hollinek, 1970.

Reports on documents in the Haus-, Hof- und Staatsarchiv in Vienna concerning the debts and institutional confinement of Haydn's brother-in-law, Joseph Keller. Describes the assistance given by Haydn to Keller and his family, and explains the role played by Theresia, Keller's sister and Haydn's first love, in caring for her brother and his child.

250. Hogwood, Christopher. *Haydn's Visits to England.* London: The Folio Society, 1980. 116 pp.

An account of the visits in 1791-92 and 1794-95, based chiefly on a selection of contemporary sources: letters, diaries, newspapers, early biographies, Haydn's London notebooks, and related documents, including substantial quotation of material from Landon, items 107 and 262. Incorporates a miscellany of black-and-white illustrations.

251. Hörwarthner, Maria. "Joseph Haydns Bibliothek." In *Joseph Haydn in seiner Zeit* (item 77), pp. 172-74.

Views the substantial size and breadth of Haydn's library as the reflection of a continuous, intensive process of self-education and cultivation. Places his literary interests in the context of contemporary Austrian intellectual fashions and aspirations, and cites the importance of his English experience as a stimulus for his later interest in English aesthetics, philosophy, and poetry (see item 34).

252. Hughes, Rosemary. "Dr. Burney's Championship of Haydn." *The Musical Quarterly* 27 (1941):90-96.

An account of Burney's supportive role, with quotations from his diary and from reviews which the author attributes to him.

253. ———. *Haydn.* 5th ed. London: J.M. Dent & Sons, 1974. xiii, 271 pp.

A concise treatment of Haydn's life and works, primarily for the musically knowledgeable amateur. First appeared in 1950 (London: Dent), with subsequent revised editions, each taking into account advances in Haydn research, in 1956, 1962, and 1970. Provides an overview of his compositional output, with chapters on non-operatic vocal works, keyboard music, chamber music for strings, orchestral music, and opera. Includes a modest number of music examples, eight plates (mostly contemporary portraits), and several appendices: chronology, catalogue of works, personalia.

254. ———. "The Rediscovery of Haydn." *The Musical Times* 100 (1959):258-59.

Suggests that largely as a result of post-World War II research, a pattern in Haydn's creative life may be discerned: the intermittent inspiration of his 20s and 30s; the startling emergence of a mature and powerful idiom at about age 40; the temporary ebbing of that power in his late 40s and early 50s; then the later, renewed energy heralded by the Paris symphonies and Op. 64 quartets.

255. Hurwitz, Joachim. "Haydn and the Freemasons." *The Haydn Yearbook* 16 (1985):5-98.

A fresh, heavily documented look at Haydn's relationship to the Freemasons. Provides background on Freemasonry in Austria and discusses events surrounding Haydn's induction on 11 February 1785. Investigates a number of issues concerning Haydn and Freemasonry: the reasons Haydn became a Freemason, the extent of his participation in the lodges, the meaning Freemasonry held for him, and the question of Masonic influences on Haydn's music, particularly *The Creation* and *The Seasons.* Offers photographic reproductions of relevant documents, membership lists, printed music, and title pages. An appendix presents 23 documents pertaining to Haydn's membership in two lodges: "True Concord" and "Truth."

256. Jacob, Heinrich Eduard. *Joseph Haydn: His Art, Times, and Glory.* Translated by Richard and Clara Winston. New York: Rinehart, 1950. xv, 368 pp.

A loose-jointed, leisurely narrative, more concerned with Haydn's personality and the course of his career than with the artist and his accomplishment. Emphasizes the inseparability of the composer's life and his music, and shows how Haydn managed to preserve his inner freedom while submitting to outward servitude. Offers vivid portrayals of contemporary figures and locales, numerous biographical anecdotes, and background discussion of eighteenth-century musical customs. First appeared in English translation, though originally written in German. Among subsequent publications were a French version, translated by M. Buchet as *Joseph Haydn, son art, son époque, sa gloire* (Paris: Corrêa, 1950), and the German version, *Joseph Haydn: Seine Kunst, seine Zeit, sein Ruhm* (Hamburg: C. Wegner, 1952).

257. Jancik, Hans. "Begegnungen zwischen Joseph und Michael Haydn." *Österreichische Musikzeitschrift* 14 (1959):206-12.

A discussion of contact between the two brothers: the visits, the career and financial assistance offered by Joseph, and Michael's conducting of works by his brother. Notes the brotherly affection sustained despite many years' separation and the disparity in their way of life.

258. Karajan, Theodor Georg von. *J. Haydn in London, 1791 und 1792.* Vienna: Karl Gerold's Sohn, 1861. 118 pp.

An anecdotal, affectionately penned narrative recounting the successes and musical adventures of Haydn's first London journey. Examines Haydn's relationship with Marianne von Genzinger, quotes extensively from their letters, and reproduces the text of their correspondence of 1789-92.

259. Landon, H.C. Robbins. *Haydn: Chronicle and Works.* 5 vols. Bloomington: Indiana University, 1976-80.

By far the most ambitious, comprehensive biographical study to date. Drawing on a great wealth of documentary information, follows in Pohl's footsteps by pursuing an essentially antiquarian approach. In each of the volumes (annotated as items 260-64 below), "Chronicle" chapters, featuring extensive quotation from letters and other contemporary documents, are distinguished from chapters on musical works from the period in question. Texts of documents are often given both in the original language and in English. Incorporates material from the author's *The Symphonies of Joseph Haydn* (item 964), and includes letters not found in his *Collected Correspondence* (item 107). Offers descriptive accounts of the music, pointing out salient, historically significant features of individual works and aspects of stylistic development. While taking pains to place Haydn's music in the context of achievements by predecessors and contemporaries (with particular emphasis on various groups of Haydn imitators, or *seguaci*), tends to avoid detailed critical or stylistic analysis. Many illustrations and a substantial number of music examples throughout. Each volume has an extensive bibliography, detailed general index, and index of works cited.

260. ———. *Haydn: Chronicle and Works.* Vol. 1: *Haydn: The Early Years, 1732-1765.* Bloomington: Indiana University Press, 1980. 655 pp.

Extensive historical and biographical background, with chapters on Austria in the early eighteenth century, Haydn's family, mid-century musical practices and fashions in Vienna, and Eisenstadt and the Esterházys. Discusses the role of copyists, monasteries, and music publishers in Paris, Amsterdam, and London in the dissemination of Haydn's works. Treatment of the music emphasizes evidence of artistic and technical maturity in early compositions. Identifies J.G. Albrechtsberger and F.X. Dussek as members of a "First Haydn School."

261. ———. *Haydn: Chronicle and Works.* Vol. 2: *Haydn at Eszterháza, 1766-1790.* Bloomington: Indiana University Press, 1978. 799 pp.

Encompasses discussion of the administrative organization of Eszterháza; Haydn's role as composer of vocal music (sacred and operatic); the *Sturm und Drang* movement; Pleyel as pupil of Haydn's; the "Second Haydn School," including Vanhal, Ordonez, and (for a brief period) Mozart; Haydn and Viennese society; the dissemination of Haydn's music abroad; and the "Third Haydn School:"

Pietrowski, Wranizky, Gyrowetz, and Hayda. An appendix reproduces an extended excerpt from Nicolas Étienne Framery's *Notice sur Joseph Haydn* (1810), in the original French.

262. ———. *Haydn: Chronicle and Works.* Vol. 3: *Haydn in England, 1791-1795.* Bloomington: Indiana University Press, 1976. 640 pp.

In this first volume of the study to be published, the "Chronicle" portion divides into five chapters corresponding to the years 1791-95. Draws on Haydn's correspondence and the London notebooks, documents pertaining to his association with Salomon and other acquaintances, newspaper announcements and critiques of concerts, and concert programs. Discussion of the works subsumes three chapters--vocal music, chamber works, orchestral works--and features extended commentary on the opera *L'anima del filosofo* and the London symphonies.

263. ———. *Haydn: Chronicle and Works.* Vol. 4: *The Years of 'The Creation,' 1796-1800.* Bloomington: Indiana University Press, 1977. 656 pp.

Identifies the late oratorio as Haydn's most outstanding accomplishment and one of the greatest products of the age. Offers background chapters on events and circumstances in 1795: musical life in Vienna, Eisenstadt and the Esterházy family. Principal organization is by year (1795-1800), with extensive quotations from contemporary documents in the "Chronicle" chapters and descriptive commentary on the works completed in each year. Discussion of *The Creation* itself encompasses the libretto, sketches (reproduced in transcription), sources, and musical design (including aspects of key structure, symbolism, orchestration, and commentary on individual numbers). An appendix reproduces (after Haydn's autograph copy) the extended and prestigious list of subscribers to the first edition of *The Creation.*

264. ———. *Haydn: Chronicle and Works.* Vol. 5: *The Late Years, 1801-1809.* Bloomington: Indiana University Press, 1977. 495 pp.

Divides into alternating "Chronicle" and "Works" chapters for the years 1801-3, with subsequent chapters chronicling the years 1804-9. Features documents pertaining to early performances of *The Creation* and an extended discussion of *The Seasons*. Reproduces the contents of Haydn's first will and final will, the Elssler catalogue of Haydn's music library, the catalogue of his libretto collection, and the auction catalogue of artistic effects. An appendix, "Haydn and Posterity: A Study in Changing Values," traces the eclipse of Haydn's reputation through documents from the years following his death. Includes writings by Mendelssohn, Schumann, and Hanslick; also quotations from the diaries of Cosima Wagner in which she describes four-hand performances of Haydn symphonies with Richard.

265. ———. "Haydns erste Erfahrungen in England: Von der Ankunft in London bis zum ersten Salomon-Konzert." In *Beiträge zur Musikgeschichte des 18. Jahrhunderts* (item 69), pp. 154-81.

Translation, with some omissions, of item 262, pp. 21-49.

266. ———. *Das kleine Haydnbuch.* Salzburg: Residenz Verlag, 1967. 135 pp.

Concise volume on Haydn's life for the non-specialist reader, first published in 1967. Features numerous quotations from contemporary correspondence, newspaper reports, and other documents.

267. ———, and Jones, David Wyn. *Haydn: His Life and Music.* Bloomington: Indiana University Press, 1988. 383 pp.

Incorporates biographical material from Landon's *Haydn: Chronicle and Works* (item 259) and *Haydn: A Documentary Study* (item 136). Alternates biographical chapters with discussion of the music in different periods: to 1765, 1766-80, 1781-90, 1791-95, and 1796-1803. Strives for a balanced overview of the different genres, giving information on scoring and salient features of melody, harmony, texture, and structure. No attempt at detailed analysis or critical interpretation. Includes a substantial number of music examples in score and an index of Haydn's compositions.

268. ———, and Raynor, Henry. *Haydn.* New York: Praeger, 1972. 107 pp.

Lightweight biography for the musical amateur. Features quotation of several short works (keyboard pieces, song, vocal canon) in their entirety.

269. Larsen, Jens Peter, [and Feder, Georg]. *The New Grove Haydn.* New York: W.W. Norton, 1983. 237 pp.

A modified, corrected version of the encyclopedia article (item 63), complete with Georg Feder's work list. Includes an updated bibliography.

270. Matthews, Betty. "Haydn's Visit to Hampshire and the Isle of Wight, Described from Contemporary Sources." *The Haydn Yearbook* 3 (1965):111-21.

Drawing on Haydn's notebooks and other contemporary documents, offers a speculative reconstruction of events for the composer's July 1794 visit as guest of Thomas Orde, Governor of the Isle of Wight.

271. Molnár, Antal. "Der gestaltpsychologische Unterschied zwischen Haydn und Mozart." In *Bericht über die Internationale Konferenz zum Andenken Joseph Haydns* (item 70), pp. 95-101.

Approaches the comparison of Haydn and Mozart from the standpoint of Gestalt psychology. For each composer, examines such issues as family background and attitudes, physical appearance, notable personality traits, approach to the compositional process, and attitude toward social position and the surrounding world. Shows that whereas Haydn's art had a rational basis, Mozart's was rooted in irrationality.

272. Nettl, Paul. "The Czechs in Eighteenth-Century Music." *Music and Letters* 21 (1940):362-70.

Includes a discussion of political, social, religious, and economic circumstances bearing on the practice of music in eighteenth-century Bohemia. Citing Count Morzin's ensemble as an example, emphasizes the decentralized nature of musical activity in the region as a decisively important factor.

273. Nohl, Ludwig. *Haydn.* Leipzig: Philipp Reclam, [1882?]. 123 pp.

Among the earliest and most frequently reissued of the popular biographies. A Romantically inclined portrayal, drawing largely on Dies' account for anecdotal material. Credits Haydn with adding the minuet to the three-movement symphony and with being the first to introduce into music the "tenderer and deeper notes of the heart." Celebrates Haydn as a predecessor to Beethoven, assigns him leadership in the development of quartet and symphonic style, underscores his distinct German character, and attempts to draw connections between the man and his music. Emphasizes his optimism and the inner compulsion which produced music expressive of life and longing.

274. ———. *Life of Haydn.* Translated by George P. Upton. Chicago: A.C. McClurg, 1884. Reprint. St. Clair Shores, MI: Scholarly Press, 1970. 195 pp.

English version of item 273.

275. Nowak, Leopold. *Joseph Haydn: Leben, Bedeutung und Werk.* 3d ed. Zurich: Amalthea-Verlag, [1966]. 579 pp.

First published in 1951 (Zurich: Amalthea-Verlag). Divides Haydn's career into four phases: the seeds (1740-60), growth and ripening (1761-90), fruition (1790-95), harvest (1795-1809). Attempts to provide a unified (if not comprehensive) overview of his life and accomplishment, with brief discussion of major compositions woven into the biographical narrative. Offers a discussion of music in Vienna in the time of Charles VI (1700-1740). Numerous illustrations; several half-tone facsimiles and single-line thematic examples. Includes an abbreviated work list and a detailed chronology.

276. Oldman, Cecil B. "Haydn's Quarrel with the 'Professionals' in 1788." In *Musik und Verlag: Karl Vötterle zum 65. Geburtstag am 12. April 1968,* edited by Richard Baum and Wolfgang Rehm, pp. 459-65. Kassel: Bärenreiter, 1968.

Draws on *The World* and *The Morning Post* for quotations to describe the scandal that arose when, in response to a commission from the Professional Concerts, Haydn supplied (and was paid for) three symphonies that had already been published in London and elsewhere. Analyzes the conflicting documentation, proposes a reconstruction of the likely sequence of events, and concludes that in light of the trouble in 1788, Haydn must bear some part of the blame for controversies with the "Professionals" in 1791-92.

277. Pohl, Carl Ferdinand. *Joseph Haydn.* Leipzig: Breitkopf & Härtel, 1878-1927. Reprint. 3 vols. Vaduz, Liechtenstein: Sändig Reprint, 1970-84. xx, 422 pp.; vii, 383, 14 pp.; xii, 440 pp.

Until recently the major, definitive biography. Based on extensive examination of earlier studies and documents in Eisenstadt, Vienna, and elsewhere. Volume 1 (originally published in 1875 by A. Sacco in Berlin) deals with Haydn's ancestry, childhood, musical training, early activities in Vienna, and his employment at Eisenstadt. Volume 2 (1882) concerns his career as Esterházy kapellmeister. Narrative ends with the departure for London in 1790. Discussion of the music, organized by genre, is relegated to the end of the second volume. Offers descriptive commentary and cites outstanding features. Does not attempt any detailed or systematic stylistic criticism. Volume 3 (1927) prepared with the help of the deceased author's research materials by Hugo Botstiber, chronicles the London sojourns, the time of the late oratorios, and the composer's last years. Supplements the portrayal in volume 1 with additional information on Haydn's physical appearance, manner, and outlook, and gives a descriptive account of all major works from the late period. Provides information on circumstances under which the works were written; no critical analysis. An appendix includes letters to and about Haydn (including Rebecca Schroeter's letters and Elssler's letter on Haydn's death) and a catalogue of Haydn iconography.

278. ———. *Mozart und Haydn in London.* Part 2: *Haydn in London.* Vienna: Carl Gerold's Sohn, 1867. Reprint. New York: Da Capo, 1971. xvi, 387 pp.

Gives an overview of Haydn's two London sojourns, and provides brief biographical sketches of Johann Peter Salomon and other London acquaintances. Substantial appendix material includes an account of the first London performance of *The Creation.* Furnishes information on late eighteenth-century musical organizations, concerts, and operatic repertory, and offers a tabular listing of public virtuoso performances in London in the years 1750-95, organized by the artists' performance specialty.

279. Poštolka, Milan. "Haydn, Fasch and Count Morzin." *The Musical Times* 129 (1988):78.

Corrects a long-perpetuated error in Haydn research,

adducing evidence to show that Johann Friedrich Fasch was not a predecessor of Haydn's as kapellmeister to Count Ferdinand Maximilian von Morzin in Lucaveč, but that he actually served Count Václav Morzin in Prague.

280. Redfern, Brian. *Haydn: A Biography, with a Survey of Books, Editions and Recordings.* London: Clive Bingley, 1970. 111 pp.

A clearly written but superficial discussion of Haydn's life and works. Includes a survey of predominantly non-specialist literature on Haydn available in English or English translation, a survey of Haydn editions, and a brief discography.

281. Roscoe, Christopher. "Haydn and London in the 1780's." *Music and Letters* 49 (1968):203-12.

An account of attempts by Lord Abingdon, the Professional Concerts, and others to bring Haydn to London in the 1780s. Includes quotations from contemporary newspaper reports that concern Haydn's anticipated visits and the scandal over three symphonies presented to the Professional Concerts. Includes the text of a suggestion, published in 1785 in *The Gazeteer & New Daily Advertiser,* that Haydn be kidnapped and brought to London.

282. Rutz, Hans. *Joseph Haydn: Dokumente seines Lebens und Schaffens.* Munich: C.H. Beck, 1953. 159 pp.

A non-scholarly, idealized portrayal of the master's career, with biographical narrative interwoven with quoted correspondence and contemporary accounts. Includes the 1776 autobiographical sketch, the 1761 Esterházy contract, and the 1809 will. Includes a concise chronology.

283. Schmid, Ernst Fritz. "Josef Haydns Jugendliebe." In *Festschrift Wilhelm Fischer zum 70. Geburtstag überreicht im Mozartjahr 1956,* edited by Hans Zingerle, pp. 109-22. Innsbruck: Sprachwissenschaftliches Seminar der Univ. Innsbruck, 1956.

Traces the family history of Haydn's in-laws, the Kellers, and discusses Haydn's love for Theresia Keller, who was destined for the cloister. Cites prints and other sources for Haydn's Organ Concerto in C, written for the occasion on which Theresia took vows in 1756. (The *Salve Regina* in E may have been written for this occasion too.) Tells of Haydn's marriage in 1760 to Theresia's older sister, Maria Anna, and of Theresia's probable work with charities in Vienna, after abolition of her cloister in 1782. Notes that Maria Anna provided for Theresia in her will. Reproduces excerpts from this will, the text of Haydn's marriage contract, and other relevant documents.

284. ———. *Joseph Haydn: Ein Buch von Vorfahren und Heimat des Meisters.* Kassel: Bärenreiter, 1934. 354 pp.

An ambitious, extensively researched exploration of Haydn's roots. Divided into four parts: the father's family, the mother's family, Haydn's parents (including information on his five siblings), and Haydn's heritage (concerned with national, regional, and ethnic folk elements discernible in his melodies). Supplemented by a set of seven large-format genealogical tables.

285. Schnerich, Alfred. *Joseph Haydn und seine Sendung.* 2d ed., with style-critical appendix by Wilhelm Fischer. Zurich: Amalthea-Verlag, 1926. 282 pp.

Main body of the text offers a concise, not very colorful account of Haydn's career. An introductory chapter on his place in the history of culture and art extols his artistic legacy and the historical significance of his pathbreaking accomplishments in instrumental music as well as in sacred and secular vocal genres. Compares his influence in music with that of Leonardo da Vinci in the visual arts. Fischer's appendix (pp. 225-62) treats Haydn's artistic development against the backdrop of eighteenth-century traditions. Emphasis falls on the symphonies. Includes a catalogue of works and a list of Haydn monuments, medallions, and portraits. First published in 1922 (Zurich: Amalthea-Verlag).

286. Scholes, Percy A. "Burney and Haydn." *The Monthly Musical Record* 71 (1941):155-57, 172-78.

A discussion of Burney's relationship to Haydn, drawing upon the memoirs of Burney's daughter Fanny, letters by Burney's friends, and other sources. Takes note of the long correspondence that preceded their first encounter and the few records that remain of their meetings (Burney's reminiscences were destroyed by his daughter). Includes excerpts from a poem by Burney, written to celebrate Haydn's arrival in England, and quotes the full text of a letter from Burney to Haydn concerning the subscription to *The Creation,* a project organized by Burney.

287. ———. "A New Enquiry into the Life and Work of Dr. Burney." *Proceedings of the Royal Musical Association* 67 (1940-41):1-30.

A summary of Burney's career, followed by a series of brief sketches that address various aspects of his life and work. A short section on "Burney and Haydn" discusses Haydn's contact with Burney during his London visits.

288. Schultheiss, Emil. "Ärztliches über Haydn." *Musica* 13 (1959):291-92.

An account of Haydn's health, which the author claims was strong until his later years. Describes minor ailments that afflicted him in England, and discusses more serious illnesses from 1801 until his death. Includes Haydn's account of how Dr. John Hunter, apparently through a misunderstanding, attempted to operate on his nasal polyp in London.

289. Scott, Marion M. "Haydn in England." *The Musical Quarterly* 18 (1932):260-73.

Concerned mainly with the visit of 1791-92. Topics discussed include Haydn's first crossing of the English channel, his accommodations, his reception in England, his relationship to Rebecca Schroeter, and his prolific writing. Provides quotations from Haydn and others (sources not given), and reproduces an engraving by Hardy and the autograph of the transfer to Salomon in 1796 of the second set of London symphonies.

290. ———. "Haydn Stayed Here!" *Music and Letters* 32 (1951):38-44.

Recounts the story of how the author--having discovered that houses in which Haydn lived and worked in London no longer stood--set out to find the home of a banker named Brassey, with whom Haydn lived for a while on the outskirts of London. Describes how clues in Brassey's death notice (*The Gentleman's Quarterly,* 18 September 1798) made it possible to locate and visit the house. Describes this house (called Roxford, one mile west of

Hertingfordbury), and speculates on possible causes for Brassey's early death.

291. ———. "The Opera Concerts of 1795." *The Music Review* 12 (1951):24-28.

Clarifies for the first time the changeover from "Mr. Salomon's Concerts" at the Hanover Square Rooms to the "Opera Concerts" at the King's Theater. Calls attention to Salomon's open letter (16 January 1795) in *The Oracle and Public Advertiser,* which makes it clear that Salomon abandoned his series for financial reasons but "was not responsible for the Opera Concerts": that responsibility lay with the "Proprietor" of the King's Theater (i.e. William Taylor), as shown in an advertisement for the first Opera Concert, published alongside the letter. Reprints this letter and excerpts from the advertisement.

292. Somerset, H.V.F. "Joseph Haydn in England." *Music and Letters* 13 (1932):272-85.

An account of Haydn's musical and social life in England, incorporating quotations from contemporary documents, including love letters from Rebecca Schroeter. Alludes to the publication and performance of his works in England well before the visits of 1791-92 and 1794-95.

293. Spitta, Philipp. "Joseph Haydn in der Darstellung C.F. Pohl's." In Philipp Spitta. *Zur Musik: Sechzehn Aufsätze,* pp. 151-76. Berlin: Gebrüder Paetel, 1892. Reprint. Hildesheim: Georg Olms, 1976.

Characterizing Otto Jahn's philologically oriented Mozart study as more the work of a biographer than a historian, proposes that Pohl's approach was neither biographical nor historical, but antiquarian. Praises the wealth of factual material assembled by Pohl, notably on eighteenth-century musical practices in Vienna and southern Germany. Comments on the excessive emphasis on background information at the expense of the protagonist himself, and criticizes the inappropriate attempt to address both a specialist and a general readership. Expresses the need for a study that would place the composer's artistic accomplishment in an intensively explored historical context.

294. Strunk, W. Oliver. "Haydn." In *From Bach to Stravinsky: The History of Music by its Foremost Critics,* edited by

David Ewen, pp. 77-87. New York: W.W. Norton, 1933.

A descriptive overview of the composer and his output, with emphasis on the late works. Includes quotations from Haydn's writings and other contemporary sources.

295. Tandler, Julius. "Le crâne d'Haydn." *S.I.M. Revue musicale* 6 (1910):69-74.

An abbreviated translation of item 296.

296. ———. "Über den Schädel Haydns." *Mitteilungen der Anthropologischen Gesellschaft in Wien* 39 (1909):260-79.

Recounts the story of the theft and rediscovery of Haydn's skull, up to the time of its addition to the collection of the Gesellschaft der Musikfreunde (it has since been reunited with the remainder of his skeleton). Offers a detailed description of the skull and its condition, provides a history and description of the death mask, and examines seven Haydn portraits for the sake of comparison. Establishes criteria for identifying the skull as Haydn's and shows how they are met. Includes photographs of the skull, the death mask, portraits, and an X ray of the skull inside the mask, taken to establish the identity of the skull. An appendix reproduces the contents of four relevant letters and documents.

297. Tank, Ulrich. *Studien zur Esterházyschen Hofmusik von etwa 1620 bis 1790.* Regensburg: Gustav Bosse, 1981. vi, 523 pp.

Two chapters have direct bearing on Haydn: one concerns court music under Prince Paul Anton (1734-62); the other, court music under Prince Nikolaus. Each of the chapters is divided into four main sections: court musicians (church and chamber, with documents and lists of data; the chapter on Paul Anton contains a subsection on Haydn, with relevant documents and letters); compensation of the musicians; the repertory (church, chamber, and theater); and tables concerning the musicians (year-by-year listings of the musicians at court).

298. Tenschert, Roland. *Frauen um Haydn.* Vienna: Donau-Verlag, 1947. 202 pp.

A popular study that addresses several main topics: his relationship to women in general; female relatives, pupils, and interpreters of his music; his unfortunate marriage to Maria Anna; and his relationships with Luigia Polzelli, Marianne von Genzinger, and Rebecca Schroeter. Includes 19 photographic plates.

299. Thomas, Günter. "Haydn als Zensor?" *Haydn-Studien* 6/2 (1988):161-63.

In response to Peter Branscombe's question (in item 536) of whether or not Haydn had acted as a censor for the play *Kaspar der Rauchfangkehrer,* Thomas identifies the signature on the piece as that of "Hägelin" rather than of "Haydn"--a more appropriate choice since Franz Karl Hägelin was a theater censor appointed by Maria Theresia.

300. ———. "Haydn-Anekdoten." In *Ars Musica, Musica Scientia: Festschrift Heinrich Hüschen zum fünfundsechzigsten Geburtstag am 2. März 1980,* edited by Detlef Altenburg, pp. 435-43. Cologne: Gitarre und Laute, 1980.

Concerned with questions of error and contradiction in Haydn biography. With reference to specific examples, shows how certain details long accepted as true prove to be incorrect or problematical on closer inspection.

301. Vignal, Marc. *Franz-Joseph Haydn: L'homme et son oeuvre.* Paris: Éditions Seghers, 1964. 191 pp.

Lightweight biography offering an account of Haydn's life and a chronological overview of major accomplishments. No music examples; several illustrations and facsimiles; summary catalogue of works; discography.

302. ———. *Joseph Haydn.* [Paris]: Fayard, 1988. 1534 pp.

A detailed, factual, and reasonably up-to-date handbook. Biographical portion quotes extensively from correspondence, early accounts, and court documents. Includes substantial background on the Esterházy family and music establishment. Furnishes information on the dissemination of his works, early reception of his music, and his relationship with Beethoven. Other points of special emphasis include the London sojourns and the composition and early performances of the late oratorios. Discussion of the music separates vocal works from instrumental, divides the oeuvre into discrete periods (to 1761; 1761-65; 1766-75; 1776-84; 1785-90; 1791-95; 1796-1803), and gives descriptive, summary analyses for individual compositions and groups of works. Makes considerable reference to recent research on sources, dating, and analysis. Features an extended bibliography.

303. Webster, James. "Prospects for Haydn Biography." *The Musical Times* 123 (1982):170-75.

An assessment of the state of Haydn research following the completion of Landon's *Haydn: Chronicle and Works* (item 259). Compares Landon's approach with Pohl's, and finds Landon's a vast improvement in quantity of pertinent information, but by no means an advancement with regard to intellectual depth, refinement of interpretation, or elegance of presentation. Takes Landon to task for perpetuating Pohl's "antiquarian" approach, rather than offering critical interpretation. Denounces the inadequacy of traditional views of Haydn's personality on one hand and musical style on the other. Advocates an approach that would view stylistic and biographical interpretation as aspects of a single subject: "a real man and his work."

304. ———. "Prospects for Haydn Biography after Landon." *The Musical Quarterly* 68 (1982):476-95.

An incisive critique of Landon's *Haydn: Chronicle and Works* (item 259), especially volumes 1 and 2. Cites representative errors and inconsistencies. Discussing the history of Haydn research, compares Landon with Pohl, and cites weaknesses in Landon's hypotheses about chronology and various aspects of Haydn biography. Denounces Landon's self-centered view of Haydn scholarship and his tendency to perpetuate myths of Haydn biography, notably that of the "Papa Haydn" image. Compares the course of Haydn scholarship with the accomplishments of Mozart and Beethoven scholars, and advocates abandoning the "antiquarian" approach witnessed in Pohl and Landon in favor of Spitta's ideal of interpretation. Argues for a substantially revised, more sophisticated view of both the man and his music.

305. Weismann, Wilhelm. "Joseph Haydns menschliche Persönlichkeit." *Zeitschrift für Musik* 99 (1932):277-85.

Discusses how nineteenth-century attitudes on Haydn, colored by the spirit of the times, have helped to perpetuate a distorted view of the composer. To offer clarification, examines various aspects of the man and his personality: his appearance, sense of order, persistence, optimistic fatalism, and other qualities. Shows how these traits surfaced in Haydn's relations with the nobility, other musicians, and women. Finally, takes a look at Haydn as an elderly man. Appends a letter of 9 February 1790 to Frau von Genzinger.

Master and Scholar: Studies of Musical Influence

The following listing offers a representative selection of papers and articles concerned with the influence of Haydn's music on pupils, younger contemporaries, and composers of subsequent generations. Also noted here are studies that deal with arrangements of Haydn's music, with his impact on the music of later composers (such as Brahms), various influences to which Haydn himself was subjected (including Fux on one hand, Gottfried van Swieten on the other), and with the specific question of mutual influence between Haydn and Mozart. Attention should also be called to the extensive treatment of "Haydn schools" and *seguaci* in Landon's *Haydn: Chronicle and Works* (item 259).

306. Arnold, Denis. "Haydn's Counterpoint and Fux's 'Gradus'." *The Monthly Musical Record* 87 (1957):52-58.

Finds the influence of Fux in Haydn's symphonies and chamber music of the 1760s. Discovers that two types of contrapuntal writing occur in these works, though rarely: imitative trio sonata textures and a style of counterpoint derived from Fux's *Gradus ad Parnassum.* With the aid of music examples, describes elements of Fuxian counterpoint found--nearly always in finales--and determines that these fugal exercises were essential to Haydn's development.

307. Bernhardt, Reinhold. "Aus der Umwelt der Wiener Klassiker: Freiherr Gottfried van Swieten (1734-1803)." *Der Bär: Jahrbuch von Breitkopf & Härtel* 6/9 (1929-30):74-166.

A study of van Swieten's development and his years in Berlin (1770-77) and Vienna (1778-1803). A section on his dealings with Haydn and Beethoven addresses the role he played in writing the texts and musical instructions for Haydn's *Creation* and *Seasons.* Includes two letters of interest regarding Haydn: one from Griesinger to Gottfried

Härtel (25 March 1801), which discusses *The Creation* and other topics, and one (in excerpt) from van Swieten to Härtel (December 1798), written in response to Härtel's question concerning van Swieten's role with respect to *The Creation.*

308. Blume, Friedrich. "Beethoven und Haydn." In Friedrich Blume. *Syntagma Musicologicum II: Gesammelte Reden und Schriften, 1962-1972,* edited by Anna Amalie Abert and Martin Ruhnke, pp. 292-99. Kassel: Bärenreiter, 1973. Previously published in the *Neue Zürcher Zeitung,* 1970.

Based on an address before the International Congress of the Gesellschaft für Musikforschung, Bonn 1970. Emphasizing the lack of available information on the content of Beethoven's lessons with Haydn, reviews the known facts concerning the teacher-pupil relationship. Surveys what little is known about later exchange between the two, and cites evidence suggesting mutual respect as well as distance and mistrust. A shorter version published as "Haydn und Beethoven--Bemerkungen zum Stand der Forschung," in *Gesellschaft für Musikforschung: Bericht über den Internationalen musikwissenschaftlichen Kongress, Bonn 1970,* edited by Carl Dahlhaus, Hans Joachim Marx, Magda Marx-Weber, and Günther Massenkeil, pp. 61-64 (Kassel: Bärenreiter, [1973]).

309. ———. "Haydn und Mozart." In Friedrich Blume. *Syntagma Musicologicum: Gesammelte Reden und Schriften,* edited by Martin Ruhnke, pp. 570-82. Kassel: Bärenreiter, 1963.

A lecture for the Schleswig-Holsteinische Universitäts-Gesellschaft, Kiel, 24 October 1960. Examines the artistic relationship between Haydn and Mozart. Describes, with reference to specific works, a phenomenon of mutual influence in the genres of symphony and quartet. Briefly discusses the extent of personal contact between the two composers, and calls attention to differences in background, training, and environment that helped shape their distinctive musical traits.

310. Brown, A. Peter. "Joseph Haydn and C.P.E. Bach: The Question of Influence." In *Haydn Studies* (item 73), pp. 158-64.

After reexamination of Griesinger, Dies, and other pertinent sources, proposes that Haydn's contact with C.P.E. Bach's work may not have occurred before the 1760s at the earliest. Speculates on the identity of the "first six sonatas" mentioned by Griesinger, and points out that the earliest known references to a Haydn-Bach connection came in a biographical sketch and review of 1784 (excerpts included), while Haydn's own "acknowledgment of indebtedness" to Bach did not take place until the time of his London visits.

311. Bruce, I.M. "An Act of Homage?" *The Music Review* 11 (1950):277-83.

Examines telling similarities of design in the first movements of Mozart's Symphony in C, K. 551 (1788) and Haydn's Symphony No. 100 (1794). Proposes that the correspondence in plan between these movements, particularly in the development sections, is "so extended, so exact, and so fundamental as to be beyond any reasonable possibility of mere coincidence." Leaves open the question of whether or not this instance of influence was conscious.

312. Cherbuliez, Antoine. "Bemerkungen zu den 'Haydn'-Streichquartetten Mozarts und Haydns 'Russischen' Streichquartetten." *Mozart-Jahrbuch* (1959), pp. 28-45.

From the vantage point of the friendship between the two composers, examines the influence of Haydn's Op. 33 on Mozart's Op. 10 quartets dedicated to Haydn. Notes the fact that both sets were written after a long hiatus in the respective composers' output of quartets and speculates on the meaning of the pause. Discusses other scholars' views of the relationship between the two sets and the mutual influence of the two composers. As a basis for stylistic comparison, presents a synoptic overview, which is then summarized in two pages of tables.

313. Clapham, John. "Chromaticism in the Music of Mozart." *The Music Review* 17 (1956):7-18.

Compares Mozart's approach with Haydn's, and concludes that Mozart's usage was influenced by the older composer. Cites instances of chromaticism in earlier Haydn, notably the Op. 9 quartets and the *Sturm und Drang* instrumental works.

314. Dale, Kathleen. "Schubert's Indebtedness to Haydn." *Music and Letters* 21 (1940):23-30.

Calls attention to instances of alleged resemblance between passages in the two composers' instrumental works.

No detailed critical or stylistic analysis.

315. Dawes, Frank. "William: Or the Adventures of a Sonata." *The Musical Times* 106 (1965):761-64.

Discusses two English songs based on Haydn's Piano Sonata Hob. XV:35, first movement: a piece in the collection *Twelve English Ballads* (late 1780s), set by Samuel Arnold to a poem by Richard Graves, and the more interesting "William," published separately ca. 1787-88 in Thomas Billington's setting of an anonymous poem. Examines the use of Haydn's original material in each of the settings, and describes Willoughby Lacey's readings, a "particular type of entertainment" at which "William" was first performed. Also provides biographical notes on artists connected with "William" and the readings.

316. Derr, Elwood. "A Foretaste of the Borrowings from Haydn in Beethoven's Op. 2." In *Joseph Haydn Kongress* (item 76), pp. 159-70.

Demonstrates how Beethoven paid homage to Haydn in his Op. 2 sonatas by incorporating materials from Haydn works written around the time of Beethoven's studies with him. Discusses the borrowings with respect to Op. 2 No. 1, first movement, which draws on fragments from Haydn's songs "Fidelity" (Hob. XXVIa:30) and "The Spirit's Song" (Hob. XXVIa:41), and Op. 2 No.1, second movement, which incorporates materials from the song "The Wanderer" (Hob. XXVIa:32) and the Piano Trio in E (Hob. XV:28), slow movement. Includes two appendices: the first summarizes all Haydn material used in the three sonatas of Op. 2; the second lists quotations from Haydn in Hummel's Piano Sonata Op. 13 and points out thematic similarities within *The Creation* and between passages from *The Creation* and Haydn's Symphony No. 30.

317. Engel, Hans. "Über Mozarts Jugendsinfonien." *Mozart-Jahrbuch* (1951), pp. 22-33.

Attempting to distinguish strands of Italian, Viennese, and Haydn influence in early Mozart symphonies, presents a comparative discussion of Haydn and early Mozart against the backdrop of current practices among Italian and Viennese composers. Pointing to certain characteristics of texture and harmonic organization in Haydn's music, identifies a strong early (pre-1750-style) Italian influence.

318. Esch, Christian. "Haydns Streichquartett op. 54/1 und Mozarts KV 465." *Haydn-Studien* 6/2 (1988):148-55.

Cites resemblances between the two works, notably between the first-movement introduction of the Mozart and the slow movement of the Haydn, and between the two finales. Suggests that the 1788 Haydn work was specifically influenced by Mozart's 1785 piece. Illustrates points of resemblance through extensive thematic quotation.

319. Feder, Georg. "Stilelemente Haydns in Beethovens Werken." In *Gesellschaft für Musikforschung: Bericht über den Internationalen musikwissenschaftlichen Kongress, Bonn 1970,* edited by Carl Dahlhaus, Hans Joachim Marx, Magda Marx-Weber, and Günther Massenkeil, pp. 65-70. Kassel: Bärenreiter, [1973].

While cautioning that many aspects of Haydn's style were not adopted by Beethoven, cites instances of resemblance that attest to Haydn's inspiration: variation procedures, melodic style, motivic development, thematic repetition a whole tone lower than the initial occurrence, conclusion of a movement with a reference to its opening measures, disguised (non-dominant) retransition, superimposition of implied duple patterns in triple time, surprise modulations, explosive dynamic contrast, grand pause, trumpet calls, novel exploitation of timpani sonorities, incorporation of folk-style effects, hunt and storm music, and structural devices including the linking of a symphonic introduction with the first movement proper, introduction of a new theme in the development section, retrieval of a portion of the minuet/scherzo movement in a finale, exploitation of major/minor dualities, and the withholding of a major tonic triad for dramatic effect.

320. Fellerer, Karl Gustav. "Klavierbearbeitungen Haydnscher Werke im frühen 19. Jahrhundert." In *Festskrift Jens Peter Larsen, 14. VI. 1902-1972,* edited by Nils Schiørring, Henrik Glahn, and Carsten E. Hatting, pp. 301-16. Copenhagen: Wilhelm Hansen, 1972.

Demonstrates that in the early nineteenth century, Haydn's keyboard pieces and keyboard arrangements of his own works were widely disseminated in published editions. Draws on entries in Meysel's *Allgemeines systematisch geordnetes Verzeichnis ...* (1817) to present an overview of this dissemination, and adds to these entries a number of editions not cited by Meysel. Considers arrangements of Haydn overtures, symphonies, symphonic movements, marches and dances, and excerpts from oratorios, as well as piano pieces that originated with Haydn.

321. Finscher, Ludwig. "Joseph Haydn und das italienische Streichquartett." *Analecta Musicologica* 4/*Studien zur italienisch-deutschen Musikgeschichte* 4 (1967):13-37.

Considers the economic, social, and political circumstances that inhibited cultivation of a string-quartet repertory in Italy. Cites the Tartini circle in Padua and the music-making activities of the Doria-Pamphilj family in Rome as exceptions. Observing that Haydn's quartets remained largely unknown in late eighteenth-century Italy, cites as exceptions several quartet composers influenced by Haydn: Felice Radicati, Angelo Benincori, and Luigi Tomasini. Includes music examples from their works, and proposes that only the last of the three, stylistically closest to Haydn, is truly representative of the Classical quartet.

322. ———. "Mozart's Indebtedness to Haydn: Some Remarks on K. 168-173." In *Haydn Studies* (item 73), pp. 407-10.

Discusses the nature of Mozart's apparent imitation of Haydn's Op. 9, 17, and 20 quartets. Argues that Mozart's approach betrays an allegiance to a conventional, essentially pre-Classical Viennese idiom, and not any profound understanding or assimilation of Haydn's individualistic ingenuity.

323. Fischer, Klaus. "Einflüsse Haydns in Kammermusikwerken Boccherinis." *Studi musicali* 4 (1975):169-92.

While cautioning against overestimation of Haydn's influence on Boccherini and calling attention to Boccherini's own emphatic statements about the originality of his style, cites a variety of stylistic features that suggest a palpable connection. Cites the resemblance to Haydn's typical procedures in various experimental, uncharacteristic moments in early and middle-period Boccherini quartets (notably in the minuets). Discusses the report by Giuseppe Cambini in the *Allgemeine musikalische Zeitung* (1804), which refers to Boccherini's extended study of Haydn's quartets, and offers 1766 as a plausible date for this exposure. Concludes that whereas the younger composer may have drawn inspiration from his older contemporary, there is no sense in which he used Haydn's music narrowly as a model. Expanded version of "Einflüsse Haydns in Streichquartetten Boccherinis" in *Gesellschaft für Musikforschung: Bericht über den Internationalen musikwissenschaftlichen Kongress, Berlin 1974*, edited by Hellmut Kühn and Peter Nitsche, pp. 328-32 (Kassel: Bärenreiter, 1980).

324. Freeman, Robert N. "Robert Kimmerling: A Little-Known Haydn Pupil." *The Haydn Yearbook* 13 (1982):143-79.

Discusses activities of this Benedictine priest and nephew of the Abbot of Melk as the abbey's music director, 1761-77. Traces his acquaintance with Haydn to (possibly) as early as 1756-58. Finds little evidence of significant Haydn influence in his relatively mediocre output of mostly sacred music. Portrays him as a Haydn supporter who helped transmit Haydn's teachings into the nineteenth century.

* Friedlaender, Max. "Van Swieten und das Textbuch zu Haydns 'Jahreszeiten'." *Jahrbuch der Musikbibliothek Peters* 16 (1909):47-56.

Cited as item 520.

325. Frimmel, Theodor. *Beethoven-Handbuch.* Leipzig: Breitkopf & Härtel, 1926. Reprint. 2 vols. Hildesheim: Georg Olms, 1968. 477 pp.; 485 pp.

The entry on Haydn (1:202-4) discusses the relationship between the two composers, citing earlier authors, including Wegeler, Ries, and Aloys Fuchs.

326. Geiringer, Karl. "Carl Philipp Emanuel Bach und die Meister der Wiener klassischen Schule." *Österreichische Musikzeitschrift* 43 (1988):300-306.

The section concerned with Haydn (pp. 300-302) discusses Bach's influence and quotes from Dies, Griesinger, Friedrich Rochlitz, *The European Magazine,* and Bach himself. Describes opposing views on the nature of this influence among modern writers and provides sample passages from a Bach fantasia and a Haydn sonata to illustrate stylistic similarity.

327. Goebels, Franzpeter. "Haydn-'Revision' '82: Anregungen zum Haydn-Jahr 1982." *Musica* 36 (1982):124-30.

Examines Pleyel's publication of 36 quartets based on piano sonatas by Haydn. Shows how Pleyel, prompted by the success of his 1801 collection of Haydn's string quartets, engaged Frédéric Blasius to prepare the arrangements. Using comparative music examples, shows how adjustments were made in the originals to render them effective for strings.

* Heartz, Daniel. "Haydn's 'Acide e Galatea' and the Imperial Wedding Operas of 1760 by Hasse and Gluck." In *Joseph Haydn Kongress* (item 76), pp. 332-40.

Cited as item 863.

328. Holschneider, Andreas. "Die musikalische Bibliothek Gottfried van Swietens." In *Gesellschaft für Musikforschung: Bericht über den Internationalen musikwissenschaftlichen Kongress, Kassel 1962,* edited by Georg Reichert and Martin Just, pp. 174-78. Kassel: Bärenreiter, 1963.

Discusses the importance of this collection in transmitting Baroque music (especially Bach and Handel) to the Viennese Classical composers, notably Haydn, Mozart, and Beethoven. Shows how it was possible to partially reconstruct the collection, which was dispersed after van Swieten's death (no auction catalogue is known to survive), through notations on manuscripts and studies of handwriting and paper.

329. Horn, Hans-Jürgen. "FIAT LVX: Zum kunsttheoretischen Hintergrund der 'Erschaffung' des Lichtes in Haydns Schöpfung." *Haydn-Studien* 3 (1973-74):65-84.

Discusses and quotes from van Swieten's marginal comments on "es werde Licht" in the autograph of the libretto to *The Creation.* Shows how these comments link up with a tradition of aesthetic views on the "sublime" that have their origins in antiquity. Draws on material from Edmund Burke's treatise *A Philosophical Enquiry into the Origins of Our Ideas on the Sublime and the Beautiful* (1757), and shows how closely it relates to van Swieten's suggestions. Proposes that while van Swieten may not have copied directly from Burke's book, he is likely to have come in contact with Burke's ideas through Lessing and his circle while in Berlin.

330. Jalowetz, Heinrich. "Beethoven's Jugendwerke in ihren melodischen Beziehungen zu Mozart, Haydn und Ph.E. Bach." *Sammelbände der Internationalen Musikgesellschaft* 12 (1910-11):417-74.

Examining precedents in Haydn and Mozart for characteristic types of melodic construction found in Beethoven, cites Haydn's principle of thematic development (as exemplified in his 1781 string quartets), his use of a ubiquitous rhythmic motive, and certain sonata-form strategies, notably those involving return of primary material at the start of the recapitulation.

331. Jenkins, Newell, and Churgin, Bathia. "'Ho trovato il padre dello stile di Haydn'." *Chigiana* 12 (1977):373–77.

General discussion of the accomplishment of Giovanni Battista Sammartini, whose music, according to Carpani (item 172), provoked the quoted exclamation by Joseph Myslivicek upon hearing symphonies by Haydn in Milan. Touches briefly on the issue of Haydn's indebtedness to Sammartini.

332. Johnson, Douglas. "1794–1795: Decisive Years in Beethoven's Early Development." In *Beethoven Studies 3,* edited by Alan Tyson, pp. 1–28. Cambridge: Cambridge University Press, 1982.

Addressing the issue of Haydn's music as a stimulus for Beethoven's artistic development, cites the older composer's polyphonic textures, remote key relationships, rhythmic momentum, and organic relationship among parts of a composition. Points out evidence of Beethoven's assimilation of a Haydn symphonic model in works from the mid-1790s.

* "Joseph Haydn." *Magazin der Musik* 2/1 (1784–85):585–94. Reprint. Hildesheim: Georg Olms, 1971.

Cited as item 191.

* Kalkbrenner, Friedrich. "Memoir of Mr. Frederick Kalkbrenner Reprinted from *The Quarterly Musical Magazine and Review,* Volume VI (1824)." Submitted by Peter Riethus. *The Haydn Yearbook* 12 (1981):180–91.

Cited as item 193.

333. Kantner, Leopold M. "Francesco Basily: Tre Quartetti (Sinfonie) 'sullo stile di Haydn'." *Chigiana* 36 (1979):143–51. Also published in *Nuova rivista musicale italiana* 16 (1982):561–67.

Furnishes information on the little-known composer (1767–1850), discusses sources for the works in question, which survive in symphonic versions (the original quartet versions, mentioned as early as 1820, are lost), and examines stylistic features. While noting that the minuet and finale themes resemble those of Haydn, points out that Basily had written such themes before he came to know Haydn's music. Proposes that these works (all of which have the same five-movement format, with two minuets) are not merely derivative, but have their own genuine artistic merit.

334. Kerman, Joseph. *The Beethoven Quartets.* New York: Alfred A. Knopf, 1967. Reprint. Westport, CT: Greenwood, 1982. 386, viii pp.

Contains observations on Haydn's style and his musical influence on Beethoven's quartets. Includes specific references to Haydn quartets and symphonies.

335. Larsen, Jens Peter. "Händel und Haydn." *Händel-Jahrbuch* 28 (1982):93-99. Previously published in *Georg Friedrich Händel als Wegbereiter der Wiener Klassik,* edited by Walther Siegmund-Schultze, pp. 25-33. Halle: Martin-Luther-Universität, 1977.

Explores the question of Handelian influence in *The Creation* and *The Seasons*, and proposes ways in which the nature of Haydn's absorption of Handelian influence sheds light on his musical personality. Finds little direct imitation of Handel (in the manner of Mendelssohn), but rather a liberating source of inspiration whereby the spirit and style are purely Haydn's own.

336. ———. "Haydn and Mozart." In Jens Peter Larsen. *Handel, Haydn, and the Viennese Classical Style,* translations by Ulrich Krämer, pp. 117-22. Ann Arbor: UMI Research Press, 1988.

Translation of item 337.

337. ———. "Haydn und Mozart." *Österreichische Musikzeitschrift* 14 (1959):216-22.

Draws on contemporary sources to describe rare meetings between Haydn and Mozart, and discusses the friendship and mutual respect they sustained, despite their limited personal contact. Also examines the artistic influences on both composers, including mutual influence, which was confined to certain genres and time periods.

338. LaRue, Jan. "A 'Hail and Farewell' Quodlibet Symphony." *Music and Letters* 37 (1956):250-59.

Describes the 1798 work in question, by Paul Wranitzky (1756-1808), and calls attention to its evident similarity to Haydn's *Farewell* Symphony (performers leave the stage in the last movement as in the Haydn work; but they also enter gradually at the beginning in the course of a long crescendo). Provides background on the composer and his connection with Haydn.

* Lazarevich, Gordana. "Haydn and the Italian Comic Intermezzo Tradition." In *Joseph Haydn Kongress* (item 76), pp. 376–84.

Cited as item 877.

339. MacArdle, Donald W. "Beethoven and Haydn." *The Monthly Musical Record* 89 (1959):203–11.

A concise overview of references in the standard Beethoven literature to the relationship between the two composers. Includes discussion of Haydn's visit to Bonn in 1790, Beethoven's studies with Haydn in Vienna, their settings of folksongs for Thomson, and Haydn works in Beethoven's library.

340. Mann, Alfred. "Beethoven's Contrapuntal Studies with Haydn." *The Musical Quarterly* 56 (1970):711–26.

Takes issue with Nottebohm's conclusions about Haydn's teaching (item 351). In an incisive analysis of Beethoven's corrected lessons, demonstrates that Haydn, though hasty in examining lessons, was methodical in his approach and consistent in treating problems he chose to work on. Shows also that he was thoroughly familiar with the rules of strict counterpoint, as witnessed in his heavily annotated copy of Fux's *Gradus ad Parnassum*. Includes a description of his "Elementarbuch," in which he both condensed and supplemented Fux's teachings, and shows how Beethoven returned to Haydn's approach in his own pedagogical efforts.

341. ———. "Haydn as Student and Critic of Fux." In *Studies in Eighteenth-Century Music: A Tribute to Karl Geiringer on His Seventieth Birthday*, edited by H.C. Robbins Landon and Roger E. Chapman, pp. 323–32. New York: Oxford University Press, 1970.

A new and more extended treatment of the subject matter in item 344. Demonstrates how Haydn's annotations reveal not only a meticulous consistency but also a concern with "the adherence to fundamental and unequivocal principles."

342. ———. "Haydn's Elementarbuch: A Document of Classic Counterpoint Instruction." *The Music Forum* 3 (1973): 197-237.

Provides an edition and translation of the 17-page document, a fragmentary abstract of Fux's *Gradus ad Parnassum* prepared by the Haydn pupil F.C. Magnus in 1789. Explores its significance as an indication of materials used by Haydn in instructing Beethoven. Questions Nottebohm's negative assessment of Haydn as a teacher, appraises Haydn as a student of Fux's methods, and sees evidence in the document of his persisting interest in theoretical matters.

343. ———. "Haydns Kontrapunktlehre und Beethovens Studien." In *Gesellschaft für Musikforschung: Bericht über den Internationalen musikwissenschaftlichen Kongress, Bonn 1970,* edited by Carl Dahlhaus, Hans Joachim Marx, Magda Marx-Weber, and Günther Massenkeil, pp. 70-74. Kassel: Bärenreiter, [1973].

Shorter version, in German, of item 340.

344. ———. "Eine Textrevision von der Hand Joseph Haydns." In *Musik und Verlag: Karl Vötterle zum 65. Geburtstag am 12. April 1968,* edited by Richard Baum and Wolfgang Rehm, pp. 433-37. Kassel: Bärenreiter, 1968.

Describes and provides a sampling of the extensive annotations made by Haydn in his copy of Fux's *Gradus ad Parnassum.* (This copy was destroyed in World War II, but Haydn's annotations had been transcribed by Pohl in another copy of the manual.) Proposes that "Haydn was an editor and proofreader of simply incredible precision and conscientiousness." Haydn's annotations, written in Latin, not only point out errors and omissions, but include an array of corrections ranging from the simple rectification of typographical errors to criticism of the text.

345. ———. "Zur Kontrapunktlehre Haydns und Mozarts." *Mozart-Jahrbuch* (1978-79), pp. 195-99.

Proposes that Mozart's late writings on counterpoint, including the Attwood studies, were influenced by the marginal notations in Haydn's copy of Fux's *Gradus ad Parnassum,* and that Haydn's "strict schematization" of Fux in his "Elementarbuch" was in turn influenced by Mozart's "concentrated pedagogical work." Provides background on the manuals in question, and compares them in style and general content. Discusses evidence at hand to suggest that Haydn lent out his annotated Fux manual and his "Elementarbuch" for study purposes, for example a copy of Fux's *Gradus* (discovered by Richard Sherr) in which Haydn's notations are copied in a contemporary hand.

346. Matthews, Betty. "George Polgreen Bridgtower." *The Music Review* 29 (1968):22-26.

Presents supposedly new information on Bridgtower, and includes a report in which it is claimed that he called himself a Haydn pupil.

347. Mayeda, Akio. "Nicola Antonio Porpora und der junge Haydn." In *Der junge Haydn* (item 81), pp. 41-57.

While conceding that no convincing evidence of direct Porpora influence on Haydn can be established, proposes various possible points of contact on the basis of examples quoted from chamber and sacred vocal works of both composers. Pointing out supposedly modern tendencies evident in Porpora's mid-century vocal and instrumental music, considers the likelihood that the older composer's music may have provided a source for traits found in early Haydn.

348. Münnich, Richard. "Haydn in Wagners Schriften." *Musikalisches Wochenblatt* 40 (1909-10):147-49.

Recalling Wagner's worship of Beethoven as a preeminent figure in the prior development of music, explains that others, Haydn included, must inevitably be seen as Beethoven predecessors. Reports that Wagner perceived a close historical link between Haydn and Beethoven, and cites other observations of Wagner about the significance of Haydn's accomplishment: motivic ingenuity and expansion of the expressive scope of symphonic form; felicitous transition passages that compare favorably with Mozart's; aspects of scoring, tempo, and variation procedure. No bibliographical citations for passages from Wagner's writings.

349. ———. "J. Haydn (1732-1809) jugé par Wagner." *La Revue musicale* 9/12 (1909):314-18.

Translation of item 348.

350. Nef, Karl. "Haydn-Reminiszenzen bei Beethoven."

Sammelbände der Internationalen Musikgesellschaft 13 (1911-12):336-48.

Points to a number of borrowings from Haydn in Beethoven's music, and asserts that estimation of Beethoven is not diminished, but rather augmented, through recognition of his reliance on predecessors. Defends the value of comparative thematic studies, and refers to a related article by Jalowetz (item 330).

351. Nottebohm, Gustav. *Beethoven's Studien.* Vol. 1: *Beethoven's Unterricht bei J. Haydn, Albrechtsberger und Salieri, nach den Original-Manuscripten dargestellt.* Leipzig: J. Rieter-Biedermann, 1873. Reprint. Niederwalluf bei Wiesbaden: Martin Sändig, 1971. vi, 232 pp.

A section called "Unterricht bei Joseph Haydn" reproduces extracts from a compilation of two sources for Haydn's "Elementarbuch," his instruction book based on Fux's *Gradus ad Parnassum* (the copy used by Beethoven is apparently lost). Also transcribes a portion of the Beethoven "Uebungen im Contrapunkt," including a number of exercises for which Haydn not only made corrections, but provided written explanations for changes made. Views Haydn as deficient and lacking a systematic, thorough approach in his teachings.

352. Olleson, Edward. "Gottfried van Swieten, Patron of Haydn and Mozart." *Proceedings of the Royal Musical Association* 89 (1962-63):63-74.

Tracing van Swieten's involvement with music, describes his long-standing interest in Haydn and later influence on his music. Discusses his librettos for *The Seven Last Words, The Creation,* and *The Seasons,* and shows how his marginal notations and liking for pictorialism influenced Haydn's settings of the latter two texts. His "Gesellschaft der Associierten" sponsored performances of all three works, and he was behind the generous financial support that Haydn received.

* Parrish, Carl. "Haydn and the Piano." *Journal of the American Musicological Society* 1/3 (1948):27-34.

Cited as item 1135.

353. Pečman, Rudolf. "Der junge Haydn und die tschechische Musik des 18. Jahrhunderts." In *Der junge Haydn* (item 81), pp. 31-37.

Downplaying the notion of a direct or significant influence of Mannheim composers on Haydn, proposes Jiří Antonín Benda (1722–95) as a predecessor whose style anticipates that of the early Haydn symphonies. Argues against any direct or fundamental influence of Czech folk music on Haydn. Suggesting that no Czech national style in the present-day sense existed in Haydn's time, disputes the grounds on which Czech influence on Haydn is debated.

354. Poštolka, Milan. "Joseph Haydn und Leopold Koželuh: Ein Beitrag zur Erforschung der Beziehungen zwischen der tschechischen Musikkultur des 18. Jahrhunderts und dem Schaffen Joseph Haydns." In *Bericht über die Internationale Konferenz zum Andenken Joseph Haydns* (item 70), pp. 109–15.

Discusses the fact that Koželuh studied Haydn's works in order to develop his own compositional technique, and shows that works by the two composers were often performed side by side in concerts of the time. In outline form, proposes correspondences between the two composers with respect to the nature of their invention, the structure of their sonata cycles, the form of individual movements, and the genres cultivated by both (including harmonizations of British folk songs).

355. ———. "Two Unknown Pupils of Haydn; Two Unknown Haydn Sources." In *Haydn Studies* (item 73), pp. 177–81.

Identifies the Bohemians Josef Smrček and František Václav Tomeš as possible Haydn pupils. Analyzes the claim for Smrček, which appears in Dlabač's *Tonkünstlerlexikon* (1815), and provides evidence (though not conclusive) to link Tomeš with the "Tomisch" whom Haydn named to Dies as one of his pupils. Also describes two Haydn sources at the National Museum in Prague: a printed libretto of *The Seasons* for a performance in Prague (1803) and a manuscript for the *Surprise* Symphony with the attribution "del Sig. Vogel."

356. Rifkin, Joshua. "Ein unbekanntes Haydn-Zitat bei Mozart." *Haydn-Studien* 2 (1969–70):317.

Proposes that Mozart, whether consciously or not, derived the opening measures of his Piano Concerto K. 459, last movement, from a theme in the last movement of Haydn's Symphony No. 78.

357. Rosen, Charles. "Influence: Plagiarism and Inspiration."

19th Century Music 4 (1980-81):87-100.

Incorporates discussion of two instances of Haydn influence in the music of Mozart: that of Haydn's String Quartet Op. 20 No. 2, fourth movement, on Mozart's fugal Gigue, K. 574 and that of Haydn's Symphony No. 81 in G, first movement, on the first movement of Mozart's Symphony in D, K. 504. In addition to obvious thematic and stylistic resemblances between Haydn's fugal gigue movement and the Mozart piece, finds a telling subtle connection in a passage where Mozart's rhythmic change of accent recalls a similar event in the Haydn string quartet. In the two symphony movements, discerns various similarities of gesture and process in addition to Mozart's obvious reference to Haydn's typical approach in restating the opening theme in the dominant as a means of establishing the secondary key. Proposes that by stimulating Mozart to something that became completely his own, Haydn provided the most profound form of inspiration.

358. Saint-Foix, Georges de. "Haydn and Clementi." *The Musical Quarterly* 18 (1932):252-59.

Examines aspects of the personal, artistic, and commercial exchange between the two composers. Speculates on the possibility of Haydn influence in Clementi's late symphonies and in his sonatas of Op. 7, 9, 10, and 19.

* Schenk, Erich. "Das Weltbild Joseph Haydns." In Erich Schenk. *Ausgewählte Aufsätze, Reden und Vorträge,* pp. 86-99. Graz: Hermann Böhlaus Nachf., 1967. Previously published in *Almanach der österreichischen Akademie der Wissenschaften* 109 (1959):245-72.

Cited as item 752.

359. Schmid, Ernst Fritz. "Gottfried van Swieten als Komponist." *Mozart-Jahrbuch* (1953), pp. 15-31.

A study of van Swieten's French theater works and symphonies, with contemporary assessments of his ability as a composer. Describes two of the theater pieces in some detail, noting the wealth of programmatic elements in his *Colas toujours Colas* (ca. 1770) and recalling the influence he had on Haydn's tone-painting in *The Creation* and *The Seasons.* For the symphonies, which Haydn thought to be "as pedantic as he himself," provides background discussion, a stylistic profile, and a thematic index of the seven extant works.

360. ———. "Joseph Haydn und Carl Philipp Emanuel Bach." *Zeitschrift für Musikwissenschaft* 14 (1931-32):299-312.

Concerns C.P.E. Bach's influence on Haydn. Cites Haydn's favorable assessment of Bach's *Versuch über die wahre Art das Clavier zu spielen* through quotations from Griesinger, Dies, and Latrobe; and mentions Bach's 1785 denunciation of an article (in *The European Magazine*) that falsely claimed a hostile disposition toward Bach on Haydn's part. Examines that article's depiction of Haydn as a parodist of Bach, notes stylistic similarities between the two composers, and concludes that Haydn's art was "strongly nourished" by that of his mentor. Observes that Haydn's *Nachlass* included works by both C.P.E. Bach and his father.

361. ———. "Mozart and Haydn." *The Musical Quarterly* 42 (1956):145-61. Reprinted in *The Creative World of Mozart,* edited by Paul Henry Lang, pp. 86-102. New York: W.W. Norton, 1963.

An account of the friendship and mutual influence of the two composers. Describes their sharply contrasting origins and the different musical traditions in which they developed. Suggests that traces of Haydn's influence may be seen in Mozart's work as early as 1765, though it was not until the 1770s that there was increasing evidence of it. Discusses specific instances of this influence, which affected not only thematic material, but also compositional technique. Also makes references to the generally less pronounced influence of Mozart on Haydn.

362. Schnürl, Karl. "Haydns 'Schöpfung' als Messe." *Studien zur Musikwissenschaft* 25 [*Festschrift für Erich Schenk*] (1962):463-74.

A study of the four known mass cycles set to music from *The Creation.* All originated in the first half of the nineteenth century, and one of them--by Matthias Pernsteiner--appears to have served as a model for the others. Describes similarities and differences among the settings, and provides a tabular comparison.

363. Schwarz, Boris. "Beethovens op. 18 und Haydns Streichquartette." In *Gesellschaft für Musikforschung: Bericht über den Internationalen musikwissenschaftlichen Kongress, Bonn 1970,* edited by Carl Dahlhaus, Hans Joachim Marx, Magda Marx-Weber, and Günther Massenkeil, pp. 75-79. Kassel: Bärenreiter, [1973].

Notes the difficulty of distinguishing between the influence on Beethoven exerted by Haydn on one hand and by Mozart on the other. Suggesting that there is little Haydn influence discernible after 1800, calls attention to aspects of Haydn's individuality that were not drawn upon by either Mozart or Beethoven, notably the juxtaposition of remote keys and the so-called monothematic sonata form. Finds Haydn's influence in matters of thematic structure and motivic development, and identifies Beethoven's alternate finale to his Op. 130 as a tribute to Haydn.

* Sondheimer, Robert. *Haydn: A Historical and Psychological Study Based on His Quartets.* London: Bernoulli, 1951. viii, 196 pp.

Cited as item 1035.

364. Stein, Fritz. "Der musikalische Instrumentalkalender: Zu Leben und Wirken von Gregorius Josephus Werner." *Musica* 11 (1957):390-96.

Describes Werner's programmatic *Instrumentalkalender* (1748), which depicts the months of the year. Proposes that Prince Esterházy's request of Haydn for the 1761 programmatic symphonies may have been inspired by Werner's piece, and further, that the work had a long-lasting influence on Haydn's programmatic writing. Includes general discussion of Werner's work as a composer, and notes Haydn's considerable respect for his music.

365. Stollbrock, L. "Leben und Wirken des k.k. Hofkapellmeisters und Hofkompositors Johann Georg Reuter jun." *Vierteljahrsschrift für Musikwissenschaft* 8 (1892):161-203, 289-306.

A richly documented account that quotes extensively from court records and other contemporary documents. Concerning Reutter's alleged neglect of Haydn's musical education, observes that the task of teaching the choirboys fell outside his jurisdiction. Discerning an important influence (though one not dependent on formal instruction), proposes a parallel between Reutter's relationship to Haydn and Haydn's relationship to Beethoven. Includes a chronological listing of Reutter's major theatrical works and oratorios.

366. Sumner, Floyd. "Haydn and Kirnberger: A Documentary Report." *Journal of the American Musicological Society* 28 (1975):530-39.

Describes Haydn's marginal references to Kirnberger's *Die Kunst des reinen Satzes* in his copy of Fux's *Gradus ad Parnassum.* Includes pages in facsimile showing Pohl's transcription from Haydn's copy of *Gradus*, which is no longer extant. Observing that Haydn betrayed a preference for Fux in instances of discrepancy between the two theorists, suggests that he found Kirnberger too restrictive.

367. Tyson, Alan. "Clementi as an Imitator of Haydn and Mozart." *The Haydn Yearbook* 2 (1963-64):90-92.

Examines the publication *Clementi's Musical Characteristics, or A Collection of Preludes and Cadences for the Harpsichord or Piano Forte Composed in the Style of Haydn, Kozeluch, Mozart, Sterkel, Vanhall and The Author Opera 19.* Notes that the profusion of runs and arpeggios, as well as frequent modulations and tempo changes, make it difficult to relate these pieces to works by the composers represented. Judges the Haydn imitations to be more problematic than the Mozart, and reproduces one of the former--the "Cadenza alla Haydn"--in facsimile.

368. Unverricht, Hubert. "Die Kompositionen Johann Peter Salomons: Ein Überblick." *Studien zur Musikgeschichte des Rheinlandes* 3 [*Heinrich Hüschen zum 50. Geburtstag*] (1965):35-42.

In assessing known works in Salomon's output, makes reference to his arrangement of Haydn's 12 London symphonies for piano trio and for quintet. Proposes that while Salomon learned much from Haydn, his own virtuosity had its influence on Haydn's writing for the violin, notably in the quartets of Op. 71, 74, and 76. Notes that the solos in the London symphonies were intended for Salomon, and that there are changes in Salomon's hand for the opening measures of the slow movement to Symphony No. 102.

369. Vancea, Zeno. "Der Einfluss Haydns auf die rumänischen Komponisten des XIX. Jahrhunderts." In *Bericht über die Internationale Konferenz zum Andenken Joseph Haydns* (item 70), pp. 177-80.

Discusses the influx of Western music in Romania during a period of pronounced political and economic change in the early nineteenth century. Reveals that the folk elements and simplicity of Haydn's music made their way into Romanian singspiels derived from Viennese prototypes, and that in the second half of the century, Haydn served as a model for Romanian symphonic and chamber music, as composers combined Romanian folk music with harmonies and forms derived from the Viennese Classical school.

370. Walter, Horst. "Die biographischen Beziehungen zwischen Haydn und Beethoven." In *Gesellschaft für Musikforschung: Bericht über den Internationalen musikwissenschaftlichen Kongress, Bonn 1970,* edited by Carl Dahlhaus, Hans Joachim Marx, Magda Marx-Weber, and Günther Massenkeil, pp. 79-83. Kassel: Bärenreiter, [1973].

A summary of what is known about Haydn's relationship to Beethoven from 1792 to the winter of 1803-4.

371. ———. "Gottfried van Swietens handschriftliche Textbücher zu 'Schöpfung' und 'Jahreszeiten'." *Haydn-Studien* 1 (1965-67):241-77.

Examining the exchange of ideas between Haydn and van Swieten, emphasizes the importance of the latter's advisory role in the composition of the late oratorios as revealed in his notations and instructions as well as in contemporary correspondence. Provides an edition of both librettos based on extant authentic sources.

372. ———. "Haydn gewidmete Streichquartette." In *Joseph Haydn: Tradition und Rezeption* (item 78), pp. 17-53.

Surveys the 16 known prints of string quartets that bear a dedication to Haydn. Provides a list of the 16 composers represented, and for 15 of them (Mozart is excluded), discusses the composer and his quartets. Appends a catalogue of the 16 prints in question--arranged by composer--and for each, gives the text of the title page and (where applicable) the plate number, letter or address of dedication, *RISM* number, location of source, publication date, and references to literature, reviews, and the like.

373. ———. "Haydns Schüler." In *Joseph Haydn in seiner Zeit* (item 77), pp. 311-15.

Citing the remarkable paucity of research on the subject of Haydn's pupils and the traditional neglect of the topic on the part of earlier biographers, pulls together scattered pieces of evidence pertaining to Haydn's pedagogical activities during the period 1753-1804.

374. ———. "Haydns Schüler am Esterházyschen Hof." In *Ars Musica, Musica Scientia: Festschrift Heinrich Hüschen zum fünfundsechzigsten Geburtstag am 2. März 1980*, edited by Detlef Altenburg, pp. 449-54. Cologne: Gitarre und Laute, 1980.

According to Dies, the only Haydn composition student in service to the Esterházy court was a man named Fuchs. The author proposes three others--Johann Baptist Krumpholtz, Anton Kraft, Joseph Niemecz--and cites evidence from contemporary sources. Fuchs is identified as Johann Nepomuk Fuchs, who succeeded Haydn as kapellmeister.

375. ———. "Kalkbrenners Lehrjahre und sein Unterricht bei Haydn." *Haydn-Studien* 5 (1982-85):23-41.

Draws on the "Memoir of Mr. Frederick Kalkbrenner" (1824) and other early biographical writings, including an account by Louis Boivin (1842) and a closely related, anonymous source from the same year printed in the *Neue Zeitschrift für Musik*. Furnishes information on Kalkbrenner's first meeting with Haydn and Beethoven, and his subsequent experiences as a pupil of Haydn's and Albrechtsberger's in Vienna.

376. Webster, James. "The Falling-Out between Haydn and Beethoven: The Evidence of the Sources." In *Beethoven Essays: Studies in Honor of Elliot Forbes*, edited by Lewis Lockwood and Phyllis Benjamin, pp. 3-45. Cambridge: Harvard University Press, 1984.

Reexamines traditional views of the two composers' relationship, and furnishes copious evidence to support the conclusion that "no direct word or action of Haydn's or Beethoven's, and few reliable contemporary observers, document any falling-out or feeling of artistic incompatibility between the two." Includes a table of early sources reporting conflict, and a table that specifies elements involved in the dispute-tradition and sources to which those elements can be traced.

377. Wirth, Helmut. "Nachwirkungen der Musik Joseph Haydns auf Johannes Brahms." In *Musik--Edition--Interpretation: Gedenkschrift Günter Henle*, edited by Martin Bente, pp. 455-62. Munich: G. Henle, 1980.

Concerns Brahms' early contact and intense involvement with Haydn's music from 1857 to 1862, before his move to Vienna. Demonstrates Haydn's influence on Brahms with respect to thematic material, various tonal relationships, and the practice of invoking archaic forms; also mentions a possible influence he exerted in the use of Hungarian themes. Briefly discusses Brahms' Variations on a Theme by Haydn, Op. 56a and 56b.

* Zeman, Herbert. "Das Textbuch Gottfried van Swietens zu Joseph Haydns 'Die Schöpfung'." In *Die österreichische Literatur: Ihr Profil an der Wende vom 18. zum 19. Jahrhundert (1750–1830)*, edited by Herbert Zeman, pp. 403–25. Jahrbuch für österreichische Kulturgeschichte, 7–9. Graz: Akademische Druck- u. Verlagsgesellschaft, 1979.

Cited as item 841.

VI

HAYDN'S LEGACY

The Reception of His Music by Contemporaries and Later Generations

The history of the reception of Haydn's works has fascinated scholars in their quest of insight into the historical significance of his music and the changing attitudes and fashions by which it has been buffeted over the years. Material included here encompasses both general inquiries and specific regional studies of Haydn's popularity, the dissemination of his music, and the changing image of his personality and contribution in the minds of critics and historians.

378. Bárdos, Kornel. "Neue Forschungen zum Musikleben in der Esterházy-Familie in Tata und Csákvár." *The Haydn Yearbook* 10 (1978):29–35.

Discusses changes in eighteenth-century musical life that took place after the expulsion of the Turks, with particular attention to the counts Esterházy at Tata and Csákvár. Describes recent findings by the Hungarian Academy of Sciences on the musical activity at their courts, and compares the source situation with that for Eszterháza. In reporting on composers represented in the sources for Tata, reveals that Joseph Haydn was represented by 31 works, his brother Michael by 54.

379. Barenboim, Lew. "Haydns Stellung in der russischen Musikkultur." In *Joseph Haydn Kongress* (item 76), pp. 533–40.

Traces the growing enthusiasm for Haydn in Russia beginning with the 1780s and addresses reasons for his popularity. Limiting the study to Haydn's lifetime, discusses Russian supporters among the nobility, the sale of Haydn's music, increasing mention of Haydn in Russian literature and letters, Russian publications of his works, and public performances (with particular attention to *The Creation, The Seasons,* and *Il ritorno di Tobia*). Publishes a newly discovered letter (dated 25 April 1807) from Haydn to Neukomm concerning *Tobia,* and includes a segment of the letter in facsimile.

380. Blume, Friedrich. "Gibt es ein neues Haydn-Bild?" In Friedrich Blume. *Syntagma Musicologicum II: Gesammelte Reden und Schriften, 1962-1972,* edited by Anna Amalie Abert and Martin Ruhnke, pp. 314-24. Kassel: Bärenreiter, 1973. Previously published in *Neue Zürcher Zeitung,* 1 December 1968, and in *Musica* 23 (1969):333-37.

Suggests that the image of Haydn transmitted in the traditional literature has not been coherent, and describes contrasting portrayals in early popularizations and in literature that promulgated the "Papa Haydn" image. Discusses trends in modern Haydn research, and concludes that a "new Haydn image" has yet to be delineated: scholars must first succeed in integrating Haydn's work and personality against the musical and historical backdrop of his age.

381. ———. Der Meister der klassischen Musik." In Friedrich Blume. *Syntagma Musicologicum: Gesammelte Reden und Schriften,* edited by Martin Ruhnke, pp. 558-64. Kassel: Bärenreiter, 1963. Previously published in *Neue Zürcher Zeitung,* 31 May 1959.

Remarks on Haydn's unique popularity during his lifetime, and examines the decline in public favor he suffered in the early Romantic generation of Wackenroder, Tieck, Novalis, and E.T.A. Hoffmann, which regarded him disdainfully as simple, naive, and rational. Emphasizes the crucial role played by Haydn in the formation of a late eighteenth-century Classical style, and underscores his importance as a master of this idiom. Discusses the persistence of Romantic distortions that until recently have hindered appreciation of the composer's significance.

382. Börner, Wolfgang. "'Was eine Sache nicht im ersten

Moment enthüllt': Die Pariser Sinfonien von Joseph Haydn." *Musik und Gesellschaft* 32/3 (1982):135-40.

Argues that the Paris symphonies represent liberation from the constraint of compliance with an aristocratic patron's requests. Describes the works' reception and the circumstances of their composition. Quoting in the title from a phrase of Voltaire's concerning the meaning of French "esprit," suggests that in responding to the expectations of his Parisian middle-class audience, Haydn adopted a distinctively French manner.

* Cudworth, Charles. "The Vauxhall 'Lists'." *The Galpin Society Journal* 20 (1967):24-42.

Cited as item 92.

383. Deutsch, Otto Erich. "Festkonzerte im alten Universitätssaal: Haydn - Beethoven - Schubert." *Österreichische Musikzeitschrift* 18 (1963):428-33.

An account of notable performances given in the great hall of the old university in Vienna (the "Aula"), among them the now-famous performance of *The Creation* on 27 March 1808, under Salieri's direction. Includes a reproduction of Balthasar Wigand's representation of Haydn at the concert.

* Edelmann, Bernd. "Haydns '*Il ritorno di Tobia*' und der Wandel des 'Geschmacks' in Wien nach 1780." In *Joseph Haydn: Tradition und Rezeption* (item 78), pp. 189-214.

Cited as item 818.

384. Feder, Georg. "Joseph Haydn als Mensch und Musiker." In *Joseph Haydn und seine Zeit* (item 80), pp. 43-56.

Points out the need for a new documentary biography of Haydn, which would offer an accurate interpretation of his music and personality within an historical-cultural context. Draws a connection between the need to revise our traditional view of Haydn the man and the modification of our image of Haydn the composer on the basis of the recent source research. Other versions published in *Österreichische Musikzeitschrift* 27 (1972):57-68 and *Joseph Haydn in seiner Zeit* (item 77), pp. 291-300.

385. ———. "Joseph Haydn 1982: Gedanken über Tradition

und historische Kritik." In *Joseph Haydn Kongress* (item 76), pp. 597-611.

Examines the still narrowly restricted representation of Haydn's compositions in the traditional repertory, and observes that these works form the standard of comparison by which other Haydn compositions are judged. Affirms that Haydn research is guided by the goal of greater knowledge and understanding, and sees reliable musical texts as crucial to this goal. Rejects views on text criticism that minimize the importance of an *Urtext,* and demonstrates how a newly discovered autograph can improve upon traditional readings of a work. Also acknowledges the importance of stylistic comparison and studies in performance practice in obtaining a better understanding of Haydn.

386. ———. "Lo stato attuale degli studi su Haydn." *Nuova rivista musicale italiana* 2 (1968):625-54.

Provides a concise overview of scholarly issues and accomplishments in post-World War II Haydn research. Categories surveyed include biography, source studies, the different instrumental and vocal genres, and performance practice. Discusses the latter-day reassessment of Haydn's historical significance.

387. Fellerer, Karl Gustav. "Zum Joseph-Haydn-Bild im frühen 19. Jahrhundert." In *Anthony van Hoboken: Festschrift zum 75. Geburtstag,* edited by Joseph Schmidt-Görg, pp. 73-86. Mainz: B. Schott's Söhne, 1962.

Reviews assessments of Haydn's art and historical importance by prominent critics from the late eighteenth through the mid-nineteenth century, including Gerber, Burney, Busby, Reichardt, Arnold, Schumann, Carpani, and Fröhlich. Examines the early nineteenth-century tendency to rank Haydn below Mozart, to view him as a traditionalist, and to place higher value on his instrumental works than on the theatrical or sacred music. Cites nineteenth-century Cecilian attitudes as a hindrance to the appreciation of his church music, and shows that whereas the blinding impact of Beethoven prohibited comprehension of Haydn's originality for Schumann and his contemporaries, a deeper appreciation of his contribution as a pathbreaker can be found in the writings of Fröhlich.

388. Finscher, Ludwig. "Joseph Haydn--Ein unbekannter

Komponist?" *Neue Zeitschrift für Musik* 143/10 (1982):12-18.

Compares sample nineteenth-century critiques of Haydn, both disparaging (E.T.A. Hoffmann, Schumann) and supportive (Brahms, Richard and Cosima Wagner), and explores reasons for the sharply diverging attitudes. First examines Haydn's life, which appears unremarkable and conventional by comparison with Mozart's. Then examines the music, and finds that its highly concentrated language requires a now-lost ability to listen with comparable intensity. Sees in Haydn's music a purely musical, universal language that is complex, powerful, and many-faceted, thus difficult to understand; but because of its difficulty, it is continually open to discovery.

389. Geiringer, Karl. "Das Haydn-Bild im Wandel der Zeiten." *Die Musik* 24 (1931-32):430-36.

Sketches Haydn's rise to fame, from humble beginnings to the renown attained with *The Creation* and *The Seasons.* Describes his subsequent neglect in the Romantic period, in which the "joyful and natural" qualities in his music were not especially prized. Then notes the renewal of interest in Haydn in an age when the clarity of his style was more closely akin to that of contemporary music.

390. Graf, Max. "Haydn and the Critics." Chap. 8 in Max Graf. *Composer and Critic: Two Hundred Years of Musical Criticism,* pp. 120-29. New York: W.W. Norton, 1946. Reprint. Port Washington, NY: Kennikat, 1969.

Makes the point that musical criticism was insignificant in Haydn's achievement of fame and success. Discusses critical reactions to his work from 1766 until his death, drawing quotations from contemporary journals.

391. Gruber, Gernot. "Doppelgesichtiger Haydn?" *Österreichische Musikzeitschrift* 37 (1982):139-46.

Discusses previous inquiries into the question of a rectified image of Haydn, and examines proposals on the part of modern-day scholars on how to achieve a more appropriate, historically authentic picture of the composer. Cites the importance of the Enlightenment and the ideal of the *honnête homme* in adding a new facet to this image (see item 752). Remarks on the Janus-faced *Zeitgeist* of the eighteenth century (i.e. the tension between reason and blind adherence to privilege and dogma), and notes the Janus-like tendencies both in Haydn's music and his personality.

392. Gülke, Peter. "Nahezu ein Kant der Musik." In *Joseph Haydn* (item 75), pp. 67–73.

Reflects on Haydn's reputation and the phenomenon of changing critical assessments and reinterpretations of his artistic legacy.

393. Hanslick, Eduard. *Geschichte des Konzertwesens in Wien.* Vienna: Wilhelm Braunmüller, 1869–70. Reprint. 2 vols. Westmead, England: Gregg, 1971. xv, 438 pp.; xii, 534 pp.

Book 1 provides background on eighteenth-century patronage, concert organizations, traveling virtuosos, and the music trade in eighteenth-century Vienna. Various references to Haydn, including a substantial discussion of the late oratorios (1:25–28), their enthusiastic reception, and their prominent role in Viennese musical life.

394. Höslinger, Clemens. "Joseph Haydn--Das Nachleben." In *Joseph Haydn in seiner Zeit* (item 77), pp. 316–23.

An overview of the phenomenon of Haydn's fall from public favor in the generation following his death, the tenacity with which Viennese audiences clung to the late oratorios, aspects of the negative nineteenth-century attitudes, and the circumstances under which interest in Haydn's music eventually revived.

395. ———. "Der überwundene Standpunkt: Joseph Haydn in der Wiener Musikkritik des 19. Jahrhunderts." In *Beiträge zur Musikgeschichte des 18. Jahrhunderts* (item 69), pp. 116–42.

Examines the changing attitudes of Viennese music critics towards Haydn in the nineteenth century. Describes the early adulation, then the Romantics' rejection of Haydn: their over-familiarity with a small and poorly performed representation of his work, their opposition to his tone-painting and to secular elements in his sacred music, and their rejection of his "thoroughly antiquated artistic orientation." Discusses the revival of interest in Haydn later in the century and the role played by Brahms and Joachim in awakening this interest. Includes quotations from representative critics, among them L.A. Zellner, Eduard Hanslick, E.T.A. Hoffmann, and Gross-Athanasius.

396. Hughes, Rosemary. "Haydn at Oxford: 1773-1791." *Music and Letters* 20 (1939):242-49.

Provides a brief account of Haydn's music in the Oxford repertory beginning in the 1770s. Though records of programs are fragmentary for most of the period in question, it is known that works by Haydn were performed, among them a D-major symphony (Hob. I:53) called *Overture Festivo,* which was highly popular at Oxford. Its popularity may have contributed to the triumphant success of Haydn's visit to Oxford.

397. Ingram, Jeannine S. "Repertory and Resources of the Salem Collegium Musicum, 1780-1790." *Fontes Artis Musicae* 26 (1979):267-81.

Reconstructs the repertory and resources of the collegium during the decade of Johann Friedrich Peter's directorship. Includes tables of manuscript sources by copyist, and lists prints in the collection. According to extant sources (there may originally have been many more), the favorite composers were Leopold Hofmann, Joseph Haydn, and Johann Daniel Grimm. Speculates that Peter may have taken sources with him when he left his post.

* Jones, David Wyn. "Haydn's Music in London in the Period 1760-1790." *The Haydn Yearbook* 14 (1983):144-72.

Cited as item 466.

398. Kremljew, Julij. "J. Haydn und die russische Musikkultur." In *Bericht über die Internationale Konferenz zum Andenken Joseph Haydns* (item 70), pp. 61-67.

Drawing on Russian critics and composers (including Rimsky-Korsakov and Tchaikovsky), describes three time-periods delineated by change in attitude towards Haydn, and shows that these changes occurred in Russia as elsewhere: Haydn's great popularity in the late eighteenth and early nineteenth centuries, his decline in the second half of the nineteenth century, and the twentieth-century revival following the October Revolution.

399. La Laurencie, Lionel de. "L'Apparition des oeuvres

d'Haydn à Paris." *Revue de musicologie* 13 (1932):191-205.

Recounts the history of publications and performances of Haydn's works in Paris, 1764-84. Includes quotations from concert reviews and references to publisher's announcements.

400. Lang, Paul Henry. "The Changing Portraits of Haydn." In *Haydnfest* (item 71), pp. 5-7.

Contrasts the widespread acclaim for Haydn during his lifetime with attitudes of condescension in the nineteenth and early twentieth centuries. Searching for sources of Haydn's "solid, healthy music," considers the question of a *Zeitgeist,* and finding this insufficient, focuses instead on questions of musical style. Examines the ingredients from which Haydn forged a synthesis, notably the materials common in styles of the time, the transformation of simple ideas, and the willful, autodidactic approach in developing an idiom that gave Viennese Classical style its stamp.

401. Larsen, Jens Peter. "The Challenge of Joseph Haydn." In Jens Peter Larsen. *Handel, Haydn, and the Viennese Classical Style,* translations by Ulrich Krämer, pp. 95-108. Ann Arbor: UMI Research Press, 1988.

Translation of item 405.

402. ———. "Haydn im 20. Jahrhundert." In *Musik--Edition--Interpretation: Gedenkschrift Günter Henle,* edited by Martin Bente, pp. 319-25. Munich: G. Henle, 1980.

A concise overview of the recent history of Haydn research: the early twentieth-century initiation of a complete edition, the rebirth of Haydn scholarship in the 1930s, the major post-war accomplishments. Sees the finally foreseeable accessibility of the major part of Haydn's oeuvre as the key to a critical interpretation of his works.

403. ———. "Haydn: Repertory, Interpretation, Image." *The Musical Times* 123 (1982):163-66.

Observing that the traditional, "Papa Haydn" image has impeded understanding of the composer and his music, outlines necessary steps toward a new, more authentic picture. Points of emphasis include the availability of Haydn's music through completion of the *Joseph Haydn Werke* and improved stylistic criticism through more historically informed analytical methods. Cautions that no simplistic formula can account for the complex, multi-faceted nature of Haydn's musical personality.

404. ———. "Haydn Revival." In *Haydnfest* (item 71), pp. 38-43.

Considers the question of eclipse and revival of Haydn's works. Notes the changes in musical expression and performance medium that were disadvantageous to Haydn in the nineteenth century and the related decline in availability of Haydn editions. Describes early steps toward a revival in the twentieth century, the true revival that took place after World War II, and the crucial role of H.C. Robbins Landon in sparking this revival. Concludes by surveying the state of revival in the different genres.

405. ———. "Joseph Haydn--Eine Herausforderung an uns." In *Joseph Haydn Kongress* (item 76), pp. 9-20.

Asserts that whereas the faulty "Papa Haydn" image has now been abandoned, there is no new conception of Haydn free of old prejudices. Addresses problems regarding the new image, concentrating on three central issues: our perception of the role played by Haydn in developing the Viennese Classical idiom, old and new prejudices that exist with respect to Haydn's character and musical personality, and the extent to which Haydn's music is alive today. See item 401 for an English translation.

406. ———. "Der musikalische Stilwandel um 1750 im Spiegel der zeitgenössischen Pariser Verlagskataloge." In *Musik und Verlag: Karl Vötterle zum 65. Geburtstag am 12. April 1968,* edited by Richard Baum and Wolfgang Rehm, pp. 410-23. Kassel: Bärenreiter, 1968.

Examines the Parisian publishers' catalogues of ca. 1740-70 to determine what the headings reveal about changing preferences in musical genre and whether the composers represented reflect local trends or a more widespread development. Describes an emergence of listings for symphonies in the 1750s and quartets in the 1760s, and explains how their relative numbers reflect, over time, corresponding trends in the development of Viennese Classical music, especially Haydn's. Reveals that the composers represented mirror the strong preference for Italian music in Paris in the wake of the War of the Buffoons, and proposes that visits from Stamitz and Wagenseil may explain the emergence of Mannheim and Viennese composers.

407. ———. "A Survey of the Development of Haydn Research: Solved and Unsolved Problems." In *Haydn Studies* (item 73), pp. 14-25.

Provides a general survey of Haydn research and an assessment of recent work in the areas of documentation, form and style, and performance practice. Prefaces the survey with observations on the aims and the appropriate qualifications of the scholar who wishes to engage in research on eighteenth-century music and the life and works of individual composers.

408. Lesure, François. "Haydn en France." In *Bericht über die Internationale Konferenz zum Andenken Joseph Haydns* (item 70), pp. 79-84.

Examines Haydn's early popularity in France to ca. 1820. Presents a list of official tributes from France between 1801 and 1807, and addresses the unofficial tributes as well--the many editions and performances of his works. Discusses the popularity of his symphonic music (Haydn was regarded as a model for Parisian composers) and the less well known reception of his vocal music, which was championed by Pierre Porro. Includes the text of Haydn's response to one of the official tributes, as published in the *Mercure de France.*

409. Lowens, Irving. *Haydn in America,* and Albrecht, Otto E. *Haydn Autographs in the United States.* Detroit: College Music Society, 1979. x, 134 pp.

Begins with an essay on Haydn's reputation and popularity in the United States, accompanied by pertinent charts and tables of statistics. Includes information on musical practices in the Moravian communities of Pennsylvania (Bethlehem, Lititz, Nazareth) and North Carolina (Salem), and discusses the music-making activities of the Jefferson family. Provides catalogues of Haydn imprints in the U.S., documented performances in the U.S. during the composer's lifetime, Haydn manuscript copies acquired in Salem, Bethlehem, and Lititz, and Haydn items in the Monticello Music Collection (ca. 1775-1827) at the University of Virginia. Albrecht's listing of musical autographs includes 22 entries. A shorter version of the Lowens study appears in *Haydn Studies* (item 73), pp. 35-48.

* Mörner, C.-G. Stellan. "Haydniana aus Schweden um 1800." *Haydn-Studien* 2 (1969-70):1-33.

Cited as item 198.

410. Norton, M.D. Herter. "Haydn in America (before 1820)." *The Musical Quarterly* 18 (1932):309-37.

An account of Haydn's music in early American concerts. Describes the role played by such enthusiasts as Alexander Reinagle, Hewitt and Bergmann, and the Moravians in Bethlehem in having this music performed. Through sample concert programs and information gleaned from concert announcements, offers insight into the genres and works represented (symphonies were heavily favored). Includes information on early American editions, and provides facsimiles of three title pages.

411. Nováček, Zdenko. "Joseph Haydn und Pressburg." In *Joseph Haydn und seine Zeit* (item 80), pp. 57-63.

Describes various circumstances pertaining to the connection of Haydn and his musical works with the city of Pressburg [Bratislava]. Refers to performances of his operas in that city, including *La canterina* and *La fedeltà premiata,* and discusses his association with the Pressburg Theater as well as several noble courts, among them that of Count Anton Grassalkovics (son-in-law of Paul Anton Esterházy), who may have played a more important role in his life than has been assumed. Emphasizes the importance of the daily paper *Pressburger Zeitung* as a source of information on Haydn and his music.

412. Nowak, Leopold. "Joseph Haydn und die Weltgeltung seiner Musik." *Österreichische Musikzeitschrift* 25 (1970):210-13.

An overview of Haydn's universality of appeal. Mentions early performances, publications, and other signs of acclaim in England, Italy, Russia, Scandinavia, and the New World. Identifies his output as a reflection of the transition from Austrian Baroque to Viennese Classical. Cites folk music and variation principle as key ingredients of his art.

413. Pandi, Marianne, and Schmidt, Fritz, compilers. "Musik zur Zeit Haydns und Beethovens in der Pressburger Zeitung." *The Haydn Yearbook* 8 (1971):165–293.

A selection of excerpts from the *Pressburger Zeitung*, covering the period 7 February 1767 to 6 November 1829. Includes references to Haydn, important contemporaries, musical events and publications, instruments, and further material that might offer insight into the musical life of the period. Some excerpts given in English translation.

414. Pierre, Constant. *Histoire du concert spirituel, 1725–1790.* Paris: Société française de musicologie, 1975. 372 pp.

Covers the administrative history of the organization and provides a chronological account of the programs. Richly supplied with tables and statistics. Includes reference to 256 performances of Haydn's vocal and instrumental works in the years 1777–90.

415. Rutz, Hans. "Joseph Haydn in Our Time." *The Music Review* 11 (1950):180–83.

Comments on the deplorable state of oblivion into which most of Haydn's output had fallen, save for the oratorios and a small number of symphonies and string quartets. Discusses the Haydn Society of America's proposal to undertake a new collected edition. Observes that the "living influence" of a composer has traditionally depended on the availability of the complete works in print. Notes that neo-Classical tendencies of the day suggest a potential spiritual affinity for Haydn's music. Sees the impetus toward a complete edition as the first open manifestation of an incipient era in which Haydn's music would take on fresh importance.

416. Schaffner, Anne. "The Modern String Quartet in America before 1800." *The Music Review* 40 (1979):165–67.

Reports that there was "little or no time lag" between Europe and America with regard to the development of enthusiasm for the string quartet, and that by 1786, the genre was well established within regular concert series. Haydn and Pleyel were the favorite composers. Includes mention of musicians important in cultivating the quartet in America, several of whom had had contact with Haydn while in Europe.

* Schenk, Erich. "Das Weltbild Joseph Haydns." In Erich Schenk. *Ausgewählte Aufsätze, Reden und Vorträge,* pp. 86-99. Graz: Hermann Böhlaus Nachf., 1967. Previously published in *Almanach der österreichischen Akademie der Wissenschaften* 109 (1959):245-72.

Cited as item 752.

* Schering, Arnold. "Künstler, Kenner und Liebhaber der Musik im Zeitalter Haydns und Goethes." In Arnold Schering. *Von grossen Meistern der Musik,* pp. 90-123. Leipzig: Koehler & Amelang, 1940. Previously published in *Jahrbuch der Musikbibliothek Peters* 38 (1931):9-23.

Cited as item 753.

417. Schrade, Leo. "Das Haydn-Bild in den ältesten Biographien." *Die Musikerziehung* [Königsberg] 9 (1932):163-69, 200-213, 244-49.

Disputes the contention that Haydn was not held in esteem by the Romantics. Citing Ludwig Tieck's apotheosis of the symphony, argues that they accepted him with "open and comprehending ears." Examines the Romantic formulation of Haydn's image, chiefly in the years 1800-1810, by such writers as Gerber, Siebigke, Bertuch, and above all Griesinger. Addresses the further contribution of Arnold, who in 1810 added to this image the characterization of Haydn through his symphonies and quartets. Attributes the success of the folksong settings to a Romantic interest in the folk idiom, and discusses E.T.A. Hoffmann's view that Haydn understood in a Romantic sense the "human" in human existence. Quotes a relevant passage from Hoffmann depicting Romantic images evoked by Haydn's symphonies.

418. Schroeder, David P. "Audience Reception and Haydn's London Symphonies." *International Review of the Aesthetics and Sociology of Music* 16 (1985):57-72.

Discusses Haydn's interest in learning about English musical tastes during his visits to England and his attempt to appeal to those tastes in writing his London symphonies. Considers various sources for this knowledge, including Haydn's friends Burney, Salomon, and others. Also examines the writings of selected contemporary authors on the function and aesthetics of music.

* Somfai, László. "The London Revision of Haydn's Instrumental Style." *Proceedings of the Royal Musical Association* 100 (1973-74):159-74.

Cited as item 768.

419. Steinpress, Boris. "Haydns Oratorien in Russland zu Lebzeiten des Komponisten." *Haydn-Studien* 2 (1969-70):77-112.

Describes circumstances surrounding early performances of *The Creation* and *The Seasons* in St. Petersburg and Moscow. Quotes extensively from contemporary accounts. Furnishes background information on the early dissemination and publication of Haydn's works in Russia, and discusses Haydn's contacts with Russian patrons.

420. Tank, Ulrich. "Joseph Haydns geistliche Musik in der Anschauung des 19. Jahrhunderts." In *Joseph Haydn: Tradition und Rezeption* (item 78), pp. 215-62.

Examines nineteenth-century views on Haydn's sacred music, drawing on commentary by well-known composers and writers on music. Comments on composers' apparent lack of interest in the sacred works, and shows that while lexicons gave them more attention, this attention declined, and opinions grew more reserved, with the progress of nineteenth-century Cecilianism. Offers examples of elements in Haydn's sacred music to which reformers objected, and provides background on Cecilianism and dissenting views. In a study of dissemination and performance of this music, includes an inventory of works published during the nineteenth century in German-speaking lands, and points out the notable decline in representation of hymns, cantatas, offertories, and masses from ca. 1860 on.

421. Therstappen, Hans Joachim. "Die deutsche Sendung Joseph Haydns." *Zeitschrift für Musik* 105 (1938):969-73.

Hailing the dawn of a Haydn renaissance, laments the relatively small quantity of works accessible at that time. Notes the composer's transmission of the North German heritage through C.P.E. Bach and credits him with giving definitive voice to a folk-inspired German spirit.

* Weismann, Wilhelm. "Joseph Haydns menschliche Persönlichkeit." *Zeitschrift für Musik* 99 (1932):277-85.

Cited as item 305.

The Editing of Haydn's Music

Related to the larger question of appreciation and dissemination, but isolated here as a separate category, items listed below have to do with various editing endeavors, early as well as more recent, with special emphasis on the *Joseph Haydn Werke,* still in progress but nearing completion (see the list of published volumes of the *JHW,* Appendix 1) under the direction of Georg Feder and the Joseph Haydn Institute in Cologne. Also represented here are comparative studies that concern editions within the different genres of Haydn's output.

* Badura-Skoda, Paul. "Über Haydns Klavierwerke." *Österreichische Musikzeitschrift* 14 (1959):370-76.

Cited as item 1052.

422. Brown, A. Peter. "A Re-introduction to Joseph Haydn's Keyboard Works." *The Piano Quarterly* 21/79 (1972):42-47.

A survey of keyboard works by genre (solo keyboard sonatas, miscellaneous keyboard pieces, keyboard trios, and accompanied divertimentos), with information on editions, recent research, and issues of authenticity and chronology. Includes three helpful tables: comparative numberings in different editions of the solo sonatas, a comparable table for the keyboard trios, and a list of editions of accompanied divertimentos and concertinos.

423. Burkat, Leonard. "Haydn's Symphonies: A Collation." *Notes,* no. 15 (1942), pp. 39-55.

Presents in tabular form the different numberings for each of 104 symphonies, with the Mandyczewski numberings taken as standard. These numberings are derived from catalogues, editions, and concert series, all but one of which are described in the text that precedes the table.

424. Drabkin, William. "Haydn's Piano Sonatas." *The Musical Times* 128 (1987):8-15.

A description and assessment of nine editions of Haydn's keyboard sonatas, from the Schirmer edition of 1894 (edited by Ludwig Klee and Sigmund Lebert) to the Associated Board edition of 1984-85 (edited by Howard Ferguson). Singles out those by Christa Landon and Georg Feder as the most reliable, though overtaken by recent research.

425. Feder, Georg. "Aus der Werkstatt der Haydn-Ausgabe." *Österreichische Musikzeitschrift* 14 (1959):195-98.

Describes procedures employed and problems encountered in the preparation of volumes of the *Joseph Haydn Werke*.

426. ———. "The Collected Works of Joseph Haydn." In *Haydn Studies* (item 73), pp. 26-34.

Defines the term "collected edition," and elaborates on "some actual problems and historical implications of this definition." Points to the need for historical correctness, as realized through techniques of diplomatic evaluation, philological filiation, or a combination of both. Emphasizes the scholarly, rather than practical, function of *Joseph Haydn Werke,* and notes the indispensability of critical commentary in such an edition.

427. ———. "From the Workshop of the Haydn Edition." *The Musical Times* 123 (1982):166-69.

Discusses prospects for completion of the *Joseph Haydn Werke* (44 volumes remained to be completed at the time of writing). Acknowledging that the editing process has taken more time than anticipated, defends the essential method applied as reflected in the volumes of critical commentary: the reporting of variant readings and the listing and evaluation of all sources with respect to provenance, notational style and musical plausibility, and filiation. Presents a sample source situation for operas and baryton music.

428. ———. "Gedanken über den kritischen Apparat aus der Sicht der Haydn-Gesamtausgabe." In *Colloquium Amico-*

rum: Joseph Schmidt-Görg zum 70. Geburtstag, edited by Siegfried Kross and Hans Schmidt, pp. 73-81. Bonn: Beethovenhaus, 1967.

Suggests that it is not the function of a critical commentary to enable the reader to reconstruct the sources. Indicates that the aim of the editor should be to offer the reader more knowledge in fewer words, and proposes guidelines for limiting the size of the commentary. This may be done by indicating more changes and variants directly in the musical text, limiting the sources used for revision, being selective about the differences to record, and making use of systematic summaries.

429. ———. "Haydns Opern und ihre Ausgaben." In *Musik--Edition--Interpretation: Gedenkschrift Günter Henle,* edited by Martin Bente, pp. 165-79. Munich: G. Henle, 1980.

A survey of available editions of the operas. Opens with brief discussion of the revival of interest in these works and of Haydn's activity as an opera composer. In the survey itself, operas are grouped by genre, and for each, the author provides a descriptive paragraph and, where applicable, a list of editions (including editions of the text).

* ———. "Joseph Haydn 1982: Gedanken über Tradition und historische Kritik." In *Joseph Haydn Kongress* (item 76), pp. 597-611.

Cited as item 385.

430. ———. "I melodrammi di Haydn e le loro edizioni." *Chigiana* 36 (1979):5-20.

Italian version of item 429.

431. ———. "Textkritische Methoden: Versuch eines Überblicks mit Bezug auf die Haydn-Gesamtausgabe." *Haydn-Studien* 5 (1982-85):77-109.

Evaluates important studies on methodology in classical, medieval, and German philology, and shows how philological principles apply to editorial methods in music. Cites the exemplary use of such principles by Jahn and Spitta, both of whom were in fact philologists, and quotes from a discussion of Jahn's on philological methodology. Provides an historical overview of this methodology as it applies to text criticism, and demonstrates its use in examples from Haydn. Follows a comparable approach in examining the genealogical study of sources.

432. ———. "Zur Textkritik von Haydns Streichquartetten." *Concerto* 2/6 (1985):25–31. Also published in *Festschrift Arno Forschert zum 60. Geburtstag am 29. Dezember 1985,* edited by Gerhard Allroggen and Detlef Altenburg, pp. 131–41. Kassel: Bärenreiter, 1986.

Discusses the extent of corruption in editions of the quartets, and with the aid of examples, demonstrates the introduction of errors, even in early authorized editions. Describes the methodology used in text criticism for the *Joseph Haydn Werke* editions.

433. Hase, Hermann von. *Joseph Haydn und Breitkopf & Härtel: Ein Rückblick bei der Veranstaltung der ersten vollständigen Gesamtausgabe seiner Werke.* Leipzig: Breitkopf & Härtel, 1909. 64 pp.

A history of the relationship between the firm and Haydn. Discusses Haydn works published or announced, with particular attention to the *Oeuvres complettes* published between 1800 and 1806. Also considers Griesinger's role as mediator in the years 1799–1809. Includes the texts of newspaper announcements and letters, and reproduces samples of autograph letters and music. An appendix discusses the monumental edition begun in 1907.

434. Mitchell, William J. "The Haydn Sonatas." *The Piano Quarterly* 15/58 (1966–67):9, 20–23.

Offers a table of thematic incipits for the sonatas that collates the Päsler numbers with numberings in the Peters (Martienssen) and Breitkopf & Härtel (Zilcher) editions. Specifies a level of difficulty for each sonata.

435. Ohmiya, Makoto. "Text and Performance: The Treatment of *Ossia* Variants in Haydn Critical Scores." In *Haydn Studies* (item 73), pp. 130–33.

Examines the problem of *ossia* variants with specific reference to editorial shortcomings in a performing edition of *VI Scherzandi* (Hob. II:33–38) and the critical edition of the Violin Concerto No. 1. Suggests that performers would be better served if critical reports "included all the relevant readings for *ossia* variants and also took parallel passages into account."

436. Redlich, Hans F. "The New Haydn Edition." *Music and Letters* 31 (1950):220-25.

Describes preliminary work on the Haydn Society's projected complete edition, the first two volumes of which were about to appear. Discusses issues specific to these volumes, and addresses the general question of archival research undertaken for the Society's project. Notes the importance of the Austrian monasteries for this undertaking.

437. Scott, Marion M. "Haydn's '83': A Study of the Complete Editions." *Music and Letters* 11 (1930):207-29.

Provides a detailed list of complete editions of the quartets, from Pleyel's early edition to Kistner's (Leipzig, 1896). Prefaces the list with a thematic index of first movements and a survey of both early prints and complete editions (pays particular attention to Pleyel's). Does not raise the issue of authenticity within the traditional canon.

438. Shulman, Laurie. "The Breitkopf & Härtel *Oeuvres complettes de J. Haydn.*" In *Haydn Studies* (item 73), pp. 137-42.

Offers background on the *Oeuvres complettes,* and discusses problematical aspects of the edition. Provides an inventory of works (identified by Hoboken number) in each of the 12 volumes.

439. Somerset, H.V.F. "Some Lesser Known Works of Haydn in Modern Editions." *Music and Letters* 14 (1933):36-39.

Cites a number of new publications and republications--chiefly by German and Austrian publishers--of the then lesser-known Haydn works. Though merely intended as a current report in 1933, it serves today to underscore the primitive state of Haydn research at the time.

440. Taves, Jeanette. "A Study of Editions of Haydn's Piano Sonata Hob. XVI:52 (ChL. 62) in E-flat Major." In *Haydn Studies* (item 73), pp. 142-44.

Offers several examples to illustrate two kinds of editorial problem: the perpetuation of errors when one edition is based on another and the question of differences in interpretation of the same autograph source.

441. Walter, Horst. "Haydns Klavierkonzerte aus textkritischer Sicht." In *Joseph Haydn Kongress* (item 76), pp. 444-51.

Considers problems in text criticism for three keyboard concertos: Hob. XVIII:3 (F major), Hob. XVIII:4 (G major), and Hob. XVIII:11 (D major). Discusses the application of philological principles to known sources in order to arrive at reliable readings for the editions in *Joseph Haydn Werke.* Provides filiation for each set of sources, and for the G-major concerto, offers three examples of text deterioration. Closes with brief description of contemporary cadenzas for the G-major and D-major works and a sample facsimile.

VII

MUSICAL SOURCES; AUTHENTICITY AND DATING; CHRONOLOGY

Covering a wide spectrum of genres and areas of inquiry, this section subsumes such major studies as the Bartha/Somfai book on Haydn's duties and accomplishments as opera kapellmeister (item 535) as well as narrowly specialized articles having to do with a specific composition. Items worthy of special note within the all-important area of authenticity include inquiries that have utilized Jan LaRue's "Union Thematic Catalogue of the 18th-Century Symphony" (see item 44), the astonishing story of Haydn's attempt to pass off another composer's pieces as his own (item 638), and the extensively researched question of the spurious Op. 3 string quartets (see for example items 594 and 608).

General

This subdivision comprises studies that address general issues of dating and authenticity, as well as specific inquiries concerned with more than one genre. Also included are writings on such source-related topics as sketches, paper, early prints, autograph manuscripts, copies and copyists. Featured here is the David-and-Goliath encounter of the 1930s played out in the pages of *Acta Musicologica* and the *Zeitschrift für Musik* between a young Jens Peter Larsen and the senior scholar Adolf Sandberger. Deserving special mention is Larsen's landmark contribution to Haydn research on the eve of World War II, *Die Haydn-Überlieferung* (item 478), with its panoramic view of the legacy of Haydn sources. The reader's attention is also called to the data on printed sources furnished by Irmgard Becker-Glauch in *RISM* A/I/4 (item 8) and to the indispensable wealth of information supplied in the critical notes that accompany the volumes of the *Joseph Haydn Werke* (see the list of published volumes of the *JHW*, Appendix 1).

442. Becker-Glauch, Irmgard. "Die Haydniana der Lannoy-Sammlung: Eine archivalische Studie." *Haydn-Studien* 3 (1973-74):46-52.

Attempts to reconstruct relationships among Haydn sources in the Lannoy collection. Traces a number of early materials (chiefly manuscripts) to the Viennese firm of Johann Traeg.

443. Biba, Otto. "Haydn-Abschriften von Johannes Brahms." *Haydn-Studien* 4 (1976-80):119-22.

Lists certain Brahms holdings in the Gesellschaft der Musikfreunde that contain Haydn's music copied by Brahms for study purposes. Reveals that nearly all the copies involve music with contrapuntal work and includes a one-page facsimile from Brahms' copy of Hob. I:16, second movement.

* ———. "Haydniana in den Sammlungen der Gesellschaft der Musikfreunde in Wien." *Österreichische Musikzeitschrift* 37 (1982):174-78.

Cited as item 89.

444. Deutsch, Otto Erich. "Curious Title-Pages of Works by Haydn." *The Musical Times* 73 (1932):516-18.

Describes five title pages pertinent to Haydn's relations with England, and provides photographic reproductions.

445. ———. "'Leider nicht von mir!' Musikalische Kuckuckseier." *Österreichische Musikzeitschrift* 11 (1956):348-55. Reprinted as "Musikalische Kuckuckseier" in Otto Erich Deutsch. *Musikalische Kuckuckseier und andere Wiener Musikgeschichten*, edited by Rudolf Klein, pp. 13-20. Vienna: Jugend und Volk, 1973. Previously published in *Basler National-Zeitung*, 29 May 1938.

Recalls well-known spurious works attributed to famous composers, among them two attributed to Haydn: the wind band divertimento in B flat, which contains the *St. Anthony Chorale* theme used by Brahms (it may be by a pupil, possibly Pleyel); and the *Toy* Symphony, composed by Leopold Mozart.

446. ———. "'Unfortunately Not by Me' (Musical Spuriosities)." *The Music Review* 19 (1958):305-10.

Translation of item 445.

447. Feder, Georg. "Die Bedeutung der Assoziation und des Wertvergleiches für das Urteil in Echtheitsfragen." In *International Musicological Society: Report of the Eleventh Congress, Copenhagen 1972,* edited by Henrik Glahn, Søren Sørensen, and Peter Ryom, 1:365-77. Copenhagen: Wilhelm Hansen, 1974.

Explores the use of qualitative comparative analysis to address the problem of authentication when the musical sources prove inconclusive. To demonstrate a comparative approach, examines 25 music examples--in which excerpts drawn from early Haydn chamber pieces are compared with those of contemporaries and apocryphal "Haydn" works--and shows qualitative differences among pairs or groups of examples that contain similar motives. Queries whether perceived qualitative differences might be measured quantitatively.

448. ———. "Bemerkungen zu Haydns Skizzen." *Beethoven-Jahrbuch* (1973-77), pp. 69-86.

Describes the nature of Haydn's sketches, and presents a chronological table of known sketches. Proposes that the wide variety of genres represented and the fragmentary nature of the sketches themselves suggest that Haydn may have sketched far more works and in more complete fashion than previously thought; he may in fact have sketched everything, not only major works or difficult sections. Provides facsimiles, and transcribes multiple sketches for a passage from Piano Trio No. 17.

449. ———. "Die Eingriffe des Musikverlegers Hummel in Haydns Werken." In *Musicae Scientiae Collectanea: Festschrift Karl Gustav Fellerer zum siebzigsten Geburtstag am 7. Juli 1972,* edited by Heinrich Hüschen, pp. 88-101. Cologne: Arno-Volk-Verlag, 1973.

Indicates that Hummel did not publish authorized editions of Haydn, but instead used circulating manuscripts and published editions as his sources. Shows that Hummel's readings often contain changes, some of which affect the substance of the music. Includes music examples that illustrate representative changes, such as insertion or deletion of measures and rewriting of articulation points (generally to produce symmetry where there was none), and alterations in harmony or even tonality. Proposes that Hummel's changes, which are "conventional, banal, or even deforming," cast Haydn's original text in a new light.

450. ———. "Drei Publikationen zur Haydn-Forschung." *Die Musikforschung* 17 (1964):62-66.

Offers substantive corrections and addenda to an article (item 544) in *The Haydn Yearbook,* volume 1, and Landon's supplement to *The Symphonies of Joseph Haydn* (item 964), in a critique of these volumes and Vernon Gotwals' translation of Griesinger and Dies (item 183, 1963 edition).

451. ———. "Haydn-Entdeckungen." *Musica* 19 (1965):189-92.

A concise survey of the status of Haydn source research in the various genres. Includes mention of newly discovered works and the resurfacing of previously lost compositions. Discusses problems encountered in evaluating works of questionable authenticity.

452. ———. "Manuscript Sources of Haydn's Works and Their Distribution." *The Haydn Yearbook* 4 (1968):102-39.

Translation of item 455.

453. ———. "Nachricht über die Krakauer Haydn-Autographen." *Haydn-Studien* 5 (1982-85):135-36.

Reports on the rediscovery in the Biblioteka Jagiellońska in Cracow of autographs sent during World War II from the former Preussische Staatsbibliothek to Grüssau in Silesia. Lists the 18 sources in question.

454. ———. "Über Haydns Skizzen zu nicht identifizierten Werken." In *Ars Musica, Musica Scientia: Festschrift Heinrich Hüschen zum fünfundsechzigsten Geburtstag am 2. März 1980,* edited by Detlef Altenburg, pp. 100-111. Cologne: Gitarre und Laute, 1980.

Outlines recent conclusions about Haydn's sketches (see item 448), and examines sketches for unidentified works:

30 dance movements and 25 miscellaneous pieces, 2 of them newly discovered at the Biblioteka Jagiellońska in Cracow. Gives 4 pages in facsimile.

455. ———. "Die Überlieferung und Verbreitung der handschriftlichen Quellen zu Haydns Werken (Erste Folge)." *Haydn-Studien* 1 (1965-67):3-42.

An authoritative survey of Haydn manuscript sources, based on early researches of the Joseph Haydn Institute in Cologne. Covers collections in Hungary (Budapest and Sopron), Czechoslovakia, and elsewhere in Eastern Europe, Italy, and the Iberian Peninsula. Reflects the author's concern for a comprehensive survey of sources as a basis for the complete edition. For an English translation, see item 452.

456. ———. "Zur Datierung Haydnscher Werke." In *Anthony van Hoboken: Festschrift zum 75. Geburtstag,* edited by Joseph Schmidt-Görg, pp. 50-54. Mainz: B. Schott's Söhne, 1962.

Describes several means of dating autographs of early works (apart from sketches and very early autographs, dates are absent mainly from sources that survive in incomplete form). 1) Appearance of grace notes: up to 1762 they took the form of eighth notes; from 1763 they regularly took half the value of the following main note. 2) Spelling of the word "Minuet": beginning in 1760, Haydn appears to have begun using "Menuet"; before then, "Minuet" seems to have been used exclusively. 3) Absence of dates (from manuscripts that are obviously complete): Haydn apparently did not date works at the time of composition until 1760.

457. Fellinger, Imogen. "Haydnsche Kompositionen in periodischen Musik-Publikationen des 18. Jahrhunderts." In *Joseph Haydn Kongress* (item 76), pp. 526-33.

Discusses publication of Haydn works in periodic music editions and musical supplements to journals and almanacs. Reports that while some works appear in their original form, most suffer alteration: reduction of large-scale works (especially symphonies) for keyboard or other instruments; shortening of movements by omission of segments or even entire sections; omission of entire movements (especially the minuet/trio); and recombining of movements from different works and genres. Addresses reasons for the publication of arrangements, and describes changes in quantity and type of work published after Haydn's death.

458. Fisher, Stephen C., and Boer, Bertil H. van, Jr. "A Viennese Music Copyist and His Role in the Distribution of Haydn's Works." *Haydn-Studien* 6/2 (1988):163–68.

Discusses the Viennese music copyist known as "Silverstolpe A," as yet unidentified, but so-named because he prepared a number of manuscripts for Fredrik Samuel Silverstolpe. Includes a table of Haydn copies by "Silverstolpe A" and his associates as well as reproduction of a page in the copyist's hand.

459. Fruehwald, Scott. *Authenticity Problems in Joseph Haydn's Early Instrumental Works: A Stylistic Investigation.* New York: Pendragon, 1988. viii, 275 pp.

Concentrates on pre-1770 instrumental compositions attributed to Haydn but of doubtful authenticity. Repertoire includes keyboard sonatas, keyboard trios, string trios, string quartets, miscellaneous divertimentos, and solo concertos for horn, violin, and keyboard. Surveys the scholarly literature dealing with stylistic analysis and authenticity, and offers a fresh approach involving isolation and quantification of various stylistic traits, compilation of statistical profiles, and analysis of the profiles within the framework of control groups and test groups. Results obtained, including a determination that the two Raigern sonatas (Hob. XVI:Es2 and Es3) are authentic, variously corroborate or contradict assessments by Larsen, Landon, and Feder. Asserts that stylistic methods may be no less reliable than those obtained by documentary evidence, and that they may constitute a decisive factor when external evidence proves ambiguous.

460. Geiringer, Karl. "Eigenhändige Bemerkungen Haydns in seinen Musikhandschriften." In *Anthony van Hoboken: Festschrift zum 75. Geburtstag,* edited by Joseph Schmidt-Görg, pp. 87–92. Mainz: B. Schott's Söhne, 1962.

Offers examples of the types of commentary found in Haydn's manuscripts: short Latin phrases of a religious nature (some with irregular capitalization to encode a date of composition); instructions for performers or copyists (some quite detailed); notations that call attention to contrapuntal sections; and comments, some humorous, apparently intended for Haydn himself.

461. Gerstenberg, Walter. *Musikerhandschriften von Palestrina bis Beethoven.* Zurich: Atlantis, 1960. 175 pp.

Contains one or two pages in facsimile, with commentary, for each of several Haydn works: Quartets Op. 71 No. 1 and Op. 74 No. 1; Symphonies Nos. 94, 96, and 102; the song "Trust Not Too Much"; the "Emperor Hymn"; *The Creation* and *The Seasons* (sketches); and the *Nelson* Mass.

462. *Haydn-Autographe aus dem Haydn-Haus Eisenstadt (Faksimile-Drucke).* Edited by A.J. Ohrenberger and A. Hahn. Eisenstadt: Amt der Burgenländischen Landesregierung, 1976. 13 sheets.

Items represented include the Alleluia chorus (beginning), Hob. XXIIIc:3; minuet sketches, including Hob. IX:11, No. 1; fragment from a march, Hob. VIII:7; Derbyshire March, Hob. VIII:2; aria and chorus from *Il ritorno di Tobia* ("Ah gran Dio"), with Haydn's corrections on the copyist's score; letter to Artaria (14 February 1787); letter to Griesinger (1 July 1801); sketch of a letter to an unknown addressee; sketch of a letter of Michael Haydn; sketches of correspondence from 1804; letter, probably to Nikolaus II.

463. Heussner, Horst. "Zwei neue Haydn-Funde." *Die Musikforschung* 13 (1960):451-55.

Findings consist of a manuscript for the previously lost Keyboard Concerto Hob. XVIII:5 and a source for the Piano Trio Hob. XV:40, which contains a different, hitherto unknown second movement.

464. Hoboken, Anthony van. "Zur Entstehung meiner Sammlung musikalischer Erst- und Frühdrucke." In *Beiträge zur Musikdokumentation: Franz Grasberger zum 60. Geburtstag,* edited by Günter Brosche, pp. 101-6. Tutzing: Hans Schneider, 1975.

Describes the origins of a collection of prints that is especially rich in Haydn sources (see item 37).

465. Jerger, Wilhelm. *Die Haydndrucke aus dem Archiv der 'Theater- und Musik-Liebhabergesellschaft zu Luzern'*

nebst Materialien zum Musikleben in Luzern um 1800. Freiburg in der Schweiz: Universitätsverlag, 1959. 45 pp.

Contains a catalogue of 65 early prints of works attributed to Haydn that are now housed in the archive of the Allgemeine Musikgesellschaft Luzern. Includes a concordance table that identifies contents by Hoboken number.

466. Jones, David Wyn. "Haydn's Music in London in the Period 1760-1790." *The Haydn Yearbook* 14 (1983):144-72.

Part 1 of a study on Haydn's reputation in England before his visits in the 1790s. Covers three periods: 1760-70, with background on the Bach-Abel concerts, European composers popular in London, the leading publishers, and the first English publications of Haydn's music; 1771-72, seen as "the origins of Haydn's later fame ... when ten publications of his music became available"; 1774-80, a period of few new editions of Haydn's music and few known concert performances of his works. A two-page appendix provides summary information on the 25 London publications.

467. Kast, Paul. "Die Autographensammlung Campori und ihre musikalischen Schätze." In *Gesellschaft für Musikforschung: Bericht über den Internationalen musikwissenschaftlichen Kongress, Kassel 1962,* edited by Georg Reichert and Martin Just, pp. 226-28. Kassel: Bärenreiter, 1963.

Discusses selected composers' autographs in the Campori collection of the Biblioteca Estense in Modena. Most important among these is the autograph of Haydn's insertion aria "La mia pace, o Dio, perdei," a work regarded as doubtful until the discovery of the autograph. A second Haydn autograph described is a note that accompanied a manuscript sent, presumably, to Artaria.

468. Landmann, Ortrun. "Die Dresdener Haydn-Quellen im Hinblick auf ihre Provenienzen." In *Joseph Haydn Kongress* (item 76), pp. 519-25.

Summarizes the extent of wartime losses and of current Haydn holdings at the Sächsische Landesbibliothek. Lists collections from which the manuscript sources derive, and for four of them, provides background discussion and summaries of Haydn manuscript holdings (approximately 600 Haydn sources, nearly 60 percent in manuscript).

469. Landon, H.C. Robbins. "Haydniana (I)." *The Haydn Yearbook* 4 (1968):199-206.

Collected facts on various topics: newly discovered sources for the disputed *Missa brevis "Rorate coeli desuper,"* with attributions to Reutter and Arbesser; data concerning the authenticity of 14 doubtful concertos; and discussion of 3 Haydn letters: 2 autographs (to Luigia Polzelli, 4 August 1791; and to Viotti, 19 December 1794) and a copy by Johann Elssler (to Prince Esterházy's administrator, undated). Includes facsimiles of the 2 autographs and a transcription of the letter to Viotti.

470. ———. "Neue Haydn-Quellen." *Österreichische Musikzeitschrift* 14 (1959):213-16.

A brief survey of Czech collections that contain authentic copies, eighteenth-century thematic catalogues useful for Haydn research, and sources important for dating and editing Haydn's works. Derived from item 473.

471. ———. "New Manuscript Sources of Works by Joseph Haydn, Johann Michael Haydn and Their Austrian Contemporaries." *The Haydn Yearbook* 15 (1984):199-213.

The Joseph Haydn sources described consist of manuscripts acquired by Else Radant from the collection of Louis Dité. These include the motet *O coelitum beati* in a manuscript of ca. 1765, the *Stabat Mater,* and seven other works. Of greatest interest is the manuscript for the *Stabat Mater,* which is the first known authentic score, written by Johann Elssler and another copyist, with Haydn's signature on the title page. Provides seven plates in facsimile pertaining to the *Stabat Mater:* the title page with Haydn's signature, a page each by Elssler and the other copyist, the first page of the source, and tracings of watermarks.

472. ———. "Problems of Authenticity in Eighteenth-Century Music." In *Instrumental Music: A Conference at Isham Memorial Library, May 4, 1957,* edited by David G. Hughes, pp. 31-46. Cambridge: Harvard University Press, 1959. Reprint. New York: Da Capo, 1972.

Addressing the issue of authentication, discusses a

symphony in A major once thought to be by Haydn, but later shown to be by Ordonez. Also considers the question of lost works, and retraces the steps that led to the discovery of Haydn's lost Mass in G major.

473. ———. "Survey of the Haydn Sources in Czechoslovakia." In *Bericht über die Internationale Konferenz zum Andenken Joseph Haydns* (item 70), pp. 69–77.

Calls attention to the wealth of Haydn sources in Czech libraries. Offers a survey of the important collections, summarizing the nature of their Haydn holdings and singling out sources of special interest. Includes thematic incipits for previously unknown attributions to Haydn, and discusses the role of the collections in providing information for the authentication of doubtful works.

474. ———. "Two Research Lacunae in Music of the Classic Period." In *Perspectives in Musicology: The Inaugural Lectures of the Ph.D. Program in Music at the City University of New York,* edited by Barry S. Brook, Edward O.D. Downes, and Sherman Van Solkema, pp. 136–50. New York: W.W. Norton, 1972.

Describes the centralization of provincial Czech archive materials in Prague. Makes note of recently discovered Haydn sources there, and gives an overview of archival materials at Brno and Kroměříč. Mentions important iconographical holdings at the Prague Museum.

475. Larsen, Jens Peter. "Das Echtheitsproblem in der Musik des 18. Jahrhunderts." In *Joseph Haydn und seine Zeit* (item 80), pp. 25–39. Also published in *Mozart-Jahrbuch* (1971-72), pp. 7-18, as "Über die Möglichkeiten einer musikalischen Echtheitsbestimmung für Werke aus der Zeit Haydns und Mozarts" and in *Die Musikforschung* 25 (1972):4-16 as "Über Echtheitsprobleme in der Musik der Klassik."

Identifies the period around 1760 as a uniquely difficult one for the study of authenticity, and observes that this was a time when large publishing firms in Paris, London, and Amsterdam relied on unauthentic copies from Vienna, Italy, and elsewhere. Discusses the methodological dispute among scholars regarding the relative merits of source research and stylistic examination as bases for determining authenticity. Citing his *Die Haydn-Überlieferung* (item 478), affirms the importance of source research. Quotes from Georg Feder's 1970 essay (item 622), and asserts that certainty is unobtainable solely through stylistic analysis. Setting forth cautionary guidelines for style-analytical investigation, concludes that both approaches are essential and should complement each other. An appended reply by Feder (pp. 37-39, absent from the *Mozart-Jahrbuch* and *Die Musikforschung*) seeks to clarify the context from which the passages quoted by Larsen were excerpted. See item 480 for an English translation.

476. ———. "Haydn and *Das kleine Quartbuch.*" In Jens Peter Larsen. *Handel, Haydn, and the Viennese Classical Style,* translations by Ulrich Krämer, pp. 171-83. Ann Arbor: UMI Research Press, 1988.

Translation of item 479.

477. ———. "The Haydn Tradition." In Jens Peter Larsen. *Handel, Haydn, and the Viennese Classical Style,* translations by Ulrich Krämer, pp. 185-224. Ann Arbor: UMI Research Press, 1988.

Translation of excerpts from item 478.

478. ———. *Die Haydn-Überlieferung.* Copenhagen: Einar Munksgaard, 1939. Reprint, with foreword by the author. Munich: Kraus International Publications, 1980. xviii, 335 pp.

A major landmark in the development of twentieth-century Haydn research. Concerned with imposing order on the legacy of sources and documents upon which the authentic canon of Haydn's works must rest. Gives a detailed overview of surviving autograph manuscripts, copies, and prints; and proposes criteria for distinguishing among authentic, likely, doubtful, and probably or certainly unauthentic works. Devotes a chapter to problems of chronology. Includes discussion of handwriting, paper, and watermark studies, and examines the development of Haydn's style of notation. Chapters devoted to the authentic Haydn catalogues constitute a major portion of the study. Foreword to the reprint provides a concise summary of the status of Haydn research as of 1980.

479. ———. "Haydn und das 'kleine Quartbuch'." *Acta Musicologica* 7 (1935):111-23.

In response to Sandberger (item 491), initiated the famous controversy between the two scholars (see items 491, 489, 482, 490, 483, 493, 481, 492). Describes and analyzes the contents of a thematic catalogue that once belonged to Haydn and contains his notations. Rejects Sandberger's assertion that the catalogue, found at the Esterházy archives in Budapest, was written by Elssler and represents the repertory performed by Prince Nikolaus' musical establishment under Haydn. Shows it to be a catalogue of a different, though unidentified, collection altogether, and on the basis of datable works represented, dates it ca. 1775. Compares its listing of Haydn symphonies with that of Mandyczewski, noting significant differences. Also mentions a symphony in B flat (Hob. I:B11), published under Haydn's name in an edition by Sandberger, but in fact by Vanhal. For an English translation, see item 476.

480. ———. "Problems of Authenticity in Music from the Time of Haydn to Mozart." In Jens Peter Larsen. *Handel, Haydn, and the Viennese Classical Style,* translated by Ulrich Krämer, pp. 123-35. Ann Arbor: UMI Research Press, 1988.

Translation of item 475, *Mozart-Jahrbuch* version.

481. ———. "Replik." *Acta Musicologica* 9 (1937):38-39. Also published in *Zeitschrift für Musik* 104 (1937):428-29 as "Zur 'Haydn-Kontroverse': Anmerkung zu Geh. Rat. Prof. Dr. Sandbergers Ausführungen im Januar-Heft."

An installment in the Larsen-Sandberger controversy (see item 479), in response to item 493. Addresses the question of the 78 "newly discovered" symphonies that Sandberger attributed to Haydn and of the "Göttweig sonatas," which Sandberger accepted not only as authentic, but also as being among Haydn's best keyboard works. Raises these issues to drive home the point that skepticism must be exercised in the authentication of Haydn works.

482. ———. "Replik an Professor Adolf Sandberger." *Acta Musicologica* 8 (1936):22-29. Also published in *Zeitschrift für Musik* 103 (1936):1325-30 as "Zu Professor Sandbergers Haydn-Forschung: I. Haydn und das 'kleine Quartbuch'."

Another episode in the Larsen-Sandberger debate (see item 479), in response to item 489. Reports the author's discovery of a number of manuscripts at Melk monastery written in the same hand as that of the "kleines Quartbuch" scribe and bearing the notation "ad usum Joan: Nep: Weigl." Adduces evidence to suggest Melk as the Quartbuch's place of origin, and proposes that the catalogue represents sources at Melk or a monastery with close ties to Melk. Also presents further evidence that the B-flat symphony (Hob. I:B11) attributed by Sandberger to Haydn is indeed by Vanhal. Considers the question of "unknown Haydn."

483. ———. "Zu Prof. Sandberger's Haydn-Forschung." *Acta Musicologica* 8 (1936):149-54. Also published in *Zeitschrift für Musik* 103 (1936):1331-34 as "Zu Professor Sandbergers Haydn-Forschung: II. Abschliessende Bemerkungen."

A further installment in the Larsen-Sandberger dispute (see item 479), in response to item 490. Asserts that Sandberger has produced no evidence to support his contentions regarding the "kleines Quartbuch," the B-flat symphony, the number of Haydn works in various early catalogues, or "unknown Haydn" and the 78 symphonies newly discovered by Sandberger.

484. Matthäus, Wolfgang. "Das Werk Joseph Haydns im Spiegel der Geschichte des Verlages Jean André." *The Haydn Yearbook* 3 (1965):54-110.

Discusses how publishers' privileges, among other factors, influenced the nature of André's position as a publisher of Haydn's works. Offers an annotated listing of all Haydn prints published by André. Early prints appear in an approximate chronological order based on secondary datings, chiefly from announcements in the *Frankfurter priviligiertes Staats-Ristretto,* and information is provided on their publication history. Lists mid- and late nineteenth-century publications according to genre.

485. Ohmiya, Makoto. "Zur Entstehungsgeschichte von Haydns Werken für Lira organizzata." In *Joseph Haydn Kongress* (item 76), pp. 452-57.

A discussion of works written for King Ferdinand IV of Naples between 1786 and 1790, with four tables that summarize information on sources, settings, and origins. Proposes that the five surviving concertos originated as two sets of three works each; the missing composition, ostensibly in C major, would have been No. 1 of the second set. Similarly proposes that the eight *Notturni* were conceived as two sets of six and three works each, with a missing C-major work as No. 1 of the second set. Provides datings and documentary evidence to support the proposed groupings.

486. Pilková, Zdeňka. "Haydn and His Czech Contemporary Antonín Kammel." In *Haydn Studies* (item 73), pp. 171-77.

Offers a biographical sketch of Kammel, a Bohemian who worked in London for many years. Notes how in the early 1770s, works of Kammel and Haydn were often linked in performances and advertisements, and cites stylistic similarities between them from around this time. Describes three instances of conflicting attribution involving the two composers (Hob. V:Es12, F2, F6; Hob. VI:G1; Hob. III:C11), and concludes with a discussion of features in Kammel's music that may help to distinguish it from Haydn's.

487. Poole, H. Edmund. "Music Engraving Practice in Eighteenth-Century London: A Study of Some Forster Editions of Haydn and Their Manuscript Sources." In *Music and Bibliography: Essays in Honour of Alec Hyatt King*, edited by Oliver Neighbour, pp. 98-131. New York: K.G. Saur, 1980.

Discusses Haydn's relationship with William Forster, the first English publisher with whom he established a direct relationship. Quotes a 1767 description of the music-engraving process from the French *Encyclopédie* (with illustrations of the engraver's implements), then proceeds to a comparative examination of existing manuscript copies of Haydn works from which the Forster engravings were made. Notes idiosyncrasies of individual engravers and discrepancies between the manuscript copies and the prints, notably with respect to dynamic indications, articulation marks (especially the stroke and dot), and slurs.

* Poštolka, Milan. "Joseph Haydn und Leopold Koželuh: Ein Beitrag zur Erforschung der Beziehungen zwischen der tschechischen Musikkultur des 18. Jahrhunderts und dem Schaffen Joseph Haydns." In *Bericht über die Internationale Konferenz zum Andenken Joseph Haydns* (item 70), pp. 109-15.

Cited as item 354.

488. Radice, Mark A. "Haydn and His Publishers: A Brief Survey of the Composer's Publishing Activities." *The Music Review* 44 (1983):87-94.

Deals chiefly with Haydn's relationship to Artaria and Breitkopf & Härtel. Using quotations from Haydn and Griesinger, describes editorial procedures Haydn applied to compositions printed by these publishers. Concludes that in general, Artaria editions from 1780 to 1789 may be regarded as both authorized and authentic, thereafter only as authorized. Identifies the Breitkopf & Härtel editions, mainly from 1799 on, as merely authorized and problematic. Also draws conclusions about editions of Bland, Forster, Thomson, and Longman & Broderip, and furnishes a summary table of findings on authorization and authenticity.

489. Sandberger, Adolf. "Haydn und das 'kleine Quartbuch'." *Acta Musicologica* 8 (1936):18-22. Also published in *Zeitschrift für Musik* 103 (1936):1104-11 as "Fortsetzung einer Haydn-Kontroverse."

An installment in the Larsen-Sandberger controversy (see item 479). Takes issue with points made in Larsen's article (item 479), and reasserts the author's opinion that the "kleines Quartbuch" represents Haydn's repertory catalogue and that the B-flat symphony (Hob. I:B11) is authentic.

490. ———. "Haydn und das 'kleine Quartbuch': Erwiderung auf die Replik des Herrn Magister Larsen." *Acta Musicologica* 8 (1936):139-49.

Part of the Larsen-Sandberger controversy (see item 479). Argues against Larsen's assertions (item 482) regarding the "kleines Quartbuch," the B-flat symphony (Hob. I:B11), and "unknown Haydn."

491. ———. "Neue Haydniana." *Jahrbuch der Musikbibliothek Peters* 40 (1933):28-37.

The article that gave rise to the Larsen-Sandberger controversy (see item 479). The original source of contention was the second part of the article ("Zu Haydns Repertoir in Eisenstadt und Esterhazy"), in which Sandberger described the "kleines Quartbuch" as a catalogue of Haydn's repertory in Eisenstadt and Eszterháza, claiming that it was written in Elssler's hand and that it contained 61 authentic Haydn symphonies. Sandberger then used the contents of this alleged Haydn repertory to support the claim of Mannheim influences on Haydn. The first and unrelated part of the article transcribes and comments on some Haydn correspondence, giving particular attention to Gottfried Christoph Härtel's 18 July 1800 letter to Haydn.

492. ———. "Schlussreplik." *Acta Musicologica* 9 (1937):39-41. Also published in *Zeitschrift für Musik* 104 (1937):534-36 as "Nochmals zur Haydn-Kontroverse: Schlusswort von Geh. Rat. Prof. Dr. Adolf Sandberger."

Sandberger's concluding remarks in the Larsen-Sandberger controversy (see item 479).

493. ———. "Zu den Bemerkungen des Herrn Magister Larsen in Sachen der Haydn-Kontroverse." *Acta Musicologica* 9 (1937):31-38. Also published in *Zeitschrift für Musik* 104 (1937):38-43 as "Weiter zur 'Haydn-Kontroverse'."

A continuation of the Larsen-Sandberger controversy (see item 479). Addresses the four main issues raised by Larsen in item 483.

494. ———. "Zu den unbekannten Sinfonien von Joseph Haydn." *Neues Beethoven-Jahrbuch* 7 (1937):5-16.

Examines two spurious symphonies discovered by Sandberger at the Thurn und Taxis library in Regensburg and declared by him to be authentic: one in E flat (Hob. I:Es11), the other in D major (Hob. I:D14). Against the backdrop of a discussion that addresses Haydn's popularity in France, the French liking for tone painting and programmatic music, and Haydn's Paris symphonies, describes at length the E-flat symphony, in particular the slow movement, for which Sandberger finds a counterpart in Haydn's *La reine* Symphony. Comments on the D-major work are more succinct.

495. Schünemann, Georg. *Musikerhandschriften von Bach bis Schumann.* Berlin: Atlantis, 1936. 106 pp., 96 facsimiles.

Using quotations from contemporaries and from Haydn himself, discusses the composer's work habits and approaches to composition. Takes a page from the autograph of *The Seasons* to confirm a quotation from Griesinger regarding Haydn's compositional process. Describes features of Haydn's musical script and finds few essential differences between early and late samples. Reproduces autograph pages from two symphonies, a canon, a string quartet, and *The Seasons.*

496. Scott, Marion M. "Haydn: Thereabouts or There." *Music and Letters* 21 (1940):319-27.

A critique of Larsen's *Die Haydn-Überlieferung* (item 478) that takes exception to his methodology regarding printed editions and chronology, for example, his decision to discredit Haydn publications prior to 1779 and to regard the Artaria publications as standard authentic sources. In this context, discusses the early publication history of Op. 1 and Op. 20. With regard to the latter set, cites earlier readings that are closer to Haydn's autograph than post-Artaria prints by Pleyel and Trautwein.

497. Searle, Arthur. "Haydn Autographs and 'Authentic' Manuscript Copies in the British Library." *Early Music* 10 (1982):495-504.

A description of sources in the Department of Manuscripts, including those on loan from the Stefan Zweig collection and Royal Philharmonic Society. Describes several letters and documents in addition to the more numerous autographs and copies of musical works. Contains a summary table of the music represented, providing (where applicable) the Hoboken number (except for symphonies), shelf number, number of folios (for autographs), information on previous ownership, and acquisition date. Also includes six facsimile pages of music and documents.

498. Somfai, László. "Haydn Autograph Scores Reconsidered." *The New Hungarian Quarterly* 21/77 (1980):205-12.

Advocates study of Haydn's autographs as a source of insight toward authentic interpretation and an understanding of his compositional techniques. Examines several pertinent issues: Haydn's three-stage creative process, details of his handwriting that give clues to his speed, aspects of paper that merit study, writing order within a multi-work opus or within a single work, and the matter of written instructions and inconsistent markings in the autographs. Supplies illustrative calligraphic examples as well as facsimiles of two autograph pages.

499. ———. "How to Read and Understand Haydn's Notation in Its Chronologically Changing Concepts." In *Joseph Haydn Kongress* (item 76), pp. 23-34.

Divides the development of Haydn's notational practices into two phases, with the years 1780-81 marking the separation between manuscripts prepared mainly for self-directed performance and those prepared for publishers. Considerations addressed include ornamentation; conventions regarding dotted rhythm and triplets; articulation, bowing, and touch; dynamics and accents; and tempo. Examines the evolution of Haydn's practices in notating certain ornaments, and includes numerous passages with examples of ornaments and proposed realizations. Emphasizes the need for further study of different chronological and genre-related tendencies in Haydn's notation. Advocates rejection of conventional legato performance in favor of crisp articulation and vitality in the interpretation of ornaments and bowings.

500. Tyson, Alan. "Paper Studies and Haydn: What Needs to Be Done." In *Joseph Haydn Kongress* (item 76), pp. 577-92.

Surveys methods of classifying papers used by Haydn, with emphasis on watermarks and rastrology. Identifies "total span" as the vertical distance from the top line of the top stave to the bottom line of the bottom stave. Explaining ways in which information gleaned from paper characteristics can be used to help establish chronology, shows how the link between the paper used for the autograph manuscript of the Trumpet Concerto and that used for the song "Als einst mit Weibes Schönheit" helps to date the latter. Underscores the potential value of a census of Haydn paper-types. Appends numerous facsimiles of watermarks.

501. Unverricht, Hubert. "Haydn und Bossler." In *Festskrift Jens Peter Larsen, 14. VI. 1902-1972,* edited by Nils Schiørring, Henrik Glahn, and Carsten E. Hatting, pp. 285-300. Copenhagen: Wilhelm Hansen, 1972.

Citing Bossler's announcement of Haydn's commission to publish three symphonies and six divertimentos, proposes that various Haydn prints published by Bossler between 1783 and 1794 may be regarded as authentic. Asserts that in the absence of extant correspondence between composer and publisher, information taken from title pages, announcements, and source comparisons provides data important to the assessment of the editions. Of works cited in the announcement, the identity of the divertimentos has long been known (Hob. XI:123, 103, 101, 114, 124, 108), though that of the symphonies is open to question (Larsen proposes 76-78; see Rifkin, item 120).

502. Webster, James. "External Criteria for Determining the Authenticity of Haydn's Music." In *Haydn Studies* (item 73), pp. 75-78.

Examines various types of sources: authentic and indirectly authentic manuscripts, authenticated and authorized prints, good sources, and mediocre or poor sources. For works that do not survive in authenticated sources, offers criteria for assessing which of those in the "doubtful" category might be assessed as "plausible."

503. Zahn, Robert von. "Der fürstlich Esterházysche Notenkopist Joseph Elssler sen." *Haydn-Studien* 6/2 (1988):130-47.

Discusses a copyist who served the Esterházy court from 1764 to 1782 and prepared copies of numerous Haydn works. Lists the known documents pertaining to Elssler, and describes (with illustrations) various features of his script. Demonstrates how these features may be used in the dating of Haydn's works. Incorporates tables and lists that summarize the copies known to have been prepared by, or which have been misattributed to, Elssler.

Sacred Works

504. Becker-Glauch, Irmgard. "Haydns Cantilena pro adventu in D." *Haydn-Studien* 1 (1965-67):277-81.

Explains how this piece has survived in copies with different texts and variant readings of the music. Tracks down a text in local dialect as the likely original ("Herst nachbä hä sag mir was heut") and proposes that the reading in an eighteenth-century source at Prague may come closest to Haydn's original music.

505. ———. "Joseph Haydn's *Ave Regina* in A." In *Studies in Eighteenth-Century Music: A Tribute to Karl Geiringer on His Seventieth Birthday,* edited by H.C. Robbins Landon and Roger E. Chapman, pp. 68–75. New York: Oxford University Press, 1970.

On the basis of documentary and stylistic evidence, places the work at the time of Haydn's studies with Porpora in the mid-1750s. Proposes resemblances to the *Salve Regina* of 1756 and to the Neapolitan style to which Haydn was exposed as Porpora's accompanist and copyist. Cites the relatively large number of sources (11 manuscript copies) as evidence of the work's popularity, and concludes on the basis of awkwardness in text-underlay that the *Salve Regina* text found in some sources is not the original.

506. ———. "Joseph Haydns Te Deum für die Kaiserin: Eine Quellenstudie." In *Colloquium Amicorum: Joseph Schmidt-Görg zum 70. Geburtstag,* edited by Siegfried Kross and Hans Schmidt, pp. 1-10. Bonn: Beethovenhaus, 1967.

Underscores the importance of authentic performance parts in supplying information on the original character of a piece. Describes three sets of such parts for the *Te Deum* (whose autograph is lost): one set at Eisenstadt, one at Prague, and another newly discovered at Graz. Shows that the Graz source provides a link between those at Eisenstadt and Prague: apparently based on the Eisenstadt parts, as was the Prague manuscript, it contains autograph corrections by Haydn, from which Elssler's corrections in the Prague source clearly derive. Compares the sources with the first edition (Breitkopf & Härtel, 1802) and several additional manuscripts.

507. ———. "Neue Forschungen zu Haydns Kirchenmusik." *Haydn-Studien* 2 (1969–70):167–241.

Concentrating on smaller, miscellaneous compositions, apart from the masses, examines questions of dating and authenticity that pertain to the extant sources. Works featured include Viennese compositions up to 1756 (*Missa brevis* in F, *Rorate coeli desuper* Mass, *Lauda Sion* in C, *Salve Regina* in E, *Ave Regina* in A); such early Esterházy compositions as the *Motetto de Sancta Thecla,* the cantata *Destatevi, o miei fidi,* and the early *Te Deum;* and the late English Psalms. Based on a presentation before the Haydn Institute, May 1967.

508. ———. "Wiederaufgefundene Kirchenmusikwerke Joseph Haydns." *Die Musikforschung* 17 (1964):413-14.

Reports on the rediscovery of two sacred pieces, which have survived in eighteenth-century manuscript copies: the *4 Responsoria de Venerabili*, cited in both the "Entwurf-Katalog" and the Elssler "Haydn-Verzeichnis," and a *Cantilena pro adventu*, cited in the "Entwurf-Katalog" only.

* Berkenstock, James T. "The Smaller Sacred Compositions of Joseph Haydn." 2 vols. Ph.D. dissertation, Northwestern University, 1975. viii, 230 pp.; 126 pp.

Cited as item 788.

* Brand, Carl Maria. *Die Messen von Joseph Haydn*. Würzburg-Aumühle: Konrad Triltsch, 1941. Reprint. Walluf bei Wiesbaden: Martin Sändig, 1973. 548 pp.

Cited as item 790.

509. Dack, James. "The Dating of Haydn's *Missa Cellensis in Honorem Beatissimae Virginis Mariae:* An Interim Discussion." *The Haydn Yearbook* 13 (1982):97-112.

Reviews perplexing questions surrounding the existing autograph materials, including the Bucharest fragment of 1766 (discovered in 1975) and the Budapest fragment of 1769-73. Summarizes arguments previously advanced by Feder, Landon, Brand, and others regarding the date of the work. Calls attention to stylistic discrepancies as well as external considerations in formulating the hypothesis that there may be two versions in question: an original composition (Kyrie, Gloria, and Credo) and a later completion which may have involved the reconstruction of a partially destroyed score.

510. Eby, John. "A New Missa Brevis Attributed to 'Heyden'." *Studies in Music from the University of Western Ontario* 3 (1978):127-56.

Calls attention to a *missa brevis* (*Missa in D à 7 voci*) that survives at the university library in Warsaw in a manuscript copy dated 1768. Compares the work stylistically with Joseph Haydn's *missae breves,* and concludes on the basis of style and circumstantial evidence that the work is not by Joseph. Proposes instead that his brother Michael is the likely composer, and develops an argument to support his view. Includes a modern score of the mass.

511. Feder, Georg. "Ein Kanon-Autograph von J. Haydn in Leningrad." *Haydn-Studien* 4 (1976-80):52-55.

Describes a previously unknown source at the Institute for Russian Literature. It contains a setting of the Fifth Commandment, in canon, that has bold harmonies and modulations, and differs from the simpler, more Classical canon published in the set of Ten Commandments. A facsimile and edited transcription of the canon are included.

512. ———. "A Newly Found Authentic Source for Joseph Haydn's *Missa in honorem B.V.M.*" In *Music in the Classic Period: Essays in Honor of Barry S. Brook*, edited by Allan W. Atlas, pp. 61-68. New York: Pendragon, 1985.

Places the manuscript in question, from the cathedral archive in Györ, in the context of recent source research pertaining to the work, which includes trumpet and timpani parts in approximately half the extant sources (including Györ but not Haydn's autograph manuscript for the Sanctus, Benedictus, and part of the Agnus Dei). Identifying the copyist as Joseph Elssler senior, declares this to be the "only doubtlessly authorized copy of an authentic version" of the work. Includes three pages from the source in facsimile.

* Geiringer, Karl. "The Small Sacred Works by Haydn in the Esterhazy Archives at Eisenstadt." *The Musical Quarterly* 45 (1959):460-72.

Cited as item 795.

513. Landon, H.C. Robbins. "Eine aufgefundene Haydn-Messe." *Österreichische Musikzeitschrift* 12 (1957):183-85.

Reports on the discovery of the previously lost *Missa "Rorate coeli desuper,"*--first the incipit, found among "Incogniti" in the Göttweig catalogue, then the actual source, located in the monastery library. Offers a description of the source (a manuscript copy) and a brief assessment of the musical style. Landon's claim for

Haydn's authorship is disputed by Erich Schenk in item 518.

514. ———. "Haydn's Newly Discovered *Responsorium ad absolutionem* 'Libera me, Domine'." *The Haydn Yearbook* 4 (1968):140-47, 228-35.

Speculates on circumstances surrounding composition of the piece, designed to be sung after the main body of the Requiem mass. Proposes that it may have been written in connection with the death of Princess Marie Elisabeth (25 February 1790), wife of Nikolaus II. Describes paper, watermarks, and parts, which show evidence of having been used in performance (all four vocal parts and organ are in Haydn's hand; copyist Johann Schellinger did violin and bass parts). Includes a modern edition, also a facsimile of parts in Schellinger's hand and Haydn's.

515. ———. "A Lost Autograph Re-discovered: Missa 'Sunt bona mixta malis,' Joseph Haydn." *The Haydn Yearbook* 14 (1983):5-8.

Addresses a variety of topics concerning the autograph and the work itself: the disappearance of the mass after its purchase by Novello from Artaria in 1829, the lack of known extant copies, possible reasons for the existence of only two movements, and the austerity of the musical style.

516. ———. "The Newly Discovered Autograph to Haydn's Missa Cellensis of 1766 (Formerly Known as 'Missa Sanctae Caeciliae')." *The Haydn Yearbook* 9 (1975):306-27.

Tells of the discovery at the Central State Library in Bucarest of the first twenty pages of the autograph and reproduces them in facsimile. Observes that the new source provides a correct title and places the beginning date of composition earlier than previously thought. Since a fragment at the Esterházy archives in Budapest bears watermarks thought to be later than 1766, advances theories to account for the discrepancy.

517. MacIntyre, Bruce C. "Haydn's Doubtful and Spurious Masses: An Attribution Update." *Haydn-Studien* 5 (1982-85):42-54.

Provides a supplement, in tabular form, to the doubtful

and spurious masses cited in volume 2 of Hoboken's catalogue (item 28). Information given for each entry includes the Hoboken number (if available), attribution, and sources (catalogue references or locations of manuscript copies and autographs). Thematic incipits are given for items not listed by Hoboken. Where feasible, judgments are given on authenticity. Includes an index by composer, lists of sigla, and a bibliography.

* Pfannhauser, Karl. "Glossarien zu Haydns Kirchenmusik." In *Joseph Haydn Kongress* (item 76), pp. 496-501.

Cited as item 813.

518. Schenk, Erich. "Ist die Göttweiger Rorate-Messe ein Werk Joseph Haydns?" *Studien zur Musikwissenschaft* 24 (1960):87-105.

Recounts Landon's discovery (item 513) of a mass attributed to Haydn at Göttweig, but long known from other sources as a work by Georg Reutter. Disputes Landon's arguments for Haydn's authorship, pointing out that most of the numerous "copyist's errors" Landon cites in his edition (Haydn-Mozart Press, 1957) occur also in the Reutter sources, and represent practices found in his works. Questions Landon's claim that the opening notes of the Kyrie occur in varied form in the "Entwurf Katalog" and the Elssler "Haydn-Verzeichnis," arguing that an initial figure is insufficient to identify a work. Describes features of the mass that are typical of Reutter's style.

Oratorios

519. Feder, Georg. "Haydns Korrekturen zum Klavierauszug der 'Jahreszeiten'." In *Festschrift Georg von Dadelsen zum 60. Geburtstag,* edited by Thomas Kohlhase and Volker Scherliess, pp. 101-12. Neuhausen-Stuttgart: Hänssler, 1978.

Concerns a manuscript discovered in 1969 that transmits Haydn's revisions and corrections in the keyboard score prepared by A.E. Müller. Concludes from examination of corrections that they were not necessarily made with reference to the score, that ease of playing was an important criterion, that light textures were preferred, and that certain departures from the score were evidently motivated by aesthetic considerations.

520. Friedlaender, Max. "Van Swieten und das Textbuch zu Haydns 'Jahreszeiten'." *Jahrbuch der Musikbibliothek Peters* 16 (1909):47-56.

Recounts the discovery of van Swieten's autograph libretto, and describes the appearance of the source, with its emendations and marginal notes. Discusses the work by James Thomson on which the text was based, and examines the relationship between text and model. Indicates that through his marginal notes, van Swieten had more influence on Haydn's compositional process than previously suspected. Reproduces marginal notes from the autograph, and for each, describes how Haydn followed van Swieten's suggestions in realizing the music.

521. Geiringer, Karl. "Haydn's Sketches for 'The Creation'." *The Musical Quarterly* 18 (1932):299-308.

Proposes that the sketches reveal an "extraordinarily intense labor" behind the "spontaneous freedom of expression" that marks this work. Examines sketches for numbers 1, 16, 17, 19, and 29 to demonstrate how Haydn worked toward achieving "noble simplicity and tranquil grandeur." Offers general comments on Haydn's compositional procedures, which in later years allegedly involved greater amounts of revision and the use of preliminary sketches.

522. Sandberger, Adolf. "Zur Entstehungsgeschichte von Haydns 'Sieben Worte des Erlösers am Kreuze'." In Adolf Sandberger. *Ausgewählte Aufsätze zur Musikgeschichte,* 1:266-81. Munich: Drei Masken, 1921. Reprint. Hildesheim: Georg Olms, 1973. Previously published in *Jahrbuch der Musikbibliothek Peters* 10 (1903):45-59.

Reports on the discovery in Passau of the autograph for Joseph Friebert's vocal arrangement of Haydn's *Seven Last Words.* Indicates that Friebert based his arrangement on a manuscript copy of Haydn's original version, which contained bass recitatives that were omitted from Artaria's edition. Shows that Haydn borrowed heavily from the music and text of Friebert's arrangement in preparing part 1 of his own vocal setting. Includes a biographical sketch of Friebert.

* Schmid, Ernst Fritz. "Haydns Oratorium 'Il ritorno di Tobia', seine Entstehung und seine Schicksale." *Archiv für Musikwissenschaft* 16 (1959):292-313.

Cited as item 834.

523. Schünemann, Georg. "Ein Skizzenblatt Joseph Haydns." *Die Musik* 8/16 (1908-9):211-22.

Supposedly the first study of a Haydn sketch. Draws upon quotations from Griesinger and Dies to address the question of Haydn's compositional process, and compares Haydn's approach with Beethoven's. Transcribes two sheets of sketches for *The Seasons* and places the final version above the transcription.

524. Searle, Arthur. "Two Recent Manuscript Acquisitions. I: British Library: Mare Clausum." *The Haydn Yearbook* 15 (1984):219-20.

Reports on a copy, in score, of the Haydn oratorio fragment on loan from the Royal Philharmonic Society. Gives a history and description of the source, the earliest known copy of the music.

Theater Works

525. Badura-Skoda, Eva. "The Influence of the Viennese Popular Comedy on Haydn and Mozart." *Proceedings of the Royal Musical Association* 100 (1973-74):185-99.

Related in content to item 526 and derived from it in part. Sketches the history of the Viennese popular comedy and the critical roles played by Josef Stranitzky and Kurz-Bernardon. Discusses the manuscript "Teutsche Arien," a four-volume collection of 1,700 aria texts from 260 comedies (much of the music for the last volume is extant) and the "Teutsche Comedie Arien," a collection of 33 arias and ensemble pieces. With respect to Haydn, addresses the question of his authorship of this music, then discusses his association with Kurz-Bernardon and his first opera, the still problematic *Der krumme Teufel.* Observes that Haydn's interest in composing music for

Hanswurst continued into the 1770s, as evidenced by his *Die Feuersbrunst.*

526. ———. "'Teutsche Comoedie-Arien' und Joseph Haydn." In *Der junge Haydn* (item 81), pp. 59-72.

Describes the manuscript collection of "Teutsche Arien" texts (1737-58) in the Österreichische Nationalbibliothek, and traces the early history of the popular Viennese theater with which the songs in question were associated. Regarding pieces in the music collection "Teutsche Comedie-Arien," speculates on the possibility that some may have been composed by Haydn. While calling attention to melodic, rhythmic, and textural resemblances to contemporaneous instrumental works by the composer, offers no conclusive evidence for or against his authorship.

527. ———. "An Unknown Singspiel by Joseph Haydn?" In *International Musicological Society: Report of the Eleventh Congress, Copenhagen 1972,* edited by Henrik Glahn, Søren Sørensen, and Peter Ryom, 1:236-39. Copenhagen: Wilhelm Hansen, 1974.

Describes the discovery of a setting of *Die reisende Ceres,* with a text by Maurus Lindemayr, in the archives at the Benedictine abbey of Seitenstetten. While furnishing no evidence to support the ascription to Haydn which appears on the cover of the source, asserts that there can be little doubt of Haydn's authorship from the vantage point of musical style.

528. ———. "Zur Entstehung von Haydns Oper 'La vera costanza'." In *Joseph Haydn Kongress* (item 76), pp. 248-55.

Discusses circumstances surrounding the postponement and eventual staging of the work, and reviews accounts of its composition in Dies and Griesinger. Refers to a passage from Dies, cited by Hoboken as grounds for revising Pohl's chronology (Hoboken places it in 1777-78, after *Il mondo della luna* rather than before). Defending Hoboken's revised dating, disagrees with Landon's proposal that Haydn may have misremembered in his account to Dies. A shorter version published in *Österreichische Musikzeitschrift* 37 (1982):487-90 as "Zur Entstehungsgeschichte von Haydns Oper 'La vera costanza'."

529. ———. "Zur Salzburger Erstaufführung von Joseph

Haydns Singspiel 'Die reisende Ceres'." *Österreichische Musikzeitschrift* 32 (1977):317–24.

Provides biographical information on the librettist, speculates on the origins of the work, and proposes 1767 as a possible date of composition. Offers no new documentary evidence in support of the work's authenticity (see item 527).

530. Bartha, Dénes. "Haydn als Opernkapellmeister." In *Festschrift Heinrich Besseler zum sechzigsten Geburtstag,* edited by the Institut für Musikwissenschaft der Karl-Marx-Universität, pp. 361–65. Leipzig: VEB Deutscher Verlag für Musik, 1961.

Emphasizing the intensity of Haydn's operatic activities, furnishes a chronological overview of the Eszterháza opera repertory from 1776 through 1790.

531. ———. "Haydn als Opernkapellmeister: (Ein Forschungsbericht aus dem Material der gleichnamigen Monographie von Dénes Bartha und László Somfai, zur Herausgabe geplant Budapest 1960)." In *Bericht über die Internationale Konferenz zum Andenken Joseph Haydns* (item 70), pp. 17–23.

Discusses the previous neglect of Haydn's activity as opera kapellmeister, and explains how Haydn himself was in fact to blame. Describes the nature of materials examined in the preparation of item 535, and presents a chronological table of 92 operas premiered at Eszterháza from 1776 to 1790, as well as a list of 10 operas whose scores Haydn examined, presumably with an eye toward performance.

532. ———. "Haydn's Italian Opera Repertory at Eszterháza Palace." In *New Looks at Italian Opera: Essays in Honor of Donald J. Grout,* edited by William W. Austin, pp. 172–219. Ithaca: Cornell University Press, 1968.

Offers a revised chronology of first performances conducted by Haydn from 1776 to 1790, collating information in Harich (items 541, 542), Landon (item 544), Bartha and Somfai (item 535), Horányi (item 543), and Pohl (item 277). Includes remarks on sources, and for each item listed, refers the reader to relevant passages in the above studies. For each year, lists the number of premieres and the operatic genres represented. Furnishes information on operatic practices at the Esterházy court during Haydn's tenure (1761-90). Portrays Eszterháza as an important center for Italian opera, and discusses the relationship of its repertory to those of opera theaters in Vienna, Venice, and Naples.

533. ———. "Haydn, the Opera Conductor: An Account of the Newly Disclosed Sources in Budapest." *The Music Review* 24 (1963):313-21.

Reports on the author's effort, in collaboration with László Somfai, to make a thorough investigation of the Esterházy opera material, deposited during the Second World War at the Budapest National Archives and later incorporated in the Széchényi National Library. Accounts for 88 premieres and 5 newly rehearsed productions between 1776 and 1790, and provides a chronological list of opera premieres, based on a study of the sources. Discusses copyists, and calls attention to the wealth of directorial editing by Haydn. Categorizes different kinds of alteration made by the composer, and provides a list of 21 of his insertion arias.

534. ———. "The Unknown Haydn: Haydn as an Opera Conductor at Esterháza." *The New Hungarian Quarterly* 1/1 (1960):139-46.

Offers a description of material relevant to Haydn research at the Esterházy archives: autographs, documents, and musical sources for the opera collection, the latter having been neglected prior to the research conducted by Bartha and Somfai. Discusses Haydn's extensive work in revising scores for operas he conducted. Explains the process of organizing the sources and describes the methods employed, especially the study of authentic copyists. Provides statistics concerning opera performances, and gives a sampling of facts unearthed in the course of research. Includes three facsimiles from insertion arias by Haydn.

535. ———, and Somfai, László. *Haydn als Opernkapellmeister: Die Haydn-Dokumente der Esterházy Opernsammlung.* Budapest: Ungarische Akademie der Wissenschaften, 1960. 470 pp.

Recounts the authors' efforts to impose bibliographical control on the Esterházy opera collection in the Széchényi National Library in Budapest. Distinguishes three historical layers of archival materials: 1) Italian opera scores from 1711 to 1762; 2) performance materials employed in Eszterháza productions, 1776-90; 3) German-language operas from 1804 to 1812. Discusses Haydn's efforts as opera kapellmeister, and surveys documents pertaining to conditions under which he worked. Offers a chronicle of operatic activities, 1776-90, with information on works performed, singers, libretti, extant performance materials, letters, and other pertinent documents. Gives an alphabetically organized table of Eszterháza singers and instrumentalists, 1776-90. Other features include a chapter on copyists, with pages of their work in facsimile; information on paper and watermarks; catalogue of musical sources in the collection, ordered by date of first performance; and a catalogue of Haydn's insertion arias, 1776-90. Provides indexes of opera titles, roles, and aria text incipits.

536. Branscombe, Peter. "Hanswurst Redivivus: Haydn's Connexions with the 'Volkstheater' Tradition." In *Joseph Haydn Kongress* (item 76), pp. 369-75.

Reviews and supplements available information on Haydn's links with the popular theatrical tradition following the start of his Esterházy employment. Reexamines questions pertaining to the authenticity of *Die Feuersbrunst* and *Die reisende Ceres.* Hitherto unknown documentary material cited includes a quotation from an 1831 "Journal of a Nobleman," and an excerpt from John Moore's anonymously published "A View of Society and Manners in France, Switzerland, and Germany" (1779).

537. ———. "Music in the Viennese Popular Theatre of the Eighteenth and Nineteenth Centuries." *Proceedings of the Royal Musical Association* 98 (1971-72):101-12.

Traces the history of the popular theater and the roles played by Stranitzky, Prehauser, Kurz-Bernardon, La Roche, Schikaneder, and others in its development. Reports that composers of musical pieces for the earlier plays are largely unknown: Haydn's name is the only one that has surfaced (in connection with *Der neue krumme Teufel*) for any performance before 1769, the year in which a regular company was first established. Extant music from the early theater consists of 33 "Teutsche Comedie Arien," which bear stylistic resemblance to music in Haydn's marionette opera *Die Feuersbrunst* and may be by Haydn.

538. Brown, A. Peter. "Tommaso Traetta and the Genesis of a Haydn Aria (Hob. XXIVb:10)." *Chigiana* 36 (1979):101-42.

Begins with a general discussion of Haydn's sketches and compositional processes. Then examines in detail his replacement *scena* for Act 1 of Traetta's *Ifigenia in Tauride,* explaining its relationship to Traetta's original and to Haydn's own sketches. Offers a list of the musical documents, which are ample enough to "provide a complete history of the compositional process," and gives descriptions of the sketches and autographs as well as transcriptions of the sketches. Proposes reasons for Haydn's decision to replace Traetta's original *scena,* and describes differences in compositional approach between Haydn and Traetta.

539. Haas, Robert. "Die Musik in der Wiener deutschen Stegreifkomödie." *Studien zur Musikwissenschaft* 12 (1925):3-64.

A detailed exploration of intermezzo and improvised comedy in Vienna through the mid-eighteenth century. Surveys the activities of Josef Felix von Kurz (Bernardon), describes extant text sources, and examines the two "Teutsche Comedie Arien" music manuscript volumes in the Österreichische Nationalbibliothek. Ponders Haydn's acquaintance with Kurz and the extent of their collaboration. Discusses the lost *Der neue krumme Teufel* and speculates on Haydn's authorship of music in the "Teutsche Comedie Arien."

540. ———. "Teutsche Comedie Arien." *Zeitschrift für Musikwissenschaft* 3 (1920-21):405-15.

Identifies for the first time the contents of two manuscript volumes of "Teutsche Comedie Arien" at the Österreichische Nationalbibliothek as pieces performed in Kurz-Bernardon's comedies. Comparison of these pieces with a manuscript collection of "Teutsche Arien" texts at the library make it possible to identify (with a few exceptions) the comedies from which they derived. Provides a list of contents for "Teutsche Comedie Arien" and another for comedies represented by these arias. Suggests that Haydn is likely to have written the music, and presents (inconclusive) evidence to support this view. Includes a general description of the music, and reprints the texts for five arias omitted from the "Teutsche Arien" collection.

541. Harich, János. *Esterházy-Musikgeschichte im Spiegel der zeitgenössischen Textbücher: Festgabe anlässlich der 150. Wiederkehr des Todestages von Joseph Haydn.* Eisenstadt: Burgenländisches Landesarchiv, 1959. 92 pp.

A study of theatrical productions of the Esterházy court, based on detailed information from librettos once housed in the family library. Includes significant discussion of the Haydn years. Indexes the librettos by title, composer, librettist, and place of publication/publisher.

542. ———. "Das Repertoire des Opernkapellmeisters Joseph Haydn in Eszterháza (1780-1790)." *The Haydn Yearbook* 1 (1962):9-110.

Presents an annotated, chronological inventory of all operas performed, distinguishing between premieres and repeat performances. Provides a summary table for each year, and includes an appendix with a tabular chronology of performances, as well as various lists of operas and composers represented. Severely criticizing what he perceives as the shortcomings of *Haydn als Opernkapellmeister* by Bartha and Somfai (item 535), draws on documents from the Esterházy archives in providing corrections and substantial additions. Includes a summary in English.

543. Horányi, Mátyás. *The Magnificence of Eszterháza.* Translated by András Deák. London: Barrie and Rockliff, 1962. 260 pp.

A history of theater at the Esterházy court, based on scores, archival documents, and librettos. Concentrates heavily on the Haydn years, with discussion of theatrical life at Eisenstadt and Eszterháza, Eszterháza castle, the new theater and its stage at Eszterháza, the opera repertory of the new theater, and the decline of Eszterháza and return to Eisenstadt. Appendices include an inventory of 113 extant librettos (1715-1810) once owned by the Esterházy family, a list of operas performed at Eszterháza in 1778, and a list of the 82 lavish illustrations. Provides indices of names and theatrical works. Also published in German as *Das Esterhazysche Feenreich: Beitrag zur ungarländischen Theatergeschichte des 18. Jahrhunderts* (Budapest: Ungarische Akademie der Wissenschaften, 1959), a translation from the original Hungarian.

544. Landon, H.C. Robbins. "Haydn's Marionette Operas and the Repertoire of the Marionette Theatre at Esterház Castle." *The Haydn Yearbook* 1 (1962):111-97.

A study that purports to set aright the errors in names, dates, titles, and other data concerning the marionette operas. Provides a background study of the marionette theater at Eszterháza and of its highpoint (1776-77) under the direction of Pauersbach. Discussion of the operas themselves concentrates on early bibliographical sources, extant librettos, and extant music. A documented, chronological catalogue includes musical incipits for extant works; and for lost works, takes text incipits from librettos, if available.

545. ———. "Haydns Oper 'La fedeltà premiata': Eine neue authentische Quelle." In *Beiträge zur Musikdokumentation: Franz Grasberger zum 60. Geburtstag,* edited by Günter Brosche, pp. 213-32. Tutzing: Hans Schneider, 1975.

German version of item 547.

546. ———. "Das Marionettentheater auf Schloss Esterház." *Österreichische Musikzeitschrift* 26 (1971):272-80.

Translation of the first part of item 544.

547. ———. "A New Authentic Source for *La Fedeltà Premiata* by Haydn." *Soundings,* no. 2 (1971-72), pp. 6-17.

Announces the discovery of a source thought to be Haydn's conducting score for the revival of *La fedeltà premiata* in 1782, and describes circumstances at court that made a revision of the work necessary. Discusses extant sources and copyists' receipts for performances of the work at Eszterháza from 1781 to 1784, and shows why the newly found manuscript, which contains corrections in Haydn's hand, appears to be the composer's conducting score. Proposes that the scribe, identical to Anonymous 48, is none other than the young Johann Elssler.

548. LaRue, Jan. "A Haydn (?) Première at Yale." *The Music Review* 24 (1963):333-34.

Describes a production at Yale of the previously lost marionette opera *Die Feuersbrunst.* Endorsing neither

Landon's authentication nor Hoboken's skepticism, suggests that the work, discovered in a source at Yale, may be partly by Haydn.

549. Thomas, Günter. "Haydns deutsche Singspiele." *Haydn-Studien* 6/1 (1986):1-63.

A detailed, meticulously documented account of source problems and questions of authenticity involving singspiel-related music attributed to Haydn. Includes extensive treatment of *Der krumme Teufel,* performances associated with the Eszterháza marionette theater, and *Die Feuersbrunst.* Includes facsimiles of title pages from pertinent eighteenth-century librettos and programs.

550. ———. "Zur Frage der Fassungen in Haydns *Il mondo della luna.*" *Analecta Musicologica* 22/*Studien zur italienischen Musikgeschichte* 13 (1984):405-25.

Describes the surviving sources and discusses the multiple versions or variants that exist for most numbers. Provides a tabular summary of source information for the first 18 numbers, groups the different versions chronologically, and shows how paper studies confirm the proposed grouping. Examines three different versions, reproduced in facsimile, of a passage from Ecclitico's aria "Un poco di denaro," and comments on the abandonment of the original *colla voce* accompaniment. Cites an additional example to illustrate that the rejection of *colla voce* textures proves significant for the revision process in this opera.

551. ———. "Zwischen Notation und Interpretation: Einige Beobachtungen an Haydns 'Il mondo della luna'." In *Joseph Haydn Kongress* (item 76), pp. 352-59.

Asserts that despite the often-cited clarity and order in Haydn's autographs, much remains ambiguous. Demonstrates the point with examples drawn from *Il mondo della luna.*

552. Walter, Horst. "On the History of the Composition and the Performance of *La vera costanza.*" In *Haydn Studies* (item 73), pp. 154-57.

Adduces evidence to show that Haydn wrote *La vera costanza* for the Esterházy company in the second half of 1778, not for the Imperial court in 1776, as hitherto believed. Explains that a score in partial autograph, dated

1785, was a reconstruction for a revival in 1785-86, the original performance materials having been unavailable (there had been a fire at Eszterháza in 1779).

* Zeman, Herbert. "Das Theaterlied zur Zeit Joseph Haydns, seine theatralische Gestaltung und seine gattungsgeschichtliche Entwicklung." In *Joseph Haydn und die Literatur seiner Zeit* (item 79), pp. 35-59.

Cited as item 903.

Secular Vocal Works

553. Angermüller, Rudolph. "Neukomms schottische Liedbearbeitungen für Joseph Haydn." *Haydn-Studien* 3 (1973-74):151-53.

Describes Neukomm's neglected manuscript of 23 Scottish song arrangements he prepared for Haydn. Compares this source with Elssler's copy, and provides evidence to support Neukomm's authorship of the two additional songs that appear in the Elssler manuscript.

554. Becker-Glauch, Irmgard. "The Apparently Authentic Version of the *Motetto de Sancta Thecla* (Hob. XXIIIa:4)." In *Haydn Studies* (item 73), pp. 82-84.

Describes the text and manuscript parts in a source at Eisenstadt (St. Martin's cathedral) that bears Haydn's signature. Proposes that this secular cantata (it survives in sacred versions also) was composed for Prince Nikolaus' entry into Eisenstadt on 17 May 1762.

555. ———. "Haydns Schottische Liedbearbeitungen für Thomson." In *Joseph Haydn Kongress* (item 76), pp. 110-16.

Drawing on a substantial array of extant documents, places the groups of song-arrangements in proper chronological order within the years 1800-1801. Includes a chronologically organized table and two manuscript facsimiles.

556. ———. "Some Remarks about the Dating of Haydn's

Settings of Scottish Songs." In *Haydn Studies* (item 73), pp. 88-90.

Describes and illustrates an approach to the dating of Haydn's arrangements that involves evaluation of the musical sources (autograph fragments, engravers' copies) in conjunction with letters, payment receipts, and other documents.

557. Deutsch, Otto Erich. "Haydns Kanons." *Zeitschrift für Musikwissenschaft* 15 (1932-33):112-24, 172.

A discussion chiefly of the secular canons. Suggests that the Breitkopf & Härtel edition of 42 canons (1810), regarded as the first, may have been preceded by Gombert's print of 6 canons, probably taken from Johann Nepomuk Hummel's manuscript copy of 40 canons. Reports that for the Breitkopf & Härtel edition, Christian Schreiber altered or replaced many of the original texts. Includes a table of 44 secular canons, with variant numberings, title, original text incipit, number of voices, poet, indication of whether text changes were made, and location of autographs. Prints 2 unpublished canons preserved in the Breitkopf & Härtel archives.

558. Feder, Georg. "Zu Haydns Schottischen Liedern." *Haydn-Studien* 1 (1965-67):43.

Addresses the question of whether Haydn knew the Scottish folksong texts and whether he supplied figured basses for the songs. In this connection, describes a manuscript fragment for No. 32 ("Dainty Davie") of the edition of Scottish folksongs for the *Joseph Haydn Werke*, and reports that the fragment (bars 1-11) has neither text nor figured bass.

* Friedlaender, Max. *Das deutsche Lied im 18. Jahrhundert: Quellen und Studien.* Stuttgart: J.G. Cotta'schen Buchhandlung Nachfolger, 1902. Reprint. 3 parts in 2 vols. Hildesheim: Georg Olms, 1962. lviii, 384 pp./vii, 360 pp.; 630 pp.

Cited as item 909.

559. Geiringer, Karl. "Haydn and the Folksong of the British Isles." *The Musical Quarterly* 35 (1949):179-208. Reprinted as the introduction to item 19.

Examines Haydn's working relationship with Napier, Thomson, and Whyte, the publishers of his British folksongs. Discusses the early editions in relation to the manuscripts, usually copies, that Haydn sent them (most surviving manuscripts are for Thomson, the most important of the three). Analyzes the 365 folksong listings in the Haydn-Elssler catalogue (1805), and finds more than 80 to be missing. Of those listed, Nos. 201-365 have no titles, but the author supplies the correct titles and sources. There is also discussion of characteristics of the arrangements. Two pages of facsimiles from Thomson editions are included.

560. Helms, Marianne. "Zur Entstehung des zweiten Teils der 24 Deutschen Lieder." In *Joseph Haydn Kongress* (item 76), pp. 116-23.

Examines sources and documents pertaining to the history of the publication. Contrasts the relative homogeneity of the first part with the less coherent assemblage of material that constitutes the latter part.

561. Hoboken, Anthony van. "A Rare Contemporary Edition of Haydn's 'Hymn for the Emperor'." In *Studies in Eighteenth-Century Music: A Tribute to Karl Geiringer on His Seventieth Birthday,* edited by H.C. Robbins Landon and Roger E. Chapman, pp. 292-96. New York: Oxford University Press, 1970.

Discusses a rare English edition of Haydn's hymn published by Monzani and Cimador, with an English translation by Charles Burney. Compares it with the edition by Broderip and Wilkinson, noting differences in the readings of Burney's text and its underlay: the 10-line verses of the translation, 2 lines longer than those of the original, require musical repetition, which is handled differently in the 2 editions (see item 908).

562. Landon, H.C. Robbins. "Auf den Spuren Joseph Haydns." *Österreichische Musikzeitschrift* 31 (1976):579-81.

Reports on the discovery of a program--from Joseph Banks' collection at the British Museum--that contains the text of Haydn's lost aria for Giacomo David. Includes facsimiles of the ticket and program for the concert and a depiction of the Hanover Square Rooms, where the concert took place on 16 May 1791.

563. Mies, Paul. "Joseph Haydns 'Abschiedslied'--von Adalbert Gyrowetz." *The Haydn Yearbook* 2 (1963-64):88-89.

Reports on Alexander Weinmann's discovery that the lied is by Gyrowetz, and describes the sources in question. Calls attention to still-problematical issues concerning Haydn and the song.

564. Sandberger, Adolf. "Ein Lied-Autograf von Josef Haydn." *Zeitschrift für Musik* 109 (1942):535-38.

Reports on the autograph for Haydn's lied "Ein kleines Haus" in the Czartoryski collection of the state library in Crakow. Includes a facsimile, a translation of W. Hordynski's description in the newspaper *Polska Zachonia,* and an edited transcription in the *Notenbeilage,* No. 12.

565. Wirth, Helmut. "Ein unbekanntes Schriftstück von Johann Elssler aus dem Jahre 1811." *Haydn-Studien* 5 (1982-85):137-39.

Cites a document in which Elssler certifies that Haydn had claimed to him on numerous occasions that the 40 vocal canons were original. Provides a facsimile, and elaborates on the canons, on people named in the document, and on Elssler and his family.

Orchestral Works

566. Davis, Shelley. "Regarding the Authenticity of the 'Haydn' Keyboard Concerto Hob. XVIII:F3." In *Haydn Studies* (item 73), pp. 121-26.

Concerns two sources for F3 unknown to Hoboken: an edition of keyboard arrangements (Longman, Lukey, & Company), with an attribution to Johann Stamitz, and a manuscript at the Staatsbibliothek Preussischer Kulturbesitz, Berlin, with an attribution to Johann Georg Lang. Stylistic evaluation and assessment both of these sources and the Einsiedeln manuscript that bears Haydn's name lead the author to propose Lang as the probable composer.

567. Fisher, Stephen C. "A Group of Haydn Copies for the Court of Spain: Fresh Sources, Rediscovered Works, and New Riddles." *Haydn-Studien* 4 (1976-80):65-84.

Suggests the possibility that two orchestral pasticcios for Hob. Ia:1 and Ia:6 at the Library of Congress (Martorell Collection) are authentic. Reveals that on the basis of the scribes represented, the group of Haydn manuscripts in which the pasticcios occur may be traced to the Spanish court of Carlos III. Discusses evidence of Haydn's contact with the court. Includes two tables that list known Haydn sources (at the Library of Congress and Archivo del Palacio Real in Madrid) identified with the court.

568. Gerlach, Sonja. "Die chronologische Ordnung von Haydns Sinfonien zwischen 1774 und 1782." *Haydn-Studien* 2 (1969-70):34-66.

Identifying the time-span in question as a particularly nebulous period, examines the issue of chronology from different standpoints, both documentary and stylistic. Establishes correlations between scoring requirements of particular works and changes in the Esterházy orchestral personnel. Drawing on such criteria as order of movements, presence of a slow introduction, and formal characteristics of slow movements as confirming indications, assigns a *terminus ante quem, terminus post quem,* and probable date of composition for each work in question.

569. ———. "Drei Korrekturen im Autograph von Joseph Haydns Hornkonzert von 1762." In *Festschrift Rudolf Elvers zum 60. Geburtstag,* edited by Ernst Herttrich and Hans Schneider, pp. 207-12. Tutzing: Hans Schneider, 1985.

Examines three corrections made by Haydn in his 1762 horn concerto and determines what was accomplished musically by the changes.

570. ———. "Ein Fund zu Haydns verschollener Sinfonie." *Haydn-Studien* 3 (1973-74):44-46.

Reports on the discovery of the first movement to Hob. I:106, a previously lost work listed in the "Entwurf-Katalog" and thought to have been a symphony. Suggests a composition date of ca. 1770, and proposes that it represents the first of two movements for the lost overture to *Le pescatrici.*

571. Halm, Hans. "Eine unbekannte Handschrift der 'Kinder-Symphonie'." In *Anthony van Hoboken: Festschrift zum 75. Geburtstag,* edited by Joseph Schmidt-Görg, pp. 101-2. Mainz: B. Schott's Söhne, 1962.

Describes a copy of the *Toy* Symphony that belonged to Adolf Sandberger. It bears the attribution "Del Sigr Hayden" and appears to have originated ca. 1780. Of special interest for its detailed, and apparently unknown, performance directions, which the author includes.

572. Heussner, Horst. "Joseph Haydns Konzert (Hoboken XVIII:5): Marginalien zur Quellenüberlieferung." *Die Musikforschung* 22 (1969):478-80.

Arguing that it is difficult to distinguish unequivocally between Haydn concertos for organ on one hand and those for cembalo on the other, describes two manuscript sources for the work in question: one from the Hessen-Philippsthal-Barchfeld collection (on which the author's 1959 edition was based; see item 463), the other, a Brno source found by Landon (see item 470), who claimed this to have been a newly discovered organ concerto. Disputes the claim made by Feder in a previous article (item 455) that the Brno manuscript, with added wind parts, should be regarded as the better source.

573. Idaszak, Danuta. "Eine Haydn-Sinfonie in Gnesen?" *Die Musikforschung* 20 (1967):287-88.

Provides a detailed physical description of the manuscript of the Gniezno symphony that had been attributed to Haydn (see item 578). Expresses doubt about the possibility that it could be his work, and offers speculation on its origin and false ascription. Includes incipits for each movement.

574. Kinsky, Georg. "Eine frühe Partitur-Ausgabe von Symphonien Haydns, Mozarts und Beethovens." *Acta Musicologica* 13 (1941):78-84.

Reports on a rare subscription series: a set of symphonic scores published by Cianchettini and Sperati (London) between 1807 and 1809. Offers a description of the series and its contents, which include 18 works by Haydn (17 symphonies and the overture to *Armida*), 6 symphonies by Mozart, and 3 by Beethoven. The Haydn editions are all reprinted from Leduc, whereas those of Beethoven and Mozart (except for one) represent the earliest known published scores for the works in question.

575. Landon, H.C. Robbins. "The Original Versions of Haydn's First 'Salomon' Symphonies." *The Music Review* 15 (1954):1-32.

Offers an account of the authentic sources, including surviving autograph manuscripts, Elssler copies, and Artaria prints. Discusses their filiation and notes discrepancies in modern performing editions. Places much of the blame for early departures from authentic readings on the Breitkopf & Härtel scores (1806-8). Urging rectification of errors in performance, supplies a partial list of corrections. Includes the original trumpet and timpani parts for No. 98, and reproduces the original version of No. 94, second movement, bars 1-16, from Haydn's autograph.

* ———. *The Symphonies of Joseph Haydn.* London: Universal Edition & Rockliff, 1955. xvii, 863 pp. *Supplement.* London: Barrie and Rockliff, 1961. 64 pp.

Cited as item 964.

576. ———. "Two Orchestral Works Wrongly Attributed to

Mozart." *The Music Review* 17 (1956):29-34.

Deals with the general problem of misattribution and demonstrates the role of fortuitous discovery in determining the correct authorship of two misattributed works. One of them has direct bearing on Haydn: a *Schlittenfahrt* symphony--closely related to Leopold Mozart's--attributed to both Haydn and W.A. Mozart. The correct author was found to be Johann Georg Franz Wassmuth, for whom attributions survive in the Lambach catalogue and a source at Regensburg (Thurn und Taxis library). The symphony is also listed in Wassmuth's *Nachlassverzeichnis* as a work of 1753. It thus preceded Leopold Mozart's *Schlittenfahrt* (1755), for which it provided a model.

577. Larsen, Jens Peter. "Haydn's Early Symphonies: The Problem of Dating." In Jens Peter Larsen. *Handel, Haydn, and the Viennese Classical Style,* translations by Ulrich Krämer, pp. 159-70. Ann Arbor: UMI Research Press, 1988. Previously published in *Music in the Classic Period: Essays in Honor of Barry S. Brook,* edited by Allan W. Atlas, pp. 117-31. New York: Pendragon, 1985.

Surveys the recent history of research on the topic and distinguishes two points of view: 1) determine a date that can be definitely confirmed by a reliable source (often substantially later than the actual date of composition), and 2) rely on conjecture in order to arrive at a date as close as possible to the time of composition. Observing that Feder applies the first approach in dating early symphonies in *The New Grove Dictionary,* and that Landon espouses the latter view in the first volume of *Haydn: Chronicle and Works* (item 260), advocates an approach that combines both. Summarizes the current state of documentary and conjectural evidence, and divides the works in question into three groups: 1) pre-Esterházy symphonies, 2) chronologically fixed works of 1761-65, and 3) symphonies of 1765-72 listed in the "Entwurf-Katalog"; and cites *termini ante quem* for works whose chronological placement remains uncertain.

* ———. "Haydn und das 'kleine Quartbuch'." *Acta Musicologica* 7 (1935):111-23.

Cited as item 479.

578. LaRue, Jan. "The Gniezno Symphony not by Haydn." In

Festskrift Jens Peter Larsen, 14. VI. 1902-1972, edited by Nils Schiørring, Henrik Glahn, and Carsten E. Hatting, pp. 255-60. Copenhagen: Wilhelm Hansen, 1972.

Recounts the 1964 discovery of a manuscript copy of this F-major work in the cathedral archive of Gniezno, Poland, where it is ascribed to Haydn. Stressing the importance of style analysis as part of the basic scholarly apparatus for identification and authentication, compares the work's regular, predominantly four-bar phrasing with the far more varied phrasing seen in a sampling of Haydn symphonies; also compares the extent of exact or varied repetition with that found in authentic Haydn. Shows with the aid of the Union Thematic Catalogue locator (see item 44) that the composer is identified as Ernst Graf in the Breitkopf supplement for 1768. Reports that it was printed by Hummel, and that a copy of the print survives in Regensburg.

579. ———. "A New Figure in the Haydn Masquerade." *Music and Letters* 40 (1959):132-39.

Identifies the true composer of an E-flat symphony attributed to Haydn in a source at the Thurn und Taxis library, Regensburg: Baron Theodor von Schacht, whose autograph score also survives at Regensburg. Discusses the controversy between Sandberger and Larsen over Haydn's authorship of the work. Provides a brief biographical sketch of Schacht and a survey of his musical output. Concludes with a description of the "has-been Haydn" symphony.

580. ———. "Three Notes of Non-Authenticity." *Haydn-Studien* 2 (1969-70):69-70.

Reports findings in the Union Thematic Catalogue that further support classification as spurious for three works attributed to Haydn in one or more sources: Hob. I:D23, also attributed to Nasolini; Hob. I:D27, to Hoffmann; and Hob. XVIII:F3 to Lang.

581. Matthäus, Wolfgang. "Die Frühdrucke der Londoner Sinfonien Joseph Haydns: Ein Versuch der Darstellung ihrer Zusammenhänge." *Archiv für Musikwissenschaft* 21 (1964):243-52.

Detailed filiation for early editions of the London symphonies (orchestral originals and arrangements). Considers such issues as precedence, shared rights, and the question of Salomon's involvement with various editions. Summarizes findings with the aid of filiation schemes for each group of six symphonies. Places heavy reliance on datings, and for the first time, draws on entries in the *Frankfurter priviligiertes Staats-Ristretto* as an aid to dating the prints.

582. ———, and Unverricht, Hubert. "Zur Abhängigkeit der Frühdrucke von Joseph Haydns Londoner Sinfonien." *Archiv für Musikwissenschaft* 24 (1967):145-48.

Summarizes the results of a discussion between Matthäus and Unverricht concerning issues raised in items 581 and 591.

583. Nowak, Leopold. "Das Autograph von Joseph Haydns Cello-Konzert in D-dur, op. 101." *Österreichische Musikzeitschrift* 9 (1954):274-79. Also published in *Biblios: Österreichische Zeitschrift für Buch- und Bibliothekswesen, Dokumentation, Bibliographie und Bibliophilie* 3/3 (1954):80-86 as "Ein Haydn-Autograph und sein Schicksal: Das Cello-Konzert in D-dur op. 101."

Concerns the perpetuation of an erroneous 1835 attribution to Anton Kraft and the discovery of the Haydn autograph, which resolved the issue of authenticity. Provides a description of the source and facsimiles of two sample pages.

584. ———. "Die Skizzen zum Finale der Es-Dur-Symphonie GA 99 von Joseph Haydn." *Haydn-Studien* 2 (1969-70):137-66.

Subjects the four-page manuscript, housed in the Österreichische Nationalbibliothek, to critical examination. Observing that Haydn worked out different thematic portions separately, connecting them through a system of 30 numbers to indicate their proper sequence, traces a path in the progress of composition that involved two versions, the second of which formed the basis for the autograph score, with still more changes. An appendix attempts a reconstruction of the first version, as represented in the sketches. Includes a facsimile reproduction of the source.

585. Nys, Carl de. "A propos du concerto pour deux cors et orchestre en mi bémol majeur." In *Bericht über die*

Internationale Konferenz zum Andenken Joseph Haydns (item 70), pp. 103-8.

Proposes that a work found in the Oettingen-Wallerstein collection at Harburg represents Haydn's lost Concerto in E flat for Two Horns, Hob. VIId:2, listed in Elssler's "Haydn-Verzeichnis" (1805). Offers hypotheses to explain why the opening theme differs from that of the "Verzeichnis," and points to the close ties between Haydn and the Oettingen-Wallerstein court that account for the heavy representation of Haydn's music in the collection.

* Sandberger, Adolf. "Zu den unbekannten Sinfonien von Joseph Haydn." *Neues Beethoven-Jahrbuch* 7 (1937):5-16.

Cited as item 494.

586. Schmid, Ernst Fritz. "Leopold Mozart und die Kindersinfonie." *Mozart-Jahrbuch* (1951), pp. 69-86.

Discusses publications and early performances of the *Toy* Symphony under Joseph Haydn's name. The work is also known as *Sinfonia Bertholgadensis,* apparently a reference to the Berchtesgaden toy industry, which made children's instruments of the type used in the symphony. Ludwig Schiedermair proposed that the work was by a Salzburg musician, either Leopold Mozart or Michael Haydn. Attributions exist for both composers, and the sources are discussed; but Leopold is considered to be the likely author for several reasons: he probably had official contact with Berchtesgaden, we know from a letter by Wolfgang that toy instruments were played at home, a pupil of Leopold's wrote pieces for these instruments, and Leopold had a proclivity for jesting with instruments. An addendum to this article in *Mozart-Jahrbuch* (1951), pp. 117-18 ("Nochmals zur 'Kindersinfonie'") reports on Landon's finding of a copy of the *Toy* Symphony at Stams monastery with an attribution to P. Edmund Angerer, a Benedictine monk at Fiecht.

587. Searle, Arthur. "The Royal Philharmonic Society Scores of Haydn's 'London' Symphonies." *The Haydn Yearbook* 14 (1983):173-86.

Concerns a set of scores willed to William Ayrton by Johann Peter Salomon and sold to the Philharmonic Society in 1847. Those for Symphonies Nos. 95 and 96 are autographs; the remainder were prepared by two English copyists. Both autographs and copies include corrections made in a fourth hand, the role and identity of which are seen as problematic. The article contains five facsimiles: Ayrton's receipt from the sale, two pages in the hand of the first copyist (Symphony No. 97), and two pages in the hand of the second copyist (Symphony No. 103).

588. Sehnal, Jiří. "Das Musikinventar des Olmützer Bischofs Leopold Egk aus dem Jahre 1760 als Quelle vorklassischer Instrumentalmusik." *Archiv für Musikwissenschaft* 29 (1972):285-317.

A study of Egk's musical establishment and his inventory, which provides the earliest known dating for Haydn's first symphony (it was among the sources purchased on 15 November 1759).

589. Thomas, Günter. "'Gioco filarmonico'--Würfelmusik und Joseph Haydn." In *Musicae Scientiae Collectanea: Festschrift Karl Gustav Fellerer zum siebzigsten Geburtstag am 7. Juli 1972,* edited by Heinrich Hüschen, pp. 598-603. Cologne: Arno-Volk-Verlag, 1973.

Discloses Maximilian Stadler as composer of the "Gioco filarmonico," a musical dice game attributed to Haydn in a print by Marescalchi of Naples. Reports that a 1781 Artaria print assigns the piece to Stadler, who names it in his manuscript autobiography, where the game is listed among works composed between 1759 and 1763.

590. Unverricht, Hubert. "Die Simrock-Drucke von Haydns Londoner Sinfonien." *Studien zur Musikgeschichte des Rheinlandes* 2 [*Karl Gustav Fellerer zum 60. Geburtstag*] (1962):235-59.

Discusses Simrock's connection with Haydn and Salomon, and his dealings with Salomon over publication rights for the 12 London symphonies. Provides a detailed account of circumstances surrounding Simrock's publication of the orchestral parts and of Salomon's trio and quintet arrangements. Includes extensive quotation from Simrock's correspondence.

591. ———. "Zur Frage nach den Frühdrucken von Joseph Haydns Londoner Sinfonien." *Archiv für Musikwissenschaft* 23 (1966):61-70.

Takes issue with a number of conclusions drawn by Matthäus in item 581. While crediting Matthäus with the first use of the *Frankfurter priviligiertes Staats-Ristretto* as a dating tool, objects that he relied almost exclusively on it, while ignoring earlier literature on the London symphonies and failing to undertake comparative source studies.

592. Weinmann, Alexander. "Bericht über einen Fund." *Haydn-Studien* 1 (1965-67):201-2.

Reports on the rediscovery of Haydn's Concertino Hob. XVIII:10 in a copy formerly housed at the Gesellschaft der Musikfreunde.

Chamber Music for Strings

593. Bloxam, M. Jennifer. "A Sketch for the Andante Grazioso of Haydn's String Quartet 'Opus 103'." *The Haydn Yearbook* 14 (1983):129-43.

Concerns a previously unknown, three-page sketch for the quartet fragment housed in the Yale Music Library. Relates the sketch to two previously known autographs for Opus 103: a score of both the *Andante grazioso* and minuet movements, preserved in a photograph at the Österreichische Nationalbibliothek, Vienna; and a draft for the minuet at the Sächsische Landesbibliothek, Dresden (the New Haven sketch is identified as a continuation of this Dresden source). Analytical discussion includes comparison of contrasting procedures followed by Haydn in sketching the two movements, a description of the function and contents of the New Haven sketch, and speculation on the chronology of Op. 103. Gives a facsimile and transcription of one page of the new source.

594. Brantley, Daniel L. "Disputed Authorship of Musical Works: A Quantitative Approach to the Attribution of the Quartets Published as Haydn's Op. 3." Ph.D. dissertation, University of Iowa, 1977. v, 92 pp.

Uses the spurious Op. 3 quartets as the subject of an experiment in computer-assisted discriminant analysis. Supplies background on Op. 3, with references to the pertinent scholarly literature, and discusses previous applications of statistical methods, notably in English literature, to the study of attribution based on style. Specifies as his central purpose the development of computer-oriented methods to address problems of double attribution, and explains his tools and procedures: employment of the DARMS encoding system and the application of software designed in SNOBOL4 and FORTRAN IV. Supplies detailed tables reporting the results of his automated analyses, which affirm the attribution of the quartets to Hoffstetter.

595. Brook, Barry S. "Determining Authenticity through Internal Analysis: A Multifaceted Approach (with Special Reference to Haydn's String Trios)." In *Joseph Haydn Kongress* (item 76), pp. 551-66.

Proposes that in the absence of conclusive documentary evidence, determination of authenticity requires an examination of stylistic traits that draws on a broad comparative base and applies rigorous statistical methods. Summarizing procedures employed to determine which of the doubtful string trios may be authentic, concludes that Hob. V:C2 is not by Haydn. Includes appendices that identify the multiplicity of facets examined individually by graduate students participating in the project.

596. ———. "Haydn's String Trios: A Misunderstood Genre." *Current Musicology,* no. 36 (1983), pp. 61-77.

Describes procedures followed in a City University of New York graduate seminar on authentication of trios ascribed to Haydn. After evaluation of external evidence, internal study involved comparison of characteristics seen in the 18 authentic trios and a representative group of 30 trios by Haydn contemporaries. Traits present in or absent from these groups were then applied as criteria for measuring 30 doubtful works. Concludes that 11 or 12 of the doubtful trios will prove to be authentic. Emphasizes the importance of the genre as a factor in the musical life of the age. Describes the trios as an area requiring further investigation, and tentatively proposes relatively late datings (ca. 1755-65) on stylistic grounds.

597. Eckhoff, Øivind. "The Enigma of 'Haydn's Op. 3'." *Studia Musicologica Norvegica* 4 (1978):9-45.

Expresses astonishment that the set had been attributed to Haydn for so long, and that scholars had even recently passed favorable judgment on the works. Proposes that while five of the six betray consistencies that support Hoffstetter's authorship, No. 5 must be by a different, much better composer: someone influenced by Haydn but not Haydn himself. Subjects the others to stylistic analysis of harmony, melody, phrasing, tonal organization, form, and texture, and finds crudities that prohibit Haydn's authorship: limited invention, inferior workmanship, lack of variety, and the failure of individual movements to cohere as a cycle. Finds traces of possible Haydn influence by comparing No. 3, first movement, with Haydn's Op. 9 No. 6, first movement.

598. Feder, Georg. "Apokryphe 'Haydn'-Streichquartette." *Haydn-Studien* 3 (1973-74):125-50.

Originally prepared for the Appendix to the critical commentary for series 12, volume 1 of the *Joseph Haydn Werke* (early string quartets). Contributes further unauthentic string quartets to those listed by Hoboken: nearly 100 works in all. Provides a catalogue, arranged by key. Includes a detailed overview of sources for the unauthentic Op. 3 quartets, beginning with the 1777 Bailleux print.

599. ———. "Aus Roman Hoffstetters Briefen." *Haydn-Studien* 1 (1965-67):198-201.

Presents several quotations from Hoffstetter's letters pertinent to Haydn. Proposes that his acknowledgment of Haydn's influence--and the improbability that he ever saw the editions of the Op. 3 string quartets with their attribution to Haydn--help to support Hoffstetter's probable authorship of the set.

600. ———. "Haydn's Corrections in the Autographs of the Quartets Opus 64 and Opus 71/74." In *The String Quartets of Haydn, Mozart, and Beethoven: Studies of the Autograph Manuscripts. A Conference at Isham Memorial Library, March 15-17, 1979,* edited by Christoph Wolff, pp. 99-110. Cambridge: Harvard University Press, 1980.

Reports that for the corrections in question (written over the original or placed at the bottom, in the margins, or on a separate sheet), original readings can usually be deciphered. Specifies different kinds of correction: minor lapses subjected to immediate correction, instances of substantial alteration before continuing, and changes evidently made after a manuscript was completed. Observing that orthographic and grammatical corrections are easiest to explain, proposes a critical interpretation for each correction cited. Makes note of evident compositional improvements, involving change from the more to the less predictable, as well as instances of self-restriction whereby an idea was replaced by something more normal or conventional.

601. Gerlach, Sonja. "The Reconstructed Original Version of Haydn's Baryton Trio Hob. XI:2." In *Haydn Studies* (item 73), pp. 84-87.

Proposes that Hob. XI:2 (A major) was based on another trio in A from which Hob. XI:2bis, a cello trio in G, also derived. Supports the thesis of an A-major original by pointing to Daube's printing (1770) of the variation movement from No. 2bis in A major (it contains one more variation than No. 2) and by drawing a connection with other early baryton trios that likewise survive in versions for cello (in G major) and, as with No. 2bis, for flute (in D major). Provides a tabular summary of relationships among the different versions of Nos. 2 and 2bis.

602. Kartomi, Margaret J. "Haydn Autograph Manuscripts Verified in Melbourne: String Quartets Opus 50 Nos. 3-6, of 1787." *Musicology* 7 (1982):139.

Reports on Georg Feder's verification of these autographs, long believed lost, and sketches a brief history of their ownership.

603. Landon, H.C. Robbins. "On Haydn's Quartets of *Opera 1* and *2:* Notes and Comments on Sondheimer's *Historical and Psychological Study.*" *The Music Review* 13 (1952):181-86.

Identifying Sondheimer's as the first book in English dealing exclusively with the music of Haydn (item 1035), declines to take issue with the substance of the study but instead provides amplification on the nature, chronology, and early publication history of the works in question. Points out Sondheimer's mistaken inclusion of Op. 1 No. 5 and Op. 2 Nos. 3 and 5 as true quartets, and corrects his erroneous assumption that entries in Haydn's "Entwurf-Katalog" fall in chronological order of composition.

604. Marrocco, W. Thomas. "The String Quartet Attributed to Benjamin Franklin." *Proceedings of the American Philosophical Society* 116 (1972):477-85.

Examines sources of the work (including one bearing an attribution to Haydn); suggests that the probable composer is Ferandini; and gives an English translation of the scathing review the piece received in the *Allgemeine Literatur Zeitung* (1799). Includes numerous facsimiles of pages from manuscript and printed sources.

605. "Problems of Authenticity--'Opus 3'." In *Haydn Studies* (item 73), pp. 95-106.

Examines documentary and stylistic evidence for the authorship of Op. 3 in contributions by Alan Tyson, Hubert Unverricht, James Webster, Jan LaRue, Ludwig Finscher, and Reginald Barrett-Ayres. Describes curious aspects of the only surviving primary source: a 1777 print by Bailleux, which ascribes the set to Haydn but which originally attributed two of the quartets to Hoffstetter. Establishes documentary criteria that would have to be met for confirmation of Hoffstetter as the composer, and presents both detailed and generalized stylistic assessments that appear to argue against Haydn's authorship. Concludes that the quartets are probably not authentic Haydn works and that the question of Hoffstetter's authorship requires further research.

606. Somfai, László. "'Ich war nie ein Geschwindschreiber ...': Joseph Haydns Skizzen zum langsamen Satz des Streichquartetts Hoboken III:33." In *Festskrift Jens Peter Larsen, 14. VI. 1902-1972,* edited by Nils Schiørring, Henrik Glahn, and Carsten E. Hatting, pp. 275-84. Copenhagen: Wilhelm Hansen, 1972.

Provides a facsimile and transcription of the sketches in question. Examines Dies' and Griesinger's descriptions of a two-step compositional process that involved an initial, spontaneous setting forth of an idea, followed by a phase of reflection, modification, and correction. Studies the sequence in which notes were entered on the page, and ponders questions of compositional process as reflected in the appearance of the sketches.

607. ———. "An Introduction to the Study of Haydn's Quartet Autographs (with Special Attention to Opus 77/G)." In

The String Quartets of Haydn, Mozart and Beethoven: Studies of the Autograph Manuscripts. A Conference at Isham Memorial Library, March 15-17, 1979, edited by Christoph Wolff, pp. 5-51. Cambridge: Harvard University Press, 1980.

Areas of inquiry addressed include the question of order of composition within a given opus, style of notation, paper, and compositional process as reflected in the sources. Citing the absence of a full chain of sources (including proofs with the composer's corrections) for any opus, cautions against overestimating the authority of the extant autographs. Includes numerous facsimiles.

608. ———. "Zur Echtheitsfrage des Haydn'schen 'Opus 3'." *The Haydn Yearbook* 3 (1965):153-65.

Presents documentary and stylistic evidence that undermines the authenticity of Op. 3. With regard to documentation, shows among other things that Bailleux, publisher of the set, had had no contact with Haydn and had published known spurious works under Haydn's name; that while the authenticity of Pleyel's edition and thematic catalogue of Haydn's quartets was supposedly confirmed by Haydn, Pleyel's publication apparently made no use of autographs or authentic copies; and that the listing of the set in Elssler's "Haydn-Verzeichnis" was based on Pleyel. With regard to style, concludes that the works are uncharacteristic of Haydn, as determined from the number and succession of movements, the tonality of the slow movements, character of the movements, and the instrumental layout. Contains a summary in English.

609. Tyson, Alan, and Landon, H.C. Robbins. "Who Composed Haydn's Op. 3?" *The Musical Times* 105 (1964):506-7.

Reviews the deficient evidence supporting Haydn's authorship of the Op. 3 quartets, and offers new information to cast doubt on their authenticity. Shows that Bailleux's edition of 1777, the earliest print of the set, contains two quartets in which an attribution to Hoffstetter was deleted and overprinted. Suggests that all six quartets could have originated with Hoffstetter, noting that a number of his works had been misattributed to Haydn.

* Unverricht, Hubert. *Geschichte des Streichtrios.* Tutzing: Hans Schneider, 1969. 363 pp.

Cited as item 1041.

610. ———. "Haydn and Franklin: The Quartet with Open Strings and Scordatura." In *Haydn Studies* (item 73), pp. 147-54.

Deals with the confusion surrounding two related, curious quartets, one attributed to Haydn in a Zittau manuscript, the other to Benjamin Franklin in a manuscript at the Bibliothèque nationale in Paris. Lists these and five additional sources: three anonymous, the others with attributions to Ferandini and Pleyel. Also mentions a reference in Kunzen and Reichardt's *Studien für Tonkünstler und Musikfreunde* (1792) to two quartets of this type published under obvious pseudonyms (Martinez and Roller). Gives a filiation of the sources, with the Martinez and Roller prints as hypothetical originals, and indicates variants in tuning and combination of movements. Proposes that the works were composed ca. 1790 by a minor South German composer.

611. ———. "Zur Chronologie der Barytontrios von Joseph Haydn." In *Symbolae Historiae Musicae: Hellmut Federhofer zum 60. Geburtstag,* edited by Friedrich Wilhelm Riedel and Hubert Unverricht, pp. 180-89. Mainz: B. Schott's Söhne, 1971.

Examines the chronology of the baryton trios, taking into account information that had recently appeared in *Joseph Haydn Werke* XIV/5, *Kritischer Bericht.* Includes the texts of letters, bills, and other documents that enable the author to trace the progress of Haydn's output from September/October (?) 1765 to March/April 1774. Shows that the first 100 were composed in quick succession, in groups of a dozen or half dozen, from 1765 to December 1771, while the remainder came in smaller groups with longer spans of time intervening. Considers the numbering of the trios in the "Entwurf-Katalog" and Elssler "Haydn-Verzeichnis." Tables summarize the dates of origin for numbers 101-14 in the "Entwurf-Katalog" and the chronology of trios 97-126 plus several works listed as doubtful by Hoboken.

612. ———, in collaboration with Gottron, Adam, and Tyson, Alan. *Die beiden Hoffstetter: Zwei Komponisten-Porträts mit Werkverzeichnissen.* Mainz: B. Schott's Söhne, 1968. 80 pp.

Provides a comprehensive overview of the documentary and stylistic grounds for questioning Haydn's authorship of the Op. 3 quartets and supporting Roman Hoffstetter's. Examines 14 quartets from the years 1765 to 1780 securely attributable to Hoffstetter, and reproduces a series of letters from Hoffstetter to Silverstolpe (1800-1802). Observing that the Bailleux print gave "Hoffstetter" without supplying a first name, entertains the idea that the composer might not have been Roman but the obscure dilettante Johann Urban Alois, possibly a twin brother, whose few surviving compositions reveal a talent inferior to Roman's. Furnishes thematic catalogues of works by both Hoffstetters.

* Webster, James. "The Bass Part in Haydn's Early String Quartets and in Austrian Chamber Music, 1750-1780." Ph.D. dissertation, Princeton University, 1974. xii, 429 pp.

Cited as item 1153.

613. ———. "The Chronology of Haydn's String Quartets." *The Musical Quarterly* 61 (1975):17-46.

Undertakes to date each set of quartets as precisely as possible on the basis of dated autographs (Op. 17, 20, 64, 71/74, and 77), letters, catalogue entries, and other contemporary documents. Points out that Haydn tended to compose quartets in isolated periods of intense activity: 10 works in the late 1750s; the sets from ca. 1770-72; the Op. 33 quartets of 1781; then the more continuous stream beginning with Op. 50 in 1787. Proposes that whereas each of the earlier groups featured different solutions to stylistic problems encountered, not until Op. 50 were all the features associated with mature Classical quartet style finally brought together. Furnishes a chronology of the 68 authentic quartets and a table that lists authentic sources for each.

Solo Keyboard Music and Chamber Music with Keyboard

614. Benton, Rita. "A Resumé of the Haydn-Pleyel 'Trio Controversy' with Some Added Contributions." *Haydn-Studien* 4 (1976-80):114-17.

Brings to light further sources with attributions to Pleyel for two disputed "Haydn" trios, the first two works of Hob. XV:3-5 (in C and F major, respectively; see items 634 and 638). To reinforce the attribution to Pleyel, reports that a symphony of his in F (Benton 136) has a second movement in which the first eight bars are identical thematically to those of the F-major trio, second movement. Observes that Pleyel is known to have re-used material in this manner.

615. Biba, Otto. "Two Recent Manuscript Acquisitions. II: Gesellschaft der Musikfreunde: *F-moll Variationen.*" *The Haydn Yearbook* 15 (1984):220-22.

Reports on the 1983 acquisition of a manuscript of the variations in Johann Elssler's hand, with Haydn's autograph signature on the title page. Includes discussion of the source and photographic reproductions of the Portal & Bridges watermarks.

616. Boer, Bertil H. van, Jr. "The Sonatina with Twelve Variations by J. Haydn (sic)." *Haydn-Studien* 5 (1982-85): 139-41.

Identifies the composer of the sonatina as Joseph Martin Kraus on the basis of Swedish sources: two authentic manuscript copies, transcribed by Wikmanson (a friend and student) and Silverstolpe (Kraus' first biographer), and an edition published in the magazine *Musikaliskt Tidsfördrif* (a facsimile of the first page is included). The attribution to Haydn occurs in a print by Goulding, Phipps, D'Almaine & Co.

617. Brown, A. Peter. "A Country Dance by Haydn." *The Musical Times* 127 (1986):17-18.

Reports on the discovery of a Gow print containing a keyboard piece previously unknown in the Haydn literature: *Haydn's Strathspey.* Proposes that this 16-bar piece, reproduced in the article, may be one of the lost country dances. Gives evidence supporting Haydn's authorship.

618. ———. "Haydn and the Gows." *The Musical Times* 129 (1988):459-60.

Updates information in item 617 with the discovery of a later Gow edition, "corrected and improved," which attributes the strathspey to "Mr. McIntyre," presumably Duncan McIntyre, the musician and dancing master. Also discusses a piece in this edition called "The Pic Nic," which contains material attributed to Nathaniel Gow, Giornovichi, and Haydn.

619. ———. "Haydn's Keyboard Idiom and the Raigern Sonatas." In *Haydn Studies* (item 73), pp. 111-15.

Examines the "control of thrust" in these sonatas by comparing their rhythmic interactions, weight of articulation, and phrase structure with those of selected authentic works. Discovers points of similarity as well as difference, but concludes that the Raigern sonatas "do not convincingly exemplify either his [Haydn's] keyboard style or his high level of craftsmanship."

* ———. *Joseph Haydn's Keyboard Music: Sources and Style.* Bloomington: Indiana University Press, 1986. xxiv, 450 pp.

Cited as item 1054.

620. ———. "Problems of Authenticity in Two Haydn Keyboard Works (Hoboken XVI:47 and XIV:7)." *Journal of the American Musicological Society* 25 (1972):85-97.

For Hob. XVI:47, describes four significantly different versions, none of which is known to be authentic. Drawing on external evidence and information on Haydn's cyclic construction, concludes that the configuration of movements in a source at the Gesellschaft der Musikfreunde appears most likely: it conforms in succession of movements to a number of works in Hoboken's groups XI, X, and V; and its three movements, unlike the other versions, contain similar thematic material. But this version is likely to have been transposed to E from an original in F. For Hob. XIV:7, describes a version for keyboard alone and one for keyboard, two violins, and cello. On stylistic grounds, suggests that the accompanying string parts probably did not originate with Haydn.

* ———. "The Solo and Ensemble Keyboard Sonatas of Joseph Haydn: A Study of Structure and Style." 3 vols. Ph.D. dissertation, Northwestern University, 1970. viii, 259 pp.; 172 pp.; unpublished scores.

Cited as item 1055.

621. Eibner, Franz. "Die authentische Klavierfassung von Haydns Variationen über das 'Gott erhalte'." *The Haydn Yearbook* 7 (1970):281-306.

Discusses circumstances surrounding the neglect of this hitherto unnoticed piece. Shows that while an autograph survives, Artaria took no steps to confirm Haydn's authorship: the first edition (1799) failed to name Haydn as the arranger, its reading differed in details from the autograph, and it replaced the keyboard arrangement of the theme with the keyboard setting of the song; in a reissue, with a new title page, the publisher named Gelinek as the arranger. Entries in Artaria's title inventory and publishers' catalogues merely confuse the issue, while mention in an authors list of a "fair copy by [or from] Haydn" effectively eliminates Gelinek as the arranger. Advances hypotheses to explain the attribution of this authentic Haydn piece to Gelinek. Supplies facsimiles of the first page of the autograph, the two Artaria title pages, and a summary in English.

622. Feder, Georg. "Haydns frühe Klaviertrios: Eine Untersuchung zur Echtheit und Chronologie." *Haydn-Studien* 2 (1969-70):289-316.

Applying stylistic criteria as well as available documentary evidence, designates the following as authentic: Hoboken XV:1, 2, 34-38, 40, 41, C1, f1, as well as the lost 33 and (possibly) the lost D1. In proposing a chronology, explains the necessity of relying heavily on idiosyncrasies of notation in extant manuscripts, as well as on stylistic criteria. Observes that the works contain significant expressive content, anticipating the composer's later "Romantic crisis." Makes special note of the wide range of keys employed (extending from F minor to E), in contrast to the narrow spectrum found in the early solo keyboard sonatas. Proposes that the early trios represent the composer's most important examples of keyboard music up to ca. 1760. Notes that Haydn's contributions reflect the late eighteenth-century vicissitudes of the genre: waning interest in the course of the 1760s and 70s, followed by reemergence in the 80s.

623. ———. "Eine Haydn-Skizze in Ostiglia." *Analecta Musicologica* 12/*Studien zur italienisch-deutschen Musikgeschichte* 8 (1973):224-26.

Reports on a sketch housed at the Biblioteca musicale Greggiati in Ostiglia, and includes a source description by Claudio Sartori as well as a facsimile and transcription. Shows why the sketch represents a solo keyboard work, probably the first movement of a sonata, and suggests, among other possibilities, that it may have been intended for a sonata in a Breitkopf & Härtel edition announced in 1789 but never published. Determines that the sketch is likely to have originated before 1800.

624. ———. "Haydn's Piano Trios and Piano Sonatas." In *Haydnfest* (item 71), pp. 18-23.

Probes the two categories of keyboard composition most notable in terms of number and quality. For the trios, defines two main groups: early works (written before and ca. 1760), for which authentication is problematic, and 29 mature works, comprising those written at Eszterháza (1784-90) and commissioned by publishers, and those from London (1794-95), dedicated to individuals. Also addresses matters of instrumentation, texture, and cyclic structure. Treats the sonatas in similar fashion, discussing authentication in the early works, publishers or individuals for whom subsequent works were written, and stylistic issues. Includes facsimiles from the "Entwurf-Katalog" and printed editions.

625. ———. "Probleme einer Neuordnung der Klaviersonaten Haydns." In *Festschrift Friedrich Blume zum 70. Geburtstag,* edited by Anna Amalie Abert and Wilhelm Pfannkuch, pp. 92-103. Kassel: Bärenreiter, 1963.

Modifies the listing of piano sonatas in Hoboken's catalogue (item 28), Group XVI. Adds divertimentos with piano and piano trios, drawn from Groups XIV and XV, that survive in authentic versions for piano; several piano pieces in Hoboken's Groups XVII and XVIIa; and sonatas attributed to Haydn that do not appear in Hoboken. Omits works not properly designated as piano sonatas. Within the newly constituted list, regards 58 pieces as authentic and an additional 7 as authentic with reservations. Provides information on dating, and divides the authentic works into three chronological groups.

626. ———. "The Sources of the Two Disputed Raigern Sonatas." In *Haydn Studies* (item 73), pp. 107-11.

Manuscripts in question include a copy by Rutka that

attributes both sonatas to Haydn (see item 627); one by Roskovszky (see Hatting, item 629) that contains the second sonata, but with an attribution to Mariano Romano Kayser; and one that contains neither, but suggests derivation of this and the Rutka manuscript from a common, lost source. Offers hypotheses to explain the conflicting attribution, and concludes that Haydn's authorship of the sonatas should now be viewed as doubtful.

627. ———. "Zwei Haydn zugeschriebene Klaviersonaten." In *Gesellschaft für Musikforschung: Bericht über den Internationalen musikwissenschaftlichen Kongress, Kassel 1962,* edited by Georg Reichert and Martin Just, pp. 181–84. Kassel: Bärenreiter, 1963.

Reports the discovery of two piano sonatas (*Es2* and *Es3*) in a manuscript from the Benedictine monastery of Raigern (Rajhrad). Describes the source, which consists of five sonatas attributed to Haydn, and proposes that it may date from the 1760s, and probably not later than 1770. Concludes that the mode of transmission as well as stylistic features make the attribution credible.

* Fillion, Michelle. "The Accompanied Keyboard Divertimenti of Haydn and His Viennese Contemporaries (c. 1750–1780)." Ph.D. dissertation, Cornell University, 1982. xvi, 570 pp.

Cited as item 1059.

628. ———. "Eine bisher unbekannte Quelle für Haydns frühes Klaviertrio Hob. XV:C1." *Haydn-Studien* 5 (1982–85):59–63.

Discusses a Salzburg manuscript that attributes the trio to Wagenseil. Compares it with other known sources--in which Haydn is named as composer--and suggests that all go back to a common source, now lost. Concludes that the work, regarded by some as suspect, was rightly attributed to Haydn, and supports the claim with a discussion of style. Proposes that a Leopold Mozart letter (18 August 1771) raises the possibility that the Salzburg manuscript once belonged to the Mozart family.

629. Hatting, Carsten E. "Haydn oder Kayser?--Eine Echtheitsfrage." *Die Musikforschung* 25 (1972):182–87.

Concerns a Budapest source for a keyboard divertimento ascribed to Mariano Romano Kayser, but attributed to Haydn in a manuscript at Brno. Discusses the Budapest source and its scribe, Pantaleon Roskovszky, and explains why neither musical nor documentary evidence is strong enough to confirm either Haydn or Kayser as the composer, though the work has been published as authentic by Georg Feder on the strength of the Brno source (see item 626).

630. Landon, H.C. Robbins. "Joseph Haydn: A Sketch to Piano Trio No. 30 (Hob. XV:17)." *The Haydn Yearbook* 13 (1982):220-27.

The privately owned sketch, in oblong format on handmade northern Italian paper, concerns the first-movement development section, beginning with material of bar 40. Representing a more complicated version than the final one, it was possibly too complicated for amateur performers for whom the work was primarily intended.

631. Larsen, Jens Peter. "Eine bisher unbeachtete Quelle zu Haydns frühen Klavierwerken." In *Festschrift Joseph Schmidt-Görg zum 60. Geburtstag,* edited by Dagmar Weise, pp. 188-95. Bonn: Beethovenhaus, 1957.

Describes a previously neglected manuscript collection at the Gesellschaft der Musikfreunde in Vienna. Notes that the first part, consisting mainly of keyboard works by Haydn, incorporates a version of Hob. XVI:47 significantly different from that of the 1788 Artaria edition. Speculates on which version may have been first, and provides a facsimile for the hitherto unknown finale from the newly found version.

* Newman, William S. *The Sonata in the Classic Era.* 3d ed. Chapel Hill: University of North Carolina Press, 1983. xxii, 933 pp.

Cited as item 1073.

632. Roy, Klaus G. "The So-Called Violin Sonatas of Haydn." *Bulletin of the American Musicological Society,* nos. 11-13 (Sept. 1948), pp. 38-40.

An abstract of a December 1947 paper read before the New England chapter of the American Musicological Society. Speculates that the Violin Sonata Op. 70 (Hob.

XV:32), regarded by Larsen as the only real violin sonata, may be the sonata *Jacob's Dream.* The latter was supposedly written by Haydn to trick a musical dilettante in London who liked to display his virtuosity in the highest registers of the violin. Points out that the publication date 1794 is the year in which the *Jacob's Dream* episode was thought to have taken place, and discusses further coincidences that may link the two works.

633. Schmid, Ernst Fritz. "Franz Anton Hoffmeister und die 'Göttweiger Sonaten'." *Zeitschrift für Musik* 104 (1937):760-70, 889-95, 992-1000, 1109-17.

Presents evidence for ascribing the sonatas to Hoffmeister. Offers a biographical sketch of Hoffmeister and surveys early editions of the sonatas. Undertakes a stylistic comparison with other Hoffmeister works and finds close similarities in the treatment of theme and harmony.

634. Schwarting, Heino. "Über die Echtheit dreier Haydn-Trios." *Archiv für Musikwissenschaft* 22 (1965):169-82.

Undertakes a stylistic examination to determine to what extent the trios Hob. XV:3-5 are characteristic of Haydn (Haydn had attributed No. 3 to his brother, Framery had attributed Nos. 3-5 to Pleyel, and Leduc had published the three works under Pleyel's name in 1797). Looks at such aspects as texture, large-scale form, themes, periodic structure, and sonata form, and concludes that Nos. 3 and 4 differ fundamentally from Haydn's approach, but that No. 5 is clearly by Haydn. Rejects the attribution to Michael Haydn but proposes that Pleyel's authorship of Nos. 3 and 4 merits further study.

635. Steglich, Rudolf. "Eine Klaviersonate Johann Gottfried Schwanbergs (Schwanenberg[er]s) in der Joseph Haydn-Gesamtausgabe." *Zeitschrift für Musikwissenschaft* 15 (1932-33):77-79.

On the basis of catalogue references and a Berlin source, proposes that Hob. XVI:17 is by Johann Gottfried Schwanenberger, and that the opening of the first movement was modeled on the beginning of a sonata by Johann Christian Bach. Notes that it does not resemble Haydn's music stylistically, and questions the authenticity of Hob. XVI:16 on similar grounds.

636. Straková, Theodora. "Josef Antonín Štěpán und Haydns Divertimento in Es dur." *Acta Musei Moraviae: Scientiae Sociales* 46 (1961):132-36.

Examines a divertimento (Hob. XIV:Es1) preserved in two versions at Kroměříž: a setting for keyboard, two violins, and bass attributed to Haydn and another for keyboard alone attributed to Štěpán. Proposes Štěpán as the likely composer on the basis of style.

637. Strunk, W. Oliver. "Notes on a Haydn Autograph." *The Musical Quarterly* 20 (1934):192-205.

Draws on the autograph of Hob. XVI:52 to resolve the question of conflicting dedications in two early editions: one to "Fraülein von Kurzböck," one to "Mrs. Bartolozzi." The autograph, dated 1794, is dedicated to Therese Jansen, who became Mrs. Bartolozzi in 1795, and whose name appears in the edition published in 1799 or 1800. Biographical information from the memoirs of her daughter, the actress Madame Vestris, combined with other sources, enables the author to propose a chronology for Haydn's last keyboard works, as summarized in a table.

638. Tyson, Alan. "Haydn and Two Stolen Trios." *The Music Review* 22 (1961):21-27.

Examines the question of authenticity for three piano trios published by William Forster as Op. 40 (Hob. XV:3-5). Shows that the first two were actually by Pleyel and that this was a known fact in the eighteenth century. Cites a contemporary book in which Pleyel's authorship is acknowledged (Dr. John Callcott's *A Musical Grammar,* 1806), and names several editions--including Pleyel's own--in which the two works are attributed to Pleyel. Provides two conflicting accounts--one by Framery (*Notice sur Joseph Haydn,* 1810), one anonymous--of how Haydn came to send the Pleyel works to Forster under his own name and of the lawsuit that followed. Suggests that Haydn later attributed one of the trios to his brother to relieve a guilty conscience.

639. ———. "New Light on a Haydn Trio (XV:32)." *The Haydn Yearbook* 1 (1962):203-5.

Discusses the relative merits of prints by both Preston and Bland as authentic editions for a piano trio by Haydn. Until publication of Hoboken's catalogue, the trio was known as a violin sonata, the only such work by Haydn. Also examines printed sources for the sonata and uncertainties surrounding its date of origin.

640. ———. "One of Haydn's Lost 'Contrydances'?" *The Musical Times* 102 (1961):693. Also published in *The Haydn Yearbook* 1 (1962):202.

Proposes that a piece called *The Princess of Wales's Favorite Dance* by "Dr. Haydn," published between 1796 and 1801 by the Edinburgh firm of Gow & Shepherd, may in fact be a mutilated version of one of the six "lost" country dances by Haydn. Reasons cited in favor of its authenticity include the care normally taken by the Gows in their ascriptions, the fact that spurious editions were much less common in the 1790s and 1800s than earlier, and Haydn's frequent invitations ca. 1795 to attend the Prince. The 16-measure piece is printed in *The Musical Times* and in facsimile in *The Haydn Yearbook.*

Miscellaneous Instrumental Music

641. Feder, Georg. "Das Autograph von Haydns Divertimento in C-Dur für 2 Klarinetten und 2 Fagotte." *Haydn-Studien* 6/2 (1988):156-58.

Discusses the autograph source for Hob. II:14, dated 1761, recently made available on microfilm by the Saltykov-Ščedrin State Library in Leningrad. Shows how certain features of the source conform to expectations for autographs from the period 1756-62. Describes characteristics of the paper and their use as an aid to dating Hob. II:24, which uses similar paper.

642. Gerlach, Sonja. "Haydn's Works for Musical Clock (*Flötenuhr*): Problems of Authenticity, Grouping, and Chronology." In *Haydn Studies* (item 73), pp. 126-29.

Discusses the surviving clocks and extant sources for the 32 pieces attributed to Haydn. Compares the ranges of these pieces in an attempt to link them to particular clocks, including those no longer available. Groups the pieces by range in a table, and provides assessments of authenticity (genuine, probably genuine, probably spurious, or spurious).

643. ———. "Neues zu Haydns Baryton-Oktet No. 5 (Hob. X:1)." *Haydn-Studien* 5 (1982-85):125-34.

Reports on the newly rediscovered autograph manuscript in the Biblioteka Jagiellońska at Crakow. Describes the relationship between the arrangements (on which the *Joseph Haydn Werke* edition of 1969-70 had relied) and the original work, and supplements the *Joseph Haydn Werke* critical commentary with new information gained from the autograph. Includes a page of the manuscript in facsimile.

644. Hellyer, Roger. "Mozart's 'Harmoniemusik' with Bibliographical Notes on Haydn and Pleyel." *The Haydn Yearbook* 9 (1975):349-57.

Makes reference to Haydn attributions for the wind band piece C 17.09 in the appendix to Köchel's catalogue of Mozart's works. These consist of manuscript copies in the Ordo militaris Crucigerorum cum rubea stella in pedapontis Pragensis, in Brno, and in the Moravian Music Archive at Winston Salem, North Carolina.

* Schmid, Ernst Fritz. "Joseph Haydn und die Flötenuhr." *Zeitschrift für Musikwissenschaft* 14 (1931-32):193-221.

Cited as item 1139.

645. ———. "Neue Funde zu Haydns Flötenuhrstücken." *Haydn-Studien* 2 (1969-70):249-55.

Describes three extant mechanical instruments for which Haydn wrote compositions, and offers biographical information on the builder Joseph Niemecz, who supplied dates (1792 and 1793) for two of the instruments. Concerning the third, undated instrument (traditionally thought to have been built as early as 1772), argues that it must have originated much later, and reports on the discovery of an autograph manuscript for the fugue from Hob. XIX:16 (dated 1789), which plays on both the 1792 instrument and the undated one.

646. Smith, Carlton Sprague. "Haydn's Chamber Music and the Flute." *The Musical Quarterly* 19 (1933):341-50, 434-55.

Provides descriptive commentary on a wide range of authentic, doubtful, and spurious works, including original compositions and arrangements. Citing Haydn's statement to Kalkbrenner that he first learned to understand wind instruments late in life, proposes that the London trios are the best of his compositions for flute, but that he lacked real enthusiasm for the instrument.

647. Thomas, Günter. "Haydns Tanzmusik--zeitgebunden oder persönlich geprägt?" *Musica* 36 (1982):140-47.

Examines the style of Haydn's dances in relation to that of his contemporaries. Concludes that essential features of the dances are shared with those of other composers. Though Haydnesque elements are to be found also, these are not distinctive enough to be used as criteria to establish the authenticity of dances whose authorship is uncertain.

648. ———. "Joseph Haydns Tanzmusik." In *Joseph Haydn und seine Zeit* (item 80), pp. 73-85.

Examines the question of authenticity for ballroom dances preserved under Haydn's name: 111 such dances (minuets and German dances) survive in autograph and other reliable sources, but the authenticity of about 200 others cannot be substantiated. Considers examples of problematic attribution and the issue of genre. For authentic dances, describes general stylistic traits (phrase structure, keys, orchestration). Also discusses Haydn's activity as a composer of ballroom music.

649. ———. "Studien zu Haydns Tanzmusik." *Haydn-Studien* 3 (1973-74):5-28.

An expanded version of item 648, with new information on authentication and the social aspects of ballroom dances.

650. ———. "Die zwölf Deutschen Tänze Hob. IX:13--echt oder gefälscht?" *Haydn-Studien* 4 (1976-80):117-18.

Argues against Landon's claim that 12 German dances in a source at Donaueschingen are authentic. Shows that Haydn is not known to have written dances for the Redoutensaal in 1792, as stated on the title page, and that the copyist Schallinger, who prepared the first two pages and thus supplied the attribution, is known to have falsely attributed other works to Haydn.

VIII

MUSIC ANALYSIS AND CRITICISM

In the selection of items for inclusion in this category, preference has been given to relatively recent writings whose authors have been able to draw on the results of post-World War II studies of sources, authenticity, and chronology. In keeping with long-standing traditions of Haydn research and appreciation, interest in the vocal genres has lagged behind that devoted to instrumental music. The amount of material on the oratorios is disproportionately small in light of the popularity that *The Creation* and *The Seasons* have always enjoyed; and while Haydn as composer of operas does have his apologists, exploration in this area has been clouded by persisting doubts about the composer's gift as a musical dramatist, doubts underscored not only by the inevitable comparison with Mozart's theatrical genius, but by Haydn's own self-deprecatory remarks. Yet even within the field of instrumental music, the number of major, significant studies concerned with critical or stylistic analysis is remarkably small: apart from dissertations, it scarcely encompasses a handful of published book-length studies of substantial scholarly interest.

General

Listed here are writings by major scholars in the twentieth century, including those of Guido Adler, Friedrich Blume, Wilhelm Fischer, Jens Peter Larsen, Leonard Ratner, and Charles Rosen, which attempt to assess Haydn's contribution within the context of Viennese Classicism.

Also included are items involving more than one genre, those concerned with a work with versions belonging to different genres (*The Seven Last Words*), and studies that examine style from a particular vantage point such as harmony, melody, rhythmic organization, structure, or musical wit and humor.

651. Ackermann, Peter. "Struktur, Ausdruck, Programm: Gedanken zu Joseph Haydns Instrumentalmusik über *Die Sieben letzten Worte unseres Erlösers am Kreuze.*" In *Studien zur Instrumentalmusik: Lothar Hoffmann-Erbrecht zum 60. Geburtstag,* edited by Anke Bingmann, Klaus Hortschansky, and Winfried Kirsch, pp. 253-60. Tutzing: Hans Schneider, 1988.

Argues that while contemporaries looked for programmatic underpinnings in Haydn's music, this work was not programmatic in intent. Cites examples from selected expositions, developments, and recapitulations to show that the musical themes were derived from spoken language. Argues that while they held no extra-musical significance, they served as the musical substance from which the forms of the respective movements developed.

652. Adler, Guido. "[Festrede]." In *Haydn-Zentenarfeier: III. Kongress der Internationalen Musikgesellschaft, Wien, 25. bis 29. Mai 1909,* pp. 45-54. Vienna: Artaria, 1909. Published separately as *Josef Haydn: Festrede gehalten am 26. Mai 1909 im grossen Musikvereinssaale.* Vienna: Artaria, 1909. 14 pp.

Depicts Haydn as a seeker in search of a new approach, which he attained in the organic unity embodied in the 1781 quartets. Addresses the principles that underlie his instrumental music, speaks of the *Gottesfreude* in his sacred music and the lyricism of his vocal music, and briefly treats his operas. Determines that the main challenge he faced was to achieve a balance between the elements of two contrasting styles, galant and Baroque, and that he was the first to synthesize these elements into a new style. Notes his reliance on the example of others, particularly C.P.E. Bach.

653. ———. "Haydn and the Viennese Classical School." *The Musical Quarterly* 18 (1932):191-207.

Portrays Haydn's individuality against the backdrop of a Classical style, characterized by a metaphysical blend of the serious and light-hearted. Alludes to an idealized humor (rooted in the Austrian or Viennese folk character) that his works embody and describes him as a seeker and explorer. Provides a concise overview of his accomplishment in the major genres.

654. ———. "Haydn und die Wiener Klassik." *Österreichische Musikzeitschrift* 14 (1959):185-87.

Excerpt from item 652.

655. ———. "Die Wiener klassische Schule." In *Handbuch der Musikgeschichte,* 2d ed., edited by Guido Adler, 2:768-95. Berlin-Wilmersdorf: Heinrich Keller, 1930.

A wide-ranging essay that portrays Haydn as a paternalistic figure with respect to his influence on Mozart and Beethoven. Emphasizing features of style and technique in instrumental music, attempts to place the accomplishments of the Classical masters in the context of the social, economic, political, and philosophical environment of which they were a part.

656. Amato, Bruno. "Mutation: An Examination of its Structural Uses in Selected Works of Haydn, Mozart, and Beethoven." Ph.D. dissertation, Princeton University, 1973. vii, 69 pp.

Defining "mutation" as change of mode, from major to minor or the reverse, examines instances in local context, and analyzes the interaction of mutation with other structural elements over the course of an entire movement. Haydn works studied include first movements of the Sonata in E flat (Hob. XVI:52), the *Oxford* Symphony, and Symphony No. 100.

657. Barford, Philip T. "The Sonata-Principle: A Study of Musical Thought in the Eighteenth Century." *The Music Review* 13 (1952):255-63.

Designating "sonata-principle" or "sonata style" as a ubiquitous, defining characteristic of late eighteenth-century music, not sufficiently explained by traditional accounts of sonata form or the multi-movement sonata cycle, calls attention to the pertinent concepts of organic wholeness, unity through opposition of forces, and the thread of continuity that ideally animates a work. Describes sonata-principle as something that embraces both the abstract sonata-form idea and the unity and variety of particular materials within a given movement. Proposes that in certain Haydn keyboard sonatas, like those of C.P.E. Bach, and contrary to Haydn's own quartets and symphonies, fanciful contrasts are not imaginatively fused into a significant unity.

658. Bartha, Dénes. "Song Form and the Concept of 'Quatrain'." *Haydn Studies* (item 73), pp. 353-55.

Draws a connection between the structure typical of many eighteenth-century popular songs with four-line stanzas and a thematic design found in instrumental music of Haydn, Mozart, Beethoven, and others, in which an AABA pattern can be discerned (i.e. initial statement, restatement, contrast, restatement). Cites instances of this pattern in Haydn's orchestral and chamber music.

659. Becking, Gustav. *Studien zu Beethovens Personalstil: Das Scherzothema, mit einem bisher unveröffentlichten Scherzo Beethovens.* Leipzig: Breitkopf & Härtel, 1921. 166 pp.

Chapter 2 ("Vergleichende Betrachtungen zu Haydn und Mozart"), pp. 52-76, examines aspects of phraseology, melodic design, development, structure, and rhythm in Haydn's minuet movements (principally symphonies and string quartets). Pays particular attention to the Op. 33 scherzo movements, and speculates on the significance of Haydn's use of the term. Classifies compositional procedures in Haydn's minuets and compares Haydn with Beethoven. Numerous music examples.

660. Bellingardi, Luigi. "Sull'incidenza non occasionale del melos popolare tzigano sulla produzione di F.J. Haydn." *Chigiana* 36 (1979):227-34.

Discusses the general issue of folk influence in Haydn's instrumental music, but focuses principally on the gypsy element. Cites numerous instances from his string quartets, symphonies, and keyboard music that appear to contain specific allusions to gypsy material.

661. Blume, Friedrich. "Fortspinnung und Entwicklung: Ein Beitrag zur musikalischen Begriffsbildung." In Friedrich Blume. *Syntagma Musicologicum: Gesammelte Reden und Schriften,* edited by Martin Ruhnke, pp. 504-25. Kassel: Bärenreiter, 1963. Previously published in *Jahrbuch der Musikbibliothek Peters* 36 (1929):51-70.

Attempting to define and categorize basic compositional principles, examines the *Liedtypus* and *Fortspinnungstypus* proposed by Wilhelm Fischer (item 693) and the related distinction between *Ablauf* and *Entwicklung* advanced by Hans Mersmann; then presents the dichotomy announced in the title as an alternative. Explains that whereas *Fortspinnung* involves juxtaposition of substantially unrelated ideas whose connection emerges only in a larger context, the latter term applies to the chain of internal relationships that results from a continuously unfolding development of material from an initial idea.

Examines Mozart's preference for the former process, in contrast to Haydn's predilection for the latter. Citing the first movement of the quartet Op. 33 No. 3 as a model, emphasizes Haydn's open-ended, dynamic approach to creating a musical design.

662. ———. "Haydn, der Klassiker." In Friedrich Blume. *Syntagma Musicologicum: Gesammelte Reden und Schriften,* edited by Martin Ruhnke, pp. 552-58. Kassel: Bärenreiter, 1963. Previously published in *Hausmusik* 23 (1959):153-58.

Examines Haydn's style in the context of the history of German literature and culture as well as music, and places his contribution at the center of a development from pre-Classical exploration to a fully ripened Classicism. Relates Haydn's phenomenal success to his gift for achieving a perfect blend of popular expression and high art. Identifies the simplicity of his thematic style as the reason for his being labeled patronizingly as "Papa" by the younger Romantics. Elaborates on the change in social circumstance of the musician from court employee to free artist, depicts Haydn as a reflection of the process, and contrasts his state of equilibrium between the old order and new to Mozart's more radical break with convention.

663. ———. "Joseph Haydn in der Musikgeschichte der Wiener Klassik." In Friedrich Blume. *Syntagma Musicologicum II: Gesammelte Reden und Schriften, 1962-1972,* edited by Anna Amalie Abert and Martin Ruhnke, pp. 306-14. Kassel: Bärenreiter, 1973.

An address for the Schweizerischen Rundfunk, Studio Basel, recorded 19 March 1971. Contrasting Haydn's relatively autodidactic development with Mozart's thorough schooling in the Italian tradition, emphasizes the older composer's early dependence on the Austrian-Czech idiom of composers residing in Vienna. Suggests that Haydn brought about a high Classic phase otherwise unimaginable, and that without his accomplishment, the pre-Classical Austrian-Czech Viennese style could have remained a provincial phenomenon, like that of Mannheim.

664. ———. "Joseph Haydns instrumentales Spätschaffen." In Friedrich Blume. *Syntagma Musicologicum II: Gesammelte Reden und Schriften, 1962-1972,* edited by Anna Amalie Abert and Martin Ruhnke, pp. 299-306. Kassel: Bärenreiter, 1973.

An address for the Schweizerischen Rundfunk, Studio Basel, recorded 19 March 1970. Ponders different phases in Haydn's stylistic development. Associates the year

1780 with the replacement of a period of experimentation by a fully matured, personal idiom that proved decisively important for the history of eighteenth-century music. Elaborates on Haydn's decision to bring his activity as a composer virtually to an end around the year 1800.

665. Bonds, Mark Evan. "Haydn's False Recapitulations and the Perception of Sonata Form in the Eighteenth Century." Ph.D. dissertation, Harvard University, 1988. 430 pp.

Explores the concept of the false recapitulation in light of eighteenth-century discussions of large-scale form and musical rhetoric. Arguing that composers' use of conventional patterns promotes intelligibility, observes that the listener's expectations are based on conventions, and that the false recapitulation thwarts certain expectations. In this sense, the false recapitulation sheds light on the nature of eighteenth-century conventions. Shows that from approximately 1768 to 1774, Haydn's ideas about articulating the point of recapitulation solidified, and that in this same period, he experimented intensively with the false recapitulation in symphonies and string quartets. Discusses eighteenth-century critics' comparisons of Haydn with Laurence Sterne, and discerns fundamental similarities between the two in their cultivation of ironic devices as an essential aspect of their art.

666. Brook, Barry S. "Sturm und Drang and the Romantic Period in Music." *Studies in Romanticism* 9 (1970):269-84.

Attempts to place the phenomenon of *Sturm und Drang* in music of the late 1760s and 1770s in the context of literary, philosophical, and political thought of the age. Observes parallels between Haydn and Goethe with respect to their creative activity during this time, and detects a pervasive air of "distress, disenchantment and melancholy." Isolates *Sturm und Drang* traits in music, including minor mode, syncopated rhythm, tensional harmony, dissonance, extended modulations, emphasis on accentuation and change in dynamics, and contrapuntal devices. Argues that the *Sturm und Drang,* along with the *Empfindsamer Stil* of C.P.E. Bach and the Mannheim experiments with dynamics, form part of a continuous thread of early Romantic thought that led into the nineteenth century.

667. Brown, A. Peter. "Critical Years for Haydn's Instrumental Music: 1787-90." *The Musical Quarterly* 62 (1976):374-94.

Arguing that the dependence of various scholars "on certain historiographical viewpoints tends to de-emphasize, or distort, the results of style analysis," focuses on the previously unrecognized period of experimentation identified in the title. Draws parallels between Haydn's *crise romantique* (late 1760s-early 1770s) and the years in question, describing how the latter phase constitutes a structural (rather than Romantic) crisis, "concerned primarily with proportion and identity of function." Speculates on reasons behind Haydn's emphasis on keyboard music during these critical years, and on reasons why scholars have overlooked the phenomenon.

668. Broyles, Michael. "Organic Form and the Binary Repeat." *The Musical Quarterly* 66 (1980):339-60.

Examines more than 300 pieces dating from 1780 to 1810, and demonstrates the trend toward elimination of the repeat in the second part of a sonata-form movement. Relates this tendency to the replacement of an older, mechanistic aesthetic by a new, organic ideal. Describes the development as a radical transformation of aesthetic foundations on which composers made their choices. Proposes that as witnessed in works of Haydn and Mozart from the late 1780s and 1790s, the phenomenon is linked to the start of a new phase of musical evolution.

669. Busch, Ulrich. "'Ein brandneues Menuett': Das Menuett beim späten Haydn in Symphonie und Quartett." *Musica* 36 (1982):148-51.

Provides incipits and brief analyses for 11 minuets to illustrate how Haydn managed to make the traditional form seem fresh.

670. Chew, Geoffrey. "The Night-Watchman's Song Quoted by Haydn and Its Implications." *Haydn-Studien* 3 (1973-74):106-24.

Identifies sources of the melody, which the author traces to Bohemian origins, and speculates on the processes of transmission reflected by variants from one source to another. Observing that Haydn tolerates folk allusion more than Mozart, proposes that Haydn's procedure characteristically involves placing a borrowed melody in relief, discontinuous with the surrounding texture, in a manner that suggests the *pastorella* tradition. Cites the Baryton Trio No. 35 (designated *pastorella* in some sources) as an example. Provides an overview of the song and its history, and identifies various Haydn works (including Symphony No. 60 and the Keyboard Sonata in C-sharp minor Hob. XVI:36 in addition to the baryton trio cited above) in which it is quoted.

671. Cobb, Charlotte E. "Poetic Rhythms in the Works of Joseph Haydn." Ph.D. dissertation, University of Iowa, 1971. xii, 228 pp.

Proceeding from the assumption that aspects of Haydn's compositional technique are rooted in predecessors' practices, as reflected in eighteenth-century treatises and manuals, examines the correlation between poetry and oratory on one hand and musical accent, rhythmic patterning, and structure on the other. Theorists discussed include Mattheson, Rousseau, Quantz, Leopold Mozart, C.P.E. Bach, Türk, Mersenne, Marpurg, and Riepel. Issues discussed, in addition to the application of poetic meters to selected passages of Haydn's music, include slurs, dots, accent marks, embellishment signs, and other aspects of notation; variation techniques; thoroughbass practice; and symmetrical forms.

672. Cole, Malcolm S. "The Development of the Instrumental Rondo Finale from 1750 to 1800." 2 vols. Ph.D. dissertation, Princeton University, 1964. ix, 279 pp.; 120 pp.

Discusses relevant eighteenth-century writings and early manifestations of rondo form and procedure, then examines late eighteenth-century instances, including extensive discussion of Haydn's. Traces an evolutionary process in Haydn toward a complex, highly integrated form, and observes that Haydn's late rondos differ from sonata form only in their reprise structure and in formal details. Notes the consistency with which Haydn applies a ternary reprise structure (involving a developmental transition to the first couplet) and finds the influence of Mozart in later works.

673. ———. "Rondos, Proper and Improper." *Music and Letters* 51 (1970):388–99.

Cites A.F.C. Kollmann's observation, in *An Essay on Practical Musical Composition* (1799), that in an "improper rondo" the recurrence of the main subject need not be in tonic key. Arguing that this practice is not forbidden by eighteenth-century writers, suggests that the term may apply to certain ambiguous movements in Haydn, Mozart, and Beethoven, notably those in which closing material at the end of an exposition constitutes a varied restatement of the main theme, in the dominant.

674. Cone, Edward T. "The Uses of Convention: Stravinsky and His Models." *The Musical Quarterly* 48 (1962):287–99.

Compares Stravinsky's approach with Haydn's, and emphasizes the latter's tendency to use a conventional pattern itself as the subject for creative development. Draws on the finale of Haydn's Quartet Op. 54 No. 2 to demonstrate the process by which an apparently incongruous turn of events proves to be integrally connected to the whole. Suggests that Haydn avoids both the obvious and the arbitrary as he modifies conventions and extends the techniques of the existing musical language through continuous questioning and reexamination of its premises.

675. Conrat, Hugo. "Joseph Haydn und das kroatische Volkslied." *Die Musik* 4/7 (1904-5):14-29.

Supports Kuhač's outdated theory of Haydn's Croatian origins. Describes something of Croatian culture, then, drawing on examples from Kuhač, compares musical themes from Haydn with Slavic folk melodies.

676. Cooper, Grosvenor W., and Meyer, Leonard B. *The Rhythmic Structure of Music.* Chicago: University of Chicago Press, 1960. 212 pp.

Applies the traditional terminology of prosody (iamb, anapest, trochee, dactyl, and amphibrach) to the interpretation of rhythmic groupings on different architectonic levels. Haydn compositions treated to multi-level analysis include Symphonies Nos. 92, 94, 97, 100, 102, and 104; and String Quartets Op. 33 No. 3 and Op. 54 No. 3.

677. Cushman, Daniel S. "Joseph Haydn's Melodic Materials: An Exploratory Introduction to the Primary and Secondary Sources Together with an Analytical Catalogue and Tables of Proposed Melodic Correspondence and/or Variance." Ph.D. dissertation, Boston University, 1973. xxiv, 787 pp.

Follows an elaborately devised method for identifying the transmission of folk materials and the contributions of specific composers in Haydn's melodic repertory. Offering disclaimers about the validity of correspondences cited, finds avenues of influence from certain composers and from compilations that appeared between 1650 and 1780, with important evidence from the era of Melchior Franck. Divides into three main parts: 1) identification and evaluation of primary and secondary source materials; 2) analytical presentation of the music itself in catalogue form: proposed sources, corresponding Haydn works, summary and appraisal of prior research (includes ca. 500 melodic examples, classified into 140 "affinity groups"); 3) tabular appendices: a) Haydn entries, with Haydn variants, primary and secondary proposed sources; b) primary sources, with secondary sources, Haydn usage; c) unverifiable source-citations; d) title index; bibliography.

678. De Angelis, Enrico. "Haydn: Il mestiere dell'illuminista." *Chigiana* 36 (1979):31-51.

Ponders Haydn's approach to his art and his audience in the light of historians' concepts of the Enlightenment. Emphasizes Haydn's commercial success in the pursuit of his metier; discusses Carpani's assessment of Haydn's musical personality; examines Haydn's capacity (especially in the quartets) to create foreseeable surprises within the framework of a coherent structure; and discusses the synthesis of opposed, seemingly irreconcilable elements, notably in the late oratorios.

679. Drury, Jonathan Daniels. "Haydn's *Seven Last Words:* An Historical and Critical Study." Ph.D. dissertation, University of Illinois, 1975. iv, 371 pp.

Offers historical background, and recounts the history of scholarship pertaining to the work. Examines sketches, provides critical analysis, undertakes a comparative study of different versions, and compares the work with Joseph Friebert's. Interprets the piece as a coherent, nine-movement instrumental cycle that draws on the oratorio tradition as a conceptual model, and that employs programmatic and depictive devices associated with the Passion of Christ. Citing an ill-fitting text, judges the choral version to be less successful. Provides an extensive bibliography.

680. Eibner, Franz. "Joseph Haydns musikalische Sendung: Die Bedeutung der österreichischen Volksmusik für die musikalische Klassik." *Österreichische Musikzeitschrift* 22 (1967):540-49.

Examining melodic structures with the aid of reductive analytical sketches, detects fundamental connections between characteristic structural features of Austrian folksong and Haydn's approach to melodic design.

681. Einstein, Alfred. "Haydn." In Alfred Einstein. *Von Schütz bis Hindemith: Essays über Musik und Musiker,* pp. 49-62. Zurich: Pan-Verlag, 1957.

Based on a 1939 lecture. Deplores the extent to which a traditionally simplistic view of Haydn the man had persisted and had colored perceptions of his music. Argues that he was a true revolutionary who had achieved an original and profoundly influential synthesis from the fragmented mixture of old and new discernible in the music of his immediate predecessors. While designating the idiom of the Op. 33 quartets as the great discovery of his life, proposes that the symphonies, with their greater diversity of available materials and greater possibilities to be realized, surpassed the quartets as an artistic legacy.

682. Engel, Hans. "Haydn, Mozart und die Klassik." *Mozart-Jahrbuch* (1959), pp. 46-79.

Examines the notion of Classicism, particularly Viennese Classicism, in literature and music. Investigates forerunners of the new musical style, recognizing the importance of sonata form and thematic duality in its development. Views the symphony as the most important instrumental genre, and explores the different symphonic movements, with particular reference to Haydn and Mozart. Offers a variety of examples from their music as well as that of contemporaries and predecessors. Concludes that the term "Classical" can be applied only to music, not to the epoch.

683. ———. "Die Quellen des klassischen Stiles." In *International Musicological Society: Report of the Eighth Congress, New York 1961,* edited by Jan LaRue, 1:285-304. Kassel: Bärenreiter, 1961.

Traces the origins of Haydn's and Mozart's Classical style to the influence of the Italians as well as that of the Viennese, Mannheim, North German, and French schools. Concentrating on the symphony, briefly sketches the development of sonata form and the symphonic cycle. Then examines in more detail the notable features of each movement in the cycle, citing practices of Haydn and Mozart as well as those of contemporaries and predecessors.

684. Eppstein, Hans. "Geist und Technik in der Musik der Wiener Klassik." *Österreichische Musikzeitschrift* 32 (1977):486-96.

Contrasts the essential incomprehensibility of true polyphony with the interactive, conversation-like, comprehensible texture typical of Viennese Classicism. Cites the cultivation of this new approach, in which the parts are comprehensible both in themselves and as part of a unified design, in the string quartets of Haydn, and notes its further development by Mozart, Beethoven, and Schubert.

685. Feder, Georg. "Die beiden Pole im Instrumentalschaffen des jungen Haydn." In *Der junge Haydn* (item 81), pp. 192-201.

To specify stylistic contrasts discernible between one genre and another, and within particular genres, proposes a loose concept of polarity: lighter, galant, and amateur-oriented vs. learned, connoisseur-oriented, and monumental. Acknowledging that the poles are neither clear-cut nor sharply delineated, applies the concept to various genres, including concertino and divertimento, keyboard sonata, trio, organ concerto, and symphony. Emphasizing Haydn's parallel cultivation of different tendencies, questions premises on which chronological orderings of early works have hitherto been proposed.

686. ———. "Bemerkungen über die Ausbildung der klassischen Tonsprache in der Instrumentalmusik Haydns." In *International Musicological Society: Report of the Eighth Congress, New York 1961,* edited by Jan LaRue, 1:305-13. Kassel: Bärenreiter, 1961.

Locates a foundation for Haydn's early idiom in the Italian-Austrian divertimento, as represented by Galuppi, Rutini, Wagenseil, and others, and attempts to identify aspects of this style that anticipate the development of a mature Classical language. Cites C.P.E. Bach's influence as a factor in the individualization and expressive deepening of Haydn's style, and proposes that in his first peak of creativity, reached with the symphonies and string quartets of 1772, the Classical language was fully realized.

687. ———. "Haydns Paukenschlag und andere Überraschungen." *Österreichische Musikzeitschrift* 21 (1966):5-8.

Defines musical surprise in the sense applicable to Haydn as a possibility anticipated only remotely by the listener, if at all, within the framework of a given convention or style. Examples cited include the seventh variation of the Symphony No. 31 finale (for contrabass, not cello, as correctly indicated in the new complete edition) and instances involving a visual, pantomimic aspect, including the finales of Symphonies Nos. 45, 60, and 98, and also the vocal quartet *Die Beredsamkeit.*

688. ———. "Eine Methode der Stiluntersuchung, demonstriert an Haydns Werken." In *Gesellschaft für Musikforschung: Bericht über den Internationalen musikwissenschaftlichen Kongress, Leipzig 1966,* edited by Carl Dahlhaus, Reiner Kluge, Ernst H. Meyer, and Walter Wiora, pp. 275-87. Kassel: Bärenreiter, 1970.

Examines the phenomenon whereby conventional figures, mannerisms, and turns of phrase enter and leave a musical style. Observing that each instance of a customary device must have originated as a new idea, proposes that whereas composers' drawing on a reservoir of such materials is basic to the continuity of music history, progress is accomplished through composers' fresh contributions to that reservoir. Cites various examples of conventional figures in Haydn, including change of mode for the repetition of a theme, melodies built over a falling series of first-inversion chords, and oscillating melodic seconds ornamented with trills.

689. ———. "Similarities in the Works of Haydn." In *Studies in Eighteenth-Century Music: A Tribute to Karl Geiringer on His Seventieth Birthday*, edited by H.C. Robbins Landon and Roger E. Chapman, pp. 186-97. New York: Oxford University Press, 1970.

Shows that while it was rare for Haydn to rework his own pieces consciously for later use (as did Bach, for example), thematic similarities occur commonly in his works. Distinguishes between different types of similarity (direct imitation, reminiscence, or use of materials common to the period) and between different underlying creative processes involved (deliberate, conscious, or partly conscious). Gives examples illustrating various kinds of similarity.

690. ———. "Typisches bei Haydn: Eine Methode der Stiluntersuchung." *Österreichische Musikzeitschrift* 24 (1969):11-17.

Based on item 688.

691. Federhofer, Hellmut. "Johann Joseph Fux und Joseph Haydn." *Musica* 14 (1960):269-73.

Specifies parallels between the two, notably in their relationship to inherited traditions. Places both in the context of musical, political, and cultural history of eighteenth-century Austria, and discusses the synthesis of late Baroque style and newer forms of expression in early Haydn.

692. Fischer, Kurt von. "Zur Theorie der Variation im 18. und beginnenden 19. Jahrhundert." In *Festschrift Joseph Schmidt-Görg zum 60. Geburtstag*, edited by Dagmar Weise, pp. 117-30. Bonn: Beethovenhaus, 1957.

Citing passages from numerous theorists (including Neidt, Walther, Scheibe, Mattheson, Grassineau, Marpurg, Rousseau, Daube, Schulz, Koch, Vogler, Momigny, Milchmeyer, and Reicha), traces changing concepts of variation as form and procedure. Among references to composers' practices are critiques by Koch, Vogler, and Reicha that mention Haydn's mastery of variation technique.

693. Fischer, Wilhelm. "Zur Entwicklungsgeschichte des Wiener klassischen Stils." *Studien zur Musikwissenschaft* 3 (1915):24-84.

Applying the author's basic distinction between *Fortspinnungstypus* and *Liedtypus,* examines characteristic eighteenth-century melodic processes at the level of phrase, period, and theme. Compares procedures witnessed in Haydn and Mozart, and gives examples from expositions and development sections of quartets, sonatas, and symphonies.

694. ———. "Zwei neapolitanische Melodietypen bei Mozart und Haydn." *Mozart-Jahrbuch* (1960-61), pp. 7-21.

Cites passages in Pergolesi's *La serva padrona, Stabat Mater,* and in various instrumental works attributed to the composer that illustrate the two types of construction in question: the "reversed period" whereby the antecedent phrase cadences on I, the consequent on V; and the "A 2B" design, which involves the statement of a motive, a contrasting motive, then repetition of the latter. Shows that comparable patterns can be found in mid-century Viennese works by M.G. Monn, Wagenseil, and Haydn. Cites an example of the second type from the opening of Haydn's late Piano Sonata in E flat.

695. Forchert, Arno. "'Klassisch' und 'romantisch' in der Musikliteratur des frühen 19 Jahrhunderts." *Die Musikforschung* 31 (1978):405-25.

Surveys the diverse and contradictory connotations of the terms "Classic" and "Romantic" among late eighteenth- and nineteenth-century critics and aestheticians. Cites early nineteenth-century German attempts to establish the music of Haydn and Mozart (and later, Beethoven as well) as stylistic models, and notes the importance of nineteenth-century French criticism in the evolving concept of a "Romantic" period. Elaborates on the growing early nineteenth-century consciousness of a no-longer-abstract principle of composition, and links this consciousness with critics' articulation of a distinction between Classic and Romantic approaches.

696. Forschner, Hermann. *Instrumentalmusik Joseph Haydns aus der Sicht Heinrich Christoph Kochs.* Munich: Emil Katzbichler, 1984. 289 pp.

Draws on Haydn's music as a basis for probing the significance of Koch's precepts, classifications, and prescriptions regarding meter, phraseology, and musical form. Pieces analyzed include the Keyboard Sonatas Nos. 2 in B (first movement), 27 in G (minuet), 32 in B minor (first movement), 50 in C (*Adagio*), 52 in E flat (first movement), String Quartet in C, Op. 33 No. 3 (first movement), Symphony No. 104 in D (first movement), and Keyboard Concerto in D (first movement). Substantial number of music examples, mostly from keyboard sonatas and string quartets.

697. Fubini, Enrico. "Haydn, l'Illuminismo e la forma-sonata." *Chigiana* 36 (1979):21-30.

Proposes that Haydn's approach to sonata form, narrative and conversational rather than dialectic, represents an ideal musical language of the Enlightenment. Citing compositions such as the quartets of Op. 33, 54, and 76, as well as post-1780 symphonies, finds structural logic, accessibility, the capacity to express complex sentiments, and a characteristic balance of reason and fantasy.

698. Garner, Chet H. "Principles of Periodic Structure in the Instrumental Works of Haydn, Mozart, and Beethoven." Ph.D. dissertation, University of Iowa, 1977. xvii, 279 pp.

Concerned with the phenomenon of antecedent-consequent relationships. Proposes an archetypal periodic progression: paired four-bar phrases with the underlying harmonic formula I-V, I-V-I. Observes that disequilibrium within the archetypal framework yields instability, which in turn constitutes the basis for musical elaboration and consequent enlargement of the scope of the musical discourse. Proposes that periodicity in Haydn and Mozart operates as a system in which basic "properties remain constant as a prerequisite of the style," and identifies a prevailing mode of organization in the two composers' binary and sonata forms that involves interplay of regular and non-regular period structures. Haydn works examined include String Quartets Op. 2, 9, 50, 71, 74, 76, 77, and 103; Sonata in E flat, Hob. XVI:52; and Symphonies Nos. 101, 102, 103, and 104.

699. Geiringer, Karl. "Joseph Haydn, Protagonist of the Enlightenment." *Studies on Voltaire and the Eighteenth Century* 25 (1963):683-90.

Viewing Haydn's age as a time of remarkable interaction among the realms of theory, practical music, and philosophy, suggests that Haydn exemplified essential aspects of the Enlightenment in his personality and his music. Cites his early allegiance to the then-progressive *style galant;* the later gain in profundity and expressive power achieved in works from the *Sturm und Drang* period, in which an evident striving for truth and authentic expression of the passions reflects Rousseau's ideals; the democratic spirit inherent in the string quartets, which accomplish a departure from the Baroque concept of distinction between leading and accompanying parts; the cosmopolitan character of his output, which involved commissions from many nations for music whose supranational character embraces East European folksong, Italian opera, French chanson, and British vocal music; and the church music, which reflects spiritual detachment, an objective view of liturgical precepts, and a fundamentally optimistic frame of mind.

700. Georgiades, Thrasybulos. "Zur Musiksprache der Wiener Klassiker." *Mozart-Jahrbuch* (1951), pp. 50-59.

A sequel to the author's article "Aus der Musiksprache des Mozarttheaters" (*Mozart-Jahrbuch,* 1950). Concerned with the phenomenon of complex interaction between meter and rhythmic patterning in the music of Haydn and his contemporaries.

701. Gjerdingen, Robert O. *A Classic Turn of Phrase: Music and the Psychology of Convention.* Philadelphia: University of Pennsylvania Press, 1988. x, 299 pp.

Traces the history of a standard melodic-harmonic formula, or "schema," through manifestations in music of the eighteenth and nineteenth centuries. The formula in question most typically comprises a matched pair of events: the first involves melodic descent from tonic to seventh scale degree while the harmony moves from tonic to dominant; the second features melodic descent from fourth to third scale degree as the harmony returns from dominant to tonic. Appearing sporadically in the early eighteenth century, then with greater frequency in the 1750s and 60s, the phenomenon reached its peak of popularity during the 1770s. Works by Haydn (especially the symphonies) are well represented among the eighteenth-century instances discussed. Includes numerous music examples and analytical sketches.

702. Göllner, Theodor. *"Die Sieben Worte am Kreuz" bei Schütz und Haydn, vorgetragen am 13. Januar 1984.* Munich: Bayerische Akademie der Wissenschaften, 1986. 130 pp.

A study and comparison of the settings by Schütz and Haydn, introduced by discussion of settings prior to

Schütz. The chapter on Haydn considers the background and substance of both his orchestral and vocal versions, analyzing the works movement by movement. Noting that the instrumental version was the first of its kind, explores ways in which thematic designs were influenced by the cadence of the text. For the vocal work, which was inspired by Joseph Friebert's vocal setting of the Haydn orchestral piece, offers comparisons with both the Friebert work and the instrumental version.

703. ———. "Vokal und Instrumental bei Haydn." In *Joseph Haydn Kongress* (item 76), pp. 104-10.

Cites the first (instrumental) and final (vocal) version of *The Seven Last Words* as the basis for speculating on the extent to which Haydn's concept of instrumental expression derives ultimately from text-oriented inspiration.

704. Gwilt, Richard. "Sonata-Allegro Revisited." *In Theory Only* 7/5-6 (1983-84):3-33.

Examines hierarchic structure, phraseology, tonal organization, and thematic distribution in the twelve London symphonies from the vantage point of A.F.C. Kollmann's *An Essay on Musical Harmony* (1796) and *An Essay on Practical Musical Composition* (1799). Pursues the application of Kollmann's hierarchic model (encompassing measure, period, section, and overall two-part design) in the first movements. Scrutinizes the interaction of Kollmann's structural model (two parts, each divided in two) and his reference to a three-part rhetorical design (statement, continuation, conclusion), and discovers that both schemes are relevant to Haydn. Suggests that neither plan necessarily conforms to the nineteenth-century conception of exposition-development-recapitulation, and proposes that form was not regarded by eighteenth-century writers as a "thing-in-itself," but rather as a context for rhetorically satisfying discourse.

* Hadow, William H. *A Croatian Composer: Notes Toward the Study of Joseph Haydn.* London: Seeley & Co., 1897. Reprint. Freeport, NY: Books for Libraries, 1972. 98 pp. Another reprint in William H. Hadow. *Collected Essays,* pp. 65-106. London: Oxford University Press, 1928.

Cited as item 247.

705. Hailparn, Lydia. "Haydn: *The Seven Last Words.* A New Look at an Old Masterpiece." *The Music Review* 34 (1973):1-21.

Traces the history of this work from Haydn's commission in 1785 for an orchestral Good Friday piece to its transformation into an oratorio. Examines the structure of the original version, then compares it with Haydn's string-quartet transcription and oratorio. Provides, in tabular form, a movement-by-movement comparison of orchestration in the original and oratorio versions. Includes material from Haydn's preface to the Breitkopf & Härtel edition of the oratorio (1801), which describes how the original work was designed to conform to practices at the Cathedral of Cádiz, for which it was commissioned.

706. Haimo, Ethan. "Haydn's Altered Reprise." *Journal of Music Theory* 32 (1988):335-51.

Explains that in the 1780s and 90s, Haydn made sweeping changes in his approach to sonata form and, in particular, to his treatment of the recapitulation, which underwent substantial alterations with respect to the exposition. Links Haydn's altered reprises with his cultivation of monothematic sonata form (which he began to favor in the 1780s), his longer development sections, and his interest in achieving unity among movements. Demonstrates the large-scale coherence attained through this type of reprise in the *Military* Symphony and in String Quartets Op. 76 No. 3 and Op. 77 No. 2.

707. Harutunian, John M. "Haydn and Mozart: A Study of Their Mature Sonata-Style Procedures." Ph.D. dissertation, University of California at Los Angeles, 1981. xii, 380 pp.

Comparative analysis features isolation of five centrally important stylistic problems faced by both composers: tonic-dominant polarity (more important to Haydn); tonal deflections in expositions (practices are similar, though Mozart's major-minor shifts are distinctly different from Haydn's procedures); nature of harmonic language at structural junctures (Haydn uses more key-juxtaposition than Mozart, more sudden shifts of tonal center, and more frequent non-dominant retransitions to the recapitulation); treatment of developments (Haydn's are longer, more sectionalized, and more organically constructed); handling of recapitulations (striking differences of procedure, with Haydn favoring extensive departure from the exposition). Haydn repertoire examined includes the Paris and London symphonies, string quartets from Op. 33 on, six keyboard sonatas, and numerous keyboard trios.

708. Hatting, Carsten E. "The Enlightenment and Haydn." In *Haydn Studies* (item 73), pp. 434-40.

With particular emphasis on the views of Carl Dahlhaus, examines correspondences between social change and change in musical style in the eighteenth century. Discusses the phenomenon of "simplification," citing its relevance to the music of Haydn's *Creation.*

709. Henneberg, Gudrun. "Heinrich Christoph Kochs Analysen von Instrumentalwerken Joseph Haydns." *Haydn-Studien* 4 (1976-80):105-12.

Identifies the Haydn works cited in Koch's *Versuch einer Anleitung zur Composition* (1782-93) as illustrations of fundamental principles of phrase and period structure, formal design, and tonal organization (four of the five pieces are minuets). Gives locations of excerpts cited in the text and summarizes observations made with regard to the music discussed. Special emphasis falls on the *Andante* of Symphony No. 42 in D, which exemplifies techniques of melodic extension through repetition and variation.

710. Hübler, Klaus-K. "'zusetzen, wegschneiden, wagen': Anmerkungen zu einigen 'Versuchen' Joseph Haydns." In *Joseph Haydn* (item 75), pp. 24-46.

Concerned with ways in which Haydn's creative energies confronted the resistance offered by existing conventions. Cites examples of experiment and revolutionary conception: pieces that begin without a true beginning, metrically or harmonically; palindromes; and various examples of originality in tone color, harmony, tonal relationship, and structure that contribute to Haydn's status as an experimental spirit among the Viennese Classicists. Offers extensive music examples in score.

711. Katz, Adele T. *Challenge to Musical Tradition: A New Concept of Tonality.* New York: Alfred A. Knopf, 1945. Reprint. New York: Da Capo, 1972. xxviii, 408 pp.

Devotes a chapter to Haydn (pp. 99-143), crediting him with definitive examples of the hitherto vaguely defined sonata, trio, quartet, and symphony. Cites such factors as thematic impulse, functional specialization, and the concept of the development section. Centering the analytical discussion on devices of harmonic prolongation, proposes imagination rather than technique as the driving force behind Haydn's expansion of form.

712. Koller, Walter. *Aus der Werkstatt der Wiener Klassiker: Bearbeitungen Haydns, Mozarts und Beethovens.* Tutzing: Hans Schneider, 1975. 221 pp.

Studies arrangements of the melody "O Can Ye Sew Cushions" by Haydn and Beethoven; the melody of the song "D' Bäurin hat d' Katz verlor'n" as a keyboard fantasy by Haydn and a divertimento by Mozart; and Haydn minuets from Symphony No. 101 and String Quartet Op. 54 No. 2 as musical clock pieces. Compares Mozart's Divertimento, K. 131, first minuet, and the later version as K. 176 No. 6, with the related Haydn minuet from Symphony No. 56. Points out differences among them that reflect contrasts in characteristic style and genre to which they belong. Analytical discussion involves questions of texture, bass line, meter, and phrasing.

713. Krones, Hartmut. "Das 'hohe Komische' bei Joseph Haydn." *Österreichische Musikzeitschrift* 38 (1983):2-8.

With the aid of contemporary critiques and pertinent excerpts from Griesinger and Dies, discusses the wealth of comic effects found in Haydn's music. Examines techniques he applied both in vocal music (sacred and secular) and in instrumental genres where there was no text to clarify meaning. For the instrumental music, notices the heavy reliance on dynamics, rhythm, and sonority to achieve desired effects.

714. Kunze, Stefan. "Die Wiener Klassik und ihre Epoche: Zur Situierung der Musik von Haydn, Mozart und Beethoven." *Studi musicali* 7 (1978):237-59.

A critical examination of the historical roles of the three masters with respect to culture and musical practices of the eighteenth and early nineteenth centuries. Ponders the historian's dilemma in generalizing with regard to the characteristics of an epoch; questions the validity of the "epoch" concept, the extent to which works of art within a given time-span represent a style, and the extent to which an epoch in music history can be related to an epoch in political or cultural history.

715. Lang, Paul Henry. *Music in Western Civilization.* New York: W.W. Norton, 1941. xxii, 1107 pp.

Proclaims that Haydn, "the musician who opened the classical era ... was permitted to accompany a new world of art from its inception to its supreme flowering." Although unusually coherent and incisive, the discussion of Haydn, pp. 625-35, fails to integrate sacred and theatrical music in the appraisal of his career and contribution.

716. Larsen, Jens Peter. "A Challenge to Musicology: The Viennese Classical School." *Current Musicology*, no. 9 (1969), pp. 105-12.

Remarks on the insufficiency of knowledge with regard to chronology for works by Haydn and his contemporaries, especially in the time of the "breakthrough of the Classical style," ca. 1770. Advocating improvement in the application of tools for stylistic analysis, argues for a flexible concept of sonata form and procedure, and expresses his belief that Wilhelm Fischer's categorization of theme-types (*Liedtypus* and *Fortspinnungstypus*) could be used to greater advantage.

717. ———. "On Haydn's Artistic Development." In Jens Peter Larsen. *Handel, Haydn, and the Viennese Classical Style*, translations by Ulrich Krämer, pp. 109-15. Ann Arbor: UMI Research Press, 1988.

Translation of item 725.

718. ———. "Some Observations on the Development and Characteristics of Viennese Classical Instrumental Music." In Jens Peter Larsen. *Handel, Haydn, and the Viennese Classical Style*, translations by Ulrich Krämer, pp. 227-49. Ann Arbor: UMI Research Press, 1988. Previously published in *Studia Musicologica Academiae Scientiarum Hungaricae* 9 (1967):115-39.

Considers problematic aspects of eighteenth-century music: the question of finding a missing link between Bach and Haydn, and the remaining problems in authentication, chronology, and characterization. Defines the Classical style as well as phases leading up to and following it. Regards Haydn and Mozart as *the* representatives of the Classical era, and views Classical style as their synthesis of Baroque and mid-century elements. Concludes with a discussion of form (primarily sonata form) in Haydn and Mozart, and notes differences between the two composers' approach.

719. ———. "Sonata Form Problems." In Jens Peter Larsen.

Handel, Haydn, and the Viennese Classical Style, translations by Ulrich Krämer, pp. 269–79. Ann Arbor: UMI Research Press, 1988.

Translation of item 720.

720. ———. "Sonatenform-Probleme." In *Festschrift Friedrich Blume zum 70. Geburtstag,* edited by Anna Amalie Abert and Wilhelm Pfannkuch, pp. 221-30. Kassel: Bärenreiter, 1963.

Ruminates on modern-day assumptions about sonata form, and denounces those assumptions as a basis for understanding eighteenth-century practices. Recalls the contributions of Wilhelm Fischer, Hans Mersmann, Kurt Westphal, and Rudolf von Tobel toward revised thinking on the subject, then proceeds to examine the phenomenon of sonata-form exposition from the standpoint of typical features in Haydn's instrumental works. Concludes that the tonal order of the exposition (forming either a two- or three-part design) should take precedence over thematic content as the decisive element of construction. Arguing for a looser, more flexible, and more historically oriented approach, underscores crucially important factors often suppressed in conventional sonata-form analysis, for example the influence of the ritornello principle in the design of a symphony movement.

721. ———. "Der Stilwandel in der österreichischen Musik zwischen Barock und Wiener Klassik." In *Der junge Haydn* (item 81), pp. 18–30.

Examines reasons for the difficulty in defining style change from Baroque to Classical: lack of familiarity with musical sources for the years in question (1740–70) and the absence of a research tradition for this transitional period. Gives an overview of the musical environment in which the young Haydn developed during his years in Vienna, grouping the relevant composers by generation. Surveys changes in musical tradition from the time of Karl VI to Joseph II, concentrating on instrumental ensemble music: *sonata da chiesa,* stylized dance music, and most especially the symphony. Briefly investigates Haydn's symphonies to 1770 and discusses how they fit into various coexisting traditions. Notes the changes after 1765 that culminated in the Viennese Classical style around 1770.

722. ———. "The Style Change in Austrian Music between the Baroque and Viennese Classicism." In Jens Peter Larsen. *Handel, Haydn, and the Viennese Classical Style,* translations by Ulrich Krämer, pp. 301-13. Ann Arbor: UMI Research Press, 1988.

Translation of item 721.

723. ———. "Traditional Prejudices in Connection with Viennese Classical Music." In Jens Peter Larsen. *Handel, Haydn, and the Viennese Classical Style,* translations by Ulrich Krämer, pp. 281-91. Ann Arbor: UMI Research Press, 1988.

Translation of item 724.

724. ———. "Traditionelle Vorurteile bei der Betrachtung der Wiener klassischen Musik." In *Symbolae Historiae Musicae: Hellmut Federhofer zum 60. Geburtstag,* edited by Friedrich Wilhelm Riedel and Hubert Unverricht, pp. 194-203. Mainz: B. Schott's Söhne, 1971.

Points to the need for a "renewal of research on Viennese Classicism," and outlines problems to be addressed. With emphasis on instrumental style, considers misconceptions about the delineation of the Classical period and the need to develop different ways of categorizing the music; problems concerning the misunderstanding of large-scale cyclical forms and the nature of sonata-form movements; the question of how to examine musical processes, specifically the need to reach beyond "one-sided theme analysis" and look at other features such as harmonic rhythm, tonal plan, and the distinction between *Liedformung* and *Fortspinnungsformung.*

725. ———. "Zu Haydns künstlerischer Entwicklung." In *Festschrift Wilhelm Fischer zum 70. Geburtstag überreicht im Mozartjahr 1956,* edited by Hans Zingerle, pp. 123-29. Innsbruck: Sprachwissenschaftliches Seminar der Univ. Innsbruck, 1956.

An outline of Haydn's internal development as a composer, intended as a guide for further research on periodization. Proposes the existence of eight major periods, and describes prominent features of each. Regards the span from 1765 to 1772 as the most critical, since it witnessed the emergence of the Viennese Classical style. For an English translation, see item 717.

726. LaRue, Jan. "A Haydn Specialty: Multistage Variance." In *Joseph Haydn Kongress* (item 76), pp. 141-46.

Explains Haydn's propensity for causing ideas to grow and become differentiated in the manner of a "musical protoplasm." Illustrates his highly flexible manner of making variants of variants by tracing stages in the evolution of an appoggiatura gesture in the Sonata in E flat, Hob. XVI:49, first movement. Contrasts Haydn's technique to procedures witnessed in sonatas by Platti, Agrell, Alberti, and Dittersdorf.

727. ———. "Multistage Variance: Haydn's Legacy to Beethoven." *The Journal of Musicology* 1 (1982):265-74.

Concerned with Haydn's procedure of deriving variants from variants of a thematic idea. Devises a system of symbols for representing such relationships and cites examples in several Haydn keyboard sonatas. While contrasting this technique to Mozart's typically clear distinction between ornamental and structural variance and his avoidance of remote derivations, underscores the similarity between the Haydn approach and that seen in Beethoven.

728. ———. "Significant and Coincidental Resemblance between Classical Themes." *Journal of the American Musicological Society* 14 (1961):224-34.

Observes that the homogeneity typical of thematic material in Classical music gives rise to family resemblances, and cautions against grafting nineteenth-century conceptions about intentional thematic relationship onto the criticism of eighteenth-century music. Makes specific reference to Sondheimer's *Haydn* (item 1035), where the composer is credited with borrowing from Stamitz, Beck, and Boccherini. Sets forth two considerations relevant to determination of significant resemblance: a) statistical background, i.e. the extent to which themes in question belong to a characteristic type; and b) structural similarity (specifically with respect to melodic contour, rhythmic function, and tonal and harmonic background). Offers the relationship between the opening *Adagio* and the *Allegro* of Haydn's Symphony No. 103 as a model of significant resemblance.

729. Levy, Janet M. "Gesture, Form, and Syntax in Haydn's

Music." In *Haydn Studies* (item 73), pp. 355-62.

Remarks on the pervasive use of an archetypal closing gesture in the first movement of String Quartet Op. 50 No. 1. Shows that the gesture appears in its complete, normative form only at the end of the movement, where it is finally matched with the appropriate structural context.

730. Major, Ervin. "Ungarische Tanzmelodien in Haydns Bearbeitung." *Zeitschrift für Musikwissenschaft* 11 (1928-29):601-4.

Examines four Haydn pieces that attest to his connection with Hungarian music: an *Alla ongarese* (1772) for a mechanical instrument; the *Rondo all'ongarese* movements from the D-major Keyboard Concerto (1784) and the G-major Piano Trio (1795); and the *Hungarischer Nationalmarsch* (1802). Speculates on sources for melodic material in the *Rondo all'ongarese* of the G-major trio.

731. Marx, Karl. "Über die zyklische Sonatenform: Zu dem Aufsatz von Günther von Noé." *Neue Zeitschrift für Musik* 125 (1964):142-46.

In response to the Noé article, "Der Structurwandel der zyklischen Sonatenform" (pp. 55-62 in this volume of the journal), which dealt principally with nineteenth- and twentieth-century manifestations of the thematically or structurally unified instrumental cycle, argues that the concept need not exclude the idiom of Haydn and Mozart. Examples of cyclic unification cited in Haydn include Symphony No. 46; Keyboard Sonata in E flat, Hob. XVI:49; Cello Concerto in D; and Symphony No. 104.

732. Neubacher, Jürgen. *'Finis Coronat Opus': Untersuchungen zur Technik der Schlussgestaltung in der Instrumentalmusik Joseph Haydns, dargestellt am Beispiel der Streichquartette, mit einem Exkurs: Haydn und die rhetorische Tradition.* Tutzing: Hans Schneider, 1986. x, 278 pp.

Using as a frame of reference the concept of period structure put forth in Koch's *Versuch einer Anleitung zur Composition* (1782-93), examines intermediate and final closing passages. Considers aspects of harmony, voice-leading, embellishment, tempo, rhythm, and meter. Discusses the concept of the coda, and characterizes different kinds of closing gesture in accordance with the terminology of rhetoric. Draws principally on the string quartets, with occasional reference to other instrumental genres.

733. ———. "'Idee' und 'Ausführung': Zum Kompositionsprozess bei Joseph Haydn." *Archiv für Musikwissenschaft* 41 (1984):187-207.

Notes Haydn's use of the terms in his correspondence with Artaria regarding the 1780 publication of Keyboard Sonatas Hob. XVI:20 and 35-39. Drawing on descriptions of musical structure and process found in Koch, Riepel, and Vogler, and on Griesinger's discussion of Haydn's compositional technique, examines two sonata movements (from Hob. XVI:36 and 39) based on the same idea, but with a different *Ausführung*. Cites sketches to the finale of Symphony No. 99 in identifying three phases of a compositional process (invention of the main parts, the secondary parts, the working-out of the finished composition), and applies this three-phase model to the keyboard sonatas in question.

734. Nicolosi, Robert Joseph. "Formal Aspects of the Minuet and *Tempo di Minuetto* Finale in Instrumental Music of the Eighteenth Century." Ph.D. dissertation, Washington University, 1971. vii, 194 pp.

Ponders the historical process whereby the minuet persisted in later eighteenth-century instrumental cycles, and explores the significance of its occasional inclusion as a final movement. Examines various options chosen: two minuets in the same key, two in contrasting keys (i.e. minuet-trio), minuet with multiple trios, and single minuets. Considers aspects of phraseology and structural organization within the form. Pays particular attention to processes of expansion and enlargement to which the dance model is subjected. Includes extended discussion of variation and rondo forms. Haydn works cited include keyboard sonatas, keyboard trios, string trios, and symphonies.

735. Noske, Frits. "Le principe structural génétique dans l'oeuvre instrumental de Joseph Haydn." *Revue belge de musicologie* 12 (1958):35-39.

Proposes that in addition to thematic polarity and dialectic treatment of certain melodic and rhythmic elements, the principle identified in the title constitutes a third foundation of structural technique for Viennese Classicism. Associates this principle with the process of generating subsequent themes from the substance of the foregoing. Includes consideration of rhythmic as well as melodic relationships, and links the process with affinities between themes in a movement, between a minuet and its trio, and between a slow introduction and the *Allegro* proper.

736. Paul, Steven E. "Comedy, Wit, and Humor in Haydn's Instrumental Music." In *Haydn Studies* (item 73), pp. 450-56.

Ferrets out early critical references to aspects of humor in Haydn's music, and offers representative instances in which Haydn mocks convention to produce a striking, unexpected effect. Cites examples of understatement as well as overstatement, witty uses of silence, false endings, rhythmically ambiguous passages, surprise returns, pianissimo endings, and musical puns (for example, the recurrence of an opening phrase at the close). Identifies Wranitzky's *Sinfonia Quodlibet* as an example of extramusical comedy inspired by the example of Haydn's *Farewell* Symphony.

737. ———. "Wit, Comedy, and Humour in the Instrumental Music of Franz Joseph Haydn." Ph.D. dissertation, Cambridge University, 1981. 491 pp.

Features critical analysis of notable special effects and compositional strategies. Distinguishes between comic effects involving overstatement and incongruity on one hand, and structural and formal wit, characterized by understatement and ambiguity, on the other. Pays particular attention to manifestations of humor as an organic ingredient that plays an integral role in the structure of a composition, and underscores the extent to which Haydn's instrumental music may embody humor without any exterior, programmatic reference. Includes background on theories of humor in philosophy, literature, and music; humor in music before Haydn; discussion of early critical writings on humor in Haydn; examination of Haydn's own writings and early biographical accounts that reflect his propensity for humor; and brief discussion of influence of Haydn's wit on other composers. Many music examples in score.

738. Perry-Camp, Jane. "A Laugh a Minuet: Humor in Late

Eighteenth-Century Music." *College Music Symposium* 19/2 (1979):19-29.

Pursues elements of humor in instrumental music, where humorous effect must depend on deviation from a predictable musical language or on "non-musical association with the sounds we hear." Concentrates on examples from Haydn and Mozart, with passing reference to other composers.

739. Petrobelli, Pierluigi. "Haydn e lo *Sturm und Drang.*" *Chigiana* 36 (1979):65-72.

Questions the reasoning of scholars who attempt to link the German literary movement with well-recognized stylistic peculiarities in works by Haydn from around 1770. Argues that whereas *Sturm und Drang* stood for rebellion against all forms of organization and rationality in favor of complete spontaneity of emotion, Haydn's fundamental approach to composition, including works from the period in question, requires rigorous logic and adherence to rational principles of construction. As an example, cites the thematically unified design that embraces all four movements of the allegedly "Sturm und Drang"-style Symphony No. 49.

740. Preussner, Eberhard. *Die bürgerliche Musikkultur: Ein Beitrag zur deutschen Musikgeschichte des 18. Jahrhunderts.* 2d ed. Kassel: Bärenreiter, 1954. 210 pp.

First published in 1935 (Hamburg: Hanseatische Verlagsanstalt). Portrays Haydn, standing between C.P.E. Bach and Beethoven, as a key figure in the development of a modern bourgeois music culture. Perceives an historically significant synthesis of folk-like, enlightened, and artistic elements in his music; emphasizes the international scope of his acclaim in later years, and identifies the early performances of *The Creation* for the benefit of charities as the reflection of contemporary middle-class ideals.

741. Prey, Stefan. "Originalität in Haydns Harmonik." *Musica* 36 (1982):136-39.

Contends that in most works by Haydn, but especially late ones, there are harmonic features that "show Haydn to be one of the most inspired and original composers in the history of music." Examines one passage each from the String Quartet Op. 54 No. 1 and *The Creation* and explains unusual harmonic elements, how they relate to the musical language of the period, and (for *The Creation*) how they serve an extramusical purpose.

742. Ratner, Leonard G. "*Ars combinatoria:* Chance and Choice in Eighteenth-Century Music." In *Studies in Eighteenth-Century Music: A Tribute to Karl Geiringer on His Seventieth Birthday,* edited by H.C. Robbins Landon and Roger E. Chapman, pp. 343-63. New York: Oxford University Press, 1970.

Explores the process of *ars combinatoria,* as used in random selection or by design. With specific reference to theorists and composers (including Haydn), describes different aspects of the process as applied to figures and motives, phrase and period structure, order of keys, and substitution or paraphrase for complete movements. Shows that it offered a means of construction well suited to musical materials of the eighteenth century.

743. ———. *Classic Music: Expression, Form, and Style.* New York: Schirmer Books, 1980. xvii, 475 pp.

A systematically organized exploration of stylistic ingredients. Includes discussion of dance-types, march, French overture, Turkish music, strict style, and fantasia; also rhetoric, texture, notation, articulation, ornamentation, formal stereotypes, national and regional styles, and stylistic dichotomies: high and low, serious and comic. Treatment of individual topics features quotation from contemporary theoretical sources and illustrative examples drawn from the repertory. Includes an extended analysis of Haydn's Keyboard Sonata in E flat, Hob. XVI:52, as well as references to numerous other Haydn sonatas, quartets, and symphonies.

744. ———. "Harmonic Aspects of Classic Form." Ph.D. dissertation, University of California at Berkeley, 1947. 184 pp.

A pathbreaking inquiry into the grammatical resources, devices, mannerisms, and conventions of late eighteenth- and early nineteenth-century harmony in instrumental music with respect to musical organization on the levels of phrase, period, theme, and larger design. Places major emphasis on aspects of harmony basic to the Classical conception of sonata form. Haydn works cited include Symphonies Nos. 101-4 and String Quartets Op. 20 Nos. 2

and 5, Op. 55 No. 1, Op. 74 No. 3, Op. 76 Nos. 2-5, and Op. 77 Nos. 1 and 2.

745. ———. "Theories of Form: Some Changing Perspectives." In *Haydn Studies* (item 73), pp. 347-51.

Drawing the distinction between nineteenth-century concepts of musical form as plan and the eighteenth-century prescriptive approach emphasizing process, argues that application of nineteenth-century, bi-thematic models to Haydn represents a contradiction of the generating forces of Classical form. Detects three aspects of eighteenth-century musical process central to Haydn's accomplishment: strict counterpoint; *style galant* (concentrated motivic play involving short melodic figures); and *ars combinatoria* (rearrangement, combination, and permutation of figures).

746. Reed, Carl H. "Motivic Unity in Selected Keyboard Sonatas and String Quartets of Joseph Haydn." Ph.D. dissertation, University of Washington, 1966. xi, 178 pp.

Examines processes whereby initial thematic kernels provide material for subsequent elaboration. Reviews the pertinent literature on the topic, and proposes the term "unimotivic" in place of "monothematic" to describe movements that exemplify the procedure. Delineates four types of motive in Haydn (primary, secondary, introductory, and rhythmic), and analyzes movements from 15 keyboard sonatas and 25 string quartets. Many music examples in score.

747. Reti, Rudolph. "The Role of Duothematicism in the Evolution of Sonata Form." *The Music Review* 17 (1956):110-19.

Proposes that in a coherent, unified movement, contrasting themes must betray some underlying similarity in motivic content and contour, and senses that such connections are essential to the fulfillment of the potential of duothematic sonata form. With respect to Haydn, distinguishes several alternatives, including a real second theme, an unschematic succession of different groups, a unithematic design, and the recurrence of a primary theme toward the end of an exposition. Discerns vacillation and experimentation in Haydn's approach, and a tendency to waver between uni- and duothematic approaches without settling on a definitive solution.

748. Rosen, Charles. *The Classical Style: Haydn, Mozart, Beethoven.* 2d ed. New York: Viking, 1972. 467 pp.

Through the examination of telling or distinctive passages in selected representative works, offers a wide-ranging portrayal of compositional procedures that inform the works of the masters. Includes introductory chapters on eighteenth-century musical language, theories of form, origins of the style, its coherence, and the relationship between structure and ornament. Chapters devoted to Haydn feature the genres of string quartet, symphony, piano trio, and church music. First published in 1971 (New York: Viking).

749. ———. *Sonata Forms.* New York: W.W. Norton, 1980. 344 pp.

Highlighting the major instrumental works of Haydn, Mozart, Beethoven, and Schubert, with some representation by predecessors, lesser contemporaries, and successors, offers chapters on ternary and binary forms, aria, and concerto in addition to discussions of the evolution of sonata form proper. Devotes attention to Haydn's development sections, his concept of the "premature reprise," his mass movements, and the phenomenon of relationship between thematic motive and larger structure. Shows how Haydn's "unorthodox structures fulfill the expectations of the form as well as the more common procedures do, and how he uses one theme to the same purpose that another composer uses many." Defends Haydn's disparaging assessment of Sammartini as a "Schmierer." Many music examples, including some in score.

750. Rudolf, Max. "Storm and Stress in Music." *Bach* 3/2 (1972):3-13; 3/3 (1972):3-11.

Takes Théodore de Wyzewa to task for incautious speculation on the apparent phenomenon of a "Romantic crisis" mirrored in some of Haydn's music from the 1770s and for uninformed generalizations on the significance of a *Sturm und Drang* movement in the arts. Incorporates relevant quotations from the Wyzewa article (item 783). Scolds Geiringer (item 242) for following Wyzewa's lead and making sweeping generalizations about Haydn's being influenced by a contemporary *Zeitgeist.* Describes the Klinger play, originally entitled *Wirrwarr,* and places it in the context of German, English, and French literary currents of the time. Cites early uses of the term *Sturm und Drang* to describe a movement, and points out the inadequacy of the word "stress" (suggesting an exterior force) as a translation of "Drang" (implying internal compulsion). Isolates traits associated with "storm and stress" in eighteenth-century music, and proposes a list of representative theatrical and instrumental works composed between 1738 and 1781 that prominently display these qualities. In a parallel column, lists literary works recognized as having exerted influence on the movement. Proposes that the phenomenon as witnessed in Haydn represents part of a prolonged evolutionary development and not a sudden change undergone under some exterior influence.

751. Russell, Tilden A. "Minuet, Scherzando, and Scherzo: The Dance Movement in Transition, 1781-1825." Ph.D. dissertation, University of North Carolina, 1983. 329 pp.

Beginning with Haydn's Op. 33 quartets and ending with Mendelssohn's Octet, Op. 20, examines this period of artistic transition from the vantage point of the dance movements: their historical background and their manifestations within the specified time-span. Offering background discussion of the relevant specialist literature, takes issue with Nicolosi's dissertation (item 734) on *tempo di minuetto* finales, and attempts to compensate for its deficiencies, particularly in the area of tempo. Adopts a semantic approach, tracing the history of the terms, "by whatever principles they might be governed," rather than an evolutionary approach that would try to match the terms with the purported development of a genre. Recounts the history of the terms and their application, delineates traditional procedures, examines aspects of style (including tempo, meter, key, aspects of structure, and the contrast between minuet and trio), and examines pertinent issues of late eighteenth-century aesthetics, notably the comic element and British influence on German thought. Numerous references to Haydn; extensive bibliography.

752. Schenk, Erich. "Das Weltbild Joseph Haydns." In Erich Schenk. *Ausgewählte Aufsätze, Reden und Vorträge,* pp. 86-99. Graz: Hermann Böhlaus Nachf., 1967. Previously published in *Almanach der österreichischen Akademie der Wissenschaften* 109 (1959):245-72.

Discusses the multiplicity of influences on Haydn, both

musical and nonmusical, in the successive phases of his career. Explains the established traditions and contemporary fashions that contributed to his compositional synthesis.

753. Schering, Arnold. "Künstler, Kenner und Liebhaber der Musik im Zeitalter Haydns und Goethes." In Arnold Schering. *Von grossen Meistern der Musik*, pp. 90-123. Leipzig: Koehler & Amelang, 1940. Previously published in *Jahrbuch der Musikbibliothek Peters* 38 (1931):9-23.

Contrasts the characteristic seventeenth- and early eighteenth-century distinction between the musical specialist and non-specialist to the later eighteenth-century phenomenon of dynamic interaction among artist, connoisseur, and amateur. Links Haydn's world-wide success with his inexhaustible talent for appealing to the latter two groups. Views *The Creation* as a work whose universality eradicated the boundaries between sacred and secular, between Enlightenment and Romantic, between high and low, and between connoisseur and amateur.

754. Schmalzriedt, Siegfried. "Charakter und Drama: Zur historischen Analyse von Haydnschen und Beethovenschen Sonatensätzen." *Archiv für Musikwissenschaft* 42 (1985):37-66.

In quest of an improvement over the application of standard sonata-form models as a yardstick for criticism, surveys the descriptions of instrumental form in Francesco Galeazzi's *Elementi teorico-pratici di musica* (vol. 2, 1796) and Anton Reicha's *Traité de haute composition musicale* (1826). Works studied from this vantage point include Haydn's String Quartet in B flat, Op. 64 No. 3.

755. Schmidt, Leopold. "Joseph Haydn, Volksgesang und Volkslied." In *Joseph Haydn und die Literatur seiner Zeit* (item 79), pp. 25-33.

Demonstrates that Gottfried van Swieten had no need to advise Haydn on the use of folksongs and folk instruments in *The Seasons:* long before composing the oratorio, Haydn knew and made use of folk materials. Representative examples are discussed, in addition to melodies by Haydn that made their way into the folk repertory.

* Schnerich, Alfred. *Joseph Haydn und seine Sendung.* 2d

ed., with style-critical appendix by Wilhelm Fischer. Zurich: Amalthea-Verlag, 1926. 282 pp.

Cited as item 285.

756. Scholz, Gottfried. "Zu Haydns Menuetten." In *Joseph Haydn Kongress* (item 76), pp. 465-70.

Explores Haydn's treatment of the minuet in light of the contemporary social environment for ballroom dancing. Distinguishes between functional dances and the stylized dances of multi-movement instrumental works.

757. Schrade, Leo. "Joseph Haydn als Schöpfer der Klassischen Musik." In Leo Schrade. *De Scientia Musicae Studia atque Orationes,* edited by Ernst Lichtenhahn, pp. 506-18. Bern: Paul Haupt, 1967. Previously published in *Universitas* 17 (1962):767-78 and in *Basler National-Zeitung,* 24 May 1959.

Depicts Haydn as an autodidactic spirit and as the first composer to overcome Baroque style. Credits him with causing German music to outgrow its provincialism through the originality of his genius. Discusses the development of Haydn's quartets, and sees in these works the strongest concentration of his creativity. Places the birth of Classical style in 1781, the year of the Op. 33 quartets. Ponders the effects of isolation on Haydn's originality and the consequences of his view that form is dependent on thematic invention.

758. Schroeder, David P. "Haydn and Gellert: Parallels in Eighteenth-Century Music and Literature." *Current Musicology,* no. 35 (1983), pp. 7-18.

Suggests parallels between the literary aims of Gellert as a proponent of middle-class enlightenment and certain ideals reflected in Haydn's instrumental music of the 1780s. Citing Gellert's belief that literature should promote the improvement of society through moral, aesthetic, and educational means, identifies the realization of enlightenment goals in Haydn's works: for example the Op. 33 quartets, with their metaphorical engagement of four individuals in a strong sense of unified purpose, and the first movement of Symphony No. 83, where opposition proves inevitable, and the highest form of unity is shown to be one in which opposing forces coexist.

759. ———. "Melodic Source Material and Haydn's Creative Process." *The Musical Quarterly* 68 (1982):496-515.

Concentrating on a notion of the dramatic representation of opposites, notably in the contrast of thematic content between slow introduction and first-movement *Allegro* proper of the late symphonies, explores the terrain of possible melodic source materials in search of insight into Haydn's creative process. More interested in Haydn's spontaneous exploitation of a national heritage than in specific sources for specific melodies, proposes a link between the relative darkness and ambiguity of the introductions and their possible sources in plainchant, folksong, and hymn traditions that have to do with death, sin, and sorrow; and contrasts this association with the "life-reinforcing characteristics of folk dancing" suggested by the *Allegro* themes. Includes substantial bibliographical information on hymn books, collections of spiritual songs, and folksong collections.

760. Schwarting, Heino. "Ungewöhnliche Repriseneintritte in Haydns späterer Instrumentalmusik." *Archiv für Musikwissenschaft* 17 (1960):168-82.

Observes that whereas the transition to the recapitulation in Mozart typically involves an organic, natural continuity, the approach witnessed in Haydn and Beethoven features confrontation and tension. Examines structural and expressive implications of the point of recapitulation in late Classical sonata form, and discusses the historical question of alternatives to the normal dominant preparation. Citing elements of tension, surprise, and deception in Haydn's characteristic solutions, concludes that he provided an essential stimulus for Beethoven, and that the younger composer, rather than copying Haydn, applied the spirit of his approach in an original fashion.

761. Scott, Marion M. "Haydn: Fresh Facts and Old Fancies." *Proceedings of the Royal Musical Association* 68 (1941-42):87-105.

Goes back to an idea found in Carpani (item 172) about a secret method of composing that Haydn had developed. Claims to have uncovered the secret, which involves derivation of an entire work, even its proportions, from an initial motto. Attempts to apply this theory to Symphony No. 103 and Piano Sonata No. 52.

762. Sidorowicz, Alexander E. "The Proportional and Spatial Analysis of the First Movement Sonata-Allegro Form of Mozart, Haydn, and Beethoven." Ph.D. dissertation, Kent State University, 1981. iii, 93 pp.

Constitutes the second, separately paginated part of a two-part dissertation, the first, unrelated part of which is titled "'The Stroke of an Oar,' A Triptych for Narrator, Soprano, Baritone, and Chamber Ensemble." Computes proportions of introduction, exposition, development, recapitulation, and coda for a sampling of first movements of solo keyboard sonatas, string quartets, and symphonies. Concludes that Haydn has relatively longer development sections than either Mozart or Beethoven, so that whereas the placement of the recapitulation in Mozart and Beethoven approximates the Golden-Section proportion (.618), in Haydn it tends to fall closer to a point three-fourths of the way through the movement.

763. Širola, Božidar. "Haydn und Beethoven und ihre Stellung zur kroatischen Volksmusik." In *Beethoven-Zentenarfeier, Wien, 26. bis 31. März 1927; Internationaler musikhistorischer Kongress*, pp. 111-15. Vienna: Universal, 1927.

Discusses and criticizes Kuhač's study on Haydn's national origins and use of folk materials, and names three Croatian folksongs incorporated in works by Haydn.

764. Sisman, Elaine R. "Haydn's Hybrid Variations." In *Haydn Studies* (item 73), pp. 509-15.

Favors two broad categories, strophic and hybrid, as a framework for discussion of Haydn's compositional procedure in variation movements. Includes a table that associates 61 hybrid-variation movements with specific subcategories: "rondo-variation," "alternating rondo-variation," "alternating strophic-variation," "ternary," and "unusual."

765. ———. "Haydn's Variations." Ph.D. dissertation, Princeton University, 1978. xvii, 340 pp.

Uses structural and terminological guidelines derived from eighteenth-century theorists, principally Koch, to classify and examine about 150 variation movements in Haydn's instrumental oeuvre. Classifies different procedures employed and traces changes in Haydn's approach to variation design in the course of his career. Determines that more than half the movements may be classified as strophic variations, but that after 1772 Haydn betrays an increasing tendency to employ hybrid types and to explore new alternatives for the integration of variation procedures in a unified composition. Cites "rondo-variations" that are in effect strophic variations with inserted couplets. Includes detailed description of procedures in representative works singled out for discussion.

766. ———. "Small and Expanded Forms: Koch's Model and Haydn's Music." *The Musical Quarterly* 68 (1982):444–75.

Considers the concept of internal expansion as expounded in theoretical writings of Riepel and Koch as a foundation for examining related procedures in Haydn. Examples discussed include the slow movement of Symphony No. 14, which constitutes an expansion of the theme from the variation set in Divertimento Hob. II:11 (fourth movement), and the first movement of Piano Trio Hob. XV:19, which involves variations on two themes, one in minor, one in major, with a concluding *Presto* that expands the major theme into a coda-like variation.

767. Somfai, László. "Haydn's Eszterháza: The Influence of Architecture on Music." *The New Hungarian Quarterly* 23/87 (1982):195-201.

Offers background on Haydn's architectural environment in Vienna, Eisenstadt, and (especially) Eszterháza. Considers the impressions that the new palace may have exerted on Haydn, especially during the years 1768–72, as he encountered it on a daily basis. Notes the remarkable symmetries of the edifice and its exaggerated grandeur in the context of a spacious rural landscape. Speculates on a link with Haydn's search for an ideal balance of inner movements in his Op. 20 and Op. 33 quartets.

768. ———. "The London Revision of Haydn's Instrumental Style." *Proceedings of the Royal Musical Association* 100 (1973-74):159–74.

Discerns important reasons for the revision of Haydn's style for London: to attract the attention of his audience; to take account of the different social makeup, concert conventions, and acoustics in London (particularly the Hanover Square Rooms); and to use the security of his reputation to take risks and experiment. Examines samples from different genres to identify features characteristic of the London works, and determines which of these were preserved in works that post-date the London sojourns.

769. ———. "Opus-Planung und Neuerung bei Haydn." *Studia Musicologica Academiae Scientiarum Hungaricae* 22 (1980):87-110.

Explores from several vantage points (historical, documentary, analytical, and creative) the question of actual order of composition within planned sets of instrumental works. Focusing mainly on the quartets (e.g. Op. 17, 20, 64) finds characteristic patterns of tonal planning, and detects a certain "intensity curve" in the flow of inspiration as Haydn executes such a cycle: concentration on the challenge of a new artistic conception, temporary exhaustion of creative energy, then the recapturing of innovative inspiration toward the end of a set.

770. ———. "Vom Barock zur Klassik: Umgestaltung der Proportionen und des Gleichgewichts in zyklischen Werken Joseph Haydns." In *Joseph Haydn und seine Zeit* (item 80), pp. 64-72.

Traces the organization of Haydn's early multi-movement works with respect to the juxtaposition of different meters, tempos, and form-types; then proceeds to an intricately reasoned conclusion regarding the six quartets of Op. 33: they represent two models (the B minor, E-flat, C, and B major constituting one, the quartets in G and D belonging to the other). Both models reflect an apparently conscious attempt to achieve a large-scale, uniquely well-balanced architectural equilibrium, one that achieves independence from the lopsided proportions of earlier works, while differing from the likewise lopsided Classical model characteristic of the later quartets. Identifies the time of composition of these works as a moment of complete independence before the establishment of Classical conventions.

771. Steinbeck, Wolfram. *Das Menuett in der Instrumentalmusik Joseph Haydns.* Edited by Hans Heinrich Eggebrecht. Munich: Emil Katzbichler, 1973. 175 pp.

Traces the development of novel and individualistic approaches to the minuet genre in Haydn's symphonies and string quartets. Comments on the relationship between Haydn's manner and the tradition represented by his predecessors, notably Telemann. Analytical discussion concentrates on questions of period structure, phraseology, and metrical emphasis. Supplies numerous music examples and structural diagrams.

772. Sutcliffe, W. Dean. "Haydn's Musical Personality." *The Musical Times* 130 (1989):341-44.

In searching for the artistic and emotional sources of Haydn's creative accomplishment, finds that both performances and critiques of his music lack coherence and "affective focus." Counters traditional assessments, with their emphasis on purity, directness of expression, and ingenuous simplicity, by pointing out qualities of strategic complexity, irony, ambiguity, and contradiction. Shows that no available view of the composer satisfactorily encompasses these aspects. Deplores the tendency to comprehend Haydn's music not on its own terms, but from the vantage point of Mozart on one hand and Beethoven on the other, and defends Sondheimer's controversial study (item 1035) by showing that it at least acknowledges "the intellectual power of Haydn's formal structures."

773. Szabolcsi, Bence. "Joseph Haydn und die ungarische Musik." *Beiträge zur Musikwissenschaft* 1/2 (1959):62-73. Reprinted in *Bericht über die Internationale Konferenz zum Andenken Joseph Haydns* (item 70), pp. 159-75.

A study of Hungarian folk elements in Haydn's music. Examines earlier studies concerned with Hungarian and East European influences, and discusses the virtual lack of sources for early Hungarian folk music. Names works by Haydn that contain Hungarian elements, and shows that Haydn is known to have owned some Hungarian national dances. Speculates on the types of folk music Haydn is likely to have heard (instrumental, dance, gypsy, and to a lesser extent, vocal), and presents evidence that folk music was performed at Eszterháza. Analyzes music examples drawn from Haydn's works and Hungarian music. Abbreviated version in *Österreichische Musikzeitschrift* 21 (1966):589-94.

774. ———. "Ein melodiegeschichtlicher Beitrag zu Haydn." *Studia Musicologica Academiae Scientiarum Hungaricae* 2 (1962):281-82.

Concerns the "Nachtwächter" melody whose quotation in an early divertimento and in Symphony No. 60 had been noted by Landon in the *Supplement* (1961) to *The Symphonies of Joseph Haydn* (item 964). Traces the ancestry of the melody to a song heard in the Danube region since the 16th century. Cites this as an instance of Haydn's drawing upon the stimulus of a common language of folk traditions.

775. Tobel, Rudolf von. *Die Formenwelt der klassischen Instrumentalmusik.* Bern: Paul Haupt, 1935. xvi, 357 pp.

An ambitious attempt to categorize and describe approaches to structure and compositional procedure in instrumental music by the eighteenth- and nineteenth-century masters. Includes consideration of meter and tempo contrast, periodicity, thematic differentiation, development, connection between themes, recurrence and recapitulation. Many references to Haydn throughout (principally symphonies and string quartets). Hampered by a dearth of music examples or diagrams.

776. Todd, R. Larry. "Joseph Haydn and the *Sturm und Drang*: A Revaluation." *The Music Review* 41 (1980):172-96.

Indicates that the *Sturm und Drang* elements normally associated with Haydn's minor-key works occur also in many major-key compositions. Associates Haydn's output of the late 1760s and early 1770s with a "confrontation between two distinctly different instrumental styles," those of the late Baroque and early Classical periods, rather than "expressions of a *crise de l'âme.*" Examines this stylistic clash with respect to Symphonies 39, 49, and 59, and traces some of Haydn's "erratic mannerisms" in the late 1760s to the influence of C.P.E. Bach.

777. Vignal, Marc. "Die goldene Zahl in Werken Joseph Haydns." In *Joseph Haydn Kongress* (item 76), pp. 146-53.

Discovers instances in which structural punctuation within themes and sections conforms to Golden Section proportions. Works cited include the first movements of Keyboard Sonata Hob. XVI:52, Symphony No. 92, and Symphony No. 101. Offers diagrams and thematic quotations.

778. Webster, James. "Binary Variants of Sonata Form in Early

Haydn Instrumental Music." In *Joseph Haydn Kongress* (item 76), pp. 127-35.

Reports on the examination of 289 movements from Haydn's symphonies, divertimentos, string quartets, string trios, and works with keyboard (divertimentos, trios, and sonatas) composed no later than 1765. Provides a summary table representing salient features of structure in movements where tonal return is not coordinated with the reprise of the primary theme.

779. Wheelock, Gretchen A. "Wit, Humor, and the Instrumental Music of Joseph Haydn." Ph.D. dissertation, Yale University, 1979. 314 pp.

Aiming to place the phenomenon of Haydn's musical wit and humor in a suitable historical context, incorporates results of an extensive and penetrating background study. Includes well-documented chapters on theories of the comic in music, eighteenth-century concepts of taste, eighteenth- and early nineteenth-century views of wit and humor, and contemporaries' views of Haydn's style. Discussion of the music, focused principally on minuets and finales, features instances of surprise and thwarted expectation. Examines both the manipulation of conventional procedures and "incongruities specific to the materials presented in a given movement." Making note of a connection between Haydn's late eighteenth-century popularity and an appetite for novelty, originality, and individuality among his middle-class audiences, characterizes his compositional personality as a "disposition for unconventional uses of conventions."

780. Williams, Peter. "Encounters with the Chromatic Fourth ... or, More on Figurenlehre." *The Musical Times* 126 (1985):276-78, 339-43.

Makes the point that composers' use of the chromatic fourth need not necessarily involve programmatic significance. Discusses the question of composition by *figurae* in Haydn, and cites Haydn compositions that employ the chromatic fourth, including the motet *Insanae et vanae curae* and the slow movement of Symphony No. 92.

781. Willner, Channan. "Chromaticism and the Mediant in Four Late Haydn Works." *Theory and Practice* 13 (1988):79-114.

Underscores the importance of the major mediant as a tonal goal in development sections of Haydn's sonata-form movements. Cites instances in which the mediant serves as the "voice-leading anchor of the development," and finds that while it acts less often as the principal goal of the section, it tends to function as the "development's focal point" and last tonal goal before the retransition. With the aid of Schenker sketches and music examples, examines in detail four movements in which the mediant plays a significant role: Piano Sonata in C (Hob. XVI:50), first movement; Symphony No. 90, finale; Symphony No. 101, first movement; and Symphony No. 104, finale.

782. Winkler, Klaus. "Alter und neuer Musikstil im Streit zwischen den Berlinern und Wienern zur Zeit der Frühklassik." *Die Musikforschung* 33 (1980):37-45.

Cites passages from Haydn's 1776 autobiographical sketch that allude to negative criticism of his chamber music on the part of Berlin critics. Examines the conflict in point of view between Berlin (where attitudes were still shaped by a contrapuntal, trio-sonata tradition) and South German and Viennese circles (influenced by Italian tastes and the newer homophonic style). Proposes a connection between early criticism endured and Haydn's studies of counterpoint, and examines his application of fugal technique in the baryton trios and Op. 20 quartets. Finds in the latter works an integration of contrapuntal technique and personal idiom that opened new expressive possibilities and contributed to the ripening of Classical style.

783. Wyzewa, Théodore de. "A propos du centenaire de la mort de Joseph Haydn." *Revue des deux mondes* 79 (1909): 935-46.

Extols Haydn's greatness, deprecates C.F. Pohl's incomplete biography, comments on the standard, paternal image of the composer, and welcomes the prospect of a complete critical edition of his works. Observes that the three volumes of early symphonies represented in Eusebius Mandyczewski's edition betray a virile energy that contradicts common perceptions of Haydn's artistic personality. Focuses particular attention on a stunning change of style perceived in the 1772 symphonies, which feature unprecedented expressive urgency and passionate content. Hypothesizes that the stimulus for this break with the past, heralded in the 1771 C-minor Sonata (Hob. XVI:20) and followed by the retreat to a *galant* idiom by

1773, must lie in some crisis in the composer's personal life. Notes that while no obvious source for this Romantic inspiration can be documented, the works in question point to some personal tragedy, perhaps involving an unknown "immortal beloved." Links the artistic manifestations of Haydn's Romantic crisis with the contemporaneous *Sturm und Drang* movement prevalent in the arts in Germany. Concerning the untypical, but characteristically Mozartean qualities of Haydn's Symphony No. 99, proposes that this work reflects Haydn's supposed encounter with Mozart's late works upon his return to Vienna after the first London sojourn. Perceiving the symphony as a tribute to the artistic spirit of the deceased composer, cites its unusually lyrical phraseology and rhythmic continuity.

784. Zeller, Hans Rudolf. "Abweichungen vom Thema." In *Joseph Haydn* (item 75), pp. 47-66.

Uses the first movement of Keyboard Sonata Hob. XVI:50 as a basis for exploring the concept of theme: theme as entity; thematic elaboration, variation, and development; and the function of the theme within a larger design.

785. Županović, Lovro. "L'Influence du chant populaire des Croates, spécialement de Burgenland, sur la création de Joseph Haydn." In *Joseph Haydn Kongress* (item 76), pp. 209-17.

A concise overview of issues pertinent to the question of Croatian influence in Haydn's music: sources, the nature and extent of Haydn's borrowings, the possibility of Haydn influence on regional popular melody, and the significance of Haydn's evident interest in folk music as a precedent for practices of later composers. Includes numerous examples of Croatian melodies and related passages in Haydn's instrumental works.

Sacred Works

786. Becker-Glauch, Irmgard. "Die Kirchenmusik des jungen Haydn." In *Der junge Haydn* (item 81), pp. 74-84.

Refers to item 507. Examines the earliest known sacred

works from the composer's early years in Vienna: two masses (*Missa brevis in F a due soprani* and *Missa Rorate coeli desuper* in G) and the *Lauda Sion*. Proposes that the *Rorate* Mass predates the F major, and that *Lauda Sion*, whose fresh, folk- or songlike thematic style anticipates Haydn's mature, personal idiom, is the most advanced of the three. Makes note of stylistic similarities between the 1756 *Salve Regina* and the *Ave Regina* in A.

787. ———. "The Masses of Joseph Haydn." In *Haydnfest* (item 71), pp. 32-37.

A chronological survey of the masses, with updated information on chronology. Includes background on the individual works, miscellaneous observations on the music, and biographical material. Contains illustrations and facsimiles, including sample pages from the autographs of the *Mariazell* Mass and *Creation* Mass.

788. Berkenstock, James T. "The Smaller Sacred Compositions of Joseph Haydn." 2 vols. Ph.D. dissertation, Northwestern University, 1975. viii, 230 pp.; 126 pp.

Concerned with sacred works other than masses and oratorios. With regard to the intertwining of sacred and secular features in this repertory, examines Haydn's personal attitudes toward religion and the range of acceptable stylistic choices available to composers of the time. Argues that Haydn's approach was not inappropriate in light of his personal nature and creative environment. Discusses dating, authenticity, and source transmission. Treatment of style and structure places emphasis on matters of vocal technique, tonal organization, the manipulation of text to accommodate structural design, and the composer's use of ritornello procedure and sonata-binary form.

789. Biba, Otto. "Die kirchenmusikalischen Werke Haydns." In *Joseph Haydn in seiner Zeit* (item 77), pp. 142-51.

Relating Haydn's approaches to existing traditions and models, provides brief descriptions of major sacred compositions. Places particular emphasis on pre-1786 works.

790. Brand, Carl Maria. *Die Messen von Joseph Haydn*. Würzburg-Aumühle: Konrad Triltsch, 1941. Reprint. Walluf bei Wiesbaden: Martin Sändig, 1973. 548 pp.

A chronologically organized discussion of the masses, divided into two main parts: works written between 1750 and 1782 and the six late masses, 1796-1802. The work-by-work treatment includes documentary as well as historical discussion, but emphasis falls on description of the music, supported by numerous examples. Further topics addressed include changing views on Haydn as a church composer, reasons for the hiatus in his composition of music for the church, and Haydn as Catholic and Freemason. Datings for some of the works have since been revised.

791. Chusid, Martin. "Some Observations on Liturgy, Text and Structure in Haydn's Late Masses." In *Studies in Eighteenth-Century Music: A Tribute to Karl Geiringer on His Seventieth Birthday,* edited by H.C. Robbins Landon and Roger E. Chapman, pp. 125-35. New York: Oxford University Press, 1970.

Confirms Landon's thesis that "the late Haydn Masses are in their fundamental construction symphonies for voices and orchestra" (see item 964, epilogue) by proposing that each of these works subdivides into three tonally unified "vocal symphonies"--Kyrie, Gloria; Credo; Sanctus, Benedictus, Agnus Dei--whose interior arrangement of keys, tempos, and meters proves roughly analogous to the characteristic movement-sequence of the symphony.

792. Fellerer, Karl Gustav. "Joseph Haydns Messen." In *Bericht über die Internationale Konferenz zum Andenken Joseph Haydns* (item 70), pp. 41-48.

Views Haydn's output of masses against the backdrop of enlightened thinking on appropriate sacred style. Examines the cumulative influences on Haydn, from Fux's *Gradus ad Parnassum* to symphonic orchestral style. Proposes that while Haydn did not adhere to ecclesiastical guidelines on comprehensibility of text, he did strive from the very start for a distinctly sacred type of musical expression, and that he perfected this approach in his late works.

793. ———. "The Liturgical Basis of Haydn's Masses." In *Haydn Studies* (item 73), pp. 164-68.

Shows how Joseph II's reforms and rationalistic views on liturgy during the Enlightenment not only brought about the hiatus in Haydn's output of masses but also gave Haydn cause to reflect on the problems of church music and to change his approach in the late masses of 1796-1802.

794. Geiringer, Karl. "Joseph Haydn als Kirchenmusiker: Die kleineren geistlichen Werke des Meisters im Eisenstädter Schloss." *Kirchenmusikalisches Jahrbuch* 44 (1960):54-61.

Another version of item 795, in translation.

795. ———. "The Small Sacred Works by Haydn in the Esterhazy Archives at Eisenstadt." *The Musical Quarterly* 45 (1959):460-72.

Describes a body of small sacred works preserved among performance copies at Eisenstadt. Spanning the years 1756-99, this group consists of both contrafacta of secular pieces (including the Latin cantata *Applausus,* 1768) and pieces originally written for the church. For each work, briefly discusses the music and offers information on date of composition, early performances, secular models, annotations in the source, and characteristics of the manuscript. Another version published in *Bericht über die Internationale Konferenz zum Andenken Joseph Haydns* (item 70), pp. 49-56, as "Sidelights on Haydn's Activities in the Field of Sacred Music: Small Works of Church Music in Eisenstadt."

796. Gibbs, Thomas J., Jr. "A Study of Form in the Late Masses of Joseph Haydn." Ph.D. dissertation, University of Texas at Austin, 1972. xvii, 378 pp.

Approaches the topic from the standpoint of symphonic influence on aspects of structure and compositional procedure. Subjects first, second, and fourth movements of the London symphonies to systematic analysis of structure, then examines the movements of the six late masses. Musical elements scrutinized include dynamics, orchestration, harmony, and melodic organization. Considers the interaction of the mass texts and musical design, and finds that structure in the non-polyphonic fast movements from Gloria and Credo settings is largely text-inspired, whereas in slow portions of the Gloria, Credo, Sanctus, and Agnus Dei, as well as in polyphonic sections, organization follows a more purely musical logic. Categorizing structural procedures with the aid of diagrams, finds little evidence of "symphonic character," and finds symphonic gestures usually absent. Concludes that symphonic form is not borrowed in the late masses, but that Haydn's mastery of structure evident in the late symphonies is reconstituted and reconceived for a different context and purpose.

797. Gruber, Gernot. "Musikalische Rhetorik und barocke Bildlichkeit in Kompositionen des jungen Haydn." In *Der junge Haydn* (item 81), pp. 168-91.

Identifies Haydn's adherence to traditional rhetorical figures and stylistic conventions as a decisively important factor in his early sacred works. Compositions cited include the *Missa brevis* in F (1749), *Salve Regina* in E (1756), *Stabat Mater* (1767), and the *Great Organ Mass* (1768-69). Emphasizing the need for further study, suggests that certain features associated with originality, expressive intensity, and innovation in these works actually reflect the influence of a persisting musical-rhetorical tradition.

798. Hughes, Rosemary. "Two Haydn Masses." *The Musical Times* 91 (1950):213-18.

Compares aspects of musical structure in two late masses in B flat: the *Theresienmesse* (1799) and *Harmoniemesse* (1802).

799. Kalisch, Volker. "Haydn und die Kirchenmusik: Ein analytischer Versuch am Beispiel des Benedictus aus der Schöpfungsmesse." *Musik und Kirche* 54 (1984):159-70.

An exceptionally detailed critical analysis of the movement, with particular emphasis on structural relationships between sections and thematic processes within sections. Isolates four distinct, interactive levels of compositional significance: formal/structural, content-bearing, textual, and theological.

800. Kantner, Leopold M. "Das Messenschaffen Joseph Haydns und seiner italienischen Zeitgenossen--Ein Vergleich." In *Joseph Haydn: Tradition und Rezeption* (item 78), pp. 145-59.

Points out elements in Haydn's masses that may be found in works of Italian contemporaries, predecessors, and successors. Concludes that Haydn's masses, despite a surprising stylistic similarity to these works, surpass them in quality, if only because his ideas and development of material were superior.

801. Krummacher, Friedhelm. "Symphonische Verfahren in Haydns späten Messen." In *Das musikalische Kunstwerk: Geschichte, Ästhetik, Theorie. Festschrift Carl Dahlhaus zum 60. Geburtstag,* edited by Hermann Danuser, Helga de la Motte-Haber, Silke Leopold, and Norbert Miller, pp. 455-81. Laaber: Laaber-Verlag, 1988.

Using as a point of departure Landon's often-cited characterization of the six late masses as a "symphonic legacy" (see the epilogue to item 964), examines aspects of text-setting, structure, and thematic development in various movements. Concluding that the masses achieve a synthesis of musically autonomous design and projection of text, proposes that the symphonic essence of these works resides not in structural analogies having to do with the cycle as a whole or with individual movements, but rather in the unfolding of a large-scale design using large-scale resources, vocal as well as instrumental.

802. Landon, H.C. Robbins. "Haydn Masses." In H.C. Robbins Landon. *Essays on the Viennese Classical Style: Gluck, Haydn, Mozart, Beethoven,* pp. 68-76. London: Barrie & Rockliff, 1970.

Originally a lecture for the British Broadcasting Corporation, 1967. Describes the historical and biographical circumstances associated with each of the works. Little emphasis on musical style.

803. Larsen, Jens Peter. "Beethovens C-dur-Messe und die Spätmessen Joseph Haydns." In *Beethoven-Kolloquium 1977: Dokumentation und Aufführungspraxis,* edited by Rudolf Klein, pp. 12-19. Kassel: Bärenreiter, 1978.

Examines the disparaging remark made by Prince Nikolaus II Esterházy in reaction to Beethoven's C-major Mass (the work was commissioned by the prince when Haydn was too infirm to accept such tasks). Considers possible reasons for Nikolaus' reaction, and to this end undertakes a comparison with Haydn's late masses. Analyzes large-scale structure in the six Haydn works, and finds a similarity of approach among them, shared also with the Beethoven mass. Determines, however, that within the large-scale framework, the two composers' approaches were very different: Haydn strove for unity, whereas Beethoven was concerned chiefly with intensification of expression. The C-major Mass is seen to depart from the Classical tradition, and this seems to account for the prince's reaction.

804. ———. "Beethoven's C-Major Mass and the Late Masses of Joseph Haydn." In Jens Peter Larsen. *Handel, Haydn, and the Viennese Classical Style,* translations by Ulrich Krämer, pp. 149-57. Ann Arbor: UMI Research Press, 1988.

Translation of item 803.

805. ———. "Haydn's Early Masses: Evolution of a Genre." In Jens Peter Larsen. *Handel, Haydn, and the Viennese Classical Style,* translations by Ulrich Krämer, pp. 137-48. Ann Arbor: UMI Research Press, 1988. Previously published in *American Choral Review* 24/2-3 (1982):48-60.

A chronological survey of the masses written through 1782. Describes salient features of each work, assessing its significance in Haydn's development as a composer of masses.

806. McCaldin, Denis. "Haydn's First and Last Work--The *Missa Brevis* in F Major." *The Music Review* 28 (1967):165-72.

Draws on Dies' biography (item 175) to tell of Haydn's joyful reaction to the rediscovery of his earliest mass (ca. 1749) and his work on a revision (1805). Briefly considers the nature of a *missa brevis,* and speculates on both why Haydn wrote the original work and why he changed it. The revision involved superimposing seven wind parts on the original texture of Viennese church trio and voices. The author examines the late wind writing and shows how it transformed the early version.

807. ———. "The *Missa Sancti Nicolai*; Haydn's Long *missa brevis.*" *Soundings,* no. 3 (1973), pp. 7-17.

Views the 1772 mass as a transitional work, bearing resemblance to earlier *missa brevis* procedures while foreshadowing means of expansion realized in later masses. Observes that Haydn, requiring an elaborate setting but pressed for time and lacking resources for a full-scale *missa solemnis,* chose to expand upon the *missa brevis* model. Examines methods of musical unification within separate movements, comments on the effective use of solo vocal quartet texture in the "Crucifixus pro nobis," and mentions the expansion of instrumentation to include horns and viola.

808. MacIntyre, Bruce C. "Die Entwicklung der konzertierenden Messen Joseph Haydns und seiner Wiener Zeitgenossen." *Haydn-Studien* 6/2 (1988):80-87.

Concerned with the extant Viennese repertory of masses from Haydn's generation that include solo voices in addition to four-voice chorus and orchestra. Considers form, instrumentation, handling of concerted instrumental parts and vocal *tutti* and *soli*, and customs of notation. Finds the amalgamation of such conventions as fugue and ritornello aria with sonata form to be symptomatic of a general tendency of the time; relates departures from earlier, standard instrumentation practices to the influence of other genres, notably the symphony; and discerns an increasing use of obbligato instrumental solos. Contrasts Haydn's approaches to those of his contemporaries, and observes a tendency toward less employment of *alla breve* and greater use of meters associated with dance and chamber music (3/4, 3/8, 6/8).

809. ———. "Viennese Common Practice in the Early Masses of Joseph Haydn." In *Joseph Haydn Kongress* (item 76), pp. 482-96.

Relates characteristics of Haydn's early masses to features observed in masses by Viennese composers of sacred music from 1741 (the death of Fux) to 1783 (the start of Joseph II's restrictive decrees). Covers works of 28 composers whose sacred music was performed in Vienna during this period. Concludes that Haydn's masses drew on a diverse assortment of Viennese traditions. Isolates innovative and distinctive practices of Haydn's, including unusual instrumentation, diversity of tonal plan, use of varied (rather than exact) repetition, rearrangement or omission of parts of liturgical texts in deference to musical form, and elements of surprise and drama. Includes summary tables of composers and style traits.

810. Martinotti, Sergio. "Note sulle Messe di Haydn." *Chigiana* 36 (1979):271-96.

Relates Haydn's late masses to the contemporaneous

symphonies and oratorios, and places them in the context of eighteenth-century Austrian church music. Compares their style with that of Michael Haydn's sacred music as well as Mozart's. Reviews early critiques, notably those that raise the question of appropriate sacred style. Detects in these works both the liberation from Baroque sacred-music tradition and the reflection of Enlightenment ideals. Also sees in them an anticipation of Beethoven, Schubert, and the early nineteenth-century *Biedermeier*. Addresses questions of text-setting within the different mass movements, cites aspects of symphonic influence, and notes the prominence of sonata-form procedure. Furnishes numerous music examples in score.

811. Pass, Walter. "Josephinism and the Josephinian Reforms Concerning Haydn." In *Haydn Studies* (item 73), pp. 168-71.

Inspects the musical reforms of Joseph II, and outlines main features of decrees that affected the church service and secular music. Suggests that while enlightened reform accounts for the pause in Haydn's writing of masses, the influence of the Enlightenment on Haydn himself remains unclear.

812. Pauly, Reinhard G. "The Reforms of Church Music under Joseph II." *The Musical Quarterly* 43 (1957):372-82.

Through numerous references to contemporary documents, elucidates Joseph II's attitudes and appraises the impact of his policies on Austrian church music of the 1780s. Calls attention to the emphasis on simplicity and economy, and speculates on the effect of his reforms on the sacred music of Haydn and Mozart.

813. Pfannhauser, Karl. "Glossarien zu Haydns Kirchenmusik." In *Joseph Haydn Kongress* (item 76), pp. 496-501.

A collection of miscellaneous facts concerning the late masses and the misattribution of sacred works (works falsely ascribed to Haydn and Haydn works falsely attributed to others).

814. Rosenberg, Wolf. "Weltliche Botschaften in Haydns Sakralwerken." *Österreichische Musikzeitschrift* 37 (1982):168-73.

Observes that the title of Kant's *Religion within the Limits of Reason Alone* had become a watchword for Haydn and many others, and that while Haydn's belief in God was steadfast, he bore a critical attitude toward the Bible, sacred ritual, and mysticism. Develops this idea by analyzing selected instances of secularism in Haydn's sacred music.

815. Schnerich, Alfred. "Die katholischen Glaubenssätze bei den Wiener Klassikern." *Zeitschrift für Musikwissenschaft* 8 (1925-26):231-35.

Provides background on artistic and symbolic representations of the Eucharist and Immaculate Conception, and suggests that by virtue of the available musical resources for vivid text setting, their definitive musical expression was attained in the time of Haydn and Mozart. Works singled out for discussion include Haydn's *Nelson* Mass and the *Missa in tempore belli.*

Oratorios

816. Barrett-Ayres, Reginald. "Haydn's Seven Last Words." *The Musical Times* 108 (1967):699-700.

Finds musical features which suggest that Haydn may have composed a choral version of *The Seven Last Words* before preparing his quartet arrangement in 1789. Raises the question of whether Friebert had access to such a version when composing his vocal setting, on which Haydn based a substantial portion of his own 1796 oratorio version.

* Bernhardt, Reinhold. "Aus der Umwelt der Wiener Klassiker: Freiherr Gottfried van Swieten (1734-1803)." *Der Bär: Jahrbuch von Breitkopf & Härtel* 6/9 (1929-30):74-166.

Cited as item 307.

817. Brown, A. Peter. "Haydn's Chaos: Genesis and Genre." *The Musical Quarterly* 73 (1989):18-59.

Examines sketches for the introductory movement of *The Creation* as a point of departure for critical interpretation. Pondering Haydn's thought processes and the resources and traditions he drew upon to give the work its shape and substance, discerns two compositional tiers, one involving strict counterpoint, the other suggesting free fantasia. Traces a growth process through the sequence of sketches, and examines the organization of the movement from the standpoint of traditional rhetoric. Identifies the movement as an *exordium* and in this vein proposes that the genre "ricercar," with its dual implications of improvised prelude and motet style, may be applicable. Includes facsimiles of the pertinent sketches.

818. Edelmann, Bernd. "Haydns '*Il ritorno di Tobia*' und der Wandel des 'Geschmacks' in Wien nach 1780." In *Joseph Haydn: Tradition und Rezeption* (item 78), pp. 189-214.

Shows how this oratorio was indebted to the Neapolitan opera tradition, and examines changing attitudes toward the work as that tradition waned. Offers quotations from contemporary writers on the subject of taste, and discusses how the Tonkünstler-Societät commissioned writers to shorten and reshape the oratorio librettos it used in order to conform to current tastes. Describes changes made by Haydn, then Neukomm, for revivals of the work by the Tonkünstler-Societät in 1784 and 1808.

819. Feder, Georg. "Die Jahreszeiten nach Thomson, in Musik gesezt von Joseph Haydn." In *Beiträge zur Geschichte des Oratoriums seit Händel: Festschrift Günther Massenkeil zum 60. Geburtstag,* edited by Rainer Cadenbach and Helmut Loos, pp. 185-201. Bonn: Voggenreiter, 1986.

Discusses van Swieten's sources for the libretto, and describes his transformation of the original material. Proposes that critics' condescension toward the text was undeserved, since van Swieten had provided for Haydn a wealth of "vivid and powerfully expressive images" as well as musically conceived forms that were "richly varied" and represented a "coherent whole." Observes that in structuring both *The Seasons* and *The Creation,* Haydn drew on the tradition of Handel's English oratorios, which placed great emphasis on choruses. Addresses the issue of tone painting, and describes three kinds represented in *The Seasons:* hunting calls, imitation of natural sounds, and symbolic depiction.

820. Gotwals, Vernon. "Haydn's *Creation* Revisited: An Introductory Essay." In *Studies in Music History: Essays for Oliver Strunk,* edited by Harold Powers, pp. 429-42.

Princeton: Princeton University Press, 1968.

Drawing on excerpts from Griesinger and Dies, examines the origin and early history of *The Creation.* Topics addressed include van Swieten's arrangement of Lidley's text, early performances, the work's financial success, the first edition, and Haydn's sketches. Considers the question of the English translations, and shows that for the English text that appeared in the first edition (along with the German), Haydn made careful musical adjustments. Compares excerpts from this text with subsequent translations, and concludes that the "unselfconscious original ... should be preserved in all its linguistic innocence." Discusses the sources for Lidley's text.

821. Gülke, Peter. "Worte Wortdeutung versperrend." In *Joseph Haydn* (item 75), pp. 74-78.

Reflects upon paradoxical aspects of Haydn's accomplishment in creating the oratorio version of *The Seven Last Words.*

822. Heartz, Daniel. "The Hunting Chorus in Haydn's *Jahreszeiten* and the 'Airs de chasse' in the *Encyclopédie.*" *Eighteenth-Century Studies* 9 (1976):523-39.

Observing that the traditional eighteenth-century repertory of French hunting calls came "as close to universality as any musical language of the time," calls attention to parallels between melodic materials of the hunting chorus in *The Seasons* and the hunting calls set forth in the illustrative plates that accompany Charles Georges Le Roy's 1763 article "Chasses" in the *Encyclopédie.* Suggests that Haydn expected his Viennese audience to recognize and understand the significance of numerous calls alluded to in the chorus. Examines musical subtleties involved in the interweaving of the calls, each with its specific purpose within the ritual of the hunt, in the choral and orchestral fabric. Includes four facsimile reproductions of plates from the *Encyclopédie* and numerous music examples.

823. His, Marie E. "Zu Haydn's 'Ein Mädchen, das auf Ehre hielt'." *Zeitschrift der Internationalen Musikgesellschaft* 12 (1910-11):159-61.

Cites studies by Max Friedlaender (item 909) and Georgy Calmus that reveal the connection between the text to

Hannchen's romance in Haydn's *Seasons* and a piece ("Fille d'honneur") in Mme. Favart's *Annette et Lubin.* Points to a long tradition behind the text, naming as a direct model "La Bergère rusée" (includes text and melody). Mentions as the known source for the melody of Favart's piece the folksong "La Pernotte" (see item 838).

* Horn, Hans-Jürgen. "FIAT LVX: Zum kunsttheoretischen Hintergrund der 'Erschaffung' des Lichtes in Haydns Schöpfung." *Haydn-Studien* 3 (1973-74):65-84.

Cited as item 329.

824\. Levarie, Siegmund. "The Closing Numbers of *Die Schöpfung.*" In *Studies in Eighteenth-Century Music: A Tribute to Karl Geiringer on His Seventieth Birthday,* edited by H.C. Robbins Landon and Roger E. Chapman, pp. 315-22. New York: Oxford University Press, 1970.

Asserts that Haydn had a distinct purpose in writing the second half of *The Creation*, part 3 (Nos. 31-34), often omitted in performance because of its seemingly anticlimactic character. Proposes that the second half is not only needed for structural balance, but that it also serves to parody the first half, much in the manner of parody in singspiel.

825\. Michel, Walter. "Die Tobias-Dramen bis zu Haydns Oratorium 'Il ritorno di Tobia'." *Haydn-Studien* 5 (1982-85):147-68.

Describes the biblical tale, then presents an overview of the history of its dramatic representation. Provides pertinent background on Aristotelian poetics and *Affektenlehre.* Comments on Giovanni Gastone Boccherini's text for the Haydn work, and shows that the dramatic personages function less as true characters than as vehicles for the representation of affections, as revealed notably in the numerous, prominent recurrences of the words "hope," "despair," "torment," and "fear." On the question of the text's message and edifying purpose, suggests a connection between the emphasis on "light" as a symbol and the German *Aufklärung.* Proposes that the text embodies an admonition to the young and impetuous Joseph II with regard to his implementation of Enlightenment ideals.

826\. Moe, Orin, Jr. "Structure in Haydn's *The Seasons.*" *The Haydn Yearbook* 9 (1975):340-48.

Discerning evidence of large-scale unity, most notably in the realm of tonal structure, sees the work as an instance of the pervasiveness of the sonata principle in music of the time. Identifies C as the central tonality, and suggests that the work as a whole constitutes a realization of the principle on a grand scale, the four parts of the oratorio (Spring, Summer, Autumn, Winter) corresponding to four parts of a sonata form (exposition, development, recapitulation, coda) with regard to structural procedure and tonal organization.

* Olleson, Edward. "Gottfried van Swieten, Patron of Haydn and Mozart." *Proceedings of the Royal Musical Association* 89 (1962-63):63-74.

Cited as item 352.

827. ———. "The Origin and Libretto of Haydn's *Creation.*" *The Haydn Yearbook* 4 (1968):148-68.

Offers a translation of van Swieten's letter, printed in the *Allgemeine musikalische Zeitung* (January 1799), on the origins of the work; examines the biblical and Miltonian sources of the text; studies the relationship between van Swieten's German version and the surviving English version printed in the published score; and speculates on the lost English original. Concludes that the English version in the score is not merely a retranslation, but was compiled by van Swieten directly from his English model. Casts doubt on Thomas Linley's supposed authorship of the libretto. Suggests that Linley may have played the role of middleman, and that the lost libretto may have actually been done by one of Handel's librettists, either Charles Jennens or Newburgh Hamilton.

828. Ravizza, Victor. *Joseph Haydn: Die Schöpfung.* 2 vols. Munich: Wilhelm Fink, 1981. 76 pp.; 19 pp.

Begins with general background, then examines the libretto's origins, with quotes from van Swieten's letter in the *Allgemeine musikalische Zeitung* (January 1799). Considers the intellectual climate of the times and analyzes the text. Offers a descriptive account of the non-recitative numbers, gives a general discussion of the recitatives, and addresses questions of tone painting and key characteristics. Reproduces pertinent documents, including contemporary letters and critiques. A separate pamphlet furnishes the libretto and musical incipits.

829. Riedel-Martiny, Anke. "Die Oratorien Joseph Haydns: Ein Beitrag zum Problem der Textvertonung." Ph.D. dissertation, Göttingen, 1965. 264 pp.

A detailed, multifaceted inquiry that explores the interaction of music and text in recitatives, arias, ensembles, and choruses from *Il ritorno di Tobia, The Creation,* and *The Seasons.* Also includes brief discussion of *The Seven Last Words.* Supplies background information on sources, and furnishes tables that represent key relationships, meter, tempo, length, text-form, and structural type. Strives for categorization and style-analytical portrayal of Haydn's characteristic procedures. Features an extended discussion of various types of musical symbolism and depiction.

830. ———. "Das Verhältnis von Text und Musik in Haydns Oratorien." *Haydn-Studien* 1 (1965-67):205-40.

Principally concerned with the issue of dependence of musical organization on text, briefly considers *The Seven Last Words* as a special case in which music preceded text. Distinguishes between the relatively tradition-bound Neapolitan idiom evident in *Il ritorno di Tobia* and the more individualistic interaction of music and text in *The Creation* and *The Seasons.* Scrutinizes aspects of declamation and accent. With respect to the later works, cites the effect of instrumental participation in partnership with the voices, the wide variety of text-painting devices employed, the use of major/minor polarities, and the symbolic use of keys and instruments.

831. Riemer, Otto. "Realistisches Oratorium: Zur Phänomenologie von Haydn's 'Schöpfung'." *Musica* 13 (1959):283-86.

Discusses the significance of the work's text and musical setting within the oratorio tradition. Explains its realism in terms of its turn-of-the-century historical position between Rococo on one hand and Biedermeier on the other. Dwells on its remarkable richness of text-painting, and associates this feature with the purpose of communicating an enlightened, edifying message. Argues that the text-painting details form part of a larger coherence.

832. Riethmüller, Albrecht. "Die Vorstellung des Chaos in der Musik zu Joseph Haydns Oratorium 'Die Schöpfung'." In

Convivium Cosmologicum; Interdisziplinäre Studien: Helmut Hönl zum 70. Geburtstag, edited by Anastasios Giannarás, pp. 185–95. Basel: Birkhäuser, 1973.

Addresses the question raised by Zelter in the *Allgemeine musikalische Zeitung* (1802) of whether a piece of music based on the concept of order can depict chaos. After examining assessments of Haydn's "Chaos" by Dilthey, Schenker, Botstiber, and Tovey, selects harmony as the element by which to measure the success of Haydn's depiction. Determines that given the eighteenth-century context, Haydn could not suspend the norms of musical composition, even for the depiction of chaos. Points out that his "Chaos" sounds less chaotic to modern ears accustomed to departures from eighteenth-century norms, and concludes that whether or not Haydn's representation succeeded, it proves to be an extraordinary and progressive piece of music.

833. Schenker, Heinrich. "Haydn: Die Schöpfung. Die Vorstellung des Chaos." *Das Meisterwerk in der Musik* 2 (1926):159–70. Reprinted in *Joseph Haydn* (item 75), pp. 15–23, as "'Die Vorstellung des Chaos' aus der 'Schöpfung'."

Metaphorical and technical account of voice-leading events supplementing extensive graphic analysis. Argues that "art can only express chaos through its strict media." Describes a particular arpeggiation as "the spirit of God, which, in a triad-generative manner, is already in effect in the darkness of the chaos." Includes quotation of Zelter's commentary on the piece in *Allgemeine musikalische Zeitung* (1802, col. 390) and Haydn's brief letter of response. Translated in Sylvan Kalib, "Thirteen Essays from the Three Yearbooks *Das Meisterwerk in der Musik* by Heinrich Schenker: An Annotated Translation" (Ph.D. dissertation, Northwestern University, 1973), 2:430–50.

* Schmid, Ernst Fritz. "Gottfried van Swieten als Komponist." *Mozart-Jahrbuch* (1953), pp. 15–31.

Cited as item 359.

834. ———. "Haydns Oratorium 'Il ritorno di Tobia', seine Entstehung und seine Schicksale." *Archiv für Musikwissenschaft* 16 (1959):292–313.

Describes the long tradition of oratorios based on the

Tobias theme. Offers a detailed history of the work itself, including origins, details of important performances, various revisions, contemporary reactions, and publication of popular excerpts. Discusses the felicitous source discoveries early in this century that once again made available the long-lost original version of 1775.

835. Smither, Howard E. "Haydns '*Il ritorno di Tobia*' und die Tradition des italienischen Oratoriums." In *Joseph Haydn: Tradition und Rezeption* (item 78), pp. 160-88.

Examines the work in terms of social context, libretto, and music. Sketches a brief history of the oratorio in Italy and Vienna, and shows the work to be part of a secular tradition traceable in Italy in the mid-17th century and Vienna in the mid-eighteenth. Describes the content and structure of Italian oratorio librettos; shows how Boccherini's libretto is part of a long tradition (artistic and literary) that drew on the book of Tobias, and that it follows the oratorio librettos of Zeno and Metastasio in structure and style. Points out that Haydn's music was the least traditional aspect of the work, and compares it with other oratorios performed for the Tonkünstler-Societät in the years 1772-75.

836. Stern, Martin. "Haydns 'Schöpfung'--Geist und Herkunft des van Swietenschen Librettos: Ein Beitrag zum Thema 'Säkularisation' im Zeitalter der Aufklärung." *Haydn-Studien* 1 (1965-67):121-98.

Examines *The Creation* against the backdrop of literary, philosophical, and religious thinking of the period. Describes the working relationship between composer and librettist, then explores various sources and traditions behind the libretto and its subject: the question of Lidley/Linley's text; use of the Bible and Milton's *Paradise Lost* as van Swieten's models; the metaphor of Adam's Fall in pre-Enlightenment works; the theological question of the Fall of Man in the eighteenth century; and enlightened homage to the Creation in literature prior to Haydn's oratorio. Presents an analysis of van Swieten's text, including critiques by contemporaries. Shows that *The Creation* was representative of the enlightened thinking that hastened the disintegration of Christian ideology.

837. Temperley, Nicholas. "New Light on the Libretto of *The Creation*." In *Music in Eighteenth-Century England: Essays in Memory of Charles Cudworth*, edited by Chris-

topher Hogwood and Richard Luckett, pp. 189-211. Cambridge: Cambridge University Press, 1983.

With reference to Edward Olleson's study (item 827), shows that the English text represented in the librettos for the first English performances of *The Creation* survives largely in its original form, and thus does not constitute a retranslation from the German. Concludes that the original English text was still available in London and was used as a source for the London librettos, and argues that Haydn intended this text to have equal authority with the German. Includes music examples, facsimiles of score pages, and a table of textual variants in the London librettos.

838. Tiersot, Julian. "Le Lied 'Ein Mädchen, das auf Ehre hielt' et ses prototypes français." *Zeitschrift der Internationalen Musikgesellschaft* 12 (1910-11):222-26.

Discussing the background to Hannchen's romance from *The Seasons* (see item 823), calls attention to a collection *Recueil de romances historiques ...* (1767) that contains a piece "La Villageoise avisée" by "M. Favart" and "La Bergère rusée" by "M. Nau" based on the same melody and subject. Speculates that the text of "La Villageoise avisée" was written by Monsieur Favart and set to a version of the traditional melody "La Pernotte"; then Madame Favart incorporated text and melody in her *Annette et Lubin* (1762). Next, after a translation of the text became known in the German popular theater, it was used in Haydn's oratorio.

839. Tovey, Donald Francis. *Essays in Musical Analysis.* Vol. 5: *Vocal Music.* London: Oxford University Press, 1937. vi, 256 pp.

Discusses *The Creation* and *The Seasons*, pp. 114-61. Relates the representation of chaos to the "Nebular Hypothesis" of Kant and Laplace. Dwells at length on questions of musical depiction, and proposes that the description of the animals on the Sixth Day is the "most dangerous, disputed, and in some ways the most delightful passage in the whole work." Asserting that *The Seasons* does not represent any abatement of power by comparison with *The Creation*, observes that the "whole subject is of a lower order, and its appropriate treatment represents Haydn at his best."

840. Unverricht, Hubert. "Joseph Haydns *Die sieben Worte Christi am Kreuze* in der Bearbeitung des Passauer Hofkapellmeisters Joseph Friebert." *Kirchenmusikalisches Jahrbuch* 65 (1981):83-94.

Reviews misunderstandings on the part of Carpani, Pohl, Sandberger, and others concerning various arrangements and versions of the work and the crucial role played by Friebert and his cantata setting. Lists the extant sources for Friebert's arrangement, and discusses its relationship to Haydn's later oratorio version (1795-96). Cites Gottfried van Swieten's role in improving the text used by Friebert, and elaborates on Haydn's compositional procedures in adopting Friebert's version as a model.

* Walter, Horst. "Gottfried van Swietens handschriftliche Textbücher zu 'Schöpfung' und 'Jahreszeiten'." *Haydn-Studien* 1 (1965-67):241-77.

Cited as item 371.

841. Zeman, Herbert. "Das Textbuch Gottfried van Swietens zu Joseph Haydns 'Die Schöpfung'." In *Die österreichische Literatur: Ihr Profil an der Wende vom 18. zum 19. Jahrhundert (1750-1830),* edited by Herbert Zeman, pp. 403-25. Jahrbuch für österreichische Kulturgeschichte, 7-9. Graz: Akademische Druck- u. Verlagsgesellschaft, 1979.

A study of the literary and cultural traditions behind van Swieten's libretto. Examines the four models for his history of *The Creation,* then considers the design and nature of the text, viewed as a late example of enlightened writing. Describes the close contact between Haydn and van Swieten during the composition process, and sees van Swieten as Haydn's last and most significant mentor. Also explores philosophical and other writings that may have influenced van Swieten.

Theater Works

842. Abert, Anna Amalie. "Haydn und Gluck auf der Opernbühne." In *Joseph Haydn Kongress* (item 76), pp. 296-302.

Attempts a stylistic comparison between Haydn's *L'incontro improvviso, Armida,* and *Orfeo ed Euridice* on one hand and Gluck's *La Rencontre imprévue, Armide,* and *Orfeo ed Euridice* on the other. Emphasizing the divergence of Haydn's approach from Gluck's, contrasts the former's musical orientation to the latter's attention to dramatic considerations.

843. Allroggen, Gerhard. "'*La canterina*' in den Vertonungen von Nicolà Piccinni und Joseph Haydn." In *Joseph Haydn: Tradition und Rezeption* (item 78), pp. 100-112.

Discusses forerunners of Piccinni's intermezzo, salient features of the work, and differences between Piccinni's setting and Haydn's that reflect their differing functions: Piccinni's formed part of the third act of his opera *Origille* (1760) and functioned dramatically as an opera within an opera; Haydn's *Canterina* (1766) was an independent work with no sinfonia but a more elaborate finale, and its numbers were considerably longer than those of Piccinni's piece. The works are compared in two tables, one listing individual numbers, the other presenting the texts of the two finales.

844. ———. "Piccinnis *Origille.*" *Analecta Musicologica* 15/*Studien zur italienisch-deutschen Musikgeschichte* 10 (1975):258-97.

A study of the opera *Origille* (1760): its libretto, the libretto's origins, and the music. Finds that the text to a third-act intermezzo, *La canterina,* corresponds to Haydn's *La canterina,* and proposes that Haydn derived his libretto from Piccinni's. Suggests as Piccinni's source the text to Gregorio Sciroli's two-act intermezzo *La canterina,* which was incorporated in David Perez's opera *Farnace* (1753).

845. Altenburg, Detlef. "Haydn und die Tradition der italienischen Oper: Bemerkungen zum Opernrepertoire des Esterhàzyschen Hofes." In *Joseph Haydn: Tradition und Rezeption* (item 78), pp. 77-99.

Observes that as opera kapellmeister (1762-90), Haydn "worked within that international system of Italian court opera which reached from St. Petersburg to Madrid, from Naples to Copenhagen." Shows how the musical tastes of Prince Nikolaus were reflected in a repertory that was virtually all Italian and gave strong preference to comedy. Discusses the importance of Eszterháza (1776-90) as "an opera center of European class" in terms of quality and quantity of works performed each year (80-120 performances annually). Includes a table of operas performed at Eisenstadt and Eszterháza, with information on genre, librettist, year and number of performances, date of premiere, and date of performance in Vienna.

846. Angermüller, Rudolph. "Die entpolitisierte Oper am Wiener und am Fürstlich Esterházyschen Hof." *The Haydn Yearbook* 10 (1978):5-27.

Citing the *Hochlöbliches Directorium in politicis et cameralibus* (1795) by the Viennese censor Franz Carl Hägelin (1735-1809), discusses pre-revolutionary inhibitions prevalent in Vienna in the 1780s. Describes the excising of social and political criticism from dramatic works (notably Da Ponte's version of Beaumarchais' *Le Mariage de Figaro*) in an effort not to offend the monarchy. Speculates on reasons for the cancellation of plans to perform Mozart's *Figaro* at Eszterháza in 1789.

847. ———. "Salieri-Opern in Esterháza." *Chigiana* 36 (1979):87-99.

An account of five Salieri operas that Haydn either produced (*La scuola de' gelosi* and *La fiera in Venezia*), planned to produce (*Axur, Re d'Oramus* and *La grotta di Trofonio*), or considered producing (*La secchia rapita*) at Eszterháza. Provides relevant information on each, examining *La scuola de' gelosi* most extensively: its plot, performance history, and the many changes made by Haydn, a number of them to accommodate the modest vocal talents of Luigia Polzelli; the work was performed at Eszterháza 23 times in 1780-81. Considers Haydn's relationship to Salieri and the latter's admiration for Haydn, demonstrated by the performance of numerous Haydn works under his direction and by his sonnet on Haydn, given here in the original Italian.

848. ———. "Haydns 'Der Zerstreute' in Salzburg (1776)." *Haydn-Studien* 4 (1976-80):85-93.

Attempts to resolve the question of whether Haydn's entr'acte music to *Der Zerstreute* incorporated only parts of Symphony No. 60 or the entire work. Provides a history and synopsis of the play and information on the Karl Wahr troupe, for which Haydn supplied the music to this play in 1774. Lists the troupe's repertory in Salzburg, 1775-76, and reprints in full a detailed critique of the music to *Der Zerstreute* (Salzburg *Theaterwochenblatt,* 27 January 1776). Comparison of critique and music leads to the conclusion that, for Salzburg at least, the entr'acte music consisted of the entire symphony.

849. Badura-Skoda, Eva. "Reflections on Haydn Opera Problems." In *Haydnfest* (item 71), pp. 26-31.

Considers the progress made since World War II in research on, performance of, and availability of Haydn's operas. Briefly surveys his German and Italian output, and examines his return to opera composition in 1791 (with *L'anima del filosofo*), after an extended hiatus. Recalls Haydn's regret over his relative neglect of vocal music and describes his pride in and preference for his vocal works. Includes six facsimiles, among them a predominantly autograph list of Haydn's operas and oratorios.

850. Basso, Alberto. "La rappresentazione a Torino (1804) dell' 'Armida' di Haydn." *Quadrivium* 14 (1973):235-47. Also published in *Testimonianze, studi e ricerche in onore di Guido M. Gatti (1892-1973),* pp. 235-47. Bologna: A. M. I. S., 1973.

Adduces evidence to suggest that a false rumor of Haydn's death may have begun as early as November of 1804. Citing a commemorative performance of Haydn's *Armida* in Turin on 27 December 1804 and a commemorative concert at the conservatory early in 1805, suggests that Turin may have been the first city to so honor the supposedly deceased composer. With respect to *Armida,* describes changes made in the libretto for the Turin performance, names performers and others involved in the production, and includes the text of a review from the *Journal de Turin.*

851. Feder, Georg. "Bemerkungen zu Haydns Opern." *Österreichische Musikzeitschrift* 37 (1982):154-61.

Miscellaneous pieces of information presented in chronological order. Includes examples showing the close relationship between settings of an aria from *Le pescatrici* as realized by Haydn (1769) and Gassmann (1771).

852. ———. "Einige Thesen zu dem Thema: Haydn als Dramatiker." *Haydn-Studien* 2 (1969-70):126-30.

Citing Helmut Wirth's *Joseph Haydn als Dramatiker* (item 902) as a point of departure, defends Haydn as a musical dramatist. Acknowledges that his settings tend to represent surface text more than underlying dramatic situation, and places a portion of the blame for alleged dramatic weakness on faults in the libretti. Compares the original French text of *L'incontro improvviso,* set by Gluck, with the Italian version by Karl Friberth, and judges the latter to be dramatically inferior. Cites Haydn's focus of attention on his performing personnel (reflected, for example, in the tendency toward dramatically inappropriate embellishments), and argues that the merit of his operas lies principally in the music and in the theatrical effectiveness of individual scenes.

853. ———. "Ein Kolloquium über Haydns Opern." *Haydn-Studien* 2 (1969-70):113-31.

Presents the contents of three papers read at a colloquium at the Joseph Haydn-Institute the previous year (see items 862, 898, and 852). Includes a summary table of Haydn's operas, a chronological list (with date, type of opera, number of acts, characters), and an alphabetical list of characters. Provides a summary of the discussion that followed the papers.

854. ———. "Opera seria, opera buffa und opera semiseria bei Haydn." In *Opernstudien: Anna Amalie Abert zum 65. Geburtstag,* edited by Klaus Hortschansky, pp. 37-55. Tutzing: Hans Schneider, 1975.

Devotes an extended paragraph to each of the fourteen works in question. Concludes that whereas the pure *opere serie* and pure *opere buffe* are relatively strictly stylized and limited to the traditional rules associated with their genres, the *opere semiserie* not only mix the genres but extend beyond them to a realm of greater musical diversity. Observes that the wide spectrum of expression evident in the last three of these works (*La vera costanza, La fedeltà premiata,* and *Orlando paladino*) corresponds most closely to that of Mozart's mature masterworks.

855. ———, and Thomas, Günter. "Documente zur Ausstattung von *Lo speziale, L'infedeltà delusa, La fedeltà premiata,*

Armida, und andern Opern Haydns." *Haydn-Studien* 6/2 (1988):88-115.

Reports on the contents of: 1) a 1775 inventory pertaining to the Esterházy theater, including detailed descriptions of costumes for various operas; 2) descriptions of costumes for a 1782 performance of *La fedeltà premiata;* 3) descriptions of costumes for the original production of *Armida.* Observes that there appears to be little connection between costume and inner dramatic significance associated with the roles, and argues that this circumstance reflects the loose coordination of elements (drama, poetry, music, staging, etc.) characteristic of eighteenth-century opera. Reproduces the contents of each document.

856. Geiringer, Karl. "From Guglielmi to Haydn: The Transformation of an Opera." In *International Musicological Society: Report of the Eleventh Congress, Copenhagen 1972,* edited by Henrik Glahn, Søren Sørensen, and Peter Ryom, 1:391-95. Copenhagen: Wilhelm Hansen, 1974.

Traces the text of Haydn's *Orlando paladino* to *Le pazzie d'Orlando,* written by Carlo Francesco Badini and set by Pietro Alessandro Guglielmi for the King's Theater in London, ca. 1770. Identifies a direct connection between this text and a Nunziato Porta libretto (dated 1775) at the university library in Prague entitled "Orlando paladino." Points out the close link between this source and the Viennese libretto of 1777 which provided the basis for Haydn's work.

857. ———. "Gluck und Haydn." In *Festschrift Otto Erich Deutsch zum 80. Geburtstag am 5. September 1963,* edited by Walter Gerstenberg, Jan LaRue, and Wolfgang Rehm, pp. 75-81. Kassel: Bärenreiter, 1963.

Shows that Haydn was conversant with Gluckian reform, and that apart from the early *Acide* (1762), all his serious operas incorporate reform characteristics. Describes the occurrence of these features in *Philemon und Baucis, L'isola disabitata, Armida,* and *L'anima del filosofo.*

858. ———. "Haydn as an Opera Composer." *Proceedings of the Royal Musical Association* 66 (1939-40):23-32.

A brief survey of thirteen surviving Haydn operas known

to the author. Distinguishes between Haydn's serious and serio-comic works in a chronological overview.

859. ———. "Joseph Haydn und die Oper." *Zeitschrift für Musik* 99 (1932):291-94.

Proposes that the traditional neglect of Haydn's operas had less to do with accessibility of sources than with prejudice against the works themselves. Examines different phases in Haydn's operatic writing, and concludes that his best theater compositions date from the 1760s and 1770s (before he attained a mature Classical style), when he simply juxtaposed contrasting elements: light and profound, comic and serious, burlesque and heroic. In later works, when unification and concentration permeated his thinking, his operas became less colorful and interesting.

860. Geyer-Kiefl, Helen. "Joseph Haydns vis comica: Die beiden Opernproduktionen der Wiener Festwochen." *Österreichische Musikzeitschrift* 37 (1982):225-32.

Describes the plots of *Orlando paladino* and *Die Feuersbrunst,* and discusses aspects of comedy, irony, and characterization evident in the musical settings with reference to the genres represented by the two texts (*Dramma eroicomico* vs. *Hanswurstiade*).

861. Green, Robert A. "'Il Distratto' of Reynard and Haydn: A Re-examination." *The Haydn Yearbook* 11 (1980):183-95.

Argues that relationships between Haydn's incidental music and the play are closer than suggested by Schering (item 985) or Landon (item 964). Proposes that the composer's intentions included setting the mood for each act, portraying the characters, and alluding to specific incidents in the course of the drama. Provides background information on the play, gives a plot summary for each act, and draws connections between the characters and stock types of the *commedia dell'arte.*

862. Gruber, Gernot. "Haydns Marionettenopern in ihren kulturgeschichtlichen Zusammenhängen." *Haydn-Studien* 2 (1969-70):119-22.

Discusses the favorable reception of Italian puppet theater in mid-17th-century Vienna, and shortly thereafter, of Stranitzky's marionette theater. Describes subsequent developments of such theater, including Prince Nikolaus' theater at Eszterháza and the contributions made by Haydn and Pauersbach. Points out that Haydn's marionette operas and his ballet pantomimes for Kurz-Bernardon served as an intermediate stage between Viennese *Hanswurst* and later folk comedy, and that from 1778 on, the singspiel in Vienna combined traditions such as marionette opera with elements of *opera buffa* and *opéra comique.*

863. Heartz, Daniel. "Haydn's 'Acide e Galatea' and the Imperial Wedding Operas of 1760 by Hasse and Gluck." In *Joseph Haydn Kongress* (item 76), pp. 332-40.

Examines evidence of influence on Haydn's work by Hasse's *Alcide al Bivio* and Gluck's *Tetide.* Citing Hasse's lyric gift on one hand, and Gluck's novel, dramatic inspiration on the other, suggests that Haydn faced the challenge of profiting from both without resembling either in any overt way.

864. ———. "Haydn und Gluck im Burgtheater um 1760: Der neue krumme Teufel, Le Diable à quatre und die Sinfonie 'Le soir'." In *Gesellschaft für Musikforschung: Bericht über den Internationalen musikwissenschaftlichen Kongress, Bayreuth 1981,* edited by Christoph-Hellmut Mahling and Sigrid Wiesmann, pp. 120-35. Kassel: Bärenreiter, 1984.

Reports that while Haydn's popular comedy is normally associated with the German company at the Kärntnertortheater, there is evidence that links it as well to the French company at the Burgtheater: in 1759, two performances of *Der neue krumme Teufel* were given there under the title *Le Nouveau Diable boiteux avec deux grands ballets.* Next, discloses the author's discovery that the first movement of Haydn's *Le Soir* incorporates in its entirety the new version of Gluck's tobacco song "Je n'amais pas le tabac beaucoup" from a revision in 1761 of his *Le Diable à quatre* for the Burgtheater. Proposes that Prince Nikolaus is likely to have heard this popular song at the Burgtheater and may have asked Haydn to incorporate it in a symphony.

865. Hoboken, Anthony van. "Nunziato Porta und der Text von Joseph Haydns Oper 'Orlando Paladino'." In *Symbolae Historiae Musicae: Hellmut Federhofer zum 60. Geburtstag,* edited by Friedrich Wilhelm Riedel and Hubert

Unverricht, pp. 170-79. Mainz: B. Schott's Söhne, 1971.

Shows that Porta's libretto for Haydn's *Orlando paladino* (1782) may be traced to Francesco Badini's text to Pietro Guglielmi's *Le pazzie d'Orlando* (1771), which Porta reworked and renamed *Orlando paladino* for a 1775 performance in Prague. A comparative study of texts draws on these librettos as well as those for an *Orlando palladino* by Anfossi (Vienna, 1777) and a later performance of Haydn's opera (Dresden, 1792).

866. Hunter, Mary K. "Haydn's Aria Forms: A Study of the Arias in the Italian Operas Written at Eszterháza, 1766-1783." Ph.D. dissertation, Cornell University, 1982. xv, 550 pp.

Isolating text, ritornellos, and vocal setting as principal domains of organization, and viewing aria forms from the standpoint of sonata style, examines introductory ritornellos, vocal expositions, developmental processes, and recapitulations. Includes schematic diagrams of all solo arias in Esterházy operas from *La canterina* (1766) to *Armida* (1783), and offers detailed analyses of four representative arias. Demonstrates Haydn's integration of sonata elements into arias that give the impression of complete obedience to the requirements of the text, and proposes that in such instances, application of sonata procedures both represents and creates dramatic action in a manner more typically associated with Mozart.

867. ———. "Haydn's Sonata-Form Arias." *Current Musicology,* no. 37-38 (1984), pp. 19-32.

Noting the generally close adherence to sonata procedure in Haydn's arias, compares their melodic style, structural organization, and compositional processes with those seen in the instrumental music. While finding distinctive contrasts in matters of proportion and melodic idiom, discerns similar avoidance of literal repetition and recurrence, and similarities as well as differences in the approach to thematic development. Emphasizes underlying stylistic connections between the instrumental and operatic realms, despite evident diversity on the surface.

868. ———. "Text, Music, and Drama in Haydn's Italian Opera Arias: Four Case Studies." *The Journal of Musicology* 7 (1989):29-57.

Examines two *seria* arias and two *buffa* arias from among Haydn's later comic operas: *Il mondo della luna, La fedeltà premiata,* and *Orlando paladino.* For each piece, considers aspects of dramatic circumstance and structure in relation to musical form. Notes the importance of the sonata aesthetic in Haydn's operas, especially the arias, and senses a strong association of sonata form with *seria* characters. Proposes that Haydn's skill in treating different aspects of musical form enhances his dramatic characterizations.

869. Kanduth, Erika. "Die italienischen Libretti der Opern Joseph Haydns." In *Joseph Haydn und die Literatur seiner Zeit* (item 79), pp. 61-96.

Focusing on individual operas and the nature of their texts, emphasizes the predominance of comic elements. Discusses hindrances to the quest for a full understanding of Haydn's approach to his texts, most notably the substantial number of lost and fragmentary works. In categorizing the texts and describing the traditions they represent, calls attention to underlying elements of parody and grotesque exaggeration that blur the distinction between *opera seria* and *buffa.*

870. Kolk, Joel. "'Sturm und Drang' and Haydn's Operas." In *Haydn Studies* (item 73), pp. 440-45.

Observes that Haydn, like his contemporaries, rarely employs minor keys in operatic works, but that when he does, their use is associated with sentiments of disdain, anger, storm-depiction, or outburst of invective. Proposes a link between this traditionally employed operatic procedure and the heightened intensity in the language of Haydn's instrumental music of the late 1760s and early 1770s.

871. Landon, H.C. Robbins. "Haydn und die Oper." *Österreichische Musikzeitschrift* 22 (1967):253-57.

Briefly describes Haydn's extensive duties as opera kapellmeister at the Esterházy court, and presents a chronological survey of his operas, from his work for Kurz-Bernardon in the 1750s to his last opera in London.

872. ———. "Joseph Haydn als Opernkomponist und Kapellmeister." In *Joseph Haydn in seiner Zeit* (item 77), pp. 249-54.

Discusses circumstances under which major operatic works were conceived and produced. Related in content to item 871 above.

873. ———. "The Operas of Haydn." In *The New Oxford History of Music*. Vol. 7: *The Age of Enlightenment, 1745-1790*, edited by Egon Wellesz and Frederick Sternfeld, pp. 172-99. London: Oxford University Press, 1973.

Biographical summary of Haydn's composition of the operas, followed by critical discussion. Cites the influences of Gluck and characteristic emphases on long-range coherence and continuity. Noting Haydn's emancipation from the clichés of Italian opera, proposes that his stage works represent a marriage of Italian theatrical and Viennese symphonic traditions. Offers a disparaging assessment of the libretti. Makes brief mention of the insertion arias. Numerous music examples.

874. ———. "Some Notes on Haydn's Opera *L'infedeltà delusa*." *The Musical Times* 102 (1961):356-57.

Identifies the author of the libretto as Marco Coltellini. Indicates, however, that Coltellini's libretto was rewritten for Haydn's opera, probably by someone at Eszterháza.

875. ———. "Zu Haydns 'L'infedeltà delusa'." *Österreichische Musikzeitschrift* 16 (1961):481-84.

Translation of item 874.

876. Lang, Paul Henry. "Haydn and the Opera." *The Musical Quarterly* 18 (1932):274-81.

Emphasizes the contrast between Mozart's Italianate gift for vocal music and Haydn's more instrumentally oriented style. Proposes a link between the development of the latter's mastery of polyphonic, instrumental part-writing and his alleged failure as an opera composer. Attributes that failure partially to a "lack of psychological observation and objectivity," and suggests that dramatic tension not accomplished on the stage found expression through the composer's mastery of the symphony and quartet.

877. Lazarevich, Gordana. "Haydn and the Italian Comic Inter-

mezzo Tradition." In *Joseph Haydn Kongress* (item 76), pp. 376-84.

Emphasizes Johann Adolf Hasse's role in the formation of Haydn's early comic style. Considers musical syntax, aria types, aria structure, and ensemble finale structure. Examines biographical circumstances under which Haydn may have become acquainted with intermezzi of Hasse and others.

878. Leopold, Silke. "Haydn und die Tradition der Orpheus-Opern." *Musica* 36 (1982):131-35.

Examines the tradition of Orpheus-legend settings to support a hypothesis that the fourth act of Haydn's last opera, *L'anima del filosofo,* does not represent the intended conclusion. An unsatisfactory ending, combined with other factors, leads to the proposal that a fifth act prepared by Badini was never set to music.

879. ———. "'Le pescatrici'--Goldoni, Haydn, Gassmann." In *Joseph Haydn Kongress* (item 76), pp. 341-49.

Proposes that Haydn's operas demonstrate a greater interest in musical than dramatic considerations. By way of illustration, compares examples from Haydn's setting of *Le pescatrici* (1769-70) with those from Gassmann's (first performed 1771). Shows that by comparison with Gassmann, Haydn conceived his arias in instrumental rather than dramatic terms and that his ensembles were oratorio-like rather than scenic in concept.

880. Lippmann, Friedrich. "Haydn e l'opera buffa: Tre confronti con opere italiane coeve sullo stesso testo." *Nuova rivista musicale italiana* 17 (1983):223-46.

Italian version of item 883.

881. ———. "Haydns 'La fedeltà premiata' und Cimarosas 'L'infedeltà fedele'." *Haydn-Studien* 5 (1982-85):1-15.

Describes the mixture of serious and comic elements in the Neapolitan libretto of Cimarosa's work (1779). Compares this text with that of Haydn's subsequent setting (1780), and cites numerous melodic resemblances between the two operas. Suggests that to some extent Cimarosa provided at least a springboard, though not really a compositional model, for Haydn.

882. ———. "Haydns Opere serie: Tendenzen und Affinitäten." *Studi musicali* 12 (1983):301-31.

Discusses Italian influences discerned in Haydn's setting of certain traditional types of serious-opera aria texts. Laments modern-day critics' denigration of Italian tendencies in Haydn, and proposes that his affinity for Italian models provided a basis for his individuality as a musical dramatist. Citing examples from *La canterina, Lo speziale, Le pescatrice, L'infedeltà delusa,* and *La vera costanza,* proposes that Haydn's *opera seria* style was nurtured in the realm of *opera semiseria.*

883. ———. "Haydn und die Opera buffa: Vergleiche mit italienischen Werken gleichen Textes." In *Joseph Haydn: Tradition und Rezeption* (item 78), pp. 113-40.

Compares each of three comic (i.e. "non-serious") operas by Haydn with a setting of the same or similar text by an Italian composer: *La canterina* (Piccinni), *La fedeltà premiata* (Cimarosa, with the title *L'infedeltà fedele*), and *Il mondo della luna* (Paisiello). Concludes that Haydn incorporates serious elements to a greater extent, is less inclined to parody *opera seria* or to incorporate comic scenes and slapstick, makes less use of *buffa* mannerisms such as note and motive repetition, and is more apt to highlight details of the text.

884. Loewenberg, Alfred. "Lorenzo da Ponte in London: A Bibliographical Account of His Literary Activity." *The Music Review* 4 (1943):171-89.

Makes note of an overlooked duet by Haydn in the course of a discussion of librettos associated with da Ponte in London. The duet--"Quel cor umeno e tenero," with a text by da Ponte--was one of several pieces inserted in an opera *Il Burbero di buon core* by Vincenzo Martin y Soler for a performance in 1794. This may be the duet sung at Haydn's last benefit concert in London in 1795. (Subsequently identified as a duet from *Orlando paladino*; see Hob. XXVIII:11/16 and XXVa:Anhang.)

885. McClymonds, Marita P. "Haydn and His Contemporaries: *Armida abbandonata.*" In *Joseph Haydn Kongress* (item 76), pp. 325-32.

Places Haydn's setting of the Tozzi-based libretto in the context of numerous other *Armida* texts of the 1770s and

80s. Includes a chronological list of libretti related to Haydn's *Armida.*

886. Melkus, Eduard. "Haydn als Dramatiker am Beispiel der Oper 'La vera costanza'." In *Joseph Haydn Kongress* (item 76), pp. 256-76.

Champions the opera as a reflection of Haydn's mastery as a dramatist. Offers an appraisal of his historical position as a contributor to the development of the genre between Gluck and Mozart. Compares Haydn's theatrical craft with Mozart's, and explores the former's approach to musical representation of dramatic circumstances and events. Argues that closer study and greater familiarity will permit Haydn's operas to stand alongside the instrumental genres as reflections of his compositional genius. Numerous music examples, and several diagrams and charts.

887. Müller-Blattau, Joseph. "Zu Haydns 'Philemon und Baucis'." *Haydn-Studien* 2 (1969-70):66-69.

Reveals that the libretto, presumably by Philipp Georg Bader, was a reworking of a play *Philemon und Baucis* (1763) by the Colmar writer G.K. Pfeffel. Shows that portions of Pfeffel's text were incorporated into the singspiel with virtually no change.

888. Paul, Steven E. "Wit and Humour in the Operas of Haydn." In *Joseph Haydn Kongress* (item 76), pp. 386-402.

Emphasizes the many instances of word-painting in Haydn's operas of the 1770s, and ponders the question of interaction between operatic style and instrumental music. Cites the quartets of Op. 33, in which conversational gestures, patter phrases, dramatic pauses, and motivic play suggest operatic origins. Includes several operatic examples in score.

889. Porter, Andrew. "Haydn and 'La fedeltà premiata'." *The Musical Times* 112 (1971):331-35.

Provides commentary on the text and Haydn's setting, and briefly discusses the editions by Günter Thomas and H.C. Robbins Landon. Praises the thoroughness with which available versions are represented in the former, and questions the policy in the latter of applying all cuts found in the autograph score. While applauding the outstanding musical content of the opera, concludes that it is flawed theatrically, and that while Pohl's opinion of Haydn's limitations as an opera composer needs amplification on the basis of increased understanding of the works, his verdict may stand without essential alteration.

890. ———. "L'incontro improviso." *The Musical Times* 107 (1966):202-6.

Compares the work with Gluck's *La Rencontre imprévue* (1764), identifies the Esterházy singers for whom the parts were created, and discusses Haydn's merits as an opera composer by comparison with Mozart. Cites examples to support speculation that Mozart learned from Haydn's operas, and draws a connection between the curtailment of Haydn's activities as an opera composer in the 1780s and the appearance of Mozart's *The Marriage of Figaro*. Concludes that while Haydn does not measure up to Mozartean standards as a music dramatist, his operas are richer in musical and dramatic substance than those of more popular composers such as Cimarosa, Anfossi, and Paisiello.

891. Rice, John A. "Sarti's Giulio Sabino, Haydn's Armida, and the Arrival of opera seria at Eszterháza." *The Haydn Yearbook* 15 (1984):181-98.

Based on a paper read at Riverside in May 1983. Observes that whereas *opera seria* was popular throughout most of Europe in the 1770s, it was seldom heard in Vienna, Paris, or Eszterháza. Not until 1783 was the first full-length *opera seria* performed under Prince Nikolaus. The work was Sarti's *Giulio Sabino*, discussed here at length. The success of this work is likely to have been responsible for Haydn's first *opera seria*, *Armida*, which appears to have been influenced by the Sarti work both in the choice of libretto and in the music. In a comparative discussion of the two works, attention is drawn to "similarities in structure and shape of the two librettos" and, to a lesser extent, in the music.

892. Schneider, Herbert. "Vaudeville-Finali in Haydns Opern und ihre Vorgeschichte." In *Joseph Haydn Kongress* (item 76), pp. 302-9.

Provides an overview of the genre from Rousseau, Philidor, and Monsigny, through Hiller, Gassmann, Fleischer, and Reichardt. Examines Haydn's applications in *Orlando paladino* and *L'isola disabitata,* and discusses a vaudeville-like scene in *La vera costanza.*

893. Smith, Erik. "Haydn and 'La fedeltà premiata'." *The Musical Times* 120 (1979):567-70.

A general description of the work and its background, including discussion of Eszterháza, the available resources there, and the opera's popularity.

894. Steblin, Rita. "Key Characteristics and Haydn's Operas." In *Joseph Haydn Kongress* (item 76), pp. 91-100.

Relates late eighteenth- and early nineteenth-century theoretical descriptions of different keys and the effects with which they are associated to Haydn's practice as witnessed in his operatic arias and ensembles. Noting the possibility of humorous intent in the deliberate choice of an inappropriate key, discerns in Haydn a flexible approach rather than any rigid adherence to a scheme of key associations. Includes a comparative table of key characteristics as represented by Vogler, Schubart, Knecht, and Galeazzi.

895. Strohm, Reinhard. "Zur Metrik in Haydns und Anfossis 'La vera costanza'." In *Joseph Haydn Kongress* (item 76), pp. 279-94.

Comparing Anfossi's 1776 setting with Haydn's of 1779, examines the distribution of Italian verses within the metrical and harmonic framework of the music. Includes numerous music examples comparing the two composers' settings of the same verses.

896. Thomas, Günter. "Anmerkungen zum Libretto von Haydns Festa teatrale 'Acide'." *Haydn-Studien* 5 (1982-85):118-24.

Identifies the probable author of the text as Giovanni Ambrogio Migliavacca, not Giovanni Battista Migliavacca as given in Pohl's copy of the libretto. Points out the close similarities between the text and that of Metastasio's *Galatea.*

897. ———. "Observations on *Il mondo della luna.*" In *Haydn Studies* (item 73), pp. 144-47.

Offers miscellaneous information about the work: evidence

of alternate versions for various numbers, other settings of the libretto, preparations for the first performance, possible changes in cast, important sources, Haydn's use of several numbers in other works, and arrangements by others.

898. ———. "Zu 'Il mondo della luna' und 'La fedeltà premiata: Fassungen und Pasticcios." *Haydn-Studien* 2 (1969-70):122-26.

Proposes that the second version of *Il mondo della luna*--with Ecclitico as tenor, Ernesto as alto, and Lisetta as alto--was the one performed at the first and apparently only performance on 3 August 1777. Argues that although the libretto lists Lisetta as a soprano, a change in the role was probably made after the printing, in response to the departure of soprano Maria Jermoli in June (cf. items 535, 544, and Landon's Bärenreiter edition, 1958). Suggests that multiple versions of several arias reveal that Haydn viewed his operas as more than mere occasional music. For *La fedeltà premiata,* demonstrates how changes in personnel necessitated changes in roles, and discusses three pasticcios that contain numbers from this opera.

899. Viertel, Karl-Heinz. "Joseph Haydn und das Musiktheater." *Musik und Gesellschaft* 32/3 (1982):141-45.

Emphasizes the great extent of theater-related activity in Haydn's career in the years 1776-90. Summarizes his operatic endeavors during this time, underscores the importance of this experience to the eventual accomplishment of the late oratorios, and pleas for more frequent performance of the operas.

900. Wirth, Helmut. "Gluck, Haydn und Mozart--drei Entführungs-Opern." In *Opernstudien: Anna Amalie Abert zum 65. Geburtstag,* edited by Klaus Hortschansky, pp. 25-35. Tutzing: Hans Schneider, 1975.

Discusses the popularity of Turkish elements in eighteenth-century Viennese operas and singspiels, and examines dramatic works by Gluck, Haydn, and Mozart that incorporate exotic elements. The Haydn work, *L'incontro improvviso,* a *dramma giocoso per musica* first performed in 1775, was based on Karl Friberth's adaptation of L.-H. Dancourt's libretto, which had been used for Gluck's *La Rencontre imprévue* (1764). Different from the Gluck work are the use of recitative instead of spoken dialogue, the omission of several characters, and certain changes in structure.

901. ———. "Haydns letzte Oper 'Orfeo ed Euridice'." *Österreichische Musikzeitschrift* 22 (1967):249-52.

A brief account of the opera and its history: the commission from Giovanni Andrea Gallini, the dramatic nature of Badini's libretto, the forces for which it was composed, and a summary of musical highlights.

902. ———. *Joseph Haydn als Dramatiker: Sein Bühnenschaffen als Beitrag zur Geschichte der deutschen Oper.* Wolfenbüttel: Georg Kallmeyer, 1940. 197 pp.

Topics addressed include background on theatrical activity in eighteenth-century Vienna, influence of Italian operatic traditions on Haydn's accomplishments, prior assessments of his contribution as an opera composer, comparison of Gluck's *La Rencontre imprévue* with Haydn's *L'incontro improvviso,* and an assessment of his incidental theater music. Examines structure and style, characterization, and coordination of drama and musical organization. Compares Haydn with Mozart as a musical dramatist, and depicts *Orlando paladino,* in which a comic surface masks an underlying tragic countenance, as a highpoint in Haydn's *opera buffa* technique. Identifies the late oratorios as a culminating fruition of Haydn's theatrical achievement. Lists manuscripts, prints, and libretto sources consulted.

* Zeman, Herbert. "Joseph Haydns Begegnungen mit der Literatur seiner Zeit--zur Einleitung." In *Joseph Haydn und die Literatur seiner Zeit* (item 79), pp. 7-23.

Cited as item 920.

* ———. "Literarische Perspektiven um Joseph Haydn." In *Joseph Haydn in seiner Zeit* (item 77), pp. 198-210.

Cited as item 921.

* ———. "Die österreichische Lyrik der Haydn-Zeit." In *Joseph Haydn und seine Zeit* (item 80), pp. 121-46.

Cited as item 922.

903. ———. "Das Theaterlied zur Zeit Joseph Haydns, seine theatralische Gestaltung und seine gattungsgeschichtliche Entwicklung." In *Joseph Haydn und die Literatur seiner Zeit* (item 79), pp. 35-59.

Alluding to the seamless integration of folk elements in Haydn's music, describes the flourishing of the popular Viennese theater, ca. 1750, and discusses the lost *Der neue krumme Teufel.* Describes characteristic aspects of structure and content in the aria texts as transmitted in a surviving 1758 version of the libretto. Contrasts the popular tradition represented by this text to the later German singspiel idiom associated with Christian Felix Weisse and Johann Adam Hiller. Drawing on the author's introduction to *Deutsche Komödiearien 1754-1758, 2. Teil* (*Denkmäler der Tonkunst in Österreich* 121 [Vienna, 1971]: vii-xii), describes two pertinent sources in the Österreichische Nationalbibliothek: "Teutsche Arien" (texts only), and "Teutsche Comedie Arien" (which includes some musical settings in addition to texts). Emphasizes the importance of the eighteenth-century *Komödiearie* as a form of lyric expression in German, and speculates on Haydn's possible authorship of settings in the latter collection. Offers no proof, but suggests that Haydn's contribution cannot be excluded.

Secular Vocal Works

904. Biba, Otto. *Gott Erhalte! Joseph Haydns Kaiserhymne.* Vienna: Ludwig Doblinger, 1982. 35 pp.

Official texts of the anthem, background on circumstances under which it was commissioned, discussion of its elevation to official status, and overview of its use in the nineteenth and twentieth centuries. English translation, by Eugene Hartzell, bound with the German. Separate facsimile of the 1797 edition of text and music.

905. Brown, A. Peter. "Joseph Haydn and Leopold Hofmann's 'Street Songs'." *Journal of the American Musicological Society* 33 (1980):356-83.

Regarding three poems by Karl Friberth, Hofmann's settings of which were denounced in Haydn's irate letter to

Artaria (20 July 1781), compares the two composers' approaches to the same texts. Emphasizing the manifest technical and artistic superiority of the Haydn settings, notes subtle correspondences between text and musical realization. Contrasts the directness and simplicity of the North German tradition represented by Hofmann with the greater variety, breadth of conception, and technical polish witnessed in Haydn.

906. ———. "Zur profanen Vokalmusik Joseph Haydns." In *Joseph Haydn in seiner Zeit* (item 77), pp. 282-90.

Distinguishing two divergent strands--the Italian theatrical tradition on one hand, the folk-oriented German manner on the other--offers a descriptive, chronological overview of the secular vocal repertory. Emphasizes the importance of the London sojourns as a stimulus for vocal composition, which constituted a major portion of Haydn's creative endeavor after his return from the second journey.

907. Cramer, Carl Friedrich. "Ueber die Schönheiten und den Ausdruck der Leidenschaft in einer Cantate von J. Haydn." *Magazin der Musik* 1 (1783):1073-1115. Reprint. Hildesheim: Georg Olms, 1971.

Praising "Ah, come il core" (Hob. XXIVA, Anh. 4) as a perfect whole, exemplary and inimitable, discusses the virtues of economy, restraint, melodic invention, and noble simplicity that it embodies. Calls attention to matters of structure, accentuation, choice of harmony, punctuation (poetic and musical), orchestration, texture, embellishment, and text repetition.

908. Deutsch, Otto Erich. "Haydn's Hymn and Burney's Translation." *The Music Review* 4 (1943):157-62.

Offers a short history of Haydn's "Emperor Hymn," with emphasis on Burney's translation (actually a paraphrase) of the original verses by Haschka. Describes structural departures from Haschka and Burney's omission of politically sensitive material. Includes both the Haschka and Burney texts, and describes musical differences between Haydn's original setting and the version published by Broderip and Wilkinson with Burney's text (see item 561).

909. Friedlaender, Max. *Das deutsche Lied im 18. Jahrhundert: Quellen und Studien.* Stuttgart: J.G. Cotta'schen Buch-

handlung Nachfolger, 1902. Reprint. 3 parts in 2 vols. Hildesheim: Georg Olms, 1962. lviii, 384 pp./vii, 360 pp.; 630 pp.

A study of lieder published in German-speaking countries. The first volume contains a chronological list of publications, followed by a section of commentary on entries in the chronological list. Cites four sets of Haydn songs and the "Emperor Hymn," a total of 37 pieces in all, and discusses Haydn as a composer of lieder. The second volume, which examines the texts, pays particular attention to Haydn's setting of the "Emperor Hymn."

910. Heuss, Alfred. "Haydns Kaiserhymne." *Zeitschrift für Musikwissenschaft* 1 (1918-19):5-26.

Examines the interactive relationship between melodic design and text. Points out an extant sketch for the melody, and speculates on musical and text-related reasons behind the changes made. Discusses doubts raised about the originality of the melodic opening, and considers at length the issue of coincidence versus conscious or unconscious use of a known melody. With regard to the refrain, notes the absence of the first appoggiatura from the earliest edition of the hymn and its subsequent appearance in the *Emperor* Quartet--possibly a concession to a practice adopted by the public (see item 916).

911. Lunn, Jean. "The Quest of the Missing Poet." *The Haydn Yearbook* 4 (1968):195-99.

Offers supplementary information on the texts to two vocal quartets: "Freund ich bitte" and "Lebe, liebe, trinke, lärme." Both appeared in an essay "Abhandlungen von den Liedern der alten Griechen" appended to Hagedorn's odes in *Sammlung der vorzüglichsten Werke deutscher Dichter und Prosaister,* volume 16; and both are German translations of anonymous Greek poems from Athenaeus' *Deipnosophistai.* Names Jouard de la Nauze as probable author of the essay and Johann Arnold Ebert as probable translator of the essay and its poems.

912. Mies, Paul. "Joseph Haydns Singkanons und ihre Grundidee." In *Bericht über die Internationale Konferenz zum Andenken Joseph Haydns* (item 70), pp. 93-94.

Addresses the question of why Haydn held his canons in special esteem. Examining the texts and their musical representation, concludes that he prized them because they embodied the lending of musical, artistic shape to practical wisdom.

913. ———. "Textdichter zu J. Haydns 'Mehrstimmigen Gesängen'." *The Haydn Yearbook* 1 (1962):201.

Identifies the authors of two texts in Haydn's *Mehrstimmigen Gesänge,* in which poets were not named: No. 1, "Der Augenblick," is by Johann Nikolas Götz; No. 2, "Der Vetter," by Christian Felix Weisse.

914. Reindl, Johannes. "Zur Entstehung des Refrains der Kaiserhymne Joseph Haydns." *Studien zur Musikwissenschaft* 25 [*Festschrift für Erich Schenk*] (1962):417-33.

Discusses occurrences of the refrain melody in earlier works by Haydn and in music of contemporaries. Attempts to reconstruct the emotions Haydn may have experienced and the ideas he may have linked at the time he wrote the hymn. Proposes a chain of associations that could have led him to recall (whether consciously or not) the "Alleluja" passage from Mozart's *Exultate jubilate,* K. 165 (1773) and material from Venanzio Rauzzini's Keyboard Sonata, Op. 8 No. 1 (before 1781), which in turn may have derived from Mozart. Includes a comparison of the Mozart, Rauzzini, and Haydn themes, and shows that "every note of the refrain ... is included or anticipated" in Rauzzini.

915. Riethmüller, Albrecht. "Joseph Haydn und das Deutschlandlied." *Archiv für Musikwissenschaft* 44 (1987):241-67.

Examines a variety of issues concerning the "Emperor Hymn," especially the political and nationalistic associations it holds, the question of folk influences, the significance of "God Save the King" as a model, and Haydn's intentions in writing the hymn.

916. Schnerich, Alfred. "Zur Vorgeschichte von Haydns Kaiserhymne." *Zeitschrift für Musikwissenschaft* 1 (1918-19):295-97.

With reference to Heuss' article (item 910), proposes that after much reflection, Haydn took the first four measures of the refrain directly from earlier works of his (they do not occur in sketch form). Names three instances of their occurrence: *The Seven Last Words* (1784), an aria from *Il mondo della luna* (1777), and the Benedictus--based on the aria--from his *Mariazell* Mass (1782). Offers additional comments on the Heuss article.

917. Scott, Marion M. "Some English Affinities and Associations of Haydn's Songs." *Music and Letters* 25 (1944):1-12.

After brief discussion of Haydn's earlier lieder and his relationship with the English prior to the London sojourns, examines a selection of songs that Haydn set to English-language texts. Includes background--some of it new--on associations of the songs with English acquaintances, among them Mary Ann Hodges, who is suggested in place of Haydn as the likely composer of "The Lady's Looking Glass."

918. Strommer, Roswitha. "Wiener literarische Salons zur Zeit Joseph Haydns." In *Joseph Haydn und die Literatur seiner Zeit* (item 79), pp. 97-121.

Provides biographical background on the Greiner and Arnstein families and discusses the importance of their salons as focal points of artistic and literary activity in Vienna, ca. 1780-96. Disagreeing with condescending judgments of Haydn's texts, notably in Pohl, discerns the influence of the Greiner circle in Haydn's literary orientation and his choice of verses. Cites evidence in Haydn's correspondence of an active interest in the literary quality of his songs.

919. Wünsch, Walther. "Das Volkslied als Thema der Zeit von Joseph Haydn." In *Der junge Haydn* (item 81), pp. 38-40.

Briefly sketches the history of ideas on "poetry of nature," in an attempt to view the relationship between folk and art music in a fresh light. Describes a symbiotic relationship, for which Haydn's "Emperor Hymn" provides an example.

920. Zeman, Herbert. "Joseph Haydns Begegnungen mit der Literatur seiner Zeit--zur Einleitung." In *Joseph Haydn und die Literatur seiner Zeit* (item 79), pp. 7-23.

Discusses relevant literary background for consideration of Haydn's cultural milieu as it pertains to his approach to operatic, oratorio, and song texts. Emphasizes the significance of Philipp Hafner (1731-64) and Michael Denis (1729-1800) as representatives, respectively, of an older, popular Viennese tradition and a modern, enlightened, more learned vein. Discusses Haydn's encounter with Freemasonry, and draws comparisons between the text of his *L'anima del filosofo* and those of Mozart's *Così fan tutte* and *La clemenza di Tito.*

921. ———. "Literarische Perspektiven um Joseph Haydn." In *Joseph Haydn in seiner Zeit* (item 77), pp. 198-210.

Surveys the field of Viennese literary trends and fashions in the middle and later years of the eighteenth century. With emphasis on Haydn's choice of libretti and song texts, sheds light on his literary tastes and preferences.

922. ———. "Die österreichische Lyrik der Haydn-Zeit." In *Joseph Haydn und seine Zeit* (item 80), pp. 121-46.

Furnishes a detailed overview of literary currents in eighteenth-century Vienna. Examines influential figures and their contributions; discusses the Viennese popular comedy tradition; and provides literary background information pertinent to Haydn's lieder as well as his theatrical works.

Orchestral Works

923. Alston, Charlotte L. "Recapitulation Procedures in the Mature Symphonies of Haydn and Mozart." Ph.D. dissertation, University of Iowa, 1972. ix, 230 pp.

Limiting the scope of inquiry to first movements of later works, develops a systematic comparison of the two composers' approaches. Exploring Haydn's recapitulatory use of themes in new structural roles, observes that Haydn reaches beyond Mozart in varying and developing exposition material. Stylistic features examined encompass aspects of harmony, dynamics, and orchestration. Furnishes schematic diagrams and numerous music examples. Incorporates background material on eighteenth- and nineteenth-century views of sonata form in theoretical writings.

924. Andrews, Harold L. "The Submediant in Haydn's Development Sections." In *Haydn Studies* (item 73), pp. 465–71.

Identifying the submediant as a characteristic tonal goal in Haydn's major-key symphonic development sections, examines a variety of procedures involved in its establishment.

* Angermüller, Rudolph. "Haydns 'Der Zerstreute' in Salzburg (1776)." *Haydn-Studien* 4 (1976–80):85–93.

Cited as item 848.

925. Bard, Raimund. "'Tendenzen' zur zyklischen Gestaltung in Haydns Londoner Sinfonien." In *Gesellschaft für Musikforschung: Bericht über den Internationalen musikwissenschaftlichen Kongress, Bayreuth 1981,* edited by Christoph-Hellmut Mahling and Sigrid Wiesmann, pp. 379–83. Kassel: Bärenreiter, 1984.

From the vantage point of Haydn's monothematic approaches within individual movements, explores the question of devices that lend unity to a four-movement cycle. With the aid of specific examples, examines melodic relationships, rhythmic relationships, instrumentation or sonority, and the use of related forms.

926. ———. *Untersuchungen zur motivischen Arbeit in Haydns sinfonischem Spätwerk.* Kassel: Bärenreiter, 1982. 319 pp.

Offers a critical appraisal of pertinent secondary literature as well as an examination of theoretical discussions by writers such as Marpurg, Sulzer, Gerber, and Koch. Observing that Haydn's procedures encompass and reach beyond contemporary formulations, argues that motivic elaboration, as exemplified in Haydn, constitutes a centrally important principle for the Viennese Classical style. Citing numerous examples, isolates and categorizes techniques whereby a motivic kernel generates a coherent, unified unfolding of material. Includes brief discussion of motivic procedures in the quartets and sonatas.

927. Bartha, Dénes. "Volkstanz-Stilisierung in Joseph Haydns Finale-Themen." In *Festschrift für Walter Wiora zum 30. Dezember 1966,* edited by Ludwig Finscher und Christoph-Hellmut Mahling, pp. 375-84. Kassel: Bärenreiter, 1967.

Identifies rhythmic, melodic, and structural traits associated with an eighteenth-century contredanse finale type, and examines evidence of its employment in the final movements of Symphonies Nos. 44-46, 50, 51, 55, 82, 84-86, 88, 92, and all but two of the London symphonies (95 and 101). Includes relevant thematic quotations.

928. Bawel, Frederick H. "A Study of Developmental Techniques in Selected Haydn Symphonies." Ph.D. dissertation, Ohio State University, 1972. 256 pp.

Choosing the first-movement development sections of seven symphonies from different periods of Haydn's creative output (Nos. 2, 23, 26, 56, 77, 88, 100), concentrates on the detailed analysis of motivic manipulation, phrase structure, voice-leading, harmonic succession, and tonal relationship.

929. Bedbur, Magda. "Die Entwicklung des Finales in den Symphonien von Haydn, Mozart und Beethoven." Ph.D. dissertation, University of Cologne, 1953. ii, 170 pp.

Organizes the discussion of symphonic finales chronologically within form-type (sonata form, three-part rondo, rondo with two episodes, rondo with varied refrain, and sonata rondo). Aiming to trace an evolutionary process, ca. 1760-1820, observes that while the three composers exploit procedures based on existing practices, theirs is a process of refinement in techniques of development and expressive intensification. Emphasizes the concept of a functional relationship of the finale to the other movements, an idea traced to Haydn, whose compositional strategies encompassed the cycle as a whole and involved featuring the finale as a rhetorical summary or climax. Gives descriptive thumbnail analyses of structural and thematic development in all sonata-form last movements; cites instances of variation, fugue, and minuet finales in Haydn; proposes that a highpoint in the amalgamation of sonata and rondo is reached with Symphony No. 103; and suggests that the last movement of Symphony No. 104 foreshadows Beethoven's monumental concept of the finale.

930. Beenk, Eugene. "Ländler Elements in the Symphonic Minuets of Joseph Haydn." Ph.D. dissertation, University of Iowa, 1969. 205 pp.

Furnishes historical background on the history of the dance and its music. Drawing on published collections of *Ländler,* subjects the available dances to a stylistic analysis that takes into account melodic range, conventional figures, and rhythmic organization. Uses the traits thus discerned as a basis for comparison with minuets in Haydn's symphonies. Identifies 6 that could justifiably be called *Ländler* and 35 others that betray *Ländler* influence, notably in their use of broken-chord figures, wide melodic intervals (especially sixths), yodel figures, and certain characteristic rhythmic patterns.

931. Benary, Peter. "Die langsamen Einleitungen in Joseph Haydns Londoner Sinfonien." In *Studien zur Instrumentalmusik: Lothar Hoffmann-Erbrecht zum 60. Geburtstag,* edited by Anke Bingmann, Klaus Hortschansky, and Winfried Kirsch, pp. 239-51. Tutzing: Hans Schneider, 1988.

Emphasizing the individuality and diversity of the 11 introductions, examines them from the standpoint of phraseology, harmony and tonality, motivic connection with the ensuing movement, and thematic substance. Focuses more on the introductions themselves than on their role as part of a larger structure. Compares aspects of Haydn's approach with those found in symphonies of Mozart and Beethoven.

* Bruce, I.M. "An Act of Homage?" *The Music Review* 11 (1950):277-83.

Cited as item 311.

932. Brusotti, Mizi. "Di alcuni inediti 'Klavierkonzerte' di J. Haydn." *Rivista musicale italiana* 38 (1931):525-45.

Defends Haydn's keyboard concertos against critics' negative appraisals by citing the composer's limited aspirations as well as the limitations of the medium itself. Provides descriptive commentary on four selected works: Hob. XVIII:2, 3, 9 and the doubtful Hob. XVIII:Es1.

933. Butcher, Norma P. "A Comparative-Analytical Study of Sonata-Allegro Form in the First Movements of the London Symphonies of Franz Joseph Haydn." Ph.D. dissertation, University of Southern California, 1971. vi, 172 pp.

In addition to stylistic observations that apply to the symphonies generally, offers descriptive analyses for each of the individual movements under consideration. Examines aspects of overall structure and orchestration, but concentrates on questions of motive and theme: relationship between slow introduction and first movement proper; aspects of motivic development and derivation; and thematic function. Finds pervasive use of rhythmic and melodic figures that provide continuity and tension. Appendices offer statistics on structural design in exposition and recap; derivation of material used in development sections; and location and function of pedal points. Incorporates many music examples.

934. Carse, Adam. *18th Century Symphonies: A Short History of the Symphony in the 18th Century.* London: Augener, 1951. 75 pp.

Intended in part as a companion to the author's series of editions, *Early Classical Symphonies* and *18th Century Overtures,* attempts to grasp an overview of the genre and its early development. Incorporates chapters on such topics as French overture and Italian sinfonia, the concert symphony, form of individual movements, and the issues of score, parts, and ochestration. Numerous references to Haydn throughout.

935. ———. *The History of Orchestration.* London: Kegan Paul, Trench, Trubner, 1925. Reprint. New York: Dover, 1964. xiii, 348 pp.

Discussion of Haydn occurs primarily in chapter 8 on the period of Haydn and Mozart. Describes his early orchestral textures, then traces his stylistic development. An analysis of the mature orchestration of Haydn and Mozart addresses the treatment of strings, woodwinds, horns, trumpets, and timpani. Also considers questions of color and of Haydn's "naive attempts at realism."

936. ———. *The Orchestra in the XVIIIth Century.* Cambridge: W. Heffer & Sons, 1940. Reprint. New York: Broude Brothers, 1969. 176 pp.

Contains references to features in Haydn's orchestration and to early performance of his music. Provides information on the composition of the Esterházy orchestra in 1783 and on incidental details regarding performance circumstances at court.

937. Churgin, Bathia. "The Italian Symphonic Background to Haydn's Early Symphonies and Opera Overtures." In *Haydn Studies* (item 73), pp. 329-36.

Arguing that the Classical symphony originated in Italy, presents an overview of the early Italian development of the symphony and overture. Traces the dissemination of Italian symphonic style and its influence on Viennese composers. Drawing on 39 Haydn symphonies, ca. 1757-65, underscores their connection with the Italian overture tradition (notably the use of sharp contrast in secondary key areas), and points out stylistic similarities between middle-period Sammartini and early Haydn.

938. ———. "The Recapitulation in Sonata-Form Movements of Sammartini and Early Haydn Symphonies." In *Joseph Haydn Kongress* (item 76), pp. 135-40.

Summarizes results of a comparison of 35 movements from early Haydn symphonies with 50 such movements from early and middle-period Sammartini symphonies. Categorizing different types of altered recapitulation in both composers, argues that Haydn's typical reformulation of the recapitulation, far from unique, took place in the context of an established vocabulary of procedures. Includes representative timeline analyses.

939. Cole, Malcolm S. "Haydn's Symphonic Rondo Finales: Their Structural and Stylistic Evolution." *The Haydn Yearbook* 13 (1982):113-42.

Counts a total of 5 rondo finales in Haydn symphonies before 1771, 26 thereafter. Divides them chronologically into groups: early years (ca. 1761-66), Eszterháza (1766-75), consolidation (1775-84), Haydn-Mozart exchange (1785-90), and London (1791-95). Delineates four options with regard to structure (minuet-trio type, two-couplet and three-couplet designs, and sonata-rondo) and discusses their individual shaping by Haydn. Provides schematic analyses of representative movements, and describes the 10 rondo finales of the London symphonies as models of ingenuity in exploiting various rondo elements.

940. ———. "Momigny's Analysis of Haydn's Symphony no. 103." *The Music Review* 30 (1969):261-84.

Examining this early example of a measure-by-measure analysis, incorporated in the theorist's *Cours complet d'harmonie et de composition* (1806), notes the application of a descriptive program, a detailed critique of the orchestration and its coordination with the structural divisions of the form, and the isolation of different hierarchic layers (including section, period, phrase, and motive) in the design.

941. ———. "The Rondo Finale: Evidence for the Mozart-Haydn Exchange?" *Mozart-Jahrbuch* (1968-70), pp. 242-56.

A detailed inquiry into the two composers' approaches, using Haydn's Symphony No. 85 and Mozart's Piano Concerto K. 595 as points of reference. Includes a table of reprise structures for 24 rondo finales in Haydn symphonies. Concludes that Haydn possibly received the idea of sonata-rondo form from Mozart, proposes that Haydn's influence contributed to Mozart's quest for conciseness in the sonata-rondos of his last years, and identifies aspects of Mozart's practice possibly traceable to Haydn's precedents, including the ABA reprise arrangement, abbreviated returns of the reprise, replacement of the contrasting central couplet with a contrapuntal development section, and the use of variants and rescoring in returns, recapitulations, and terminal developments.

942. ———. "The Vogue of the Instrumental Rondo in the Late

Eighteenth Century." *Journal of the American Musicological Society* 22 (1969):425-55.

Examining the theoretical and critical literature (including writings of Schubart, Vogler, Reichardt, and Cramer), as well as pertinent instrumental and vocal repertories, locates the phenomenon between 1773-74 and 1785-86. Includes a table showing the chronological distribution of 596 instrumental rondos composed in the period 1750-1800 and a table summarizing Haydn's use of the rondo in symphonies from 1750 through 1786.

943. Danckwardt, Marianne. *Die langsame Einleitung: Ihre Herkunft und ihr Bau bei Haydn und Mozart.* 2 vols. Tutzing: Hans Schneider, 1977. 435 pp.

Views the concept of the introduction from several vantage points: characteristic gestures, principles of organization, patterns of harmonic progression, and tonal organization. Examines the relationship between introduction and fast movement that follows, and compares introductions with other standard form-types: sonata, slow movement, march, French overture. Scrutinizes overture introductions in addition to symphonies and string quartets. Searching for precedents for the late eighteenth-century masters' procedures, inspects Vivaldi concerto introductions in addition to those of earlier symphonies, overtures, and chamber music. Emphasizing the importance of Italian models, argues that characteristic properties of the late eighteenth-century symphonic introduction have little to do with the French overture model usually invoked to explain its origins.

944. Della Croce, Luigi. *Le 107 sinfonie di Haydn: Guida e analisi critica.* Turin: Eda, 1975. 380 pp.

Following a biographical sketch and brief essay on the course of Haydn's career as a symphonist, divides the repertory into six categories: Italian period (1757-60), Baroque period (1761-65), Romantic period (1766-72), Classic period (1773-84), French period (1785-89), English period (1791-95). Offers a thumbnail stylistic critique of each work, and supplies incipits for each movement. Appendices include a summary of Haydn's tonal palette in the symphonies and several sets of music examples: Mannheim sighs, appoggiatura embellishments, examples of the descending chromatic tetrachord, characteristic *Sturm und Drang* melodic gestures, and instances of the "Beethovenian" rhythmic motive (short-short-short-long). Published in a French translation as *Les 107 symphonies de Haydn: Guide et analyse critique* (Brussels: Editions Dereume, 1977), with a foreword by Georg Feder.

945. Di Benedetto, Renato. "La Sinfonia n. 104 di Haydn: Una proposta d'interpretazione." *Analecta Musicologica* 22/*Studien zur italienischen Musikgeschichte* 13 (1984):427-36.

Characterizes the work as an embodiment of the composer's humanistic vision and as an example of ideal Classic style. Detects processes that signify completion and closure on one hand and those that suggest infinite open-endedness on the other. Describes aspects of melody, chord progression, tonal organization, and form in each movement, and emphasizes resemblances in motive and thematic profile, both subtle and overt, that link the movements.

946. Edwall, Harry R. "Ferdinand IV and Haydn's Concertos for the *Lira Organizzata*." *The Musical Quarterly* 48 (1962):190-203.

A vivid character sketch of the eccentric Neapolitan king and a summary description of the five surviving concertos. Describes the instrument, and reproduces a diagram from Dom François Bedos de Celle's *L'Art du facteur d'orgues* (1778). Discusses the compositional challenge inherent in concertos for an instrument with limited capacity for virtuosity, and discerns a mixture of concerto form with forms and techniques native to the divertimento.

947. Einstein, Alfred. "Haydns Sinfonie." In Alfred Einstein. *Von Schütz bis Hindemith: Essays über Musik und Musiker*, pp. 63-71. Zurich: Pan-Verlag, 1957. Previously published in *Zeitschrift für Musikwissenschaft* 91 (1924):169-74.

Originally the introduction to an Eulenburg miniature score edition of 18 Haydn symphonies. Explains earlier generations' lack of understanding for the symphonies by suggesting that their expressive realm excluded the Romantic, bourgeois, plebian, and pathos-oriented inclinations of the nineteenth century. Proposing that these works transcended the dualism of galant and learned styles, dwells on their organic coherence and their display of originality and ingenuity in thematic development.

* Engel, Hans. "Haydn, Mozart und die Klassik." *Mozart-Jahrbuch* (1959), pp. 46-79.

Cited as item 682.

948. ———. *Das Instrumentalkonzert: Eine musikgeschichtliche Darstellung.* Vol. I: *Von den Anfängen bis gegen 1800.* Wiesbaden: Breitkopf & Härtel, 1971. viii, 393 pp.

Offers general stylistic commentary on the Haydn concertos, chiefly in chapters on concertos for keyboard (see pp. 280-83), violin (pp. 241-42), and cello (pp. 314-15), but also in scattered references to concertos for other instruments and in a discussion of the *sinfonie concertante* (pp. 368-70). Useful for placing the works in historical context.

* ———. "Die Quellen des klassischen Stiles." In *International Musicological Society: Report of the Eighth Congress, New York 1961,* edited by Jan LaRue, 1:285-304. Kassel: Bärenreiter, 1961.

Cited as item 683.

949. Fisher, Stephen C. "Sonata Procedures in Haydn's Symphonic Rondo Finales of the 1770s." In *Haydn Studies* (item 73), pp. 481-87.

Challenges Landon's statement (in item 964) that the finale of Symphony No. 77 in B flat constitutes the first symphonic sonata-rondo of Haydn's. Points out three symphony finales as earlier examples that betray sonata-rondo features: Symphony No. 64 in A (ca. 1773), No. 69 in C, and No. 66 in B flat (both by 1770). Observes that all have developmental episodes employing primary-theme material, with movement to an episode in the dominant in the manner of a sonata-form transition. Concerning the question of possible Mozart influence, notes that Haydn's interest in combining sonata and rondo elements dates from approximately 10 years before his meeting with Mozart, and proposes that both composers may have hit upon the idea at about the same time.

950. Flothuis, Marius. "Die Instrumentation der 'Londoner' Sinfonien." In *Joseph Haydn Kongress* (item 76), pp. 183-89.

Specifying the historical position of Haydn's late symphonies (they follow Mozart's and precede Beethoven's), examines innovative peculiarities of orchestral usage, notably those having to do with flutes, clarinets, independent cello and contrabass, solo strings, and timpani.

951. Foster, Jonathan. "The Tempora Mutantur Symphony of Joseph Haydn." *The Haydn Yearbook* 9 (1975):328-29.

Identifies the inscription on a set of authentic manuscript parts for Symphony No. 64 as a reference to an epigram by John Owen (ca. 1565-1622). Suggests that the rhythm of the rondo-finale theme corresponds to the poetic meter of the first line of the epigram. Proposes that this device can be compared to Haydn's use of plainchant themes in instrumental works and also to the technique seen in his *Seven Last Words,* where the theme of each part fits the rhythm of its particular Latin superscription.

952. Grasberger, Franz. "Form und Ekstase: Über eine Beziehung Haydn-Schubert-Bruckner in der Symphonie." In *Anthony van Hoboken: Festschrift zum 75. Geburtstag,* edited by Joseph Schmidt-Görg, pp. 93-100. Mainz: B. Schott's Söhne, 1962.

Relates a mystical, ecstatic transcendence in Bruckner's symphonies to the cumulative, wave-like force of the composer's processes of motivic development. Cites precedents both in Schubert (e.g. in the first movement of the *Unfinished* Symphony) and in Haydn's approach to motivic development. Emphasizes the potential for expressive intensity in Haydn's symphonic technique, notably in the slow movements. Cites a moment of mystical suspension in the second movement of Symphony No. 104, bars 114-17, that foreshadows something that was to become essential for Schubert and Bruckner.

* Gwilt, Richard. "Sonata-Allegro Revisited." *In Theory Only* 7/5-6 (1983-84):3-33.

Cited as item 704.

953. Haselböck, Martin. "Die Orgelkonzerte Joseph Haydns." *Musik und Kirche* 54 (1984):17-26.

Offers miscellaneous facts on each of the seven concertos

identified by Feder in item 1108. Distinguishes between church-trio settings and those with a pronounced tutti-solo division. Includes background on organs in use in Haydn's environs and discusses eighteenth-century liturgical uses for purely instrumental pieces such as concertos and symphonies.

954. Hastings, Baird. "Vergleich der konzertanten Techniken in den Sinfonien Mozarts und Haydns." *Mitteilungen der Internationalen Stiftung Mozarteum Salzburg* 16/3-4 (1968):6-10.

Observes that while both composers used concertante elements in their symphonies, Haydn did so more extensively, generally giving them a structural function and incorporating a broader spectrum of sonorities. Proposes that Mozart favored lyrical melodies and a more brilliant concertante style, with greater emphasis on virtuosity and contrast.

955. Hauschild, Peter. "Liedthema und Entwicklung in den Expositionen von Haydns 'Londoner' Sinfonien." In *Joseph Haydn Kongress* (item 76), pp. 175-83.

Explores aspects of motivic elaboration and thematic process in the first movements of Symphonies Nos. 93, 99, 100, 102, 103, and 104, all of which feature song-like principal themes.

* Heartz, Daniel. "Haydn und Gluck im Burgtheater um 1760: Der neue krumme Teufel, Le Diable à quatre und die Sinfonie 'Le soir'." In *Gesellschaft für Musikforschung: Bericht über den Internationalen musikwissenschaftlichen Kongress, Bayreuth 1981,* edited by Christoph-Hellmut Mahling and Sigrid Wiesmann, pp. 120-35. Kassel: Bärenreiter, 1984.

Cited as item 864.

956. Heller, Friedrich. "Haydn's 'Londoner Symphonie', D-Dur: Eine Analyse." In *Beiträge zur Musikgeschichte des 18. Jahrhunderts* (item 69), pp. 182-88.

Proposes that in the Classical period, as in no other, music assumed the character of a language. Examines this notion with respect to the simplicity and unity of ideas in Haydn's Symphony No. 104. Demonstrates that the entire symphony grows out of material in the introduction.

957. Heuss, Alfred. "Der Humor im letzten Satz von Haydns Oxford-Symphonie." *Die Musik* 12/5 (1912-13):271-86.

Adopting processes of motivic development as a central focus, attempts to criticize the movement as a whole from the standpoint of its humorous content. Cites effects involving instrumentation, thematic recurrence, change of mode, surprise, and thwarted expectations.

958. ———. "Joseph Haydns Londoner Sinfonie in c-moll eine Charakter-Sinfonie?" *Zeitschrift für Musik* 99 (1932):285-90.

Describes the first-movement primary and secondary themes in terms of purported contrasts between masculine and feminine, and personifies their juxtaposition, interaction, and development. Applying the notion to subsequent movements, entertains the possibility of a reflection of the composer's own personality and amorous experiences.

959. Hodgson, Antony. *The Music of Joseph Haydn: The Symphonies.* London: Tantivy, 1976. 208 pp.

Written primarily for the non-specialist, portrays Haydn's originality of style from the vantage point of his symphonies. Provides a brief, casually assembled, and sometimes rather subjective account of each work. Includes a fair number of music examples (some in score), and several glossy illustrations, some in color.

960. Johns, Donald C. "In Defence of Haydn: The *'Surprise'* Symphony Revisited." *The Music Review* 24 (1963):305-12.

Deploring the allegedly superficial, condescending treatment of Symphony No. 94 (especially the middle movements) offered by Tovey and Landon, provides a detailed stylistic analysis of the second movement that features aspects of harmony, dynamics, melody, rhythm, and orchestration. Identifies a long-range plan of tension and relaxation that transcends the theme-and-variations scheme and divides the movement into two large sections. Finds organic unity in the minuet, notably in motivic connections to be found between minuet proper and trio. Jan LaRue's letter to the editor in *The Music Review* 25

(1964):159, defends Tovey's analysis of the *Andante* and cites an additional motivic connection within the minuet.

961. Klein, Rudolf. "Wo kann die Analyse von Haydns Symphonik ansetzen?" *Österreichische Musikzeitschrift* 37 (1982):234-41.

Observes that the procedure of thematic duality, understood as thesis and antithesis, is rare in Haydn, who prefers to design a series of related ideas, each of which forms an integral, motivically connected outgrowth of the preceding. Applies the linguistic term *Parataxe* to this process, as opposed to the *Syntaxe* principle more commonly encountered in Mozart, whose musical ideas are set in a balanced relationship to one another. Proposes that while Haydn grasped and utilized the *Syntaxe* approach on occasion, he preferred the other, thereby betraying artistic opposition to certain syntactically oriented ideals of the Enlightenment. Linking *Parataxe* to the element of surprise in Haydn, argues that whereas the thesis and antithesis of *Syntaxe* excludes structural surprise, Haydn's approach permits the generation of a continuum in which the unexpected can occur.

962. Klinkhammer, Rudolf. *Die langsame Einleitung in der Instrumentalmusik der Klassik und Romantik.* Regensburg: Gustav Bosse, 1971. vi, 206 pp.

Surveys seventeenth- and eighteenth-century precedents for the concept of the symphonic introduction. The chapter on Haydn, pp. 21-57, divides symphonic introductions into three groups: 1) Nos. 6, 7, 50, 53, 54, 57, 60, 71, 73, 75; 2) Nos. 84, 85, 86, 88, 90, 91, 92; 3) the London symphonies. Treats aspects of harmonic organization, phrase structure, thematic function, and connection with thematic material in the movements that follow. Offers numerous music examples.

963. Landon, H.C. Robbins. *Haydn Symphonies.* London: British Broadcasting Corporation, 1966. Reprint. Seattle: University of Washington Press, 1969. 64 pp.

A balanced overview of the repertory, combining biographical material with information on sources, chronology, and style. Divides into six chapters: early works (to 1761), 1761-65, 1766-74, 1775-84, 1785-89, London symphonies.

964. ———. *The Symphonies of Joseph Haydn.* London: Universal Edition & Rockliff, 1955. xvii, 863 pp. *Supplement.* London: Barrie and Rockliff, 1961. 64 pp.

Still the definitive study of the genre, divides into three parts: 1) authenticity and terminology (e.g. overture vs. symphony), sources, chronology, textual problems, questions of performance (makeup of orchestras; tempos, repetitions, ornaments, dynamics, rhythmic interpretation); 2) descriptive analysis and criticism of the works, through 1788, divided into the following groups: pre-1761, 1761-65, 1766-70, 1771-74, 1774-84, 1785-88; 3) the London symphonies: documentary account, analysis, epilogue on the late masses (1796-1802), depicted as Haydn's "symphonic legacy." Appendices include a catalogue of authentic symphonies, catalogue of doubtful and spurious works, bibliography, index of Haydn compositions cited, general index, errata and addenda, and (bound separately) the score to Hob.I:107* (previously printed only as the string quartet Hob. III:5). Offers much documentary information and background on circumstances of the works' composition. Emphasis in discussions of the music falls on criticism of individual movements and compositions rather than on a larger view of Haydn's accomplishment or the evolution of his approach to the genre. Celebrates the theatricality of the *Sturm und Drang* works (1766-70), praises the breadth and originality of the 1771-74 symphonies, and deplores the limitations of symphonies from the later 70s and early 80s. Many music examples; more than 40 plates and illustrations. The *Supplement,* published separately, incorporates corrigenda and addenda originally published in *The Music Review* 19 (1958):311-19 and 20 (1959):56-70. It also includes new information on Czech sources for authentic and spurious Haydn symphonies.

965. ———. "Die Verwendung gregorianischer Melodien in Haydns Frühsymphonien." *Österreichische Musikzeitschrift* 9 (1954):119-26.

Proposes that Haydn sought liberation from the *Fortspinnung*-type pre-Classical melodic style through two means: the use of Slavic folksong material and the borrowing of traditional liturgical melodies. Examines evidence of the latter device in Symphony No. 26 (*Sinfonia lamentatione*), quoting passages that illustrate Haydn's procedure in making the plainchant references. Alludes to the practice in Symphonies Nos. 22 and 30.

966. Larsen, Jens Peter. "Concerning the Development of the Austrian Symphonic Tradition." In Jens Peter Larsen. *Handel, Haydn, and the Viennese Classical Style,* translations by Ulrich Krämer, pp. 315-25. Ann Arbor: UMI Research Press, 1988.

Translation of item 968.

967. ———. "Haydn and the Classical Symphony." In *Haydnfest* (item 71), pp. 8-11.

Presents an overview of Haydn's symphonies in four stages: the early works (before and around 1760 to ca. 1765), which exhibited great diversity; the decisive phase (ca. 1766-72 [1775]), in which Haydn expanded his means of expression; the operatic period (ca. 1775-85), during which he cut back his production because of preoccupation with duties as opera kapellmeister and perhaps because the prince may have objected to his modernisms; and the late period, which encompasses the Paris symphonies, written for a larger orchestra, and the London symphonies, which begin to approach nineteenth-century style. Includes facsimile pages from the "Entwurf-Katalog" and from the autographs of Symphonies Nos. 35, 90, and 94.

* ———. "Der Stilwandel in der österreichischen Musik zwischen Barock und Wiener Klassik." In *Der junge Haydn* (item 81), pp. 18-30.

Cited as item 721.

968. ———. "Zur Entstehung der österreichischen Symphonietradition (ca. 1750-1775)." *The Haydn Yearbook* 10 (1978):72-80.

Concerned with stylistic developments from the time of Caldara and Fux through the mid-century accomplishments of composers such as Wagenseil, Holzbauer, and Tuma. Addresses questions of stylistic diversity and chronology in early Haydn symphonies. Depicts the emerging Viennese Classical idiom as a synthesis of ingredients traceable to the traditions of overture, parthia, sonata, and concerto.

969. Livingstone, Ernest F. "Unifying Elements in Haydn's Symphony No. 104." *Haydn Studies* (item 73), pp. 493-96.

Outlines ingredients in all four movements that contribute to thematic and structural unity. Observes subsequent recurrences of ideas from the first-movement introduction, and cites significant procedural similarities among the different movements.

970. McCaldin, Denis. "Haydn as Self-Borrower." *The Musical Times* 123 (1982):177-79.

Calls upon two concertos for two *lire organizzate* to demonstrate Haydn's use of borrowed materials from his own works (in Haydn's modest use of borrowed material, he typically drew upon ideas of other composers). Describes changes made in adapting material from Concerto No. 5 for Symphony No. 89 and from Concerto No. 3 for Symphony No. 100.

971. Marco, Guy A. "A Musical Task in the 'Surprise' Symphony." *Journal of the American Musicological Society* 11 (1958):41-44.

Examines the course of thematic and tonal events in the first movement of Symphony No. 94. Focusing on recurrences of the first main subject, shows that the "task" posed by the exposition involves expansion of a brief, essentially incomplete motive into a full-fledged musical thought. Argues that the recapitulation constitutes a structural synthesis of materials and tendencies witnessed in the exposition, and places special emphasis on the reinterpretation of the second subject, which now functions as the second, complementary half of the first subject.

972. Marillier, C.G. "Computer Assisted Analysis of Tonal Structure in the Classical Symphony." *The Haydn Yearbook* 14 (1983):187-99.

Originally read at the International Computer Music Conference, Queens College, Flushing, 13-16 November 1980. Aims to establish an appropriate model for statistical analysis of tonal organization, which would then apply to the corpus of Haydn's symphonies. Concerned in particular with a concept of "tonal distance," discerns a tendency in Haydn to balance areas in "keys sharper than the tonic" with flatter keys in development sections. Proposes that the balance of sharp and flat tonal areas in the late 1780s tips in favor of flat keys in the London symphonies.

973. Martinez-Göllner, Marie Louise. *Joseph Haydn: Symphonie Nr. 94 (Paukenschlag).* Munich: Wilhelm Fink, 1979. 37 pp. plus music appendix and examples.

Offers a movement-by-movement analysis, preceded by source information and background discussion of Haydn's first visit to London, the contract with Salomon, first performance of the work, and its subsequent popularity. Incorporates a section on Haydn and posterity, and a small selection of documentary material that includes two reviews of the first performance and Burney's poem on Haydn. An appendix provides excerpts from works that use the second-movement theme: a vocal canzonetta, a minuet version, and a passage from *The Seasons.*

974. Marx, Karl. "Über thematische Beziehungen in Haydns Londoner Symphonien." *Haydn-Studien* 4 (1976-80):1-20.

Contends that *Substanzgemeinschaft* became a creative impulse for Haydn at the height of his powers, but leaves open the question of whether it was a deliberate source of cyclical unification or an inadvertent result of the creative process. Provides 32 analytical sketches in order to demonstrate thematic relationship of varying degrees, and considers different analysts' criteria for thematic similarity.

975. Menk, Gail E. "The Symphonic Introductions of Joseph Haydn." Ph.D. dissertation, University of Iowa, 1960. 138 pp.

Following discussion of precedents in seventeenth- and eighteenth-century music, subjects 29 Haydn introductions to stylistic and structural analysis. Identifies consistent features (irregular phrasing, characteristic treatment of dissonance, unifying motives, unity through rhythmic patterning) as well as evolutionary tendencies (toward greater number of phrases, variety of phrase-length, and increasing use of minor mode). An appendix lists introductions in standard late eighteenth- and nineteenth-century symphonic repertory.

976. Monk, Dennis C. "Style Change in the Slow Movement of the Viennese Symphony: 1740-1770." 2 vols. Ph.D.

dissertation, University of California at Los Angeles, 1971. xi, 280 pp.; iii, 147 pp.

Featured composers include Raimund Birck, Josef Bonno, Florian Gassmann, Leopold Hofmann, Georg Monn, Carlos d'Ordonez, Luca Predieri, Georg Reutter, Jr., Franz Tuma, Johann Vanhal, Georg Wagenseil, and early Haydn. Considers such factors as orchestration and orchestra size, texture, melodic and thematic construction, tonal relationships between movements, cadence types, harmonic structure of primary themes, modulatory patterns, and formal patterns employed. Extensive comparison between Haydn's movements and others'. Thematic catalogue; scores of unpublished slow movements. Numerous music examples, many in score.

977. Osthoff, Wolfgang. "Trombe sordine." *Archiv für Musikwissenschaft* 13 (1956):77-95.

Speculates on the possible programmatic significance of the slow movement of Symphony No. 102, which specifies muted trumpets. Cites a choral arrangement of the movement by F.A. Schulze (ca. 1800), recalls the traditional association of muted trumpets with funereal and elegiac expression, and refers to a passage in the Dies biography about a certain symphonic *Adagio* that supposedly represented a dialogue between God and a sinner.

978. Palm, Albert. "Unbekannte Haydn-Analysen." *The Haydn Yearbook* 4 (1968):169-94.

Quotes extensively from an analysis of Symphony No. 103, first movement, in Jérôme-Joseph de Momigny's *Cours complet d'harmonie et de composition* (1806), the content of which combines structural periodization with descriptive, poetic interpretations that strive to explain sources of unity and diversity as well as irrational, expressive substance. Comparing the theorist's vantage point with those of Charles Batteux, Jean le Rond d'Alembert, and Heinrich Wilhelm von Gerstenberg, emphasizes his notion of music as an expressive language. Other Momigny analyses mentioned include those in the *Encyclopédie méthodique* (1818; articles "Rondo," "Symphonie," and "Système") dealing with Symphony No. 104 and the Piano Trio in A flat (Hob. XV:14). Compares Momigny's treatment of Haydn with his analyses of Mozart, and observes that the theorist regards Haydn as a preeminent model of formal perfection.

979. Peretti, F. de Pauer. "Nel bicentenario di Giuseppe Haydn: L'ultima sinfonia." *Rivista musicale italiana* 39 (1932):299-310.

Extolling Haydn as a symphonic master and predecessor of Beethoven, singles out Symphony No. 104 as a crowning achievement and offers a critical appraisal of the work.

980. Riehm, Diethard. "Die ersten Sätze von Joseph Haydns Londoner Sinfonien." Ph.D. dissertation, Westphalian Wilhelm's University, Münster, 1971. 144 pp.

Alert to the pitfalls of analyzing eighteenth-century music in terms of nineteenth-century concepts of form, argues that despite the extraordinary diversity of the London symphonies, these works reveal consistent practices that submit to explanation in accordance with contemporary writings, notably those of Heinrich Christoph Koch. Shows that a characteristic procedure of Haydn's, involving the contrast between animated, largely non-thematic tutti passages and lied-like thematic areas, conforms more closely to Koch's principle of unity than to any model based on a concept of thematic duality. Offers a descriptive chapter on each of the twelve symphonies and summary chapters on each main part of the first-movement form.

981. ———. "Zur Anlage der Exposition in Joseph Haydns letzten Sinfonien." *Österreichische Musikzeitschrift* 21 (1966):255-60.

Draws on the expositions of Symphonies Nos. 102 and 104 to illustrate Haydn's conceptual approach to structure. Points out the inappropriateness of textbook schemes for describing Haydn's symphonies, and rejects the principle of contrast between first and second themes as a controlling factor in favor of the contrast between period structure on one hand and loosely constructed passages (*Gänge*) on the other.

982. Ringer, Alexander L. "The *Chasse* as a Musical Topic of the 18th Century." *Journal of the American Musicological Society* 6 (1953):148-59.

Provides an historical sketch of music for the hunt and its use in art music. Describes the musical and sociological functions of the eighteenth-century *chasse*, and examines the use of hunting music by a variety of composers, including Haydn in his Symphonies Nos. 31 and 73.

983. Rywosch, Bernhard. *Beiträge zur Entwicklung in Joseph Haydns Symphonik, 1759-1780.* Turbenthal: Rob. Furrers Erben, 1934. 133 pp.

The author's Zurich dissertation, this study applies the period-concepts of Rococo, *Sturm und Drang,* and Classic as a frame of reference for tracing an evolutionary path toward the composer's perfection of a symphonic idiom. Divides the symphonies in question into three groups (1759-71; 1771-74; 1774-81), and examines them movement by movement from the standpoint of instrumentation, dynamics, theme, and structure. Isolates three notable factors implicated in Haydn's stylistic progress: concertante technique, counterpoint, and thematic contrast. Finds him to be an experimenter in these works, and proposes that devices involving dynamics and sonority are eventually assimilated to become organic components of the later masterworks. Appends a summary analysis of modulation plans in the sonata-form development sections of the first 70 symphonies.

984. Sárosi, Bálint. "Parallelen aus der ungarischen Volksmusik zum 'Rondo all'Ongarese'-Satz in Haydns D-dur Klavierkonzert Hob. XVIII:11." In *Joseph Haydn Kongress* (item 76), pp. 222-26.

Examines compositional processes in the concerto movement that resemble those associated with Hungarian folk and gypsy traditions. Includes several music examples.

985. Schering, Arnold. "Bemerkungen zu J. Haydns Programmsinfonien." In *Vom musikalischen Kunstwerk,* edited by Friedrich Blume, pp. 246-77. Leipzig: Koehler & Amelang, 1949. Previously published in *Jahrbuch der Musikbibliothek Peters* 46 (1939):9-27.

Addresses the nature and significance of extra-musical stimuli in Haydn's instrumental music, drawing on quotations from early Haydn biographers. Examines several symphonies that have programmatic titles, and discusses the underlying stimuli (if known) or speculates on what they may have been.

986. Schlager, Karl-Heinz. *Joseph Haydn: Sinfonie Nr. 104 D-Dur.* Munich: Wilhelm Fink, 1983. 55 pp.

Features a detailed, event-by-event analysis of theme, structure, and compositional process in each movement. Includes background on the late symphonies: creation, performance, and reception; and quotes from Haydn's correspondence, a review of the first performance, and the third London notebook.

987. Schröder, Gesine. "Über das 'klassische Orchester' und Haydns späte symphonische Instrumentation." In *Joseph Haydn* (item 75), pp. 79-97.

Deals with questions of novel and conventional orchestration in Haydn's London symphonies from the vantage point of historians' concepts of the Classical orchestra. Works cited include Symphonies Nos. 98 (second movement), 101 (first movement), and 102 (first movement).

988. Schwartz, Judith L. "Thematic Asymmetry in First Movements of Haydn's Early Symphonies." In *Haydn Studies* (item 73), pp. 501-9.

Surveys and categorizes different types of asymmetrical phrase patterning in early Haydn symphonies and in works of Haydn's contemporaries in Italy, Germany, and Austria, ca. 1720-65. Identifying instances of such patterning as alternatives to regular periodicity based on even-numbered multiples of a metrical unit, shows that Haydn's early symphonies reflect not merely an old-fashioned *Fortspinnung* technique, but a variety of periodic and non-periodic processes widely exploited by older contemporaries.

989. Sondheimer, Robert. "Die formale Entwicklung der vorklassischen Sinfonie." *Archiv für Musikwissenschaft* 4 (1922):85-99, 123-39.

Criticizing the narrowness of Riemann's focus on late Stamitz symphonies in his exploration of the background for the Classical symphony, aims for a relatively broad overview of the period. Composers passing in review within the time-span ca. 1730-80s include Leo, Tartini, Sammartini, Wagenseil, Monn, Stamitz, Filz, Beck, Cannabich, Toeschi, Gossec, and Haydn. Limits study to aspects of overall form and details within first movements. Furnishes numerous music examples.

* ———. *Die Theorie der Sinfonie und die Beurteilung einzelner Sinfoniekomponisten bei den Musikschriftstellern des 18. Jahrhunderts.* Leipzig: Breitkopf & Härtel, 1925. 99 pp.

Cited as item 212.

990. Sponheuer, Bernd. "Haydns Arbeit am Finalproblem." *Archiv für Musikwissenschaft* 34 (1977):199-224.

Traces the evolution of the symphonic finale in Haydn from its status as merely the last in a series of movements to its eventual position as an ingredient of a larger design with a specific function involving the equilibrium of the cycle as a whole. Discusses aspects of Haydn's innovation, experimentation, and humor in working within established norms and boundaries, and relates the issue of the evolving finale to the contemporaneous phenomenon of disintegration of an absolutist feudal order and the development of an emerging bourgeois society.

991. Therstappen, Hans Joachim. *Joseph Haydns sinfonisches Vermächtnis.* Wolfenbüttel: Georg Kallmeyer, 1941. xi, 275 pp.

Focusing on the 12 London symphonies, strives to elucidate Haydn's symphonic technique and his concept of the symphonic cycle by examining different portions of the cycle in turn: first movements (introduction, exposition, development, and recapitulation), slow movements, minuets, and finales. Within each topic, discusses common features and isolates each symphony for individual treatment. Considers thematic design and function, motivic work, proportion, harmonic organization, sources of musical coherence, and compositional logic. Many references to pertinent literature. Provides indexes to references to each movement of each symphony and to other Haydn works mentioned.

992. Torrefranca, Fausto. "Le origini della sinfonia." *Rivista musicale italiana* 20 (1913):291-346.

Protesting the excessive emphasis placed by Pohl and others on German composers in their quest for precursors to the symphonies of Haydn's generation, argues for the importance of the Italian composers, notably Sammartini. Refers to a "neo-Italian" symphonic style in Mannheim and

Vienna, and cites Italian precedents for Haydn's approach.

993. Tovey, Donald Francis. *Essays in Musical Analysis.* Vol. 1: *Symphonies.* London: Oxford University Press, 1935. viii, 223 pp.

Discussion of Haydn, pp. 138-76, includes witty accounts of 11 late symphonies (Nos. 88, 92, 94, 95, 98-104). For each work, touches on salient features of theme, structure, and compositional process. Identifies the "surprise" in Symphony No. 94 as the "most unimportant feature in all Haydn's mature works," observes that Haydn's approach to form is most nearly regular in his minor-key compositions, and suggests that the slow movement of Symphony No. 98 might be called his Requiem for Mozart. Introduces the Haydn section with an essay entitled "Haydn the Inaccessible," which calls attention to the remarkably primitive state of research on the composer up to that time.

994. Unger, Max. "The First Performance of Haydn's 'Surprise' Symphony." *The Musical Times* 73 (1932):413-15.

Publishes, with commentary, Johann Christian Firnhaber's 1825 account of Haydn's rehearsal of the "unexpected crash on the drum," second movement, and of a London audience's reaction to it in 1793. The purpose of his article was to refute a claim in the *Zeitung für die elegante Welt* (March 1825) that Haydn had introduced the startling effect to waken audiences who "quietly ... [went] to sleep during the performance of his symphonies."

995. Vinton, John. "The Development Section in Early Viennese Symphonies: A Re-valuation." *The Music Review* 24 (1963):13-22.

Appraises developmental processes in selected symphonies by Georg Matthias Monn and Georg Christoph Wagenseil, and defends the Viennese symphonists' skill in exploring development-section possibilities. Finds that Monn, in works prior to and contemporaneous with early Haydn, composed central passages that truly merit the label "development section" by virtue of their formal clarity and specialization. While conceding that development sections in early Haydn seem relatively primitive by comparison with those of monumental works from later years, argues that Haydn's earliest attempts nevertheless surpass the accomplishments of his immediate predecessors. Furnishes analytical commentary on development sections from Haydn's symphonies in the period 1757-61.

996. Walter, Horst. "Das Posthornsignal bei Haydn und anderen Komponisten des 18. Jahrhunderts." *Haydn-Studien* 4 (1976-80):21-34.

Studies post-horn signals to clarify whether the solo horn motive in Haydn's Symphony No. 31 constitutes such a signal or a local hunting call, as claimed by Hoboken. Reports on eighteenth-century descriptions of the post horn's functions, and describes the types of instrument available. Draws on signals found in art music, since extant transcriptions of functional signals are almost nonexistent before 1828. Compiles a list of 26 works with such signals, from Beer (late seventeenth century) to Beethoven (1795), and provides a corresponding set of themes. On the basis of this information, concludes that the figure in Symphony No. 31 was based on a widely disseminated post-horn signal.

997. Wolf, Eugene K. "The Recapitulations in Haydn's London Symphonies." *The Musical Quarterly* 52 (1966):71-89.

Emphasizing the developmental nature of Haydn's compositional process, compares recapitulations with expositions in terms of large- and small-scale organization. Finds numerous, highly original alterations involved in the adaptation of exposition material for recapitulatory use. Emphasizes the coordination of changes to reinforce specific redefinition of formal functions, and identifies a characteristic process involving compression in the first part of a recapitulation, followed by structural expansion.

998. Worbs, Hans Christoph. *Die Sinfonik Haydns.* Heidenau/Sa.: Ministerium für Kultur, 1956. 73 pp.

Concerned with reflections of European social evolution in the development of Haydn's symphonic style. Discusses the transformation from courtly minuet to scherzo, the changing nature of Haydn's audiences, and the changing relationship of the composer toward his art. Citing a shift in the function of music, from courtly entertainment to direct expression of middle-class experience and ideals, emphasizes Haydn's tendency toward an increasingly subjective, dynamic, and folklike musical language.

999. Zaslaw, Neal. "Mozart, Haydn and the *Sinfonia da Chiesa.*"

The Journal of Musicology 1 (1982):95-124.

Quoting from such writers as Mattheson, Scheibe, and Schulz, examines contemporary references to performances of symphonies (including works by Haydn) in church. Calls attention to Haydn symphonic works claimed by Landon to have church connections (listed in an appendix), and questions Landon's assumption that works beginning with a slow movement must belong to a church tradition. Points to the lack of evidence of such a tradition or consistent practice. Observes that a Haydn symphony with plainsong references would be redundant in a church service unless it served to replace a chant, and concludes that such works were decidedly not intended for church use.

Chamber Music for Strings

1000. Barrett-Ayres, Reginald. *Joseph Haydn and the String Quartet.* New York: Schirmer Books, 1974. xiii, 417 pp.

Following an approach that is more descriptive than critical or analytical, explores the evolution of Haydn's approach to the medium, incorporating brief discussion of his predecessors and a more extensive inquiry into the quartets of Mozart. Devotes a chapter to the question of the authenticity of Op. 3. Furnishes numerous music examples.

1001. Bartha, Dénes. "Thematic Profile and Character in the Quartet-Finales of Joseph Haydn (A Contribution to the Micro-Analysis of Thematic Structure)." *Studia Musicologica Academiae Scientiarum Hungaricae* 11 (1969):35-62.

Pursuing a line of inquiry developed in the author's "Volkstanz-Stilisierung in Joseph Haydn's Finale-Themen" (item 927), looks into aspects of metric and motivic microstructure. Attempts to isolate normative, conventional elements and to trace evolutionary tendencies. Reviews the literature on Haydn's quartets, identifies deficiencies of existing methods of stylistic criticism, and points to the need for greater emphasis on the analysis of microstructure.

1002. Blume, Friedrich. "Joseph Haydns künstlerische Persönlichkeit in seinen Streichquartetten." In Friedrich Blume. *Syntagma Musicologicum: Gesammelte Reden und Schriften,* edited by Martin Ruhnke, pp. 526-51. Kassel: Bärenreiter, 1963. Previously published in *Jahrbuch der Musikbibliothek Peters* 38 (1931):24-48.

Calling for a revision of the traditionally superficial view, by which Haydn is comprehended mainly from the vantage point of his late works, concludes that Op. 50 represents the full realization of the composer's string-quartet ideal. Contrasts the variability of Mozart's approach with Haydn's more predictable, consistent pursuit of a central stylistic concept. Emphasizing Haydn's identification with an era of rationalism and enlightenment, sees the balance of rational and *Sturm und Drang* elements in the quartets as the result of a consciously applied effort.

1003. Bowker, Barbara Ellen. "Intensification Relationships between Texture and Other Elements in Selected String Quartets of Haydn." Ph.D. dissertation, Northwestern University, 1988. 172 pp.

As a frame of reference, applies Wallace Berry's concept of "intensity." Accordingly, the change from homophony to polyphony denotes an increase in textural intensity, while the change from polyphony to homophony constitutes a decrease. Searches for correlations and interactions between textural intensity and activity involving other musical elements, including aspects of rhythm and harmony. Finds a tendency toward activity that complements textural fluctuation, especially in situations involving strong contrasts in texture. Shows, however, that later quartets reveal a greater proportion of activity that is compensatory, rather than complementary, in relation to intensity in texture.

* Cherbuliez, Antoine. "Bemerkungen zu den 'Haydn'-Streichquartetten Mozarts und Haydns 'Russischen' Streichquartetten." *Mozart-Jahrbuch* (1959), pp. 28-45.

Cited as item 312.

1004. Cuyler, Louise E. "Tonal Exploitation in the Later Quartets of Haydn." In *Studies in Eighteenth-Century Music: A Tribute to Karl Geiringer on His Seventieth Birthday,* edited by H.C. Robbins Landon and Roger E.

Chapman, pp. 136-50. New York: Oxford University Press, 1970.

Identifies examples of unusual juxtaposition of chords and keys within movements, as well as remote relationships between movements. Proposes three governing principles of pitch organization that guided Haydn's procedures: bimodality (combining the available choices of a major key and its parallel minor), mirror relationships (equidistant centers above and below a tonic), and the chromatic alteration of a diatonic relationship (e.g. D to F-sharp major).

1005. Demaree, Robert W., Jr. "The Structural Proportions of the Haydn Quartets." Ph.D. dissertation, Indiana University, 1973. x, 252 pp.

Influenced by Susanne Langer, in addition to Grosvenor Cooper and Leonard Meyer, proposes an analytical method involving multiple architectonic levels: cumulative plane (spanning an entire movement), primary plane (highest formal divisions within a movement), secondary plane (theme group), tertiary plane (period-level structure), basal plane (phrase), and sub-basal plane (motive). Supplements this framework with a method of graphic analysis and a specialized terminology for specifying structural relationships and musical processes. Employs these materials in the analysis of selected movements (encompassing characteristic first, second, third, and fourth movements), and attempts to identify processes that contribute to structural organization.

* Eppstein, Hans. "Geist und Technik in der Musik der Wiener Klassik." *Österreichische Musikzeitschrift* 32 (1977):486-96.

Cited as item 684.

* Esch, Christian. "Haydns Streichquartett op. 54/1 und Mozarts KV 465." *Haydn-Studien* 6/2 (1988):148-55.

Cited as item 318.

1006. Finscher, Ludwig. *Studien zur Geschichte des Streichquartetts.* Vol. 1: *Die Entstehung des klassischen Streichquartetts, von den Vorformen zur Grundlegung durch Joseph Haydn.* Kassel: Bärenreiter, 1974. 388 pp.

Examines instrumental-ensemble genres from the first half of the eighteenth century that furnished precedents for the string quartet, including sonata *a quattro* and sinfonia, in France, Italy, and central Europe. Discusses eighteenth-century thoroughbass practice, liberation from thoroughbass in the evolution of string-quartet texture, manifestations of soloistic texture, and the instrumentation of the bass line. Explains the synthesis of keyboard sonata, trio sonata, solo concerto, and quartet-symphony represented by Haydn's Op. 1 and 2. Offers a discussion of texture, structure, and compositional process in each set through Op. 33, and places each in an evolutionary path in Haydn's development of the genre. Includes numerous music examples in score.

1007. Germann, Jörg. "Die Entwicklung der Exposition in Joseph Haydn's Streichquartetten." Ph.D. dissertation, University of Bern, 1964. viii, 206 pp.

Concentrating on first movements, attempts to specify a pattern of stylistic evolution, to demonstrate aspects of formal and stylistic individuality, and to reveal sources of unity and continuity whereby the quartets stand as exemplary models of Classical style. Aspects discussed include thematic structure, motivic unification and development, texture, phraseology, structural organization, and harmonic usage. Devotes chapters to each of four functional areas within the exposition: principal theme, transition, contrasting area, and closing material.

1008. Griffiths, Paul. *The String Quartet.* [New York]: Thames and Hudson, 1983. 240 pp.

Deals with Haydn extensively in the first two chapters, which concern the years ca. 1759-71 and 1772-99, respectively. Gives a moderately detailed treatment of medium, audience, and the role of eighteenth-century publishers in the early evolution of the quartet. Focuses the discussion of Haydn on texture and sonority. Relates his quartets to those of contemporaries, most notably Mozart. Emphasizes stylistic generalization rather than detailed criticism.

1009. Hickman, Roger. "Haydn and the 'Symphony in Miniature'." *The Music Review* 43 (1982):15-23.

Describes a late eighteenth-century change in chamber

style (sharply reflected in Haydn's quartets of Op. 71 and 74) involving abrupt textural and dynamic contrasts, rhythmic repetition, chordal and unison passages, and the general avoidance of subtlety in favor of broad, quasi-orchestral gestures. Notes similar features in contemporaneous quartets by Gyrowetz and Wranitzky, and cites Landon's observation that Haydn's Op. 71 and 74 are the first quartets by the great masters to have been written specifically for concert-hall performance.

1010. ———. "The Nascent Viennese String Quartet." *The Musical Quarterly* 67 (1981):193-212.

Proposing a systematic distinction between orchestral and soloistic styles, argues for the recognition of a decisive break in the late 1760s between an older approach and a new, distinctly soloistic chamber idiom. Examining string ensemble music by Gassmann, Monn, Ordonez, and Vanhal, as well as Haydn, proposes that orchestral performance for pre-1770 Viennese quartets should not be excluded (especially outside Vienna). Suggests that Haydn's Op. 9, along with other quartets from this time, reflects an essentially new conception based on obligatory solo writing.

1011. Hughes, Rosemary. *Haydn String Quartets.* London: British Broadcasting Corporation, 1966. Reprint. Seattle: University of Washington Press, 1969. 55 pp.

Against the backdrop of biographical events, studies Haydn's development as a composer of string quartets. Delineates five groups representing origins (Op. 1, 2), emergence (Op. 9, 17, 20), establishment (Op. 33, 42, 50, 54, 55, 64), transitional stage (Op. 71, 74), and final maturity (Op. 76, 77, 103). Offers a concise, descriptive account of highlights in each opus. Numerous thematic quotations; some excerpts in score. Includes a chronological list of the quartets.

1012. Keller, Hans. "The String Quartet and Its Relatives." *The Music Review* 26 (1965):247-51, 340-44; 27 (1966):59-62, 228-32, 232-35.

Incorporates general stylistic discussion of Op. 9 No. 4 and Op. 20 Nos. 1-4, with examples of notable features in the music.

1013. Kirkendale, Warren. *Fugue and Fugato in Rococo and Classical Chamber Music.* Revised, expanded second edition, translated by Margaret Bent and the author. Durham, NC: Duke University Press, 1979. xxvii, 383 pp.

In this substantially expanded version of the original German study, *Fuge und Fugato in der Kammermusik des Rokoko und der Klassik* (Tutzing: Hans Schneider, 1966), identifies and explores a hitherto unexamined tradition of fugal polyphony in eighteenth-century instrumental ensemble music. Haydn works cited include Op. 20 Nos. 2, 5, 6; Op. 55 No. 1; Op. 64 No. 5; and Op. 76 No. 6. In the chapter on Haydn (pp. 137-51), discusses possible influences and the extent of Haydn's knowledge of musical and pedagogical sources. Calls attention to fugal polyphony in the baryton trios, and places the Op. 20 fugal finales in historical context as part of a viable fugal tradition rather than as stylistic aberrations.

1014. Konold, Wulf. "Normerfüllung und Normverweigerung beim späten Haydn--am Beispiel des Streichquartetts op. 76 Nr. 6." In *Joseph Haydn: Tradition und Rezeption* (item 78), pp. 54-73.

Explains how nineteenth-century critics failed to perceive in Haydn's music the complexity of structures that were veiled by an apparent simplicity. With respect to the quartets, indicates that while works such as Op. 33 represent Classical examples from which writers of the period developed rules, Haydn himself often went beyond his own Classical models in subsequent quartets. Describes the Op. 76 cycle, and examines the four movements of No. 6 to show that Haydn could sustain a facile manner in a work whose structure departed markedly from norms he established for the quartet.

1015. ———. *Das Streichquartett: Von den Anfängen bis Franz Schubert.* Wilhelmshaven: Heinrichshofen, 1980. 209 pp.

Addressing the question of precedents for Haydn's quartets, examines the pre-history and early evolution of the genre. The chapter on Haydn draws heavily on Ludwig Finscher (item 1006) and provides a concise summary of Haydn's accomplishment, a discussion of stylistic evolution evident within his string-quartet output, and brief descriptions of outstanding features in unusual or representative pieces. Translated by Susan Hellauer as *The*

String Quartet: From Its Beginnings to Franz Schubert. (New York: Heinrichshofen, 1983).

1016. Löher, Burckhard. *Strukturwissenschaftliche Darstellung der ersten und letzten Sätze der sechs Streichquartette op. 76 von Joseph Haydn.* 2 vols. Münster, 1983. 117 pp. text; 152 pp. of diagrams and music examples.

Adopts an elaborate method of structural analysis developed by Werner F. Korte and Ursula Götze. Involves a specialized vocabulary of terms, symbols, and graphics for representation of structural ingredients and relationships. Applies the method in order to categorize salient features of organization and structural processes in each movement. Draws on results to establish a summary picture of overall similarities as well as distinctive individual properties in the works analyzed.

1017. Mainka, Jürgen. "Haydns Streichquartette: 'Man hört vier vernünftige Leute sich untereinander unterhalten'." *Musik und Gesellschaft* 32/3 (1982):146-50.

An overview of Haydn's string quartet oeuvre. Emphasizes Haydn's central role in establishing the concept of the genre and the significance of these works as a reflection of his artistic personality.

1018. Moe, Orin, Jr. "The Significance of Haydn's Op. 33." In *Haydn Studies* (item 73), pp. 445-50.

Observes that Op. 33 should not be understood as Haydn's first mature quartets, and that the innovations they embody are not principally textural. Sees these works as a summation of the popularizing tendency witnessed already in Haydn's preceding symphonies. Summarizes notable features of Op. 33, including the achievement of a level of complexity in slow movements commensurate with that of other movements in the cycle, irregularities of meter, rhythm, and harmony, *Thematische Arbeit,* clear structural outlines, and folklike themes.

1019. ———. "Texture in Haydn's Early Quartets." *The Music Review* 35 (1974):4-22.

With the aid of music examples, sorts out textural features evident in the Op. 1 and 2 quartets. Discerns three principal approaches to texture that were to become important in later works: the rapid alternation of contrasting textures (particularly in fast movements); "interruption in regularity of movement"--for example, changes in upbeat and downbeat groupings and cadence placement (certain fast movements); and the use of textures with four equal parts (all movements).

1020. ———. "Texture in the String Quartets of Haydn to 1787." Ph.D. dissertation, University of California at Santa Barbara, 1970. xxi, 362 pp.

Encompasses the quartets through Op. 50 and defines "texture" as the relationship between component voices in a composition. Traits witnessed in Op. 9 and Op. 17, by contrast to earlier quartets, include a widened pitch range, greater rhythmic variety, the use of texture as a vehicle to support harmonic and formal design, increased differentiation and specialization of textures, and a generally greater skill in writing for strings. For Op. 33, cites the emphasis on motivic work whereby all instruments share the thematic substance. In Op. 50, discerns tendencies toward equal-voice texture and metrical disturbance.

1021. Niemöller, Klaus Wolfgang. "Die Bedeutung der Rhythmik für Form und Ausdruck in Haydns Streichquartetten (am Beispiel der Triole)." In *Joseph Haydn Kongress* (item 76), pp. 170-75.

Deplores the neglect of rhythmic studies of Haydn. Concentrating on the string quartets, shows that Haydn used triplets in conjunction with specific forms and with expressive intent. Notes a stylized use of triplets in the early quartets, in a manner typical of galant style and *Empfindsamkeit.*

1022. Pankaskie, Lewis V. "Tonal Organization in the Sonata-Form Movements of Haydn's String Quartets." Ph.D. dissertation, University of Michigan, 1956. vii, 331 pp.

Attempting to gain a comprehensive view of Haydn's tonal practice through examination of sonata-form movements in the quartets, organizes the inquiry in terms of essential harmonic areas within a movement (tonic key, modulation, related key, development, recapitulation). Traces the growth of Haydn's technique, with emphasis on aspects of tension and dynamism in the posing and solving of problems in contrast and relationship. Identifies underlying patterns of order and logic as well as characteristic avenues of freedom, surprise, and diversity. Finds precedents for Haydn's procedures in the Prussian and Württemberg sonatas of C.P.E. Bach. Proposes an underlying coherence of strategy where the sequence of tonal events appears mystifying, whimsical, or strange. An appendix furnishes a list of sonata movements in the string quartets. Numerous music examples in score.

1023. Pincherle, Marc. "On the Origins of the String Quartet." *The Musical Quarterly* 15 (1929):77-87.

Focusing on the question of texture (four homogeneous instrumental parts), discusses precedents for the string quartet of Haydn and his generation. Precedents cited include instrumental music of Flemish, French, and Italian schools of the sixteenth and early seventeenth century and seventeenth-century English fantasies for strings without keyboard. Proposes that the keyboard presence is not necessarily rigorously enforced in eighteenth-century keyboard works with continuo. Calls attention to the ambiguity of the term "bass" in mid-eighteenth-century chamber music, and makes note of immediate precedents for Haydn's accomplishment in the music of Boccherini, Gassmann, and Vanhal.

1024. Randall, J.K. "Haydn: String Quartet in D major, Op. 76, No. 5." *The Music Review* 21 (1960):94-105.

An intricately contrived harmonic analysis of each movement. Proposes an underlying tonal organization deriving from a "progression of tonicizations" stated in the opening section: D - B minor - G - E minor - D. Points to a consistency of harmonic procedure involving derivations from the basic pattern through transposition, retrograde, and rotation.

1025. Saint-Foix, Georges de. "Les Sonates pour violon et alto de Haydn." *La Revue musicale* 13/128 (1932):81-84.

Reports the discovery of a collection of duos published by Bailleux as Op. 46 and identified as arrangements of sonatas for violin and viola. Briefly describes the set, and suggests that Haydn may have communicated the idea of writing such pieces to his brother, whose own set of duos was completed by Mozart.

1026. Salzer, Felix. "Haydn's Fantasia from the String Quartet, Opus 76, No. 6." *The Music Forum* 4 (1976):161–94.

Emphasizing the boldness and complexity of its design, characterizes the movement as a theme (which constitutes a quasi-separate entity) followed by variations and augmentations. Associates the eighteenth-century concept of fantasy with tonal adventure and "rational deception" within a coherent framework, and applies Schenkerian techniques (including detailed analytical graphs) to uncover sources of tonal coherence. Describes the form in terms of two structurally similar sections, the second of which achieves completion of processes left incomplete in the first.

1027. Sandberger, Adolf. "Zur Geschichte des Haydnschen Streichquartetts." In Adolf Sandberger. *Ausgewählte Aufsätze zur Musikgeschichte,* 1:224–65. Munich: Drei Masken, 1921. Reprint. Hildesheim: Georg Olms, 1973. Previously published in *Altbayerische Monatshefte* (1900), pp. 1-24.

To determine why Haydn described his Op. 33 quartets as a "wholly new, special kind," examines his earlier quartets and their precedents. Traces two lines of development leading to the early Haydn quartet style: the cassation, divertimento, and notturno on one hand, the quadro on the other. Analyzes the early quartets, and in comparing them to Op. 33, determines that the latter's newness resides in the use of motivic process.

* Schrade, Leo. "Joseph Haydn als Schöpfer der Klassischen Musik." In Leo Schrade. *De Scientia Musicae Studia atque Orationes,* edited by Ernst Lichtenhahn, pp. 506–18. Bern: Paul Haupt, 1967. Previously published in *Universitas* 17 (1962):767–78 and in *Basler National-Zeitung,* 24 May 1959.

Cited as item 757.

1028. Scott, Marion M. "Haydn's Opus Two and Opus Three." *Proceedings of the Royal Musical Association* 61 (1934–35):1–19.

Provides a general description of Op. 2, its sources, and the genres it represents. Cites differences in content among the sources, and discusses a previously overlooked Cassation in F in La Chevardière's edition. Notes the "markedly experimental" nature of Op. 3 (now generally regarded as spurious), and speculates on reasons for the stylistic change it represents in relation to Op. 2.

1029. Seidel, Wilhelm. "Haydns Streichquartett in B-Dur op. 71 Nr. 1 (Hob. III:69): Analytische Bemerkungen aus der Sicht Heinrich Christoph Kochs." In *Joseph Haydn: Tradition und Rezeption* (item 78), pp. 3-13.

A look at structure and thematic process in the first movement of Op. 71 No. 1. Applies Koch's theory rather than sonata-form theory in describing the movement, and explains how Koch's model more closely reflects Haydn's manipulation of thematic material.

1030. Silbert, Doris. "Ambiguity in the String Quartets of Joseph Haydn." *The Musical Quarterly* 36 (1950):562-73.

Proposing that musical ambiguity occurs when a "counter tension" contradicts the principal tension, or when an event contributes to the main direction of movement while at the same time suggesting others, asserts that a predilection for ambiguous statement is intrinsic to Haydn's musical personality. Examples cited include passages from Op. 9, 33, 50, 64, 71, and 77.

1031. Sisman, Elaine R. "Haydn's Baryton Pieces and His Serious Genres." In *Joseph Haydn Kongress* (item 76), pp. 426-35.

Takes issue with scholars who relegate the trios to the periphery of Haydn's oeuvre, and shows that they play a central role in his artistic development. Views them as compactly organized examples of compositional procedure, and shows how a certain previously used technique may be given new formulation in a baryton trio and then be transformed again within one of the major genres.

1032. Somfai, László. "A Bold Enharmonic Modulatory Model in Joseph Haydn's String Quartets." In *Studies in Eighteenth-Century Music: A Tribute to Karl Geiringer on His Seventieth Birthday,* edited by H.C. Robbins Landon and Roger E. Chapman, pp. 370-81. New York: Oxford University Press, 1970.

Explores representative instances of a particular type of "enharmonic deception" from among development sections in later string quartets (Op. 76, 77, 103). Describes the phenomenon whereby a typically gradual and extended modulatory path leads into increasingly remote, flat regions; Haydn then cunningly changes the spelling of individual chord tones in order to return smoothly to the realm of tonic. Detects strategies aimed at preserving the integrity of intonation through the enharmonic change. Identifies the technique as an anticipation of related devices found in piano music of Schubert and Chopin.

1033. ———. "Haydns Tribut an seinen Vorgänger Werner." *The Haydn Yearbook* 2 (1963-64):75-80.

Concerns the 12 fugal quartets by Haydn's predecessor Gregor Joseph Werner that Haydn had published by Artaria in 1804. Traces the 6 introductions supplied by Haydn to instrumental introductions from oratorios by Werner (Nos. 42-53 in Haydn's library catalogue). Comparison of the edition with the Werner manuscripts reveals only a modest degree of editing apart from modernization of tempo markings and omission of the *basso continuo.* Includes a catalogue of the Werner manuscripts in question.

1034. ———. "'Learned Style' in Two Late String Quartet Movements of Haydn." *Studia Musicologica Academiae Scientiarum Hungaricae* 28 (1986):325-49.

Deplores the dearth of stylistic investigations of Haydn's music, then proceeds to examine the opening movements of the *Emperor* Quartet (Op. 76 No. 3) and the *Quinten* Quartet (Op. 76 No. 2). Proposes that the *Emperor* Quartet is a *quartetto "in tempore belli"*--an expression of Haydn's loyalty in time of war. Uncovers rhythmic and melodic patterns in the first movement that have warlike connotations. More significantly, discovers that the opening five notes represent an anagram for the text "Gott erhalte Franz den Kaiser" ("C" for Caesar replaces the "K" of Kaiser). Suggests that these features lend new meaning to the use of the "Emperor Hymn" as a basis for the second movement, and points to wartime symbolism in the final movement. Determines that the opening *Allegro* of the *Quinten* Quartet was influenced by Albrechtsberger's 1790 *Gründliche Anweisung zur Komposition,* and proceeds to demonstrate how Haydn used all the techniques for *cantus firmus* manipulation described by Albrechtsberger. Also examines characteristics of eighteenth-century pitch attack and different effects created by permutations of the *cantus firmus.*

* ———. "Opus-Planung und Neuerung bei Haydn." *Studia Musicologica Academiae Scientiarum Hungaricae* 22 (1980):87-110.

Cited as item 769.

1035. Sondheimer, Robert. *Haydn: A Historical and Psychological Study Based on His Quartets.* London: Bernoulli, 1951. viii, 196 pp.

A speculative study that invests heavily in ideas about contemporary works by which Haydn may have been influenced. Places particular emphasis on the influence of Franz Beck, and gives the score to the first movement of a symphony in E flat by Beck in an appendix. Examines Haydn's choice and application of available materials and resources in terms of psychological forces. Explores his unionist (rather than dualist) approach to the construction of a quartet, dwells on the relatively slow maturation of his creative abilities, and ponders the peculiarly scholastic manner of his musical thinking. Argues that his true artistic personality, undeveloped in earlier works, flourished only after his craftsmanship had matured. Suggests that the devil whom Haydn had summoned might have "covered his work with the ashen crust of formalism" had he not outmaneuvered him, first through rhythmic energy and wit, then by the grace of wisdom.

1036. Steinbeck, Wolfram. "Mozart's 'Scherzi': Zur Beziehung zwischen Haydns Streichquartetten op. 33 und Mozarts 'Haydn-Quartetten'." *Archiv für Musikwissenschaft* 41 (1984):208-31.

Probes the significance of the term *scherzo* as used by Haydn, and ponders Mozart's failure to adopt the idea. Discerns a conflict in Haydn's earlier quartets between the closed form and symmetry basic to the minuet and Haydn's predilection for open-ended compositional process. Sees the Op. 33 *scherzi*, with their playful transformation of conventional ingredients, as a solution to the conflict, and discerns in Mozart's approach the fulfillment of a tendency (foreshadowed in Haydn quartets prior to Op. 33) toward bending the minuet to conform to sonata-form principles. Summarized in *Joseph Haydn: Tradition und Rezeption* (item 78), pp. 14-16.

1037. Strunk, W. Oliver. "Haydn's Divertimenti for Baryton, Viola, and Bass (After Manuscripts in the Library of Congress)." *The Musical Quarterly* 18 (1932):216-51.

Citing a collection of manuscript copies acquired by the Library of Congress in 1906, describes circumstances under which the works were written, examines their style, and comments on their significance within the composer's oeuvre. Appends a discussion of the baryton and its idiomatic peculiarities, and provides a catalogue of the Library of Congress manuscripts in question.

1038. Tepping, Susan. "Form in the Finale of Haydn's *String Quartet, Op. 64, No. 5.*" *Indiana Theory Review* 4/2 (1980-81):51-68.

Observing that the Schenkerian concept of form hinges on background structure, rather than on phraseology or thematic and motivic relationships, decides that at the deepest structural level, the quartet finale's division is binary according to Schenker's precepts, but that the pattern of statement, contrast, and return leads to the perception of a ternary form.

1039. Tovey, Donald Francis. "Haydn, Franz Joseph, 1732-1809." In *Cobbett's Cyclopedic Survey of Chamber Music,* 2d ed., 1:514-45. London: Oxford University Press, 1963.

Credits Haydn with effecting a musical revolution of highest historical importance. Places primary emphasis on the string quartets, and devotes extensive space to discussion of background: texture, the question of the *basso continuo,* and precedents for the concept of string-quartet texture. Furnishes examples of Haydn quartet passages where the cello plays above the viola, and explores the question of Haydn's debt to C.P.E. Bach. Provides concise critiques of the different sets and individual quartets. Numerous music examples, some in score. First published in 1929 (London: Oxford University Press).

1040. Trimmer, Maud A. "Texture and Sonata Form in the Late String Chamber Music of Haydn and Mozart." 2 vols. Ph.D. dissertation, City University of New York, 1981. ix, 283 pp.; vi, 296 pp.

Employs a special system for graphic representation of different types of textural activity. Categories of activity delineated include accompanied melody, motivic permeation (involving motivically charged subordinate voices), and polyphonic style. Elaborates upon correlations discerned between textural change and tonal organization of first-movement expositions, and observes that in Haydn's Op. 33 quartets, the most intense textural activity takes place after the tonal transition. Other Haydn works studied include Op. 76 Nos. 1-4 and Op. 77 Nos. 1 and 2. Includes a review of pertinent literature. Volume 2 comprises annotated scores with accompanying symbols for different types of texture.

1041. Unverricht, Hubert. *Geschichte des Streichtrios.* Tutzing: Hans Schneider, 1969. 363 pp.

A study of the trio from 1750 to the twentieth century, with substantial reference to Haydn throughout the text. Relevant portions include discussions of authenticity in Haydn (pp. 69–72) and of the baryton trios (pp. 137–74). The former contains a list of string trios (by Hoboken number) incorrectly attributed to Haydn, and identifies the correct composer and source of attribution. The latter considers the relationship of Haydn's early string trios to the baryton trios, provides a chronology and miscellaneous documentary information, describes the baryton and critics' reactions to it, surveys elements of style in the baryton and early string trios, and gives five pages in facsimile, either in Haydn's hand or that of Joseph Elssler.

1042. Walts, Anthony A. "The Significance of the Opening in Sonata Form: An Analytical Study of the First Movements from Three Quartets by Joseph Haydn." Ph.D. dissertation, Yale University, 1985. v, 300 pp.

Working from the premise that both Haydn's compositional practices and Schenker's theories rest on the same foundations of species counterpoint and figured bass, delves into highly detailed Schenkerian analyses of three first movements: Op. 9 No. 1, Op. 20 No.2, and Op. 33 No. 3. Focuses on the structural point of departure: the initial interval of the fundamental background structure that generates the primary motivic material. Proposes that Haydn's essential method was to improvise an opening, and then explore its implications in the subsequent unfolding. Finds similarities among the three works, but also evidence of increasingly subtle and complicated treatment of motive and supporting structure. Concludes that the Op. 9 movement reveals a solid grasp of compositional technique, that the Op. 20 work is marked by experimentation, and that the Op. 33 quartet demonstrates full mastery of compositional resources.

1043. Webster, James. "Did Haydn 'Synthesize' the Classical String Quartet?" In *Haydn Studies* (item 73), pp. 336-39.

Argues that when viewed in the historical context of Austrian chamber music of the 1750s, Haydn's early string quartets represent an intensification of the *divertimento à quattro,* and thus a development within a local tradition, and not some synthesis of diverse pre-Classical antecedents.

1044. ———. "Freedom of Form in Haydn's Early String Quartets." In *Haydn Studies* (item 73), pp. 522-30.

Deploring scholars' habitual tendency to belittle Haydn's early compositions, discovers that many Haydnesque devices well known in later works were integral components of his style from the beginning. Cites instances from the Op. 2 quartets that illustrate imaginative and resourceful approaches to two formal situations: return to the main theme in the second half of a minuet and the reorganization of material in a sonata-form recapitulation.

1045. ———. "Haydn's String Quartets." In *Haydnfest* (item 71), pp. 12-17.

A survey of the 68 works deemed to constitute Haydn's repertory of string quartets. Divides the works into two parts, then traces their stylistic development (the first part comprises three isolated groups from the late 1750s, early 1770s, and 1781; the second represents half of Haydn's output, written mainly between 1787 and 1799). Isolates three features of the quartets important to Classical style: dramatic power, wit or humor (more appropriately, irony), and the synthesis of "complex and apparently disparate elements into higher unities." Includes facsimiles of sample pages from the "Entwurf-Katalog," printed editions, and the autograph of Op. 64 No. 5.

1046. Wiesel, Siegfried. "Klangfarbendramaturgie in den Streichquartetten von Joseph Haydn." *Haydn-Studien* 5 (1982-85):16-22.

Discovers characteristic passages (notably those that feature the individuality of one or more instruments) in which subtle juxtaposition and interplay of tone colors plays a structurally significant role. Uses the term "dramaturgy" to characterize long-range patterns of change in tone color, and suggests that these constitute a significant aspect of Haydn's procedures for variation and development.

1047. Wollenberg, Susan. "Haydn's Baryton Trios and the 'Gradus'." *Music and Letters* 54 (1973):170-78.

Describes the juxtaposition of Fuxian strict style and modern homophony within the binary-form framework of Haydn's baryton trio finales. Typical features cited include cantus-firmus style fugue subjects, fourth-species suspension chains, and Fuxian melodic clichés. Proposes that while providing Haydn the opportunity to develop his gift for concentrated development of motivic material, these works betray a ready-made, not fully assimilated language that lacks the individuality of expression seen in the Op. 20 quartet finales.

Solo Keyboard Music and Chamber Music with Keyboard

1048. Abbott, William W., Jr. "Certain Aspects of the Sonata-Allegro Form in Piano Sonatas of the 18th and 19th Centuries." Ph.D. dissertation, Indiana University, 1956. 336 pp.

Repertory included reaches from Haydn to Brahms, with numerous tables representing tonal designs, structural plans, and thematic organization. Special emphasis placed on key relationships. The chapter on Haydn (pp. 25-73) features the categorization of compositional procedures common to groups of sonatas.

1049. Abert, Hermann. "Joseph Haydns Klavierwerke." *Zeitschrift für Musikwissenschaft* 2 (1919-20):553-73; continued as "Joseph Haydns Klaviersonaten" in *Zeitschrift für Musikwissenschaft* 3 (1920-21):535-52.

Applauding the appearance of Päsler's volumes of the sonatas in the Breitkopf & Härtel complete edition, places the style of these works against the backdrop of the

North German school, as represented by C.P.E. Bach, and the South German-Austrian, exemplified in the keyboard music of Wagenseil. Noting Haydn's synthesis of these idioms, emphasizes his achievement of a decisively original, Classical style.

1050. Badura-Skoda, Eva. "Die 'Clavier'-Musik in Wien zwischen 1750 und 1770." *Studien zur Musikwissenschaft* 35 (1984):65-88.

Supplements the discussion in Bettina Wackernagel's dissertation (published as item 1088) on the relationship between early Haydn keyboard music and pre-Classical Viennese keyboard style. Argues for a broadening of the scope of inquiry into this repertory.

1051. ———. "Haydn, Mozart and Their Contemporaries." In *Keyboard Music,* edited by Denis Matthews, pp. 108-65. Newton Abbot: David & Charles, 1972.

Provides general background on changing musical tastes and practices in the second half of the eighteenth century. Examines questions of performance style, medium (harpsichord vs. fortepiano), melodic idiom, and phrasing in Haydn, Mozart, and their contemporaries. Arguing that Haydn's keyboard works are underestimated, deplores the traditional depiction of Haydn as a stepping stone to Beethoven. Suggests that Haydn's personal keyboard idiom involves a reconciliation of Austrian Baroque and galant styles.

1052. Badura-Skoda, Paul. "Über Haydns Klavierwerke." *Österreichische Musikzeitschrift* 14 (1959):370-76.

Laments the neglect of Haydn's keyboard music at the time of writing and comments on some of the keyboard sonatas and trios. Touches on a variety of topics, including Haydn's approach to ornamentation, changes in his style to accommodate the development of keyboard instruments, remarkable features of his keyboard writing, accommodations that must be made for performance on the modern piano, and the Päsler and Martienssen editions of the sonatas (supplies a concordance list of editions).

1053. Bell, A. Craig. "An Introduction to Haydn's Piano Trios." *The Music Review* 16 (1955):191-97.

Discusses the (apparently) dominant role of the keyboard

part in the trios and refutes several theories on why Haydn chose such a distribution. Points out that the keyboard instrument of Haydn's time would not have dominated the texture as does the modern piano.

1054. Brown, A. Peter. *Joseph Haydn's Keyboard Music: Sources and Style.* Bloomington: Indiana University Press, 1986. xxiv, 450 pp.

Offers a chronologically ordered, systematic discussion of structure and style, and extensive treatment of dating and authenticity. Confronts the question of keyboard idiom (fortepiano, clavichord, or harpsichord), and surveys the Viennese keyboard tradition represented by Fux, Wagenseil, Steffan, Birck, M.G. Monn, and Hofmann. Dwells on the issue of C.P.E. Bach's influence. Argues that the keyboard held a central place in Haydn's musical interests throughout his life. Includes a substantial bibliography, copious footnotes, numerous music examples, reproductions of pages from early prints and autograph manuscripts.

1055. ———. "The Solo and Ensemble Keyboard Sonatas of Joseph Haydn: A Study of Structure and Style." 3 vols. Ph.D. dissertation, Northwestern University, 1970. viii, 259 pp.; 172 pp.; unpublished scores.

Examines works in Hoboken categories XIV (accompanied divertimentos), XV (trios), XVI (solo sonatas), and XVII-XVIIa (keyboard pieces for two and four hands). Includes a survey of the genres, review of relevant literature, and discussion of chronology and authenticity. Stylistic criticism (organized according to movement type: sonata, binary, variation, rondo and other additive forms, dance movements) features aspects of change and continuity in the approach to structure, texture, harmonic usage, thematic construction, and rhythmic organization in different chronological periods.

1056. ———. "The Structure of the Exposition in Haydn's Keyboard Sonatas." *The Music Review* 36 (1975):102-29.

Traces reflections of Haydn's stylistic development in his keyboard sonatas, ca. 1750-96, and shows that characteristic procedures are associated with different creative periods in his career. Emphasizes significant correlations between the structure of an exposition and the compositional strategy of a movement as a whole. Observes that while thematic specialization is not a major factor, owing to Haydn's non-dialectical treatment of melody within a design, the principle of differentiated thematic function nevertheless applies, material typically being altered to fulfill different structural functions.

1057. Chapman, Roger E. "Modulation in Haydn's Late Piano Trios in the Light of Schoenberg's Theories." In *Haydn Studies* (item 73), pp. 471-75.

Using Schoenberg's concept of tonal regions as a frame of reference, surveys the use of key-signature changes, enharmonic reinterpretation of chords, and the juxtaposition of relatively remote relationships in Haydn's trios of the 1790s.

1058. Eibner, Franz. "Die Form des 'Vivace assai' aus der Sonate D-dur Hob. XVI:42." In *Joseph Haydn Kongress* (item 76), pp. 190-201.

Seeks insight into Haydn's compositional process through a moderately detailed analysis that employs Schenkerian reduction technique. Quotes the entire movement, and includes several reductive sketches.

* Feder, Georg. "Haydn's Piano Trios and Piano Sonatas." In *Haydnfest* (item 71), pp. 18-23.

Cited as item 624.

1059. Fillion, Michelle. "The Accompanied Keyboard Divertimenti of Haydn and His Viennese Contemporaries (c. 1750-1780)." Ph.D. dissertation, Cornell University, 1982. xvi, 570 pp.

Declaring that Haydn's early chamber music with keyboard cannot be fully appreciated without knowledge of the tradition from which it sprang, and of which his works are the finest manifestations, examines his keyboard divertimentos with accompaniment for two violins and bass (Hob. XIV) and the early trios for harpsichord, violin, and bass (Hob. XV) side by side with a repertory of such works by Viennese contemporaries. Finds the language of these works simpler than that of the contemporaneous solo sonata and symphony, and detects two distinct phases within the three decades in question: cultivation of an earlier, intrinsically Viennese idiom that draws on Viennese sonata, string trio, and concerto traditions and a post-1770 phase marked by foreign influences and culminating with the rapid rise of music publishing in Vienna after 1779. Treats questions of authenticity and dating, and offers extensive classification of form-types. Includes a thematic catalogue of the 66 non-Haydn works studied. Substantial bibliography, many music examples and tables.

1060. ———. "Scoring and Genre in Haydn's Divertimenti Hob. XIV." In *Joseph Haydn Kongress* (item 76), pp. 435-44.

Detects concerto-inspired tendencies in quartet divertimentos with keyboard by Haydn and his Viennese contemporaries. Proposes that these traits unify the group above and beyond differences between "concertino" and "divertimento," and that the works in question constitute a distinctive Viennese mid-century genre.

1061. ———. "Sonata-Exposition Procedures in Haydn's Keyboard Sonatas." In *Haydn Studies* (item 73), pp. 475-81.

Distinguishing between two-part and three-part exposition types, categorizes Haydn's procedures in terms of tonal articulation. Reports that 35 of 46 expositions conform to one model or the other, and that two-part expositions outnumber three-part by 26 to 9. Includes brief consideration of the "main theme transposition" feature (found in 16 of the first movements) whereby the secondary key area involves recurrence of primary-theme material.

1062. Graue, Jerald C. "Haydn and the London Pianoforte School." In *Haydn Studies* (item 73), pp. 422-31.

Points out general as well as specific similarities between Haydn's last three keyboard sonatas (Hob. XVI:50-52) and contemporaneous works by Dussek, J.B. Cramer, and Clementi. Senses that while Haydn's sonatas were not written in conscious imitation of a "London manner," they nevertheless reflect an artistic enrichment attributable to the London experience.

1063. Hatting, Carsten E. "Obligater Satz versus Generalbass-Satz: Einige Betrachtungen zur Satzfaktur in Klaviersonaten aus der Mitte des 18. Jahrhunderts, insbesondere zu Haydns Sonaten aus der Zeit vor 1770." In *Festskrift Jens Peter Larsen, 14. VI. 1902-1972,* edited by Nils Schiørring, Henrik Glahn, and Carsten E. Hatting, pp. 261-74. Copenhagen: Wilhelm Hansen, 1972.

Addresses the question of stylistic influences in early Haydn keyboard sonatas. Noting that Haydn possessed copies of thoroughbass manuals by Heinichen, Mattheson, and Kellner, proposes that a stimulus for his characteristic broken-chord figuration can be found in traditional thoroughbass pedagogy as represented by these theorists' methods. Quotes from sample broken-chord thoroughbass realizations found in texts by Gasparini and Heinichen.

1064. Höll, Uwe. *Studien zum Sonatensatz in den Klaviersonaten Joseph Haydns.* Tutzing: Hans Schneider, 1984. xii, 315 pp.

Offers an extensive introductory discussion of Koch's *Versuch einer Anleitung zur Komposition* (1782-93), and draws on Koch's approach to the analysis of phrasing, cadence, theme, and structural partitioning. Features seven analyses of keyboard-sonata first movements: Hob. XVI:2, 13, 20, 33, 41, 43, and 50. For each, a schematic summary of structure precedes detailed critical discussion of organization within sections into which the movement divides. An appendix provides tables representing tempo designations for all the sonatas, keys of different movements, tonal relationships between movements, and meter of the opening movement.

1065. Irving, Howard. "Haydn's *Deutscher Tanz* Finales: Style Versus Form in Eighteenth-Century Music." *Studies in Music* 20 (1986):12-26.

Studies the finales of six late keyboard trios (Hob. XV:18, 20, 24, 26, 28, 30) and observes that they resemble the minuet/trio structure, which at that time was archaic for finales. Reports, however, that most are faster than minuets in tempo, and all share a style for which the term *Deutscher Tanz* seems appropriate. Since the movements are in ternary form, examines eighteenth-century discussions of rondo as well as minuet, and reports that the terms are associated with musical character at least as much as with form. Decides that in terms of structure, the movements in question could be correctly designated as either minuets or rondos, but proposes that character, that of the *Deutscher Tanz,* should take precedence over form.

1066. Kamien, Roger. "Aspects of Motivic Elaboration in the Opening Movement of Haydn's Piano Sonata in C#

Minor." In *Aspects of Schenkerian Theory,* edited by David Beach, pp. 77-93. New Haven: Yale University Press, 1983.

With the aid of music illustrations, invokes Schenkerian procedures to clarify motivic relationships in Hob. XVI:32, first movement. Examines techniques by which motives are rhythmically altered and put to use on differing structural levels. Shows how Haydn applies "progressive motivic enlargement" (the recurrence of motives in progressively expanding modules) as a means of unification, and explores his technique of reharmonizing melodic lines when they recur in the recapitulation.

1067. Komlós, Katalin. "Haydn's Keyboard Trios Hob. XV:5-17: Interaction Between Texture and Form." *Studia Musicologica Academiae Scientiarum Hungaricae* 28 (1986):351-400.

An intensive study of two groups of trios, written in 1784-85 (Hob. XV:5-10) and 1789-90 (Hob. XV:11-17), based on a revision of part 3 of the author's dissertation (item 1068). Divides into three main sections, which discuss scoring and texture, form, and the interaction between texture and form. The first concentrates on instruments that comprise the trio: the keyboard instrument used (definitely fortepiano for the 1789-90 group, but apparently for the earlier group as well); the role of the violin (chiefly unison or parallel reinforcement of the keyboard but also independent line, whether in dialogue, counterpoint, or as filler); and the role of the cello (usually reinforcement of the keyboard bass, with differentiation in register or rhythmic figuration). A discussion of form follows, with descriptions of two- and three-movement cycles and structural types for individual movements: sonata, binary, ternary, rondo, and variation. Finally, interactions are examined, with conclusions advanced about how different textures are associated with the various forms and with tempo. Includes diagrams, numerous music examples, and summary tables on textural types, forms, and interactions.

1068. ------. "The Viennese Keyboard Trio in the 1780s: Studies in Texture and Instrumentation." Ph.D. dissertation, Cornell University, 1986. x, 482 pp.

Offers comparative analysis of original keyboard trios published in Vienna between 1781 and 1790. Composers represented include Clementi, Haydn, Hoffmeister, Koželuch, Mozart, Pleyel, Sterkel, and Vanhal. Discussion of Haydn (pp. 144-224) encompasses six works from 1784 to 1785 and seven from 1788 to 1790. Addresses keyboard idiom, and finds that the latter group displays a truly pianistic style by comparison with the 1784-85 works. Examines the roles of violin and cello, explores the interactions among the instruments, and classifies different kinds of ensemble texture. Categorizes movement-types and approaches to structure (including sonata, binary, ternary, rondo, and variation). Undertakes an extended discussion of interaction between texture and form. Incorporates a complete composition by each of the six composers whose works in this genre are not available in modern edition and a thematic catalogue of keyboard trios by each. Numerous music examples; extensive bibliography.

1069. Landon, H.C. Robbins. "Haydn's Piano Sonatas." In H.C. Robbins Landon. *Essays on the Viennese Classical Style: Gluck, Haydn, Mozart, Beethoven,* pp. 44-67. London: Barrie & Rockliff, 1970.

A descriptive, chronological overview, with numerous quotations from the Haydn sonatas and from works by Leopold Hofmann, C.P.E. Bach, and Alberti. Originally a lecture for the British Broadcasting Corporation, 1961.

1070. Lorince, Frank E., Jr. "A Study of Musical Texture in Relation to Sonata-Form as Evidenced in Selected Keyboard Sonatas from C.P.E. Bach through Beethoven." 2 vols. Ph.D. dissertation, University of Rochester, Eastman School of Music, 1966. 325 pp.; 308 pp.

Examination of Haydn works, volume 1, pp. 65-127, encompasses Sonatas Nos. 1, 14, 20, 37, 50, and 52. Formal-textural diagrams, volume 1, pp. 94-153, include representations of Sonatas 1, 14, 19, 20, 33, 35, 37, 50, and 52. Offers a descriptive summary of events from the standpoint of textural usage for each first movement. Proposing that distinctive approaches to texture enhance thematic and tonal relationships, explores the textural identity of themes and examines correlations between changes in texture and a particular order of events in a movement. Classifies textures in various ways, including pitch level, vertical span, spacing, and dynamics. Observes that a wide variety of textural settings contributes to the marked individuality of the Haydn works, and calls attention to examples of "textural transition" (involving gradual change from one textural setting to another) in Sonatas Nos. 50 and 52.

1071. Mersmann, Hans. "Versuch einer Phänomenologie der Musik." *Zeitschrift für Musikwissenschaft* 5 (1922-23):226-69.

Subjects Haydn's Keyboard Sonata in E flat, Hob. XVI:49 to a phenomenological analysis. Identifies motivic relationships and processes of motivic development, and examines the juxtaposition and working out of musical conflicts. Studies the tensional relationship between form and content. Includes analytical sketches in addition to music examples.

1072. Moss, Lawrence K. "Haydn's Sonata Hob. XVI:52 (ChL. 62) in E-flat Major: An Analysis of the First Movement." In *Haydn Studies* (item 73), pp. 496-501.

Dissects the opening gesture (dotted rhythm, movement to the subdominant, and melodic motive traversing a minor third) as a backdrop for an overview of structurally significant events involving register, harmony, and motivic development.

1073. Newman, William S. *The Sonata in the Classic Era.* 3d ed. Chapel Hill: University of North Carolina Press, 1983. xxii, 933 pp.

First published in 1963 (Chapel Hill: University of North Carolina Press). After an extended discussion of relevant background (the term, the sonata in eighteenth-century society, publishers, instruments, style and form), devotes individual chapters to regions and chronological spans. Dedicates an extended chapter to Haydn and Mozart, giving an overview of repertory (including ensemble sonatas), sources, and bibliography. Little detailed discussion of the music itself. Views Haydn as very much a man of his time despite his isolation and stylistic originality, and observes that a wide variety of influences may be discerned in his sonatas. Sparsely supplied with music examples; large bibliography.

1074. Ossberger, Harald. "Musikalischer Humor an Beispielen der Klaviermusik." *Österreichische Musikzeitschrift* 38 (1983):696-701.

Humor discerned in the third movement of Haydn's Keyboard Sonata in C, Hob. XVI:50 includes an interplay of predictable and unpredictable elements, conflict between form and the working out of content, musical irony, and self-parody.

1075. Radcliffe, Philip. "The Piano Sonatas of Joseph Haydn." *The Music Review* 7 (1946):139-48.

A chronological overview of the repertory that features the selection of random details rather than systematic stylistic discussion.

1076. Rolf, Marie. "Stylistic Influence in the Early Haydn Piano Trios." In *Haydn Studies* (item 73), pp. 459-64.

Finds rhythmic, harmonic, textural, and thematic traits in the early trios that appear to derive from Baroque trio sonata, suite, concerto, and aria traditions.

1077. Rutmanowitz, Lea M. "Haydn's Sonatas Hob. XVI:10 and 26: A Comparison of Compositional Procedures." In *Joseph Haydn Kongress* (item 76), pp. 154-59.

Compares a pre-1766 sonata with a work of 1773 to illustrate the change in orientation from a vertical to a horizontal continuum that took place in Haydn's works of the late 1760s to early 1770s.

1078. Schenker, Heinrich. *Fünf Urlinie-Tafeln.* New York: David Mannes Music School, [1933]. Reprinted as *Five Graphic Music Analyses,* with new introduction and glossary by Felix Salzer. New York: Dover, 1969. 61 pp.

Presents a multiple-level analytical sketch of Haydn's Sonata in E flat, Hob. XVI:49, first movement development section (pp. 39-43). In a 1932 foreword, identifies the analysis as a contribution to the bicentennial celebration, and expresses the wish that it may "reveal Haydn's demonic spirit which has remained unknown up to the present day."

1079. ———. "Haydn: Sonate C Dur." *Der Tonwille,* no. 4 (1923), pp. 15-18.

Concisely formulated analytical treatment of Hob. XVI:21, first movement only. Incorporates several fragmentary voice-leading sketches in the text.

1080. ———. "Haydn: Sonate Es Dur." *Der Tonwille,* no. 3 (1922), pp. 3-21.

A moderately detailed examination of harmonic structure and voice-leading in each of the three movements of Hob. XVI:52. Discussion is accompanied by graphic analyses for each movement.

1081. Shamgar, Beth F. "The Retransition in the Piano Sonatas of Haydn, Mozart, and Beethoven." Ph.D. dissertation, New York University, 1978. ii, 246 pp.

After examining descriptions of the process of transition to tonic key and recapitulation by such late eighteenth- and early nineteenth-century writers as Koch, Portmann, Momigny, Reicha, and Czerny, constructs an analytical framework for studying essential characteristics of the phenomenon. Considers structural function (extension of development or contrasting episode), characteristic quality of movement (intensification, detensification, or equilibrium), and the characteristics of the structural borders in question. Elements examined in the discussion of Haydn (pp. 36-100) include harmony, rhythm, thematic content, texture, harmonic rhythm, and tonal orientation.

1082. ———. "Rhythmic Interplay in the Retransition of Haydn's Piano Sonatas." *The Journal of Musicology* 3 (1984):55-68.

Sifts through explanations of the retransition in late eighteenth- and early nineteenth-century theoretical writings, including those of Koch, Portmann, Momigny, Reicha, and Czerny. Summarizes findings of an analytical study of the retransition in Haydn. Determining that rhythm constitutes a critical factor, isolates three states of movement that govern retransition activity (intensification, detensification, and equilibrium) and shows how Haydn sets up finely tuned interactions among a full complement of rhythmic parameters, including highly diversified surface rhythm, chord rhythm, and contour rhythm. Detects a characteristically complex interplay of forces that belies an apparent simplicity of conception, and that promotes both integration and punctuation.

1083. Somfai, László. "Stilfragen der Klaviersonaten von Haydn." *Österreichische Musikzeitschrift* 37 (1982):147-53.

Argues that stylistic tendencies and phases of development in Haydn's solo keyboard sonatas are closely linked to the circumstances of their commission and intended performers. Proposes four chronological groupings: early partita or divertimento type; mature two- and three-movement works of ca. 1766-72; published sets of six, 1773-80; individual sonatas, 1784-94. Describes shared characteristics and stylistic similarities within each group, and asserts that no truly continuous style evolution can be discerned from the second group on.

1084. Steinberg, Lester S. "A Numerical Approach to Activity and Movement in the Sonata-Form Movements of Haydn's Piano Trios." In *Haydn Studies* (item 73), pp. 515-22.

Applying a system developed by Jan LaRue, quantifies change of activity in three elements (harmony, melody, and rhythm) in order to obtain a reasonably objective measure of activity within sections and themes of a movement. Reveals differences in activity among early, middle, and late works, and illustrates the usefulness of the method as a tool for determining authenticity. Includes comparative tables of activity analysis for early, middle, and late trios.

1085. ———. "Sonata Form in the Keyboard Trios of Joseph Haydn." Ph.D. dissertation, New York University, 1976. xii, 363 pp.

A style-analytical inquiry that identifies characteristic patterns and procedures discernible in the treatment of harmony, melody, rhythm, and growth (i.e. the resultant profile of movement and shape) within sonata-form movements in each of three periods: early (1755-60), middle (1784-90), late (1790-96). Pays special attention to the measurement and comparison of activity levels, a factor that involves quantification of rates of change in different elements. Finds relatively high activity levels in the early trios, in keeping with their fast harmonic rhythm and beat-marking bass lines; lower levels in the middle-period works; and a return to high levels in the compositionally more complex, diverse late trios. In all periods, detects only moderate increase in activity in development sections. Appendices offer extensive tabulation of statistics (e.g. movement and section lengths, cadence types, tonal relationships) and an explanation of the method of activity analysis developed by Jan LaRue.

1086. Sutcliffe, W. Dean. "Haydn's Piano Trio Textures." *Music Analysis* 6 (1987):319-32.

Asserts that works in this repertory were conceived truly as trios, despite the extent of keyboard doubling; and finds the keyboard writing in the trios different from that of solo keyboard works, especially in registral focus. Discerns changes in the trio textures, and specifies a later procedure in which Haydn "alternates blocks of texture and melodic leadership." Observes that problems of balance disappear when the works are performed on early instruments.

1087. Vignal, Marc. "L'Oeuvre pour piano seul de Joseph Haydn." *La Revue musicale:* Carnet critique no. 249 (1961), pp. 7-20.

Proposing that Haydn's solo keyboard works reflect his instrumental orientation, as opposed to Mozart's vocal inclination, emphasizes the breadth of stylistic diversity that they encompass, from the realms of Scarlatti and Wagenseil to those of Beethoven and Schubert. Examines his relationship to North German and Viennese predecessors, and explores his changes of outlook and pertinent aspects of stylistic evolution.

1088. Wackernagel, Bettina. *Joseph Haydns frühe Klaviersonaten: Ihre Beziehungen zur Klaviermusik um die Mitte des 18. Jahrhunderts.* Tutzing: Hans Schneider, 1975. 211 pp.

Examines influences on Haydn's style attributable to Viennese predecessors, including Georg Christoph Wagenseil, Matthias Georg Monn, Johann Christoph Mann, and Joseph Anton Steffan; Italian composers such as Baldassare Galuppi and Giovanni Rutini; and C.P.E. Bach. Arguing against overemphasis on the importance of C.P.E. Bach in the formation of Haydn's style, suggests that its maturation in the later 1760s has little to do with Bach's music. Emphasizes the extent to which Haydn shares musical formulas and gestures with predecessors and older contemporaries while nevertheless bestowing on these materials his own unique personality. Offers extended discussion of selected movements, and devotes a chapter to a comparison of Haydn's sonatas with those of Mozart's K. 279–284.

1089. Westphal, Kurt. "Die Formung in Haydns Sonaten." *Die Musik* 24 (1931–32):419–24.

Places Haydn's characteristic sonata-exposition phraseology mid-way between the uninterrupted continuity of the late Baroque and the regular, clearly punctuated phrase rhythm of the Viennese Classical style. Contrasts Haydn's developmental, motivic processes, harnessed within often asymmetrical phrase groups, to Mozart's dualistic, hierarchic order, in which regular phrasing underlies symmetrical period structures.

1090. Wolff, Konrad. *Masters of the Keyboard: Individual Style Elements in the Piano Music of Bach, Haydn, Mozart, Beethoven, and Schubert.* Bloomington: Indiana University Press, 1983. xi, 206 pp.

Devotes a chapter to Haydn (pp. 63–75). Addressing the student performer, attempts to correct some fallacies concerning Haydn's keyboard music and to point out features of his style with the aid of music examples.

Miscellaneous Instrumental Music

1091. Kubitschek, Ernst. "Die Flötentrios Hob. IV:6-11." In *Joseph Haydn Kongress* (item 76), pp. 419-26.

Specifies the coherence of this cycle of six works in terms of movement type and key relationship. Identifies models upon which 9 of the 18 movements are based, and discusses relationships between model and trio version. Includes music examples and a tabular listing of movements and their models.

1092. Ohmiya, Makoto. "Die Instrumenten-Kombination in Joseph Haydns frühen Ensemble-Divertimenti." In *Haydn-Studien* 6/1 (1986):64-67.

Divides Haydn's ensemble divertimentos into four categories: 1) three string parts without viola (Hob. II:1, 8, 11), 2) string ensemble with one viola part (Hob. II:21, 22), 3) five string parts including two violas, 4) wind divertimentos. Discusses instrumental combinations of works that comprise subcategories within each main category.

* Thomas, Günter. "Haydns Tanzmusik--zeitgebunden oder persönlich geprägt?" *Musica* 36 (1982):140-47.

Cited as item 647.

1093. Unverricht, Hubert. "Joseph Haydns Kompositionen für Harmoniemusik." In *Joseph Haydn Kongress* (item 76), pp. 457-65.

Surveys Haydn's contribution to the wind-band medium against the backdrop of contemporary trends and fashions. Delineates three categories within Haydn's output: the *Feldpartien* of 1760-61, wind marches (such as those of the 1790s that reflect contemporary French wind-band music), and symphonically conceived works (such as the arrangement of the second movement of Symphony No. 100 and the second introduction in *The Seven Last Words*). Includes an inquiry into late eighteenth- and early nineteenth-century uses of the term *Harmoniemusik*.

IX

PERFORMANCE PRACTICE

This category embraces studies having to do with historically informed interpretation, ensemble personnel, and medium of performance (including examinations of the baryton, lira organizzata, and musical clock in addition to the basic question of harpsichord vs. fortepiano). Special mention may be made of the extraordinarily thorough and systematic explorations by James Webster (e.g. items 1152, 1153, 1156) into the milieu of mid-eighteenth-century Austrian chamber music and the performance tradition to which Haydn's early string chamber music belonged.

1094. Badura-Skoda, Eva. "Haydns Opern: Anmerkungen zu aufführungspraktischen Problemen der Gegenwart." *Österreichische Musikzeitschrift* 37 (1982):162-67.

Defends Haydn's operatic accomplishment against modern-day misunderstandings of his aims and negative impressions left by poorly executed revivals. Cites hindrances that may have prevented Haydn from greater fulfillment of his potentials, notably the dearth of opportunities to stage major works at important operatic centers. Emphasizes the need for first-class performances as a prerequisite to fair judgment, and delineates major problems confronting performers and directors: access to suitable performance material; vocal ranges; choice among different versions of a given aria; matters of tempo, dynamics, articulation, and ornamentation; and dramaturgical issues.

1095. Badura-Skoda, Paul. "Beiträge zu Haydns Ornamentik." *Musica* 36 (1982):409-18, 575.

Cites Christa Landon's observation that Haydn did not adhere strictly to the ornamentation rules of his *Lehrmeister* C.P.E. Bach, but that he combined South German and Austrian traditions with Bach's teachings, and modified them to suit his own purposes. Points to the need for examining both contemporary manuals and musical analogs in Haydn to arrive at appropriate interpretations, since Haydn provides little guidance in his writings. Examines seven different types of ornament in Haydn, and offers performance suggestions in accordance with the approach described.

1096. ———. "On Ornamentation in Haydn." *The Piano Quarterly* 34/135 (1986):38-48.

Translation of item 1095.

* ———. "Über Haydns Klavierwerke." *Österreichische Musikzeitschrift* 14 (1959):370-76.

Cited as item 1052.

1097. Barnett, Dene. "Non-Uniform Slurring in 18th Century Music: Accident or Design?" *The Haydn Yearbook* 10 (1978):179-99.

Emphasizing the general frequency of the phenomenon in eighteenth-century sources, examines instances in a sampling of Haydn symphony sources (including manuscript parts, manuscript scores, and prints). Proposes an elaborate, objective method for determining whether or not a given instance was accidental. Notes the virtual absence of cases in which non-uniform slurrings were subjected to correction (by performer, composer, or copyist), and concludes that non-uniformity was a common, intentional feature of eighteenth-century ensemble music, readily reflected in Haydn. Includes numerous examples in facsimile.

1098. Besseler, Heinrich. "Einflüsse der Contratanzmusik auf Joseph Haydn." In *Bericht über die Internationale Konferenz zum Andenken Joseph Haydns* (item 70), pp. 25-40.

Addresses the question of appropriate tempos for the

finales of mature Haydn symphonies. Proposes that in the London symphonies, finales are modeled on the contredanse and that the tempo chosen should be slow enough to accommodate dance steps. Traces the development of contredanse finales in Haydn, and shows that their use preceded the London sojourns. Also examines Mozart's use of the contredanse and notes his influence on Haydn. Includes background on the contredanse and its transmission.

1099. Biba, Otto. "Beispiele für die Besetzungsverhältnisse bei Aufführungen von Haydns Oratorien in Wien zwischen 1784 und 1808." *Haydn-Studien* 4 (1976-80):94-104.

Documents described include lists of performing personnel for sixteen oratorio concerts under the sponsorship of the Tonkünstler Societät. Offers information on the first performance of *Il ritorno di Tobia* in the second, expanded version, and furnishes commentary on the changing numbers of performers involved in oratorio performances over the years encompassed.

1100. ———. "Die 'Haydn-Instrumente' im Besitz der Gesellschaft der Musikfreunde in Wien: Provenienz und Authentizität." In *Joseph Haydn Kongress* (item 76), pp. 68-72.

Summarizes what is known about the background on four instruments identified as Haydn's by Eusebius Mandyczewski in a 1912 published inventory: a viola d'amore, a baryton, a cembalo, and a *Tafelklavier.*

1101. Bilson, Malcolm. "The Viennese Fortepiano of the Late 18th Century." *Early Music* 8 (1980):158-62.

Discusses advantages of playing Mozart, Haydn, and Beethoven on the Viennese fortepiano of the period, and supports this view with musical examples. Explains the differences between Viennese and English fortepianos. Includes a photograph of a Schanz fortepiano, thought to have belonged to Haydn, and reproduces a detail from the title page of Artaria's edition of the Haydn Trio Hob. XV:10.

1102. Brown, A. Peter. *Performing Haydn's 'The Creation': Reconstructing the Earliest Renditions.* Bloomington: Indiana University Press, 1986. xiv, 125 pp.

An incisive inquiry into the existing early sources, with discussion of forces, scoring, dynamics, embellishment, bowing, and articulation. Gives original contrabassoon and bass trombone parts as found in the Tonkünstler, Estate, and Sonnleithner sets. Includes numerous music examples, several tables, and comparative diagrams.

1103. Bryan, Paul. "Haydn's Hornists." *Haydn-Studien* 3 (1973-74):52-58.

Arranges the performers chronologically according to their time of entry into Esterházy service. Tabulates the changing number of horn players simultaneously employed by the court between June 1761 and August 1790. Describes their diverse functions, involving field and church music activities as well as the hunt. Draws connections between particular works and the personnel involved, and suggests clues to the dating of particular compositions on the basis of their horn requirements. Attempts to distinguish between first (high register) and second (low register) players, and supplies information on instrument-makers and repairers.

1104. ———. "The Horn in the Works of Mozart and Haydn: Some Observations and Comparisons." *The Haydn Yearbook* 9 (1975):189-255.

Isolates four chronological periods with regard to Haydn's treatment of horns (before 1761, 1761-ca. 1776, ca. 1777-85, ca. 1785 and later), and examines idiosyncratic horn usage in the symphonies, including clarino register, middle-register stopped notes, and low-register factitious tones. Examines the question of *alto* vs. *basso* for horns in C and B flat, and argues against the notion that when horns in C are used together with trumpets in C in the same work, the horns are meant to be *alto*. Relates Haydn's treatment of the horn to his changing concept of wind-ensemble sonority and function within the orchestra. Numerous music examples.

* Carse, Adam. *The Orchestra in the XVIIIth Century.* Cambridge: W. Heffer & Sons, 1940. Reprint. New York: Broude Brothers, 1969. 176 pp.

Cited as item 936.

1105. Czakler, Helmut. "Zum Problem der Lira organizzata." In *Joseph Haydn Kongress* (item 76), pp. 76-81.

Observing that no existing instrument is suitable for performing the Haydn works commissioned by Ferdinand IV, speculates on what characteristics the king's instrument must have had. Discusses an instrument in the Victoria and Albert Museum collection which presumably bears close resemblance to Haydn's, and includes four plates depicting it.

1106. Drabkin, William. "Fingering in Haydn's String Quartets." *Early Music* 16 (1988):50-57.

Proposes that Haydn introduces fingerings to achieve specific effects: the majority indicate performance on a single string, a number of others indicate "the rapid crossing of two strings," and rarely, they indicate open strings. Includes representative examples (with fingerings) from the quartets. Cautions the reader that Haydn's instructions were intended for early instruments and may not all be convincing on modern instruments.

1107. Eibner, Franz. "Registerpedalisierung bei Haydn und Beethoven." *Österreichische Musikzeitschrift* 20 (1965):190-96.

Describes the reverberation effect produced by the damper stop in the early fortepiano and cites a passage from C.P.E. Bach's *Versuch* (part 2, 1762) to support his view that the damper pedal may be treated as a stop (i.e. may be held down) for special purposes. Suggests that this treatment of the pedal was intended by Haydn in his indication "open pedal" for two critical passages in the C-major Sonata, Hob. XVI:50.

1108. Feder, Georg. "Wieviel Orgelkonzerte hat Haydn geschrieben?" *Die Musikforschung* 23 (1970):440-44.

In response to Heussner's rejection (item 572) of Landon's contention that Hob. XVIII:5 is an organ concerto, examines the problem from the vantage point of keyboard range. Shows that in early works known with certainty to be for organ, the keyboard part never exceeds the range C-c^3, whereas it does for early works known to be for piano/cembalo. Using range as a criterion, concludes that Hob. XVIII:5, 1, 2, 8, and 10 are organ concertos; No. 6 is a concerto for organ and violin; and No. 7, an organ concerto based perhaps on a piano trio.

1109. Fitzpatrick, Horace. "Waldhorntechnik um die Jahrhundertmitte." In *Der junge Haydn* (item 81), pp. 221-27.

Places Haydn's use of the horn against the backdrop of two performance traditions: Baroque (ca. 1690-ca. 1755-60) and Classical (1780-1830). Discusses the contribution of outstanding eighteenth-century performers, and examines interrelated aspects of performance technique, sonority, instrument construction, and pedagogy. Describes the two horn virtuosos with whom Haydn was associated, Steinmüller and Franz, and identifies the former with the older tradition, the latter with the newer approach.

1110. Fruchtman, Efrim. "The Baryton: Its History and Its Music Re-examined." *Acta Musicologica* 34 (1962):2-17.

Examines the instrument's history, the origin of its name, its structure, and the types of notation used. Describes Haydn as "by far the most prolific composer of music for this instrument." Remarks on the nature of baryton music and names some known historical performers.

1111. Gerlach, Sonja. "Haydns Orchestermusiker von 1761 bis 1774." *Haydn-Studien* 4 (1976-80):35-48.

Lists the musicians at the Esterházy court by instrument, giving information on alternative instruments played and inclusive dates of service. Describes general duties, and offers extensive commentary on the list, including speculation on deployment of various players and the use of outside musicians. Footnotes call attention to substantial differences with respect to Pohl's list (item 277, vol. 2).

1112. ———. "Haydns Orchesterpartituren: Fragen der Realisierung des Textes." *Haydn-Studien* 5 (1982-85):169-83.

Addresses questions of performance practice with regard to instrumentation and ensemble size for the symphonies. Drawing on information from autographs or authoritative copies (for instrumentation) and on Esterházy payrolls or data on the Salomon orchestra (for ensemble size), divides the symphonies into three periods (1757-74, 1775-90, 1791-95), and summarizes findings in tabular form. Discusses typical instrumentation for each period, then concentrates on questions that arise with respect to the bass line, continuo bassoon, cembalo, viola, and horns. Includes facsimiles of two autograph pages (1763, 1783).

* ———. "Haydn's Works for Musical Clock (*Flötenuhr*): Problems of Authenticity, Grouping, and Chronology." In *Haydn Studies* (item 73), pp. 126-29.

Cited as item 642.

1113. Harich, János. "Das Haydn-Orchester im Jahr 1780." *The Haydn Yearbook* 8 (1971):5-69.

Opens with a list of the 25 musicians who constituted the orchestra, including their dates and instrumental specialty or specialties. Offers brief commentary on the list, and names additional players hired for short engagements. Furnishes profiles of orchestra members, addressing the circumstances of their engagement and their activities at court. Briefly discusses the church choir at Eisenstadt, and includes similar profiles for its members. The study is heavily documented and provides an English summary.

1114. ———. "Das Opernensemble zu Eszterháza im Jahr 1780." *The Haydn Yearbook* 7 (1970):5-69.

Provides brief sketches on all the singers known to have been associated with the opera ensemble in 1780. Tells of their engagement and activities at court, including works in which they performed. Appends an English summary.

1115. Hellyer, Roger. "The Wind Ensembles of the Esterházy Princes, 1761-1813." *The Haydn Yearbook* 15 (1984):5-92.

A history of the court and military wind ensembles, beginning with Haydn's appointment as vice kapellmeister. Makes numerous references to Haydn, and quotes a number of documents (e.g. petitions, letters, receipts, reports, granting of allowances) in English translation. Includes 15 pages of facsimiles, among them a Haydn autograph of his *Hungarischer National Marsch,* Haydn's bill for the march, and a Haydn letter of 1802. An appendix discusses the repertories of the wind bands, both pre-1790 and post-1790, and it provides lists of music: Haydn's early *Harmoniemusik,* which may have been used by the *Feldmusik* (the early *Feldmusik* repertory is lost), and an inventory of the new library of *Harmoniemusik.*

1116. Hollis, Helen Rice. *The Musical Instruments of Joseph*

Haydn: An Introduction. Washington, D.C.: Smithsonian Institution Press, 1977. vi, 33 pp.

A look at Haydn's early experiences with musical instruments, his use of instruments, and instruments associated with the London years. Places heavy emphasis on keyboard instruments--drawing heavily on item 1150 to discuss the different types of keyboard instrument used by Haydn--, but also discusses winds, timpani, and the baryton. Includes 18 illustrations, all but one of which depict instruments.

1117. Karpf, Roswitha Vera. "Haydn und Carl Friberth: Marginalien zur Gesangskunst im 18. Jahrhundert." In *Joseph Haydn Kongress* (item 76), pp. 361-68.

Examines Friberth's role as Haydn's leading tenor (to 1776) and adapter of libretti for Eisenstadt and Eszterháza. Discusses his training in the Neapolitan vocal tradition, and then (with the use of examples) deduces characteristics of his voice from features peculiar to the music written for him by Haydn. Notes in particular his wide range (G-d^2) and his ability to negotiate uncommonly wide leaps and briskly-paced *parlando* passages. Observes the infrequent use of coloratura passages in his roles--but leaves open the question of whether this was Friberth's preference or whether he improvised the passages.

1118. Keller, Hans. *The Great Haydn Quartets: Their Interpretation.* New York: George Braziller, 1986. 260 pp.

Concerned with Op. 9 No. 4, and all the quartets from Op. 20 on, with the purportedly self-evident exception of Op. 33 No. 4 and the *Seven Last Words.* Intending to address the performer rather than the listener or scholar, treats each work separately, in a deliberately unsystematic way. Emphasis falls on matters of tempo, accent, and various details of performance style. Pays considerable attention to questions of theme and motive, especially in the context of interaction among performers in the ensemble. Generally wordy and self-indulgent, though rich in intuitive insight.

1119. ———. "The Interpretation of the Haydn Quartets." *The Score,* no. 24 (1958), pp. 14-35.

Epigrammatic observations on tempo, dynamics, phrasing,

and ensemble. Cites specific examples from each set except for Op. 17 (alleged to be beyond the grasp of anyone who has not mastered the entire canon). Extols Haydn as supreme master of the medium, and declares that his quartets are immeasurably greater than the symphonies.

1120. Kinsky, Georg. "Haydn und das Hammerklavier." *Zeitschrift für Musikwissenschaft* 13 (1930-31):500-501.

Takes issue with statements by Hans Engel (p. 476 of the journal) to the effect that Haydn was uninterested in the piano and had a greater affinity for the harpsichord. Cites passages from Haydn's letters to Marianne von Genzinger to show that Haydn favored the former instrument. Suggests that the Schanz instrument owned by the Gesellschaft der Musikfreunde is not Haydn's, as claimed in the catalogue, since the address given for Schanz on the inscription in the instrument differs from the purchase address given by Haydn in a letter of 1788 to Artaria (see also Luithlen, item 1124).

* Klein, Rudolf. "Der Applausus-Brief." *Österreichische Musikzeitschrift* 14 (1959):198-200.

Cited as item 105.

1121. Kleindienst, Sigrid. "Haydns Clavier-Werke: Kriterien der Instrumentenwahl." In *Joseph Haydn Kongress* (item 76), pp. 53-63.

Surveys the question of performance medium for Haydn's keyboard works: harpsichord, clavichord, or fortepiano. Discusses criteria for making a choice, and examines inherent ambiguities and contradictory evidence. Considers designations in prints and manuscript copies, references in pertinent correspondence, and information on the instruments that Haydn had at his disposal at different times in his career. Pays special attention to internal evidence, and quotes passages from various compositions that seem idiomatic to one instrument or another.

1122. Landon, H.C. Robbins. "The Place of Haydn in Early Music and the Challenge He Presents to the Early Musician." *Early Music* 10 (1982):298-99.

Describes problems facing the modern interpreter of Haydn's music.

1123. Lessing, Alfred. "Zur Geschichte des Barytons." In *Beiträge zur Musikgeschichte des 18. Jahrhunderts* (item 69), pp. 143-53.

Traces the history of the baryton, with the aid of excerpts from seventeenth- and eighteenth-century writings. Discusses and offers examples of the great variety among instruments. Names notable works, performers, and composers (among them Haydn), and includes a discussion of baryton music at the Esterházy court.

1124. Luithlen, Victor. "Haydn-Erinnerungen in der Sammlung alter Musikinstrumente des Kunsthistorischen Museums zu Wien." In *Anthony van Hoboken: Festschrift zum 75. Geburtstag,* edited by Joseph Schmidt-Görg, pp. 110-14. Mainz: B. Schott's Söhne, 1962.

Furnishes information on three instruments that purportedly once belonged to Haydn: a cembalo by Shudi & Broadwood (London, 1775), a *Tafelklavier* by Schanz, and a baryton by Stadlman (Vienna, 1732). All are owned by the Gesellschaft der Musikfreunde. Explains why the Schanz instrument cannot be identical to the fortepiano that Haydn acquired in 1788 (see also Kinsky, item 1120). Includes photographs of the instruments and of Thaler's wax bust of Haydn.

1125. Luoma, Robert G. "The Function of Dynamics in the Music of Haydn, Mozart, and Beethoven: Some Implications for the Performer." *College Music Symposium* 16 (1976):32-41.

Attempts to relate certain aspects of performance to eighteenth-century concepts of form, and proposes that dynamic emphasis be used to highlight important structural and tonal events in the music. Cites Leopold Mozart and C.P.E. Bach, who advocated dynamic emphasis of dissonances, and applies the principle of emphasis to larger structural dimensions. Provides discussion of several Haydn examples, including the minuet and trio of Symphony No. 101 and the trio of Symphony No. 71.

1126. Mahling, Christoph-Hellmut. "Orchester, Orchesterpraxis und Orchestermusiker zur Zeit des jungen Haydn (1740-1770)." In *Der junge Haydn* (item 81), pp. 98-112.

Depicts the middle years of the eighteenth century as a

time of transition and experimentation in orchestral practice. Examines orchestra size and distribution of instruments, and cites representative statistics for Vienna, Munich, Stuttgart, Kassel, Salzburg, and Esterházy orchestras. Discusses practices and customs pertaining to rehearsal, training of musicians, and their economic and social status. Cites orchestral experiments from Haydn's Symphonies Nos. 6, 7, and 8.

1127. ———. "Performance Practice in Haydn's Works for *Lira organizzata*." In *Haydn Studies* (item 73), pp. 297-302.

Discusses plausible substitutes for the *lira organizzata*, invoking Haydn's own choice of alternatives. Also considers the substitution of violins for clarinets in the notturnos, and offers guidelines on the use of cello and double bass in the *basso* parts.

1128. Mertin, Josef. "Zu den Orgelinstrumenten Joseph Haydns." In *Joseph Haydn Kongress* (item 76), pp. 72-75.

Features a listing of the disposition of registers for the Stadtpfarrkirche organ in Eisenstadt (built by Johann Gottfried Mallek) and the evidently related Esterházy palace organ in Vienna.

1129. Neumann, Frederick. "Bemerkungen über Haydns Ornamentik." *Joseph Haydn Kongress* (item 76), pp. 35-42.

Arguing the case for the many-sidedness in function and nuance of eighteenth-century ornamentation, challenges the belief that ornaments in Haydn fall generally on the beat. Cites instances where an unaccented ornament, before the beat, proves most in keeping with style and context, and points out instances of the characteristic "Haydn ornament" where anticipation of the main note seems appropriate. Claims that the present-day striving for absolute precision in re-creating authentic ornamentation is misdirected. Proposes that a relatively flexible Italian style, allowing a wide range of possible interpretations, is suitable for Haydn and his milieu.

1130. Newman, William S. "Haydn as Ingenious Exploiter of the Keyboard." In *Joseph Haydn Kongress* (item 76), pp. 43-53.

Observes that successive sets of Haydn's sonatas and

keyboard trios show increasingly challenging, subtle, and varied uses of the instrument: alternation of the hands, repeated notes (their decline after 1782 reflecting the change from harpsichord to fortepiano), rhythmically free virtuosic runs and flourishes, alternating octaves, wide leaps, different touches (finger, hand, forearm, upper arm), subtle, coloristic textures, and subtle articulation. Concludes that historians understate Haydn's mastery of the instrument and his resourcefulness in exploiting available materials. Sees him as a more ingenious exploiter of technical possibilities than Mozart, and in this respect a greater influence on Beethoven.

1131. ———. "The Pianism of Haydn, Mozart, Beethoven, and Schubert Compared." *The Piano Quarterly* 27/105 (1979):14-27, 30.

Ranks Haydn fourth among these Viennese musicians in terms of virtuosity and degree of activity as a keyboard performer. Describing his writing as comfortably idiomatic, cites instances of pianistic devices, including trill figures, hand-crossing, and alternation of the hands.

1132. Niemöller, Klaus Wolfgang. "Aufführungspraxis und Edition von Haydns Cellokonzert D-dur." In *Musik--Edition--Interpretation: Gedenkschrift Günter Henle,* edited by Martin Bente, pp. 394-409. Munich: G. Henle, 1980.

Reviews reasons given for questioning the work's authenticity before discovery of the autograph in 1954. This discovery raised new questions about the cello part, notated between the tutti viola and bass parts in downward-transposing treble clef. The author takes issue with Leopold Nowak's contention that the cello line in the autograph was intended to embody both tutti and solo parts, and adduces evidence to support his own view that it was intended only for the solo instrument. Includes music examples of four passages, for which the two interpretations are contrasted. Two of the examples are accompanied by facsimiles of corresponding passages in the autograph.

* Ohmiya, Makoto. "Text and Performance: The Treatment of *Ossia* Variants in Haydn Critical Scores." In *Haydn Studies* (item 73), pp. 130-33.

Cited as item 435.

1133. Ord-Hume, Arthur W.J.G. *Joseph Haydn and the Mechanical Organ.* Cardiff: University College Cardiff Press, 1982. 185 pp.

Detailed examination of three surviving mechanical instruments (all designed by Joseph Niemecz, librarian to Prince Nikolaus Esterházy and Haydn pupil) for which Haydn wrote compositions. Provides meticulous description for two of the instruments and gives an overview of the music. Considers questions of pitch, tempo, embellishment, and *notes inégales.* Proposes the dates 1789, 1792, and 1793 for their construction.

1134. ———. "Ornamentation in Mechanical Music." *Early Music* 11 (1983):185-93.

Includes mention of Haydn's music for mechanical instruments, notably the pieces created for Joseph Niemecz's musical clocks. Emphasizes Haydn's evident interest in the medium, and his efforts to create pieces that fully exploited its possibilities. Describes, with the aid of illustrations from F. Bédos de Celles, *L'Art du facteur d'orgues* (1766-78), the techniques involved in realizing different kinds of ornamentation on eighteenth-century mechanical instruments.

1135. Parrish, Carl. "Haydn and the Piano." *Journal of the American Musicological Society* 1/3 (1948):27-34.

Examines the question of Haydn's keyboard style, and describes characteristics that demonstrate the influence of C.P.E. Bach--an influence acknowledged by Haydn. Also points to traces of superficial Mozart and Clementi influence and to elements of idiomatic keyboard writing that seem to have originated with Haydn himself. Discusses Haydn's attitude toward the piano (see also Kinsky, item 1120), and describes several keyboard instruments he owned.

1136. Ripin, Edwin M. "Haydn and the Keyboard Instruments of His Time." In *Haydn Studies* (item 73), pp. 302-8.

Indicates that in the last third of the eighteenth century, the harpsichord, clavichord, and piano were "remarkably equivalent to one another," and contends that for this and other reasons, an "attempt to assign specific sonatas" to one instrument or another is "bound to fail." Finds no clear-cut change in Haydn's writing for keyboard to pinpoint his "change of allegiance" to the piano. But shows that beginning in 1788, Haydn is known to have written for particular instruments, and that stylistic differences can be seen between music written respectively for English and Viennese pianos.

1137. Saslav, Isidor. "The *alla breve* 'March': Its Evolution and Meaning in Haydn's String Quartets." In *Haydn Studies* (item 73), pp. 308-14.

Defines two main categories of new rhythmic notation that first appeared in the Op. 50 quartets (1787). Demonstrates how they evolved from earlier types, and describes implications this evolution had for changes in tempo. Explains how the *alla breve* march, which falls within one of the two categories, provides important clues to the evolution of tempo and its notation.

1138. Schenker, Heinrich. *Ein Beitrag zur Ornamentik, als Einführung zu Ph. Em. Bachs Klavierwerken, mitumfassend auch die Ornamentik Haydns, Mozarts, Beethovens etc.* 2d ed. Vienna: Universal, 1908. Reprint. Vienna: Universal, [1954]. 72 pp.

First published in 1903 (Vienna: Universal) and recently translated as "A Contribution to the Study of Ornamentation" by Hedi Siegel in *The Music Forum* 4 (1976):1-39. Discusses the integral, structural role of embellishment in C.P.E. Bach's keyboard music, then undertakes a comparative examination of different types of ornamentation in Bach, Haydn, Mozart, and Beethoven. Includes an extended discussion of the *Doppelschlag* Haydn ornament.

1139. Schmid, Ernst Fritz. "Joseph Haydn und die Flötenuhr." *Zeitschrift für Musikwissenschaft* 14 (1931-32):193-221.

Provides a brief history of the *Flötenuhr* and a biographical sketch of Pater Primitivus Niemecz, builder of three such mechanical instruments that play Haydn's music exclusively. Describes the three instruments, built in 1772, 1792, and 1793, and discusses known manuscripts of Haydn's *Flötenuhr* pieces, both autographs and copies. As a means of offering insight into Haydn's musical craft, provides several examples of passages for which Haydn wrote multiple versions. Then offers commentary on a number of pieces that merit special attention. Closes with remarks on the value of *Flötenuhr* pieces in the interpretation of ornaments and, to a lesser extent, in the realization of tempo.

1140. ———. "Joseph Haydn und die vokale Zierpraxis seiner Zeit, dargestellt an einer Arie seines Tobias-Oratoriums." In *Bericht über die Internationale Konferenz zum Andenken Joseph Haydns* (item 70), pp. 117-29.

Discusses the aria "Quando mi dona," from *Il ritorno di Tobia* (1775), which exists in an ornamented version in abbreviated autograph score. Suggests that the ornamentation was prepared for the second Viennese performance (1784), at which Valentin Adamberger was to have sung the part of Tobias, and that it may reflect Karl Friberth's ornamentation at the first performance. Comments on Haydn's early vocal training and the Italian vocal tradition in which both Haydn and Friberth were schooled. Includes a facsimile from the ornamented score and publishes the complete vocal line of the aria--both ornamented and unornamented--with bass.

* ———. "Neue Funde zu Haydns Flötenuhrstücken." *Haydn-Studien* 2 (1969-70):249-55.

Cited as item 645.

1141. Schwamberger, Karl Maria. "Das Baryton: Ein vergessenes Instrument aus der Barockzeit." *Neue Zeitschrift für Musik* 122 (1961):439-42.

Outlines the history, design, and performance technique of the instrument. Includes mention of Haydn's baryton requirements and its technical repertory. Provides illustrations of three instruments (one of them said to have been owned by Haydn) and an illustration of the device of string plucking on the underside of the fingerboard.

1142. Schwarz, Vera. "Malentendus dans l'interprétation de Haydn, présentés à partir d'exemples tirés de sa musique de clavier." *Schweizerische Musikzeitung/Revue musicale suisse* 116 (1976):429-37.

French version of item 1143.

1143. ———. "Missverständnisse in der Haydn-Interpretation, dargestellt an Beispielen aus seiner Klaviermusik." *Österreichische Musikzeitschrift* 31 (1976):25-35.

Addresses the question of why the terms "purely Romantic" and "fanciful," applied by E.T.A. Hoffmann to Haydn's music, no longer seem appropriate. Proposes that the answer may lie in modern interpretations of his music, which largely ignore eighteenth-century principles of musical expression. Discusses the central importance of declamation in bringing the music to life, and describes various aspects of musical declamation, such as "grammatical" accentuation, or the prolonging of notes or pauses beyond their notated value. Concludes with guidelines on the treatment of fermatas and the use of ornamentation.

1144. ———. "Die Rolle des Cembalos in Österreich nach 1760." In *Der junge Haydn* (item 81), pp. 249-56.

Traces the gradually waning popularity of the harpsichord in favor of the fortepiano through pertinent references in contemporary correspondence and critiques. Includes quotations from the letters of Haydn and Mozart.

1145. Somfai, László. "Zur Aufführungspraxis der frühen Streichquartett-Divertimenti Haydns." In *Der junge Haydn* (item 81), pp. 86-96.

With regard to Op. 1 (Nos. 1-4, 6), Op. 2, and Op. "0" (Hob. II:6), concludes that solo performance is plausible, that contrabass participation is not unequivocally necessary, and that while there are no authentic copies with figures, there are passages that could profitably use continuo. Advocates performance of the bass line on cello, despite the resulting occurrences of six-four chords. Reminds us of an even more pronounced part-writing difficulty: passages where a high viola accompaniment overlaps the violin melody. Includes discussion of variant phrasing and articulation in early prints and manuscript sources.

1146. Steglich, Rudolf. "Kadenzen in Haydns Klaviersonaten." *Zeitschrift für Musik* 99 (1932):295-97.

Laments the absence of realized cadenzas and accurate readings of Haydn's original texts in the composer's time. Provides model cadenzas for three sonatas: Nos. 6, 19, and 46.

1147. Tolstoy, Christie. "The Identification and Interpretation of Sign Ornaments in Haydn's Instrumental Music." In

Haydn Studies (item 73), pp. 315-23.

Discusses the complexity of interpreting sign ornaments in music of the Classical period. Describes general hazards for interpreters, and addresses the question of Haydn's inconsistencies, both over time and within a single work. Shows how context (melodic, rhythmic, harmonic, articulative, or affective) often permits identification and interpretation of an ornament symbol, and demonstrates the point by citing an instance in Hob. V:D3, where a problematical ornament is notated differently in each of five sources.

1148. Tung, Leslie. "Indicators of Early Piano Writing in the Haydn Sonatas." In *Haydn Studies* (item 73), pp. 323-26.

Concerned with instrumentation for Haydn's keyboard sonatas written between 1766 and 1776. Weighs stylistic factors such as dynamics, articulation, melody, and accompaniment figures. Lists sonatas from this period (including Hob. XVI:18-20, 33, 42-46) that suggest piano rather than harpsichord as intended medium.

1149. Van der Meer, John Henry. "Die Verwendung der Blasinstrumente im Orchester bei Haydn und seinen Zeitgenossen." In *Der junge Haydn* (item 81), pp. 202-19.

Offers an overview of late eighteenth-century wind instruments, their limitations, traditional functions, and characteristic exploitation in Haydn's orchestral works. Observes that while Haydn's early affinity for homophonic wind technique and concomitant rejection of "concertante" wind writing places him in the forefront of contemporary developments, his hesitancy to expand the spectrum of wind usage and sonority suggests a conservative bent. Contrasts the relative conservatism of Haydn's Esterházy works with the broader perspective evident in the London symphonies.

1150. Walter, Horst. "Haydns Klaviere." *Haydn-Studien* 2 (1969-70):256-88.

Meticulously examines evidence pertaining to keyboard instruments owned, used, or known by Haydn. Proposing that his compositions reflect a time of transition with respect to the customary and preferred choice of keyboard instruments, observes that only after 1780 does

Haydn employ keyboard dynamic markings. Discusses the Wenzel Schanz "Forte-piano" purchased by Haydn in 1788, makes note of his encounter with Broadwood instruments and others in England, and describes the surviving clavichord of Haydn's at the Royal College of Music, London (photograph included).

1151. ———. "Das Tasteninstrument beim jungen Haydn." In *Der junge Haydn* (item 81), pp. 237–48.

Surveys the range required in Haydn's early keyboard works, and considers the question of a short-octave configuration (implied by his interval-spans of a tenth). Probing the question of harpsichord vs. organ as it pertains to early Haydn keyboard concertos, finds ambivalence in their restrictive range (suggesting organ) and idiomatic suitability to the harpsichord.

1152. Webster, James. "The Bass Part in Haydn's Early String Quartets." *The Musical Quarterly* 63 (1977):390–424.

Addresses uncertainties of performance medium for Haydn quartets prior to Op. 33 by scrutinizing available information: contemporary accounts, authentic sources, and such stylistic evidence as the tessitura of the lowest part. Views Haydn as a link between Baroque and Classical style with regard to the function of the bass, and concludes that while the scoring for the quartets from Op. 17 on is secure, and that for Op. 9 is probably so, doubt remains with regard to the ten earliest quartets, for which cello plus contrabass is a possibility. Includes tables of part-crossings involving the bass parts.

1153. ———. "The Bass Part in Haydn's Early String Quartets and in Austrian Chamber Music, 1750–1780." Ph.D. dissertation, Princeton University, 1974. xii, 429 pp.

In a comprehensive attempt to solve the question of bass-line scoring for the early Haydn quartets, examines the works in the context of a repertory of Austrian ensemble music before 1780. Explores connotations of the Austrian *divertimento* within the pertinent time-span as the class of works to which Haydn's early quartets belong: soloistic, either serious or occasional, without continuo, and with the bass part designated *basso.* Reviews both documentary and stylistic evidence regarding the use of cello and double bass in soloistic chamber music, and cites corroborative stylistic evidence in support of soloistic performance with solo cello on the bass line for quartets prior to Op. 17. Surveys authentic sources for the entire Haydn canon, and attempts to order the works chronologically. Lists (by composer) more than 1,000 Austrian multi-movement ensemble works, ca. 1750 to ca. 1780. Substantial bibliography.

1154. ———. "The Scoring of Haydn's Early String Quartets." In *Haydn Studies* (item 73), pp. 235-38.

Argues that while the scoring for the ten earliest authentic Haydn quartets has never been established, available evidence (documentary, organological, and stylistic) suggests soloistic performance with solo cello performing the bass part.

1155. ———. "The Significance of Haydn's String Quartet Autographs for Performance Practice." In *The String Quartets of Haydn, Mozart, and Beethoven: Studies of the Autograph Manuscripts. A Conference at Isham Memorial Library, March 15-17, 1979,* edited by Christoph Wolff, pp. 62-95. Cambridge: Harvard University Press, 1980.

Examining Haydn's relatively casual approach to proofreading, concludes that there are virtually no viable grounds for preferring the reading of any other source to that of an extant Haydn autograph. Identifies and discusses three kinds of performance-practice problem encountered in the autographs: incompleteness (e.g. missing dynamic markings at the beginning of a movement), inconsistency (or variability, notably with regard to placement of articulation markings), and ambiguity. Objects to the common view that blames lack of uniformity in performance indications on the composer's haste, and observes that variety in performance markings may be seen as an integral aspect of the composer's style. Advocates publication of autograph manuscripts in facsimile as an aid to performers.

1156. ———. "Towards a History of Viennese Chamber Music in the Early Classical Period." *Journal of the American Musicological Society* 27 (1974): 212-47.

Reports that with respect to the repertory in question, the title "Divertimento" did not yield to "Quartet" until the 1780s, that "Divertimento" was the preferred title associated with non-orchestral scoring, that the term *basso* may apply to both orchestral and soloistic music, and that its use does not imply *basso continuo* practice. Proposes that the title "Quartet" was associated with the change from a private to a public music culture and the rise of the Viennese publishing firms around 1780, and that a work (from Op. 20, for example) with the title "Divertimento à quattro" and the designation *basso* constitutes a string quartet in all respects but name.

1157. ———. "Violoncello and Double Bass in the Chamber Music of Haydn and His Viennese Contemporaries, 1750-1780." *Journal of the American Musicological Society* 29 (1976):413-38.

Drawing on historical, documentary, organological, and stylistic information, questions the significance of the common designation *basso* for the bass part within the repertory in question. Scrutinizes issues of range and tessitura; examines the mid- and late eighteenth-century traditions of double-bass performance; and corrects Landon's assertion that the lowest double-bass string in Haydn's time was tuned to low C. Haydn works considered include the early quartets, baryton trios, and miscellaneous instrumental ensemble works. Shows that the word *Bassetl* was synonymous with cello, and that while for mixed ensemble works--especially those in manifestly orchestral style--the bass may have been for cello and double bass, solo cello was the principal bass instrument in the Viennese repertory.

1158. Zaslaw, Neal. "Toward the Revival of the Classical Orchestra." *Proceedings of the Royal Musical Association* 103 (1976-77):158-87.

Pertinent features include a comparative table specifying size and composition of selected European orchestras in the years 1774-96; a table representing ideally balanced string sections according to the theorists Quantz, Petri, Galeazzi, and Koch; and a hypothetical reconstruction of the amphitheater placement of instruments at the 1791-93 Haydn-Salomon concerts in London.

APPENDIX 1

PUBLISHED VOLUMES OF THE *JOSEPH HAYDN WERKE* EDITION

Published by G. Henle Verlag, Munich

This listing encompasses volumes available to date in the complete edition of Haydn's works undertaken by the Joseph Haydn Institute in Cologne, West Germany, under the leadership of Georg Feder. Most volumes are accompanied by separately bound critical commentaries. For each instance in which the critical commentary is bound with the edition, page references have been indicated; and where a separately bound commentary is not yet available, this has been indicated as well. Note that whereas the sequence of volumes runs approximately parallel to the work-categories in Hoboken, *Joseph Haydn: Thematisch-bibliographisches Werkverzeichnis* (item 28), the two numbering systems are independent.

1:4 *Sinfonien, 1764 und 1765.* Edited by Horst Walter. 1964.

1:6 *Sinfonien, 1767–1772.* Edited by C.-G. Stellan Mörner. 1966.

1:7 *Sinfonien, 1773 und 1774.* Edited by Wolfgang Stockmeier. 1966.

1:8 *Sinfonien um 1775/76.* Edited by Wolfgang Stockmeier, in collaboration with Sonja Gerlach. 1970.

1:12 *Pariser Sinfonien, 1. Folge.* Edited by Hiroshi Nakano. 1971.

1:17 *Londoner Sinfonien, 3. Folge.* Edited by Horst Walter. 1966.

1:18 *Londoner Sinfonien, 4. Folge.* Edited by Hubert Unverricht. 1963. Critical commentary not yet available.

2 *Concertante, 1792.* Edited by Sonja Gerlach. 1982. Critical commentary, pp. 65-75.

3:1 *Konzerte für Violine und Orchester.* Edited by Heinz Lohmann and Günter Thomas. 1969.

3:2 *Konzerte für Violoncello und Orchester.* Edited by Sonja Gerlach. 1981. Critical commentary, pp. 119-30.

3:3 *Konzerte für ein Blasinstrument und Orchester.* Edited by Makoto Ohmiya, in collaboration with Sonja Gerlach. 1985. Critical commentary, pp. 59-76.

4 *Die sieben letzten Worte unseres Erlösers am Kreuze: Orchesterfassung (1785).* Edited by Hubert Unverricht. 1959.

6 *Concerti mit Orgelleiern.* Edited by Makoto Ohmiya. 1976.

7 *Notturni mit Orgelleiern.* Edited by Makoto Ohmiya. 1971.

11:1 *Streichtrios, 1. Folge.* Edited by Bruce C. MacIntyre and Barry S. Brook. 1986. Critical commentary, pp. 165-210.

12:1 *Frühe Streichquartette.* Edited by Georg Feder, in collaboration with Gottfried Greiner. 1973.

12:2 *Streichquartette, "Opus 9" und "Opus 17."* Edited by Georg Feder. 1963. Critical commentary not yet available.

12:3 *Streichquartette, "Opus 20" und "Opus 33."* Edited by Georg Feder and Sonja Gerlach. 1974.

12:5 *Streichquartette, "Opus 64" und "Opus 71/74."* Edited by Georg Feder and Isidor Saslav, in collaboration with Warren Kirkendale. 1978. Critical commentary not yet available.

13 *Werke mit Baryton.* Edited by Sonja Gerlach. 1969.

14:1 *Barytontrios, Nr. 1-24.* Edited by Jürgen Braun and Sonja Gerlach. 1980. Critical commentary, pp. 137-71.

14:2 *Barytontrios, Nr. 25-48.* Edited by Hubert Unverricht. 1960.

14:3 *Barytontrios, Nr. 49-72.* Edited by Hubert Unverricht. 1958.

14:4 *Barytontrios, Nr. 73-96.* Edited by Hubert Unverricht. 1958.

14:5 *Barytontrios, Nr. 97-126.* Edited by Michael Härting and Horst Walter. 1968.

15:2 *Konzerte für Klavier (Cembalo) und Orchester.* Edited by Horst Walter and Bettina Wackernagel. 1983. Critical commentary, pp. 169-200.

16 *Concertini und Divertimenti für Klavier (Cembalo) mit Begleitung von zwei Violinen und Basso.* Edited by Horst Walter, in collaboration with Hiroshi Nakano. 1987. Critical commentary, pp. 115-37.

17:1 *Klaviertrios, 1. Folge: Frühe Trios für Cembalo, Violine und Streichbass und Quintett für Cembalo, Violine, Streichbass und zwei Hörner.* Edited by Wolfgang Stockmeier. 1970.

17:2 *Klaviertrios, 2. Folge: Trios für Cembalo oder Pianoforte, Violine (Flöte) und Violoncello.* Edited by Wolfgang Stockmeier. 1974.

17:3 *Klaviertrios, 3. Folge: Trios für Pianoforte, Violine und Violoncello und Sonate für Klavier und Violine.* Edited by Irmgard Becker-Glauch. 1986. Critical commentary, pp. 345-79.

18:1 *Klaviersonaten, 1. Folge.* Edited by Georg Feder. 1970. Critical commentary not yet available.

18:2 *Klaviersonaten, 2. Folge.* Edited by Georg Feder. 1970. Critical commentary not yet available.

18:3 *Klaviersonaten, 3. Folge.* Edited by Georg Feder. 1966. Critical commentary not yet available.

21 *Stücke für das Laufwerk (Flötenuhrstücke).* Edited by Sonja Gerlach and George R. Hill. 1984. Critical commentary, pp. 51-86.

23:2 *Messen Nr. 5-8.* Edited by H.C. Robbins Landon, in collaboration with Karl Heinz Füssl and Christa Landon. 1958. Critical commentary not yet available.

23:3 *Messen Nr. 9-10.* Edited by Günter Thomas. 1965.

23:4 *Messe Nr. 101: "Schöpfungsmesse," 1801.* Edited by Irmgard Becker-Glauch. 1967.

23:5 *Messe Nr. 102: "Harmoniemesse," 1802.* Edited by Friedrich Lippmann. 1966.

24:1 *Philemon und Baucis, oder Jupiters Reise auf die Erde: Deutsche Marionetten-Oper, 1773.* Edited by Jürgen Braun. 1971.

25:1 *Acide und andere Fragmente italienischer Opern um 1761 bis 1763.* Edited by Karl Geiringer and Günter Thomas. 1985. Critical commentary, pp. 213-35.

25:2 *La canterina: Intermezzo in musica, 1766.* Edited by Dénes Bartha. 1959.

25:3 *Lo speziale: Dramma giocoso, nach einem Libretto von C. Goldoni, 1768.* Edited by Helmut Wirth. 1959.

25:4 *Le pescatrici: Dramma giocoso, 1769, nach einem Libretto von Carlo Goldoni.* Edited by Dénes Bartha, in collaboration with Jenő Vécsey and Maria Eckhardt. 1972.

25:5 *L'infedeltà delusa: Burletta per musica in due atti, nach einem Libretto von M. Coltellini (1773).* Edited by Dénes Bartha and Jenő Vécsey. 1964.

25:6 *L'incontro improvviso: Dramma giocoso per musica, aus dem französischen übersetzt von Karl Friberth (1775).* 2 vols. Edited by Helmut Wirth. 1962-63.

25:7 *Il mondo della luna: Dramma giocoso in tre atti, 1777, nach einem Libretto von Carlo Goldoni.* 3 vols. Edited by Günter Thomas. 1979. Critical commentary, 3:595-660.

25:8 *La vera costanza: Dramma giocoso per musica (1778/79 und 1785), Libretto von Francesco Puttini.* Edited by Horst Walter. 1976.

25:10 *La fedeltà premiata: Dramma pastorale giocoso, 1780, nach einem Libretto von Giambattista Lorenzi.* 2 vols. Edited by Günter Thomas. 1968.

25:11 *Orlando paladino: Dramma eroicomico, 1782, Libretto von Nunziato Porta.* 2 vols. Edited by Karl Geiringer. 1972-73.

25:12 *Armida: Dramma eroico, 1783.* Edited by Wilhelm Pfannkuch. 1965. Critical commentary not yet available.

25:13 *L'anima del filosofo, ossia Orfeo ed Euridice: Dramma per musica, 1791, libretto von Carlo Francesco Badini.* Edited by Helmut Wirth. 1974.

27:2 *Applausus, 1768.* Edited by Heinrich Wiens, in collaboration with Irmgard Becker-Glauch. 1969.

28:1 *Il ritorno di Tobia: Oratorio (1775/1784), Dichtung von Giovanni Gastone Boccherini.* 2 vols. Edited by Ernst Fritz Schmid. 1963. Critical commentary not yet available.

28:2 *Die sieben letzten Worte unseres Erlösers am Kreuze: Vokalfassung.* Edited by Hubert Unverricht. 1961. Critical commentary not yet available.

29:1 *Lieder für eine Singstimme mit Begleitung des Klaviers.* Edited by Paul Mies. 1960.

29:2 *Verschiedene Gesänge mit Begleitung des Klaviers.* Edited by Marianne Helms. 1988. Critical commentary, pp. 93–118.

30 *Mehrstimmige Gesänge.* Edited by Paul Mies. 1958.

31 *Kanons.* Edited by Otto Erich Deutsch. 1959.

32:1 *Volkslied-Bearbeitungen: Nr. 1–100, Schottische Lieder.* Edited by Karl Geiringer. 1961.

APPENDIX 2

HOBOKEN NUMBERS

The following list identifies work-categories specified in Hoboken's *Joseph Haydn: Thematisch-bibliographisches Werkverzeichnis* (item 28).

Instrumental Works (Volume 1)

I	Symphonies
Ia	Overtures
II	Divertimentos for four or more instruments
III	String quartets
IV	Three-part divertimentos
V	String trios
VI	Duos for various instruments
VII	Concertos for various instruments
VIII	Marches
IX	Dances
X	Works for various instruments with baryton
XI	Baryton trios
XII	Duos for baryton
XIII	Concertos for baryton
XIV	Keyboard divertimentos
XV	Keyboard trios
XVa	Keyboard duos
XVI	Keyboard sonatas
XVII	Miscellaneous keyboard works
XVIII	Keyboard concertos
XIX	Works for flute-clock
XX/1	Instrumental music for *The Seven Last Words*

Vocal Works (Volume 2)

XX/2	Vocal version of *The Seven Last Words*
XXbis	*Stabat Mater*
XXI	Oratorios
XXII	Masses
XXIII	Other sacred works
XXIV	Secular vocal works with orchestra
XXV	Two-, three-, and four-part songs
XXVI	Lieder and cantatas with keyboard accompaniment
XXVII	Canons
XXVIII	Operas
XXIX	Marionette operas and singspiels
XXX	Incidental music to plays
XXXI	Folksong arrangements
XXXII	Pasticcios

APPENDIX 3

LIST OF HAYDN'S COMPOSITIONS

The following list of authentic Haydn compositions is provided for convenient reference and does not purport to supersede other recent, published catalogues. Information on dates of composition, scoring, and other details derives from that supplied by Georg Feder in the list of works published in *The New Grove Haydn* (item 269). In the table of contents, Roman numerals in parentheses refer to the relevant Hoboken categories (see Appendix 2).

In assigning Arabic numbers to compositions within each category, Hoboken chose to adopt existing, standard numbering where available (for example, for the symphonies and keyboard sonatas). Otherwise, his numbers correspond to those in the 1805 catalogue prepared by Johann Elssler (see Larsen, ed., *Drei Haydn Kataloge,* item 41). For works judged to be authentic, though missing from the Elssler catalogue or from standard lists, Hoboken has assigned additional numbers and identified them with asterisks.

Where known conclusively, dates of composition are supplied. Uncertain dates are preceded by a question mark. Brackets surround datings that are not documented.

References to items in the bibliography are indicated in italics. *Note:* References to items that concern numerous works within a genre or groups of works listed singly here (e.g. the string quartets of Op. 1) are provided under the appropriate genre name in the Subject Index.

Abbreviations.

A: alto solo
bc: basso continuo
bn: bassoon
B: bass solo
cbn: contrabassoon
cl: clarinet
Eng hn: English horn
fl: flute
hn: French horn
hpd: harpsichord
obbl: obbligato
ob: oboe
org: organ
perc: percussion
str: strings
S: soprano solo
ti: timpani
trb: trombone
tr: trumpet
T: tenor solo
va: viola
vle: violone
vn: violin

Contents

LIST OF HAYDN'S COMPOSITIONS

MASSES: Hob. XXII

Hob.No.	Work	Date	References
1	Missa brevis, F (2 S, chorus, 2 vn, bc)	?1749	***786,787, 797,806***
2	Missa "Sunt bona mixta malis," d (?a cappella)	?ca. 1767-69	***515***
3	Missa "Rorate coeli desuper," G	?	***469,507, 513,786***
4	Missa in honorem BVM (Great Organ Mass), Eb (S, A, T, B, chorus, 2 Eng hn, 2 hn, [2 tr, ti], 2 vn, vle, org obbl)	by 1774 [?ca. 1768-69]	
5	Missa Cellensis in honorem BVM, C (S, A, T, B, chorus, 2 ob, 2 bn, ?2 hn, 2 tr, ti, str, bc)	1766	***509,516***
6	Missa Sancti Nicolai, G (S, A, T, B, chorus, 2 ob, 2 hn, str, bc)	1772	***807***
7	Missa brevis Sancti Joannis de Deo (Little Organ Mass), Bb (S, chorus, 2 vn, b, org obbl)	by 1778 [?ca. 1773-77]	
8	Missa Cellensis (Mariazell Mass), C (S, A, T, B, chorus, 2 ob, bn, 2 tr, ti, str, bc)	1782	***787***
9	Missa in tempore belli (Mass in Time of War), C (S, A, T, B, chorus, ?fl, 2 ob, 2 cl, 2 bn, 2 hn, 2 tr, ti, str, bc)	1796	***815***
10	Missa Sancti Bernardi von Offida (Heiligmesse), Bb (S, A, T, B, chorus, 2 ob, 2 cl, 2 bn, ?2 hn, 2 tr, ti, str, bc)	1796	

MASSES: Hob. XXII *(continued)*

Hob.No.	Work	Date	References
11	Missa (Nelsonmesse), d (S, A, T, B, chorus, 3 tr, ti, str, org)	10 July-31 Aug 1798	***229,231, 461,815***
12	Missa (Theresienmesse), Bb (S, A, T, B, chorus, 2 cl, [bn], 2 tr, ti, str, bc)	1799	***798***
13	Missa (Creation Mass; Schöpfungsmesse), Bb (S, A, T, B, chorus, 2 ob, 2 cl, 2 bn, 2 hn, 2 tr, ti, str, bc)	28 July-11 Sept 1801	***787***
14	Missa (Harmoniemesse), Bb (S, A, T, B, chorus, fl, 2 ob, 2 cl, 2 bn, 2 hn, 2 tr, ti, str, bc)	1802	***798***
ii, 73	Mass, G (chorus, 2 vn, bc)	by 1779	

OTHER SACRED WORKS

Hob. No.	Work	Date	References
XXIIb:1*	Libera me, Domine, d (S, A, T, B, 2 vn, bc)	?ca. 1777-90	***514***
XXIIIa:1	Non nobis, Domine, d (Psalm 113:9; offertory motet; chorus, bc)	?	
XXIIIa:2	Animae Deo gratae, C (offertory motet; 2 S, T, chorus, 2 ob, 2 tr, ti, str/?2 vn, bc)	by 1776 [?ca. 1761-69]	
XXIIIa:3	Ens aeternum, G (offertory motet/ hymn; chorus, str, bc)	by 1772 [?ca. 1761-69]	
XXIIIa:4*	Quis stellae radius, C (motet; S, chorus, ?2 tr, ?ti, str, bc)	?1762	
XXIIIb:1	Salve regina, E (S, chorus, 2 vn, bc)	?1756	***283,507, 786,797***
XXIIIb:2	Salve regina, g (S, A, T, B, str, org obbl)	1771	

OTHER SACRED WORKS *(continued)*

Hob. No.	Work	Date	References
XXIIIb:3*	Ave regina, A (S, chorus, 2 vn, bc)	by 1763 [?ca. 1750-59]	***505, 507,786***
XXIIIb:4*	Salve regina, Eb (S, A, T, ?B, [?solo vns], str, bc)	by 1773	
XXIIIc:1	Te Deum, C (S, A, T, B, chorus, 2 tr, ti, 2 vn, bc)	by 1765 [?1762-63]	***506,576***
XXIIIc:2	Te Deum, C (chorus, fl, 2 ob, 2 bn, [2 hn], 3 tr, ti, str, bc)	by Oct 1800	
XXIIIc:3	Alleluia, G (S, A, chorus, str, bc)	by 1771 [?1768-69]	
XXIIIc:4	Lauda Sion (Responsoria de venerabili) i-iv: Bb, d, A, Eb (S, A, T, B, ?2 hn, 2 vn, bc)	?ca. 1765-69	***508***
XXIIIc:5	Lauda Sion (Hymnus/Motetto de venerabili) i-iv: C (S, A, B, chorus, 2 ob, 2 tr, str, bc)	by 1776 [?ca. 1750]	***507,786***
XXIIId:1	Ein' Magd, ein' Dienerin (Cantilena/Aria pro adventu), A (S, ?2 ob, ?2 hn, str, bc)	?ca. 1770-75	
XXIIId:2	Mutter Gottes, mir erlaube (Cantilena/Aria pro adventu), G (S, A, 2 vn, bc)	?ca. 1775	
XXIIId:3*	Herst Nachbä (Cantilena pro adventu; Pastorella) D (S, ?2 hn, str, bc)	?ca. 1768-70	***504, 508***
ii, 181	6 English Psalms, F, Eb, D, C, Eb, A (texts: J. Merrick; rev.: W.D. Tattersall; Psalms 26:5-8, 31:21-24, 41:12-16; 1:1-6; 61:6-8, 69:13-17; 2 S, B)	[1794/95]	

ORATORIOS

Hob.No.	Work	Date	References
XXbis	Stabat mater (sequence/hymn; S, A, T, B, chorus, 2 ob/Eng hn, str, bc)	1767	*177,189,191, 471,797*
XXIVa:6	Applausus (cantata; S, A, T, 2 B, 2 ob, bn, 2 hn/tr, ti, str, hpd obbl)	[by 4 April] 1768	*105,795*
XX/2	Die Sieben letzten Worte unseres Erlösers am Kreuze (text: ?J. Friebert, rev.: G. van Swieten; S, A, T, B, chorus, 2 fl, 2 ob, 2 cl, 2 bn, cbn, 2 hn, 2 tr, 2 trb, ti, str)	[1795-96]	*158,173, 177,186,197,206, 209,352,522,651, 679,702,703,705, 816,821,829, 830,840,951*
XXI:1	Il ritorno di Tobia (text: G. Boccherini; 2 S, A, T, B, chorus, 2 fl, 2 ob, 2 Eng hn, 2 bn, 4 hn, 2 tr, 2 trb, ti, str, bc)	[1774-75]	*97,177,189, 195,238,379, 462,818,829, 830,834,835*
XXI:2	Die Schöpfung (text: G. van Swieten, after Lidley, from Milton; S, T, B, chorus, 3 fl, 2 ob, 2 cl, 2 bn, cbn, 2 hn, 2 tr, 3 trb, ti, str, bc)	1796-98	*91,106,158,173, 195,197,224,243,255, 263,264,278,286,307, 329,352,359,362,371, 379,383,393,419,461, 521,708,741,753,817, 819,820,824,827-833, 836,837,839,1102*
XXI:3	Die Jahreszeiten (text: G. van Swieten, after J. Thomson, trans. B.H. Brockes; S, T, B, chorus, 2 fl, 2 ob, 2 cl, 2 bn, cbn, 4 hn, 3 tr, 3 trb, ti, perc, str, bc)	1799-1801	*91,158, 173,195,255,264, 307,352,359,371, 379,393,419,461, 519,520,523,755, 819,822,823,826, 829,830,838,839*

SECULAR VOCAL WORKS WITH ORCHESTRA

Hob. No.	Work	Date	References
XXIVa:1	Vivan gl'illustri sposi (cantata)	by 10 Jan 1763	
XXIVa:2	Destatevi o miei fidi (cantata; 2 S, T, chorus, 2 ob, 2 hn, str, bc)	[by ?6 Dec] 1763	*507*
XXIVa:3	Da qual gioia improvvisa (cantata; S, A, chorus, fl, 2 ob, bn, 2 hn, str, hpd obbl)	?1764	
XXIVa:3	Al tuo arrivo felice (cantata)	?1767	
XXIVa:4	Qual dubbio ormai (cantata; S, chorus, 2 ob, 2 hn, str, hpd obbl)	[by ?6 Dec] 1764	
XXIVa:5	Dei clementi (cantata)	?	
XXIVa:7	Miseri noi ... Funeste orror (cantata; S, 2 fl, 2 ob, 2 bn, 2 hn, str)	by 1786	
XXIVa:8	The Storm: Hark! The Wild Uproar of the Winds (madrigal; text: P. Pindar; S, A, T, B, 2 fl, 2 ob, 2 bn, str)	[by 24 Feb] 1792	
XXIVa:9	Nor can I think ... Thy great endeavours (aria and chorus; text: from "Klareamontos;" B, chorus, fl, 2 ob, 2 cl, 2 bn, 2 hn, 2 tr, ti, str)	?1794	
XXIVa:10	Berenice, che fai (cantata; S, fl, 2 ob, 2 cl, 2 bn, 2 hn, str)	[by 4 May] 1795	
XXVIa:43	Gott, erhalte Franz den Kaiser! (Volkslied; text: L.L. Haschka; voice, fl, 2 ob, 2 bn, 2 hn, 2 tr, ti, str)	1797	

SECULAR VOCAL WORKS WITH ORCHESTRA *(continued)*

Hob.No.	Work	Date	References
ii, 194	Der Sturm: Hört! Die Winde furchtbar heulen (Ger. trans. of Hob. XXIVa:8; S, A, T, B, chorus, 2 fl, 2 ob, 2 cl, 2 bn, 2 hn, 2 tr, 2 trb, ti, str)	by 1798 [?1793]	
ii, 433	Su cantiamo, su beviamo (S, chorus [3 vocal parts], fl, 2 ob, 2 hn, 2 tr, ti, str)	?1791	
XXIVb:2	D'una sposa meschinella (aria for Paisiello, La Frascatana; S, 2 ob, 2 hn, str)	?summer 1777	
XXIVb:3	Quando la rosa ... Finchè l'agnello (aria for Anfossi, La Metilde ritrovata, recitative by Anfossi; S, fl, bn, 2 hn, str)	?July 1779	
XXIVb:5	Dice benissimo (aria for Salieri, La scuola de' gelosi; B, 2 hn, str)	by ?27 July 1780	
XXIVb:7	Signor, voi sapete (aria for Anfossi, Il matrimonio per inganno; S, 2 fl, 2 ob, 2 bn, 2 hn, str)	by ?3 July 1785	
XXIVb:8	Dica pure chi vuol dire (aria for Anfossi, Il geloso in cimento; ?S, 2 ob, bn, 2 hn, str)	?1778/85	
XXIVb:9	Sono Alcina (cavatina for G. Gazzaniga, L'isola d'Alcina; S, fl, 2 ob, 2 bn, 2 hn, str)	[by 18 June] 1786	
XXIVb:10	Ah tu non senti ... Qual destra omicida (recitative and aria for Traetta, Ifigenia in Tauride; T, fl, 2 ob, 2 bn, 2 hn, str)	[by 4 July] 1786	

SECULAR VOCAL WORKS WITH ORCHESTRA *(continued)*

Hob.No.	Work	Date	References
XXIVb:11	Un cor si tenero (aria for F. Bianchi, Il disertore; B, 2 ob, 2 hn, str)	[by April] 1787	
XXIVb:12	Vada adagio, signorina (aria for P. Guglielmi, La quacquera spiritosa; 2 ob, 2 bn, 2 hn, str)	by ?3 June 1787	
XXIVb:13	Chi vive amante (aria for F. Bianchi, Alessandro nell'Indie; S, fl, 2 ob, 2 bn, 2 hn, str)	[by 25/26 July] 1787	
XXIVb:14	Se tu mi sprezzi (aria for G. Sarti, I finti eridi; T, 2 ob, 2 bn, 2 hn, str)	[by 9 March] 1788	
XXIVb:15	Infelice sventurata (aria for Cimarosa, I due sopposti conti; S, 2 ob, 2 bn, 2 hn, str)	[by Feb] 1789	
XXIVb:16	Da che penso a maritarmi (aria for Gassmann, L'amore artigiano; T, fl, 2 ob, 2 bn, 2 hn, str)	[by 14 March] 1790	
XXIVb:17	Il meglio mio carattere (aria for Cimarosa, L'impresario in angustie; S, fl, 2 ob, 2 bn, 2 hn, str)	by ?6 June 1790	
XXIVb:18	La moglie quando è buona (aria for Cimarosa, Giannina e Bernardone; S, fl, 2 ob, 2 bn, 2 hn, str)	by ?Aug/Sept 1790	
XXIVb:19	La mia pace, oh Dio, perdei (aria for Gassmann, L'amore artigiano; S, fl, 2 ob, 2 bn, 2 hn, str)	1790	
XXIVb:20	Solo e pensoso (aria; text: Petrarch; S, 2 cl, 2 bn, 2 hn, str)	1798	

SECULAR VOCAL WORKS WITH ORCHESTRA *(continued)*

Hob.No.	Work	Date	References
XXIVb:22*	Tornate pur mia bella (aria; T, fl, 2 ob, 2 bn, 2 hn, str)	by 13 Aug 1790 [?1787]	
XXIVb:23*	Via siate bonino (aria; S, fl, 2 ob, 2 bn, 2 hn, str)	?ca. 1785-95	
XXIVb:24 Add.	Cara deh torna in pace (aria for Giacomo Davide; T, ob, bn, [and ?])	by ?16 May 1791	
XXIVb:A1	Aure dolci ch'io respiro (aria; ?S/T, 2 fl, 2 ob, str)	by ?1762	
XXXII:1	for Circe, ossia L'isola incantata (pasticcio):	[by July] 1789	
a	"Son due ore che giro" (recitative; T, fl, 2 ob, 2 bn, str, bc)		
b	"Son pietosa, son bonina" (aria; S, fl, 2 ob, 2 bn, 2 hn, str)		
c	"Levatevi presto" (terzetto; 2 T, B, fl, 2 ob, 2 bn, 2 hn, str)		
--	Aria for Miss Poole	1791-95	
--	Aria with full orchestra	1791-95	

DRAMATIC WORKS

Hob.No.	Work	Date	References
XXIVb:1	? (?opera buffa; ?It. comedy; S, B, [...], 2 Eng hn, 2 hn, str, bc)	?1762	
XXVIII:1	Acide (festa teatrale; libr.: G.B. [?G.A.] Migliavacca; 2 S, A, T, B, 2 fl, 2 ob/Eng hn, 2 hn, str, bc)	1762	***857,863,896***
	[2nd version] (2 S, T, 2 B; 2 bn added)	[1773]	

DRAMATIC WORKS *(continued)*

Hob.No.	Work	Date	References
XXVIII:2	La canterina (intermezzo in musica; 3 S, T, 2 fl, 2 ob/Eng hn, 2 hn, str, bc)	1766	***411,843,844, 882,883***
XXVIII:3	Lo speziale (dramma giocoso; libr.: C. Goldoni; 2 S, 2 T, 2 fl, 2 ob, bn, 2 hn, str, bc)	[1768]	***882***
XXVIII:4	Le pescatrici (dramma giocoso; libr.: C. Goldoni; 2 S, A, 2 T, 2 B, chorus, 2 fl, 2 ob/Eng hn, bn, 2 hn, str, bc)	1769	**126,189,570,** ***851,879,882***
XXVIII:5	L'infedeltà delusa (burletta per musica; libr.: M. Coltellini; 2 S, 2 T, B, 2 ob, 2 bn, 2 hn, ti, str, bc)	[1773]	***177,189,874, 875,882***
XXVIII:6	L'incontro improvviso (dramma giocoso; libr.: K. Friberth, after Dancourt; 3 S, 2 T, 2 B, 2 ob/Eng hn, 2 bn, 2 hn, 2 tr, ti, perc, str, bc)	[1775]	***189,238,842, 852,890,900, 902***
XXVIII:7	Il mondo della luna (dramma giocoso; libr.: C. Goldoni; 2/3 S, 1/2 A, 2 T, B, 2 fl, 2 ob, 2 bn, 2 hn, 2 tr, ti, str, bc)	[1777]	***551,883,897, 898***
XXVIII:8;	La vera costanza (dramma giocoso; libr.: F. Puttini)	by 1779 [?April-Nov, 1778]	***528,552, 882,886, 892,895***
8a	2d version (3 S, 3 T, B, 1/2 fl, 2 ob, 2 bn, 2 hn, ti, str, bc)	1785	
XXVIII:9	L'isola disabitata (azione teatrale; libr.: Metastasio; 2 S, T, B, fl, 2 ob, bn, 2 hn, ti, str, bc)	1779	***857,892***

DRAMATIC WORKS *(continued)*

Hob.No.	Work	Date	References
XXVIII:10	La fedeltà premiata (dramma pastorale giocoso; libr.: after G. Lorenzi; 4 S, 2 T, 2 B, fl, 2 ob, bn, 2 hn/tr, ti, str, bc)	1780	***411,547,855, 881,883,889, 893,898***
XXVIII:11	Orlando paladino (dramma eroi-comico; libr.: C.F. Badini, N. Porta; 3 S, 4 T, 2 B, fl, 2 ob, 2 bn, 2 hn/tr, ti, str, bc)	1782	***856,860,865, 884,892,902***
XXVIII:12	Armida (dramma eroico; 2 S, 3 T, B, fl, 2 ob, 2 cl, 2 bn, 2 hn/tr, ti, str, bc)	1783	***842,850,855, ,857,885,891***
XXVIII:13	L'anima del filosofo, ossia Orfeo ed Euridice (dramma per musica; libr.: C.F. Badini; 2 S, T, B, chorus, 2 fl, 2 ob, 2 cl, 2 Eng hn, 2 bn, 2 hn, 2 tr, 2 trb, ti, harp, str, bc)	1791	***158,262,842, 849,857,878, 901,920***
XXIXa:1, XXIXb:2	Philemon und Baucis, oder Jupiters Reise auf die Erde (Singspiel/marionette opera; libr.: G.K. Pfeffel; 2 S, 2 T, chorus, ?2 fl, 2 ob, ?bn, 2 hn, ?2 tr, ti, str); for Vorspiel, see Hob. XXIXa:1a below	[1773]	***857,887***
XXIXa:1a	Der Götterrat (Vorspiel to Hob. XXIXa:1; libr.: ?P.G. Bader)	[1773]	
XXIXa:2	Hexenschabbas (marionette opera)	?1773	
XXIXa:3	Dido (Singspiel/marionette opera; libr.: P.G. Bader)	by 1778 [?1776]	
XXIXa:4	Opéra comique vom abgebrannten Haus	?ca. 1773-79	
XXIXb:1a	Der krumme Teufel (Singspiel; libr.: ?J. Kurz)	?1751	***525***

DRAMATIC WORKS *(continued)*

Hob.No.	Work	Date	References
XXIXb:1b	Der neue krumme Teufel (Singspiel; libr.: J. Kurz)	?ca. 1758	***537,539, 864,903***
XXIXb:3	Die bestrafte Rachbegierde (Singspiel/marionette opera; libr.: P.G. Bader)	?1779	
XXIXb:A	Die Feuersbrunst (Singspiel/marionette opera; S, ?5 T, B, chorus, 2 fl, 2 ob, 2 cl, 2 bn, 2 hn, 2 tr, ti, str)	?1775-78	***525,536, 537,548, 549,860***
XXX:1	Marchese (comedia; ?5 S, T, 2 fl, 2 ob, 2 hn, str)	1763	
XXX:4	Fatal amour (aria with spoken interjections; S, fl, 2 ob, 2 bn, 2 hn, str)	?ca. 1796	
XXX:5	Alfred, König der Angelsachsen, oder Der patriotische König (incidental music to play by J.W. Cowmeadow, after A. Bicknell):	1796	
a	"Triumph dir, Haldane" (chorus; [3 vocal parts], 2 ob, 2 bn, 2 tr, ti, str)		
b	"Ausgesandt vom Strahlenthrone" (aria with spoken interjections; S, 2 cl, 2 bn, 2 hn)		
c	"Der Morgen graut" (duet; 2 T, [?harp], vn solo, str)		
ii, 448	Il dottore (comedia)	?ca. 1761-65	
ii, 448	La vedova (comedia)	?ca. 1761-65	
ii, 448	Il scanarello (comedia)	?ca. 1761-65	

SOLO SONGS WITH KEYBOARD: Hob. XXVIa

Hob.No.	Work	Date	References
1-12	XII Lieder für das Clavier, i (texts: J.G. Herder, G. Leon, J.G. Jacobi, and others)	by 27 May 1781	
13-24	XII Lieder für das Clavier, ii (texts: G.E. Lessing, J.J. Engel, and others)	1781 [?1780] to [?3 March] 1784	
25-30	VI Original Canzonettas, i (texts: A. Hunter)	by 3 June 1794	
31-36	VI Original Canzonettas, ii (texts: Shakespeare, Metastasio, A. Hunter)	by 14 Oct 1795	
36bis	Der verdienstvolle Sylvius (text: J.N. Götz)	by 1 Feb 1795	
37	Beim Schmerz, der dieses Herz durchwühlet	?ca. 1765-75	
38	Der schlau(e) und dienstfertige Pudel	ca. 1780-87	
39	Trachten will ich nicht auf Erden	by 14 Dec 1790	
40	Der Feldzug	?	
41	The Spirit's Song (text: A. Hunter)	by 9 Sept 1800 [?ca. 1795]	
42	O Tuneful Voice (text: A. Hunter)	?ca. 1795	
43	Gott, erhalte Franz den Kaiser! (text: L.L. Haschka)	Oct 1796-Jan 1797	***461,561, 904,908-10,914-16,919***
44	Als einst mit Weibes Schönheit	?ca. 1796-1800	
45	Ein kleines Haus	by 30 Aug 1800	***564***
46	Antwort auf die Frage eines Mädchens	by June 1803	

SOLO SONGS WITH KEYBOARD: Hob. XXVIa *(continued)*

Hob.No.	Work	Date
47	Bald wehen uns des Frühlings Lüfte	?
48a-d	Four German Songs	?
XXXIc:17	The Lady's Looking-Glass	ca. 1791-95

OTHER VOCAL WORKS WITH KEYBOARD

Hob.No.	Work	Date
XXVa:1-2	2 Duetti of Nisa and Tirsi: Guarda/Senti qui; Saper vorrei (texts: C.F. Badini; S, T, hpd)	1796
	Aus des Ramlers Lyrischer Blumenlese (13 partsongs):	1796 (to ?1799)
XXVb:1	An den Vetter (no. 6; text C.F. Weisse; S, A, T, bc)	
XXVb:2	Daphnens einziger Fehler (no. 7; text: J.N. Götz; T, T, B, bc)	
XXVb:3	Betrachtung des Todes (no. 9; text: C.F. Gellert; S, T, B, bc)	
XXVb:4	An die Frauen (no. 11; text: Anakreon, trans. G.A. Bürger; T, T, B, hpd)	
XXVc:1	Der Augenblick (no. 1; text: J.N. Götz; S, A, T, B, bc)	
XXVc:2	Die Harmonie in der Ehe (no. 2; text: J.N. Götz; S, A, T, B, bc)	
XXVc:3	Alles hat seine Zeit (no. 3; text: Athenaeus, trans. J.A. Ebert; S, A, T, B, bc)	
XXVc:4	Die Beredsamkeit (no. 4; text: G.E. Lessing; S, A, T, B, bc)	
XXVc:5	Der Greis (no. 5; F.W.L. Gleim; S, A, T, B, bc)	

OTHER VOCAL WORKS WITH KEYBOARD *(continued)*

Hob.No.	Work	Date
XXVc:6	Die Warnung (no. 8; text: Athenaeus, trans. J.A. Ebert; S, A, T, B, bc)	
XXVc:7	Wider den Übermut (no. 10; text: C.F. Gellert; S, A, T, B, hpd)	
XXVc:8	Danklied zu Gott (no. 12; text: C.F. Gellert; S, A, T, B, hpd)	
XXVc:9	Abendlied zu Gott (no. 13; text: C.F. Gellert; S, A, T, B, hpd)	
XXVIb:2	Arianna a Naxos (cantata; S, hpd/pf)	by 9 Feb 1790
XXVIb:3	Dr. Harington's Compliment (S, chorus, pf)	?2-6 Aug 1794
XXVIb:4	The Battle of the Nile (cantata; text: E.C. Knight; voice, hpd/pf)	?6-9 Sept 1800
ii, 533	6 airs with variations (6 Admired Scotch Airs; voice, vn, vc, pf)	1801/2-3
--	Maccone (Gesänge) for Gallini	1791-95
--	Italian catch (?7 voices, [?bc])	by 2 June 1791

CANONS: Hob. XXVII

Hob.No.	Work	Date
a:1-10	Die Heiligen Zehn Gebote als Canons (3-5 vocal parts)	ca. 1791-95
b:1-47	40 [46/47] Sinngedichte als Canons bearbeitet (2-8 vocal parts)	ca. 1791-99

FOLKSONG ARRANGEMENTS: Hob. XXXI

Of 430 arrangements attributed to Haydn, 398 are regarded as authentic. Most were written for one voice and the following instruments: vn, bc; vc, vc, pf; or vn, vc, hpd. All but 27 of these occur in the following collections:

A Selection of Original Scots Songs. Compiled by W. Napier. ii-iii: London, 1792-95.

A Select Collection of Original Scottish Airs. Compiled by G. Thomson. i-iv: London and Edinburgh, 1802-5; v: London and Edinburgh, 1818; supplement to v: *25 Additional Scottish Airs.* Edinburgh, 1826.

The Select Melodies of Scotland. Compiled by G. Thomson. i, ii, v: London and Edinburgh, 1822; vi: *Thomson's Collection...united to the Select Melodies of Scotland...Ireland and Wales.* London and Edinburgh, 1824); supplement: *20 Scottish Melodies.* Edinburgh, 1839.

A Select Collection of Original Welsh Airs. Compiled by G. Thomson. i-iii: London and Edinburgh, 1809-17.

A Select Collection of Original Irish Airs. Compiled by G. Thomson. London and Edinburgh, 1814.

A Collection of Scottish Airs. Compiled by W. Whyte. i-ii: Edinburgh, 1804-7.

SYMPHONIES: Hob. I

Hob.No.	Key and Instrumentation	Date	References
1	D (2 ob, 2 hn, str)	by 25 Nov 1759	
2	C (2 ob, 2 hn, str)	by 1764 [by ?1761]	***928***
3	G (2 ob, 2 hn, str)	by 1762	
4	D (2 ob, 2 hn, str)	by 1762 [by ?1760]]	
5	A (2 ob, 2 hn, str)	by 1762 [by ?1760]	
6	D (fl, 2 ob, bn, 2 hn, str)	?1761	***962,1126***
7	C (fl, 2 fl/ob, bn, 2 hn, str)	1761	***962,1126***
8	G (fl, 2 ob, bn, 2 hn, str)	?1761	***864,1126***
9	C (2 fl/ob, bn, 2 hn, str)	?1762	
10	D (2 ob, 2 hn, str)	by 1766 [by ?1761]	
11	Eb (2 ob, 2 hn, str)	by 1769 [by ?1760]	
12	E (2 ob, 2 hn, str)	1763	
13	D (fl, 2 ob, 4 hn, [ti], str)	1763	
14	A (2 ob, 2 hn, str)	by 1764	***766***

SYMPHONIES: Hob. I *(continued)*

Hob.No.	Key and Instrumentation	Date	References
15	D (2 ob, 2 hn, str)	by 1764 [by ?1761]	
16	Bb (2 ob, 2 hn, str)	by 1766	***443***
17	F (2 ob, 2 hn, str)	by 1765	
18	G (2 ob, 2 hn, str)	by 1766	
19	D (2 ob, 2 hn, str)	by 1766	
20	C (2 ob, 2 hn, 2 tr, ti, str)	by 1766	
21	A (2 ob, 2 hn, str)	1764	
22	Eb (2 Eng hn, 2 hn, str)	1764	
23	G (2 ob, 2 hn, str)	1764	***928***
24	D (fl/2 ob, 2 hn, str)	1764	
25	C (2 ob, 2 hn, str)	by 1766 [by ?1760]	
26	d (2 ob, 2 hn, str)	by 1770	***928***
27	G (2 ob, 2 hn, str)	by 1766 [by ?1761]	
28	A (2 ob, 2 hn, str)	1765	
29	E (2 ob, 2 hn, str)	1765	
30	C (fl, 2 ob, 2 hn, str)	[by ?13 Sept] 1765	
31	D (fl, 2 ob, 4 hn, str)	[by ?13 Sept] 1765	***687,982***
32	C (2 ob, 2 hn, 2 tr, ti, str)	by 1766 [by ?1760]	
33	C (2 ob, 2 hn, 2 tr, ti, str)	by 1767 [by ?1760]	
34	d/D (2 ob, 2 hn, str)	by 1767	
35	Bb (2 ob, 2 hn, str)	1 Dec 1767	
36	Eb (2 ob, 2 hn, str)	by 1769 [?ca. 1761-65]	
37	C (2 ob, 2 hn, [/2 tr, ti], str)	by ?1758	
38	C (2 ob, 2 hn, [2 tr, ti], str)	by 1769	
39	g (2 ob, 4 hn, str)	by 1770 [?1765]	***776***
40	F (2 ob, 2 hn, str)	1763	
41	C (fl, 2 ob, 2 hn, [2 tr, ti], str)	by 1770	
42	D (2 ob, 2 bn, 2 hn, str	1771	***709***
43	Eb (2 ob, 2 hn, str)	by 1772	
44	e (2 ob, 2 hn, str)	by 1772	
45	f# (2 ob, bn, 2 hn, str)	1772	***173,687***
46	B (2 ob, 2 hn, str)	1772	***731***

SYMPHONIES: Hob. I *(continued)*

Hob.No.	Key and Instrumentation	Date	References
47	G (2 ob, bn, 2 hn, str)	1772	
48	C (2 ob, 2 hn, [/2tr, ti], str)	by ?1769	
49	f (2 ob, 2 hn, str)	1768	***739,776,962***
50	C (2 ob, 2 hn, 2 tr, ti, str)	1773	
51	Bb (2 ob, 2 hn, str)	by 1774	
52	c (2 ob, [bn], 2 hn, str)	by 1774	
53	D (fl, 2 ob, bn, 2 hn, [ti], str; occurs in several versions)	?1778/79	***396,962***
54	G (2 fl, 2 ob, 2 bn, 2 hn, 2 tr, ti, str)	1774	***962***
55	Eb (2 ob, bn, 2 hn, str)	1774	
56	C (2 ob, bn, 2 hn, 2 tr, ti, str)	1774	***712,928***
57	D (2 ob, 2 hn, str)	1774	***962***
58	F (2 ob, 2 hn, str)	by 1775 [by ?1767/68]	
59	A (2 ob, 2 hn, str)	by 1769	***776***
60	C (2 ob, 2 hn, [2 tr], ti, str)	by 1774	***670,687, 848,962***
61	D (fl, 2 ob, 2 bn, 2 hn, ti, str)	1776	
62	D (fl, 2 ob, [2] bn, 2 hn, str)	by 1781 [?1780]	
63	C (fl, 2 ob, bn, 2 hn, str)	by 1781 [?1779]	
64	A (2 ob, 2 hn, str)	by 1778 [by ?ca. 1773]	***949,951***
65	A (2 ob, 2 hn, str)	by 1778 [?ca. 1769-72]	
66	Bb (2 ob, 2 bn, 2 hn, str)	by 1779 [?ca. 1775/76]	***949***
67	F (2 ob, 2 bn, 2 hn, str)	by 1779 [?ca. 1775/76]	
68	Bb (2 ob, 2 bn, 2 hn, str)	by 1779 [?ca. 1774/75]	
69	C (2 ob, 2 bn, 2 hn, 2 tr, ti, str)	by 1779 [?ca. 1775/76]	***949***
70	D (fl, 2 ob, bn, 2 hn, 2 tr, ti, str)	by 18 Dec 1779 [?1778/79]	
71	Bb (fl, 2 ob, bn, 2 hn, str)	by 1780 [?1778/ 79]	***962***
72	D (fl, 2 ob, bn, 4 hn, [ti], str)	by 1781 [?ca. 1763-65]	

SYMPHONIES: Hob. I *(continued)*

Hob.No.	Key and Instrumentation	Date	References
73	D (fl, 2 ob, 2 bn, 2 hn, [2 tr, ti], str)	by 1782 [?1781]	*962,982*
74	Eb (fl, 2 ob, bn, 2 hn, str)	by 22 Aug 1781 [?1780]	
75	D (fl, 2 ob, bn, 2 hn, [2 tr, ti], str)	by 1781 [?1779]	*962*
76	Eb (fl, 2 ob, 2 bn, 2 hn, str)	?1782	
77	Bb (fl, 2 ob, 2 bn, 2 hn, str)	?1782	*928*
78	c (fl, 2 ob, 2 bn, 2 hn, str)	?1782	
79	F (fl, 2 ob, 2 bn, 2 hn, str)	by ?20 Nov 1784	
80	d (fl, 2 ob, 2 bn, 2 hn, str)	by 8 Nov 1784	
81	G (fl, 2 ob, 2 bn, 2 hn, str)	by 8 Nov 1784	
Paris symphonies (nos. 82-87):			*382*
82	C (fl, 2 ob, 2 bn, 2 hn/tr, ti, str)	1786	
83	g (fl, 2 ob, 2 bn, 2 hn, str)	1785	*758*
84	Eb (fl, 2 ob, 2 bn, 2 hn, str)	1786	*962*
85	Bb (fl, 2 ob, 2 bn, 2 hn, str)	?1785	*941,962*
86	D (fl, 2 ob, 2 bn, 2 hn, 2 tr, ti, str)	1786	*962*
87	A (fl, 2 ob, 2 bn, 2 hn, str)	1785	
88	G (fl, 2 ob, 2 bn, 2 hn, 2 tr, ti, str)	?1787	*928,962*
89	F (fl, 2 ob, 2 bn, 2 hn, str)	1787	*970*
90	C (fl, 2 ob, 2 bn, 2 hn, [2 tr, ti], str)	1788	*781,962*
91	Eb (fl, 2 ob, 2 bn, 2 hn, str)	1788	*962*
92	G (fl, 2 ob, 2 bn, 2 hn, [2 tr, ti], str)	1789	*656,676,777, 780,957,962*
London symphonies (nos. 93-104):			
93	D (2 fl, 2 ob, 2 bn, 2 hn, 2 tr, ti, str)	1791	*955*
94	G (2 fl, 2 ob, 2 bn, 2 hn, 2 tr, ti, str)	1791	*173,461,676, 960,971,973,994*
95	c (fl, 2 ob, 2 bn, 2 hn, 2 tr, ti, str)	1791	*587,958*

SYMPHONIES: Hob. I *(continued)*

Hob.No.	Key and Instrumentation	Date	References
96	D (2 fl, 2 ob, 2 bn, 2 hn, 2 tr, ti, str)	1791	***461,587***
97	C (2 fl, 2 ob, 2 bn, 2 hn, 2 tr, ti, str)	1792	***676***
98	Bb (fl, 2 ob, 2 bn, 2 hn, 2 tr, ti, hpd obbl, str)	1792	***687,987***
99	Eb (2 fl, 2 ob, 2 cl, 2 bn, 2 hn, 2 tr, ti, str)	1793	***584,733,783,955***
100	G ([2] fl, 2 ob, 2 cl, 2 bn, 2 hn, 2 tr, ti, perc, str)	1793/94	***656,676,928,955***
101	D (2 fl, 2 ob, 2 cl, 2 bn, 2 hn, 2 tr, ti, str)	1793/94	***698,712,744, 777,781,987***
102	Bb (2 fl, 2 ob, 2 bn, 2 hn, 2 tr, ti, str)	1794	***461,676,698,744, 955,977,981,987***
103	Eb (2 fl, 2 ob, 2 cl, 2 bn, 2 hn, 2 tr, ti, str)	1795	***698,744,761, 940,955,978***
104	D (2 fl, 2 ob, 2 cl, 2 bn, 2 hn, 2 tr, ti, str)	1795	***676,696,698,731, 744,781,955,981, 945,952,956,969, 978,979,986***
105*	Concertante, Bb (soli: vn, vc, ob, bn; fl, ob, bn, 2 hn, 2 tr, ti, str)	1792	
106*	D (2 ob, 2 hn, str)	?1769	
107*	Bb (2 ob, 2 hn, str)	by 1762 [by ?1761]	
108*	Bb (2 ob, bn, 2 hn, str)	by 1765	

MISCELLANEOUS ORCHESTRAL WORKS

Hob.No.	Work	Date	References
	6 Sinfonie:	by 29 Sept 1782	
Ia:1	Overture to L'infedeltà delusa, C (contains large-scale alterations; 2 ob, 2 hn, ti, str)		

MISCELLANEOUS ORCHESTRAL WORKS *(continued)*

Hob.No.	Work	Date	References
Ia:2	Overture to Il ritorno di Tobia, c/C (contains minor alterations; 2 ob, 2 bn, 2 hn, 2 tr, ti, str)		
Ia:6	Overture to L'incontro improvviso, D (contains changes in instrumentation; 2 ob, 2 hn, str)		
Ia:10	Overture to Lo speziale, G (fl, 2 ob, 2 hn, str)		
Ia:13	Overture to L'isola disabitata, g (fl, 2 ob, bn, 2 hn, str)		
Ia:15	Overture to La vera costanza, Bb (contains added movement; 2 ob, bn, 2 hn, str)		
Ia:4	Finale, D (from unidentified work; fl, 2 ob, 2 bn, 2 hn, str)	?1777-86 [?1782-84]	
Ia:7	Sinfonia, D (overture to unidentified work; 2 ob, 2 bn, 2 hn, str)	1777	
XX/1 A	Musica instrumentale sopra le 7 ultime parole del nostro Redentore in croce ossiano 7 sonate con un'introduzione ed al fine un terremoto (2 fl, 2 ob, 2 bn, 4 hn, 2 tr, ti, str)	by 11 Feb 1787 [?1786]	
XXX:3	Incidental music: Der Zerstreute (comedy by ?J.B. Bergopzoomer, after J.F. Regnard = Hob. I:60)	by 30 June 1774	**861**
i, 87	Menuet, Trio, Finale, C (2 ob, 2 hn, 2 tr, ti, str)	by ?1773	
i, 206	Piece for military band, C (arr. of sym. 100, mvt. II; fl, 2 ob, 2 cl, 2 bn, 2 hn, tr, serpent, perc)	?1794/95	
i, 590	?, E (b part for nine pieces)	?ca. 1763-69	
--	Overtura Coventgarden	1791-95	

DANCES AND MARCHES FOR ORCHESTRA OR MILITARY BAND

Hob.No.	Work	Date
VIII:1-2	2 [Derbyshire] Marches, Eb, C (2 cl, 2 bn, 2 hn, tr, serpent, perc)	1795
VIII:3	March, Eb (2 cl, 2 bn, 2 hn, tr, serpent)	1792
VIII:3 bis	March, Eb (2nd version of VIII:3; 2 fl, 2 cl, 2 bn, 2 hn, 2 tr, str)	1792
VIII:4	Hungarischer National Marsch, Eb (2 ob, 2 cl, 2 bn, 2 hn, tr)	[by 27 Nov] 1802
VIII:6	Marcia, Eb (2 cl, 2 hn, 2 bn)	by 1793 [?ca. 1780-90]
VIII:7	March, Eb (2 cl, 2 bn, 2 hn, tr, serpent)	?ca. 1792
IX:1	[12] Minuetti (with 3 Trios; 2 ob, 2 hn, 2 vn, b)	by ?1760
IX:3	[12] Menuetti (with 4 Trios; [?2] fl pic, [?2] fl, 2 ob, [?2] bn, 2 hn, 2 vn, b)	by 1767
IX:5	[6] Menuetti (with 2 Trios; fl, 2 ob, bn, 2 hn, 2 vn, b)	1776
IX:6a Add.	12 Menuets	by 11 Feb [by ?9 Jan] 1777
IX:6b Add.	18 Menuets	by 8 Feb [by ?9 Jan] 1780
IX:7	Raccolta de' [14] menuetti ballabili (with 6 Trios; fl, 2 ob, 2 bn, 2 hn, ti, 2 vn, b)	by 31 Jan 1784
IX:8	XII Menuets (with 5 Trios)	by 9 April 1785
IX:9	6 Allemandes (6 deutsche Tänze; fl, 2 ob, bn, 2 hn, 2 tr, ti, 2 vn, b)	by 15 Nov 1786
IX:9c	12 ganz neue Tanz Menuetts mit 12 Trios begleitet	by 11 Jan 1790
IX:9d, e, Add.	Unos 24 minués y otras tantas	by 22 April 1789
IX:11	[12] Menuetti di ballo (with 11 Trios; fl pic, 2 fl, 2 ob, 2 cl, 2 bn, 2 hn, 2 tr, ti, 2 vn, b)	by 25 Nov 1792

DANCES AND MARCHES FOR ORCHESTRA OR MILITARY BAND *(continued)*

Hob.No.	Work	Date
IX:12	12 deutsche Tänze (with Trio and Coda; 2 fl, 2 ob, 2 cl, 2 bn, 2 hn, 2 tr, ti, 2 vn, b)	by 25 Nov 1792
IX:16	24 Menuetti (with 24 Trios; fl pic, 2 fl, 2 ob, 2 cl, 2 bn, 2 hn, 2 tr, ti, perc, 2 vn, b)	?ca. 1790-1800
IX:23	?24 Dances (?12 Minuets and 12 Trios; 2 fl, 2 hn, 2 vn, b, and ?)	by ?ca. 1773
i, 541	March, Eb (str)	after 1791
i, 541	March, Eb (2 cl, 2 hn, 2 bn)	?
iii, 315	Marche regimento de Marshall, G (2 ob, 2 hn, 2 bn)	by 1772
iii, 323	4 and 2 Countrydances	1791-95
--	4 [?cycles of] Menuetti	by ?1765
--	24 Minuets and German Dances	1791-95

CONCERTOS

Hob.No.	Work	Date	References
VIIa:1	Concerto per il violino, C (orch: str)	by 1769 [?ca. 1761-65]	
VIIa:2	Concerto per il violino, D (orch: [2 ob, 2 hn], str)	?ca. 1761-65	
VIIa:3	Concerto per il violino, A (orch: str)	by 1771 [?ca. 1765-70]	
VIIa:4*	Concerto per il violino, G (orch: str)	by 1769	
VIIb:1	Concerto per il violoncello, C (orch: 2 ob, 2 hn, str)	?ca. 1761-65	
VIIb:2	Concerto per il violoncello, D (orch: 2 ob, 2 hn, str)	1783	***583,730, 731,1132***
VIIb:3	Concerto per il violoncello, C	?ca. 1761-65	
VIIc:1	Concerto per il violone	?ca. 1761-65	
VIId:1	Concerto per il corno di caccia, D	?ca. 1761-65	***569***
VIId:2	Concerto a 2 corni, Eb	by ?1784	***585***
VIId:3*	Concerto per il corno di caccia, D (no. 1; orch: 2 ob, str)	1762	

CONCERTOS *(continued)*

Hob.No.	Work	Date	References
VIIe:1	Concerto per il clarino, Eb (orch: 2 fl, 2 ob, 2 bn, 2 hn, 2 tr, ti, str)	1796	
VIIf:1	Concerto per il flauto, D	?ca. 1761-65	
VIIh:1*	Concerto per la lira organizzata, C (2 lire, 2 hn, 2 vn, 2 va, vc)	?1786-87	
VIIh:2*	Concerto per la lira organizzata, G (2 lire, 2 hn, 2 vn, 2 va, vc)	?1786-87	
VIIh:3*	Concerto per la lira organizzata, G (2 lire, 2 hn, 2 vn, 2 va, vc)	?1786-87	
VIIh:4*	Concerto per la lira organizzata, F (2 lire, 2 hn, 2 vn, 2 va, vc)	[1786]	
VIIh:5*	Concerto per la lira organizzata, F (2 lire, 2 hn, 2 vn, 2 va, vc)	?1786-87	
XIII:1-	Concerto per il pariton [baryton], D (orch: [?2 vn, b])	?ca. 1765-70	
2	Concerto per il pariton, D (orch: [?2 vn, b])	?ca. 1765-70	
XIII:3	Concerto per 2 pariton, D	?ca. 1765-70	
XVIII:1	Concerto per il clavicembalo (Concerto per l'organo, no. 1), C (org/hpd, 2 ob, [2 tr/?hn, ?ti], str)	?1756	***283,1108***
XVIII:2	Concerto per il clavicembalo, D (org/hpd, [2 ob, 2 tr, ti], str)	by 1767	***930,1108***
XVIII:3	Concerto per il clavicembalo, F (hpd, [?2 hn], str)	by 1771	***930***
XVIII:4	Concerto per il clavicembalo, G (hpd/pf, [?2 ob, ?2 hn], str)	by 1781 [?ca. 1770]	
XVIII:6*	Concerto per violino e cembalo, F (org/hpd, vn solo, str)	by 1766	
XVIII:11*	Concerto per il clavicembalo, D (hpd/pf, 2 ob, 2 hn, str)	by 1784	***696,984***

DIVERTIMENTOS FOR FOUR OR MORE INSTRUMENTS
(strings, winds, or both): Hob. II
(*See also* String quartets, Works for one or two barytons, Works for two lire organizzate)

Hob.No.	Work	Date	References
1	Divertimento [a 6], G (fl, ob, 2 vn, vc, db)	by 1768	
2	Divertimento a 5, G (2 vn, 2 va, b)	by 1763 [?1753/54]	
3	Divertimento [a 6], G (2 ob, 2 hn, 2 bn)	by 1766	
4	Divertimento a 5, F, (?D; 2 cl, 2 hn, bn)	by ?ca. 1765	
5	Divertimento a 5 (?a4), F (D?; 2 cl, 2 hn [?bn])	by ?ca. 1765	
7	Divertimento a 6, C (2 ob, 2 hn, 2 bn)	by 1765	
8	Divertimento [a 7], D (2 fl, 2 hn, 2 vn, b)	by 1767	
9	Divertimento a 9, G (2 ob, 2 hn, 2 vn, 2 va, b)	by 1764	
10	Divertimento a 6 (Der [verliebte] Schulmeister), D	by ca. 1765	
11	Divertimento a 6, C (Der Geburtstag; fl, ob, 2 vn, vc, db)	by 1765	
12	Divertimento (?a 6), Eb ([?2] Eng hn and ?)	by ca. 1765	
13	Divertimento (?a 6), D	by ca. 1765	
14	Divertimento [a 4], C (2 cl, 2 bn)	1761	**641**
15	Divertimento a 6, F (2 ob, 2 hn 2 bn)	1760	
16	Divertimento a 8, F (2 Eng hn, 2 hn, 2 vn, 2 bn),	1760	
17	Divertimento a 9, C (2 ob [?or 2 cl], 2 hn, 2 vn, 2 va, b)	by ca. 1765	
20	Divertimento a 9, F (2 ob, 2 hn, [bn], 2 vn, 2 va, b)	by 1763 [by ?1757]	
20bis	Divertimento, A	by ?ca. 1765	
21*	Divertimento a 6 (Eine Abendmusik), Eb (2 hn, 2 vn, va, b)	by 1763 [by ?1761]	
22*	Divertimento a 6, D (2 hn, 2 vn, va, b)	by 1764 [by ?1760]	
23*	Divertimento [a 6], F (2 ob, 2 hn, 2 bn)	by 1765 [?1760]	

DIVERTIMENTOS FOR FOUR OR MORE INSTRUMENTS *(continued)*

Hob.No.	Work	Date	References
24*	[V] Variations on a minuet, Eb (fl, 2 Eng hn, bn, 2 hn, vn solo, 2 vn, vc, vle)	?1761-62	***641***
33*-38*	6 Scherzandos, F, C, D, G, E, A (fl/2 ob, 2 hn, 2 vn, b)	by 1765	
D18	Divertimento [a 6], D (2 ob, 2 hn, 2 bn)	by 1765 [?ca. 1760]	
D22 Add.	Cassation, D (4 hn, vn, va, b)	?ca. 1763	
G1	Divertimento a 9, G (2 ob, 2 hn, 2 vn, 2 va, b)	by 1768 [?ca. 1760]	
G9/C12 Add.	Divertimento [a 6] G/C (2 ob, 2hn, 2 bn)	by 1766 [?ca. 1760]	

STRING QUARTETS: Hob. III

Hob.No.	Work	Date	References
II:6	Divertimento, Op. 1/0, Eb	by 1764 [?ca. 1757-59]	
1	Divertimento, Op. 1/1, Bb	by 1762 [?ca. 1757-59]	
2	Divertimento, Op. 1/2, Eb	by 1762 [?ca. 1757-59]	
3	Divertimento, Op. 1/3, D	by 1762 [?ca. 1757-59]	
4	Divertimento, Op. 1/4, G	by 1764 [?ca. 1757-59]	
6	Divertimento, Op. 1/6, C	by 1762 [?ca. 1757-59]	
7	Divertimento, Op. 2/1, A	by 1763 [?ca. 1760-62]	
8	Divertimento, Op. 2/2, E	by 1765 [?ca. 1760-62	
10	Divertimento, Op. 2/4, F	by 1762 [?ca. 1760-62]	
12	Divertimento, Op. 2/6, Bb	by 1762 [?ca. 1760-62]	
19-24	6 Divertimentos, Op. 9, C, Eb, G, d, Bb, A	by 1771 [?1769/70]	***313, 1010, 1012, 1030, 1042***

STRING QUARTETS: Hob. III *(continued)*

Hob.No.	Work	Date	References
25-30	6 Divertimentos, Op. 17, E, F, Eb, c, G, D	1771 (1772)	
31-36	6 Divertimentos, Op. 20, Eb, C, g, D, f, A	1772 (1774)	***744,767,780,1012, 1013,1042***
37-42	6 Quatuors, Op. 33, b, Eb, C, Bb, G, D	1781 (1782)	***95,312,606,652, 659,661,676,681, 696,751,757,758,767, 770,1018,1027,1030, 1036,1040,1042***
43	Quartetto, Op. 42, d	1785 (1786)	
44-49	6 Quartetti, Op. 50, Bb, C, Eb, f#, F, D	1787 [by 16 Sept] (1787)	***602,729,1030***
57-62	6 Quatuors, Op. 54, G, C, E; Op. 55, A, f, Bb	by ?22 Sept 1788 (1789, 1790)	***224,318,674, 676,712,741, 744,1013***
63-68	6 Quartetti, Op. 64, C, b, Bb, G, D, Eb	1790 (1791)	***600,754,1013, 1030,1038***
69-74	6 Quartetti, Op. 71, Bb, D, Eb; Op. 74, C, F, g	1793 (1795, 1796)	***461,600,744, 1029,1030***
75-80	6 Quartetti, Op. 76, G, d, C, Bb, D, Eb	by ?14 June 1797 (1799; Op. 76/3 by 28 Sept 1797)	***744,1013,1016, 1024,1026,1034***
81-82	2 Quartetti, Op. 77, G, F	1799 (1802)	***744,1030,1040***
83	Unfinished Quartet, Op. 103, d	by 1803 (1806)	***593***

STRING TRIOS (2 vn, vc, [b]): Hob. V

Hob.No.	Key	Date
1	E	by 1767
2	F	by 1767
3	b	by 1767
4	Eb	by 1767
5	B (instruments?)	by ?1765
6	Eb	by ?1764 [by ?1761]
7	A	by ?1765
8	Bb (vn, va, b)	by 1765
9	Eb (instruments?)	by ?1765
10	F	by 1767
11	Eb	by 1765
12	E	by 1767
13	Bb	by ?1765
14	b (instruments?)	by ?1765
15	D	by 1762
16	C	by 1766
17	Eb	by 1766
18	Bb	by 1765
19	E	by 1765
20	G	by 1766
21	D	?ca. 1765

BARYTON TRIOS (baryton, va, b): Hob. XI

Hob.No.	Key	Date	References
Book 1 (1-24):		by 14 Jan 1767	
1	A	[ca. 1765/66]	
2	A (?second version of 3-mvt. version in A)		***601***
2bis	G (spurious version of Hob. XI:2)		***601***
3	A	by 1770	
4	A		
5	A (2 additional versions in A)		
6	A	by 1769	
7	A	by 1769	
8	A		
9	A	by 1770	

BARYTON TRIOS (baryton, va, b): Hob. XI *(continued)*

Hob.No.	Key	Date	References
10	A	by 1772	
11	D	by 1772	
12	A		
13	A		
14	D		
15	A		
16	A	by 1772	
17	D	by 1772	
18	A	by 1772	
19	A		
20	D		
21	A	by 1771	
22	A		
23	D		
24	D	1766	
Book ii (25-48):		by 11 Oct 1767 [ca. 1766/67]	
25	A	by 1772	
26	G		
27	D		
28	D		
29	A		
30	G		
31	D		
32	G		
33	A		
34	D	by 1776 [by ?1775]	
35	A	by 1771	**670**
36	D	by 1776	
37	G	by 1776	
38	A	by 1776	
39	D	by 1776	
40	D		
41	D		
42	D	1767	
43	D		
44	D		
45	D		
46	A		
47	G		
48	D		

BARYTON TRIOS (baryton, va, b): Hob. XI *(continued)*

Hob.No.	Key	Date	References
Book iii (49-72):		by 7 July 1768 [ca. 1767/68]	
49	G		
50	D		
51	A		
52	d/D		
53	G	1767	
54	D		
55	G		
56	D		
57	A	1768	
58	D		
59	G		
60	A		
61	D		
62	G		
63	D		
64	D		
65	G		
66	A		
67	G		
68	A		
69	D		
70	G		
71	A		
72	D		
Book iv (73-96):		by 22 Dec 1771 [ca. 1768-71]	
73	G	by 1772	
74	D		
75	A		
76	C	by 1772	
77	G		
78	D		
79	D	1769	
80	G		
81	D		
82	C		
83	F		
84	G		
85	D		
86	A		

BARYTON TRIOS (baryton, va, b): Hob. XI *(continued)*

Hob.No.	Key	Date	References
87	a		
88	A		
89	G		
90	C		
91	D		
92	G		
93	C		
94	A	by 1774	
95	D		
96	b		
Book v (97-126*):		by 8 Nov 1778 [ca. 1771-78]	
97	D	[?1766]	
98	D		
99	G		
100	F		
101	C		
102	G		
103	A		
104	D		
105	G	1772	
106	D		
107	D		
108	A		
109	C		
110	C		
111	G		
112	D		
113	D		
114	D		
115	D		
116	G		
117	F		
118	D		
119	G		
120	D		
121	A		
122	A		
123	G		
124	G		
125	G		
126*	C		

WORKS FOR ONE OR TWO BARYTONS
(*See also* Concertos)

Hob. No.	Work	Date
X:1	Divertimento a 8, D (2 hn, 2 vn, baryton, va, vc, vle)	1775
X:2	Divertimento a 8, D (2 hn, 2 vn, baryton, va, vc, vle)	?1775
X:3	Divertimento a 8, a/A (2 hn, 2 vn, baryton, va, vc, vle)	1775
X:4	Divertimento a 8, G (2 hn, 2 vn, baryton, va, vc, vle)	?1775
X:5	Divertimento a 8, G (2 hn, 2 vn, baryton, va, vc, vle)	1775
X:6	Divertimento a 8, A (2 hn, 2 vn, baryton, va, vc, vle)	?1775
X:7	Divertimento (Quintet), D (2 hn, baryton, va, b)	ca. 1767/68
X:9	Divertimento, D (2 barytons, 2 hn)	?1765-70
X:10	Divertimento (Quintet), D (2 hn, baryton, va, b)	ca. 1767/68
X:11	Duetto, D (2 barytons)	ca. 1764-69
X:12*	Divertimento a 8, G (2 hn, 2 vn, baryton, va, vc, vle)	?1775
XII:1	Duetto, A (2 barytons)	ca. 1764-69
XII:2	Duetto, G (2 barytons)	ca. 1764-69
XII:5, 3	Duetto, D (2 barytons)	ca. 1764-69
XII:4	Duetto, G (2 barytons)	ca. 1764-69
XII:6	Duetto, G (2 barytons)	ca. 1764-69
XII:7-11, 12	6 Sonate, D, C, G, A, D, G (baryton, vc)	?ca. 1775
XII:13	Solo per il pariton, D (with vc)	?1770-75
XII:14	Solo per il pariton, D (with vc)	?1770-75
XII:15	Sonata, F (baryton, vc)	?
XII:16	Sonata, D (baryton, vc)	?
XII:17	Sonata, D (baryton, vc)	?
XII:18	Divertimento per il pariton solo, A (with vc)	ca. 1766-69
XII:19	12 Cassations-Stücke (2 barytons, b)	ca. 1765/66
XII:20	Divertimento per il pariton solo, G (?with vc)	ca. 1765/66
XII:21	Divertimento per il pariton solo, D (?with vc)	ca. 1765/66

WORKS FOR ONE OR TWO BARYTONS *(continued)*
(*See also* Concertos)

Hob.No.	Work	Date
XII:22	Divertimento per il pariton solo, A (?with vc)	ca. 1765/66
XII:23	Divertimento per il pariton solo, G (?with vc)	ca. 1765/66

MISCELLANEOUS CHAMBER MUSIC
(strings, winds, or both)

Hob. No.	Work	Date	References
IV:1-2, 3, 4*	[4?] Trios, C, G, G, G (2 fl, vc)	1794/95 (IV:1 = 1794)	
IV:5*	Divertimento a 3 per il corno di caccia, Eb (hn, vn, vc)	1767	
IV:6*-11*	6 Divertimentos a 3, D, G, C, G, A, D (vn/fl, vn, vc)	1784	***1091***
VI:1-6	6 Violin Solo mit Begleitung einer Viola, F, A, Bb, D, Eb, C	by 1777 [by ?1769]	

WORKS FOR 2 LIRE ORGANIZZATE: in Hob. II
(*See also* Concertos)

Hob.No.	Work	Date
25*	Notturno, C (2 lire, 2 cl, 2 hn, 2 va, b)	ca. 1788-90
26*	Notturno, F (2 lire, 2 cl, 2 hn, 2 va, b)	ca. 1788-90

WORKS FOR 2 LIRE ORGANIZZATE: in Hob. II *(continued)*
(*See also* Concertos)

Hob.No.	Work	Date
27*	Notturno, G: original version (2 lire, 2 hn, 2 vn, 2 va, vc);	?1790
	London version (fl, ob, 2 hn, 2 vn, 2 va, vc, db)	?1792
28*	Notturno, F: ?original version (?2 lire, ?2 hn, ?2 vn, ?2 va, ?vc);	?1790
	London version (fl, ob, 2 hn, 2 vn, 2 va, vc, db)	?1792
29*	Notturno, C: ?original version (?2 lire, ?2 cl, ?2 hn, ?2 va, ?vc);	?1790
	extant version (fl, ob, 2 vn, 2 hn, 2 va, vc/b)	?1791
30*	Notturno, G (2 lire, 2 cl, 2 hn, 2 va, vc)	?1790
31*	Notturno, C: original version (2 lire, 2 cl, 2 hn, 2 va, vc);	1790
	1st London version (fl, ob, 2 cl/vn, 2 hn, 2 va, vc);	?1792
	2d London version (fl, ob, 2 vn, 2 hn, 2 va, vc, db)	?1794
32*	Notturno, C: original version (2 lire, 2 cl, 2 hn, 2 va, b);	?1790
	London version (2 fl, 2 vn, 2 hn, 2 va, vc, db)	?1792

KEYBOARD DIVERTIMENTOS OR CONCERTINOS: Hob. XIV

Hob.No.	Work	Date	References
1	Divertimento, Eb (hpd, 2 hn, vn, b)	by 1766	
2	Divertimento, F (hpd, 2 vn, baryton)	?ca. 1767-71	
3	Divertimento, C (hpd, 2 vn, b)	by 1771 [by ca. 1767]	

KEYBOARD DIVERTIMENTOS OR CONCERTINOS: Hob. XIV *(continued)*

Hob.No.	Work	Date	References
4	Divertimento, C (hpd, 2 vn, b)	1764	
7*	Divertimento, C (hpd, 2 vn, vc)	by ca. 1767	***620***
8*	Divertimento, C (hpd, 2 vn, vc)	ca. 1768-72	
9*	Divertimento, F (hpd, 2 vn, vc)	by ca. 1767	
10*	Divertimento no. 1 con violini (hpd, [2] vn, [b])	?ca. 1764-67	
11*	Concertino, C (hpd, 2 vn, b)	1760	

KEYBOARD TRIOS: Hob. XV

Hob.No.	Work	Date	References
2	Sonata, F (hpd, vn, b)	?ca. 1767-71	***622***
5	Sonata, G (hpd, vn, b)	by 25 Oct 1784	
6-8	3 Sonatas, F, D, Bb (hpd, vn, vc)	6 = 1784, 7 = 1785, 8 = by 26 Nov 1785	
9	Sonata, A (hpd, vn, vc)	1785	
10	Sonata, Eb (hpd, vn, vc)	by 28 Oct 1785	
11-13	3 Sonatas, Eb, e, c (hpd/pf, vn, vc)	11 = by 8 March 1789 [by ?16 Nov 1788], 12 = by 8 March 1789 [1788/89], 13 = [by 29 March] 1789	
14	Sonata, Ab (hpd/pf, vn, vc)	by [?11 Jan] 1790	***448,630, 978***
15	Trio, G (hpd/pf, fl, vc)	[by 28 June] 1790	
16	Trio, D (hpd/pf, fl, vc)	[by 28 June] 1790	
17	Trio, F (hpd/pf, fl/vn, vc)	by ?20 June 1790	
18-20	3 Sonatas, A, g, Bb (pf, vn, vc)	by 15 Nov 1794	***766,1065***
21-23	3 Sonatas, C, Eb, d (pf, vn, vc)	by 23 May 1795	

KEYBOARD TRIOS: Hob. XV *(continued)*

Hob.No.	Work	Date	References
24-26	3 Sonatas, D, G, f# (pf, vn, vc)	by 9 Oct 1795	***1065***
27-29	3 Sonatas, C, E, Eb (pf, vn, vc)	[by 20 April 1797 [by ?Aug 1795]	***316,1065***
30	Sonata, Eb (hpd/pf, vn, vc)	by 7 Oct 1797 [?16 April-9 Nov 1796]	***1065***
31	Sonata, eb (pf, vn, vc)	1795	
32	Sonata, G (pf, vn, vc)	by 14 June 1794	***632,639***

KEYBOARD SONATAS: Hob. XVI

Hob.No.	Work	Date	References
2a	Divertimento, d (hpd)	[?ca. 1765-70]	
2b	Divertimento, A (hpd)	[?ca. 1765-70]	
2c	Divertimento, B (hpd)	[?ca. 1765-70]	
2d	Divertimento, Bb (hpd)	[?ca. 1765-70]	
2e	Divertimento, e (hpd)	[?ca. 1765-70]	
2g	Divertimento, C (hpd)	[?ca. 1765-70]	
2h	Divertimento, A (hpd)	[?ca. 1765-70]	
3	Divertimento, C (hpd)	[?ca. 1765]	
4	Divertimento, D (hpd)	[?ca. 1765]	
5a Add. = XIV:5	Divertimento, D (hpd)	[ca. 1767-70]	
6	Partita, G (hpd)	by 1766 [by ?1760]	
14	Parthia, D (hpd)	by 1767 [by ?1760]	***1070***
18	Sonata, Bb (hpd)	by 1788 [ca. 1771-73]	
19	Divertimento, D (hpd)	1767	
21-26	6 Sonatas, C, E, F, D, Eb, A (hpd)	by Feb 1774 (21-23, 26 = 1773; 24-25 = ?1773)	***1079***
27-32	6 Sonatas, G, Eb, F, A, E, b (hpd)	by 1776 (29 = 1774)	***696, 1066***

KEYBOARD SONATAS: Hob. XVI *(continued)*

Hob.No.	Work	Date	References
33	Sonata, D (hpd/pf)	by 17 Jan 1778	***1064***
34	Sonata, e (hpd/pf)	by 15 Jan 1784	
35-39, 20	6 Sonatas, C, c#, D, Eb, G, C (hpd/pf)	35-38 = by 31 Jan 1780 (36, 38 = [?ca. 1770-75]), 39 = by 8 Feb 1780, 20 = 1771	***670, 733, 1070***
40-42	3 Sonatas, G, Bb, D (pf)	by 1784	***1058,1064***
43	Sonata, Ab (hpd/pf)	by 26 July 1783	***1064***
44	Sonata, g (hpd)	by 1788 [ca. 1771-73]	
45	Divertimento, Eb (hpd)	1766	
46	Divertimento, Ab (hpd)	by 1788 [ca. 1767-70]	
47	Sonata, F (hpd/pf)	by 1788	***620,631***
47 bis Add.	Divertimento, e (hpd; ?original version of Hob, XVI:47)	[?ca. 1765]	
48	Sonata, C (hpd/pf)	by 5 April [by ?10 March] 1789	
49	Sonata, Eb (pf)	1789-[1 June] 1790	***726,731 1071,1078***
50	Sonata, C (pf)	[ca. 1794/95]	***696,781, 784,1062,1064, 1070,1074,1107***
51	Sonata, D (pf)	[?ca. 1794/95]	
52	Sonata, Eb (pf)	1794	***224,637,656, 694,696,698, 743,761,777, 1062,1070,1072,1080***

MISCELLANEOUS KEYBOARD WORKS

Hob.No.	Work	Date	References
XVII:1	Capriccio: "Acht Sauschneider müssen sein," G (hpd)	1765	
XVII:2	20 Variazioni, A (hpd)	by 1771 [?ca. 1765]	
XVII:3	12 Variations, Eb (hpd)	by 1774 [ca. 1770-74]	
XVII:4	Fantasia, C (pf)	[by ?29 March] 1789	
XVII:5	6 Variations, C (pf)	by 9 Feb 1791 (?Nov 1790)	
XVII:6	Sonata: Un piccolo divertimento, f (pf)	1793	***615***
XVIIa:1	Divertimento F (hpd, 4 hands)	by 1778 [?ca. 1768-70	
XXXIc: 17b	(Untitled piece), D ([pf])	[?1791-95]	

WORKS FOR FLUTE-CLOCK: Hob. XIX

Hob.No.	Work or key	Date	References
10	Andante, C	by 1792 [?ca. 1789]	
11	C;	by 1793 [?1789]	
	revised version	?1793	
12	Andante, C;	by 1793 [?1789]	
	revised version	?1793	
13	C (?original version);	?1789	
	?revised version	?1793	
14	C (?original version);	?1789	
	?revised version	?1793	
15	C (?original version);	?1789	
	?revised version	?1793	
16	Fuga, C;	1789	***645***
	revised version	?1793	
17	C	by 1792 [?ca. 1789]	
18	Presto, C	by 1792 [?ca. 1789]	
27	Allegretto, G	?1793	
31	Presto, C	by ?1794/95 [?1789]	

AUTHOR INDEX

SUBJECT INDEX

Selective rather than comprehensive in scope, this index furnishes a supplementary route of access to discussions of names and topics significant to Haydn research. As a rule, it excludes references to major biographical studies and encyclopedia articles. It also excludes major topics to which access can be most readily gained through the categorical organization of the bibliography.